THE COLLEGE WRITER'S REFERENCE

SECOND EDITION

Toby Fulwiler
University of Vermont

Alan R. Hayakawa
The Patriot News
Harrisburg, Pennsylvania

PRENTICE HALL, Upper Saddle River, New Jersey 07458

Library of Congress Cataloging-in-Publication Data

Fulwiler, Toby
  The college writer's reference / Toby Fulwiler, Alan R. Hayakawa.
  — 2nd ed.
      p.   cm.
  Includes bibliographical references and index.
  ISBN 0-13-080768-0
    1. English language — Rhetoric — Handbooks, manuals, etc. 2. Report
writing — Handbooks, manuals, etc. I. Hayakawa, Alan R. II. Title.
PE1408.F79 1999
808'.042 — dc21   98-20046
                                           CIP

Editorial Director: Charlyce Jones Owen
Editor in Chief: Leah Jewell
Executive Vice President of Production and Manufacturing: Barbara Kittle
Senior Production Manager: Bonnie Biller
Production Editor: Joan E. Foley
Copyeditor: Kathryn Graehl
Editorial Assistant: Patricia Castiglione
Manufacturing Manager: Nick Sklitsis
Prepress and Manufacturing Buyer: Mary Ann Gloriande
Director of Marketing: Gina Sluss
Art Director: Anne Bonanno Nieglos
Interior Designers: Kenny Beck & Barbara Bert/North 7 Atelier Ltd.
Cover Designer: Kenny Beck

Acknowledgements
Page 44. Brooks, Gwendolyn. "We Real Cool" from *Blacks* by Gwendolyn Brooks.
The Third World Press, 1987. Reprinted by permission.

Pages 391–403. Fulwiler/Hayakawa, *The Blair Handbook,* Second Edition, 1996, pp. 295–307.
Reprinted by permission of Prentice Hall, Upper Saddle River, New Jersey.

Page 121. By permission. From *Merriam-Webster's Collegiate® Dictionary,* Tenth Edition.
© 1997 by Merriam-Webster, Incorporated.

This book was set in 10/12 Minion by Digitype
and was printed and bound by R.R. Donnelley & Sons Company.

© 1999, 1996 by Prentice-Hall Inc.
Upper Saddle River, New Jersey 07458

Printed in the United States of America
10 9 8 7 6 5 4 3

ISBN 0-13-080768-0

Prentice-Hall International (UK) Limited, *London*
Prentice-Hall of Australia Pty. Limited, *Sydney*
Prentice-Hall Canada Inc., *Toronto*
Prentice-Hall Hispanoamerica, S.A., *Mexico*
Prentice-Hall of India Private Limited, *New Delhi*
Prentice-Hall of Japan, Inc., *Tokyo*
Prentice-Hall Asia Pte. Ltd., *Singapore*
Editora Prentice-Hall do Brasil, Ltda., *Rio de Janeiro*

CONTENTS

PART V
EDITING MECHANICS 283

PREFACE

The second edition of *The College Writer's Reference* remains portable, accessible, and easy to understand. It continues to explain and illustrate the qualities of good writing as well as the logic behind the traditional conventions of grammar and usage. And it continues to insist that good writing is a mix of inventive composing, judicious revising, and rigorous editing rather than the mechanical following of formulaic prescriptions. At the same time, the new edition features an expanded discussion of Internet research and documentation conventions, fresh samples of student writing, more complete information on publishing student writing, and (we hope) more clarity and grace throughout!

Pedagogical features

As a progressive alternative to traditional brief handbooks, this revised edition of *The College Writer's Reference* has several important features that will continue to make this book as easy for instructors to teach from as it is for students to use on their own.

Useful organization

The College Writer's Reference offers concise yet thorough coverage of all handbook concerns, uniquely organized according to the logic of the writing process: in the opening section, we urge writers to think about planning and drafting; in the later sections, we ask them to think hard about revision and editing. Traditional topics of style, grammar, punctuation, and mechanics are thus presented as "editing" choices writers make in the final stage of the writing process.

Teachable treatment of the whole writing process

The opening chapters of *The College Writer's Reference* examine the creative but frustrating messiness of the writing process, offering plenty of ideas and strategies to help writers shape, organize, and give voice to their work. This fully teachable treatment of the writing process discusses inventing, composing, revising, and keeping journals. Detailed chapters cover four common purposes for writing—recounting experiences, explaining things, interpreting texts, and arguing positions. For the second edition, each chapter includes a fresh and authentic sample of student writing to illustrate each kind of writing.

Publishing portfolios, class books, and Web pages. This edition of *The College Writer's Reference* adds a new chapter (11) explaining how students may publish their work, including guidelines for different types of writing portfolios and for organizing class editors to publish class books.

Peer editing. The new edition also provides practical advice on specific editing strategies and defines more clearly the concept of effective writing. In addition, we offer more specific ideas for peer editing from both writer's and responder's points of view.

Emphasis on effectiveness

The middle chapters focus on editing for effectiveness, for grammar, for usage, for punctuation, and for mechanics—fundamentals that also depend upon the writer's purpose, audience, and situation. Hand-edited examples illustrate at a glance how writers revise and edit, showing students proven strategies for focusing loose paragraphs, strengthening weak sentences, and finding the most precise and suitable words. Throughout the editing sections, we updated samples from the first edition, replacing ones that seemed dated and providing wherever we could ones that illustrated concepts and editing choices more clearly. For example, the discussion of recognizing and fixing fragments is much simpler and uses fewer technical grammatical terms.

Emphasis on conventions, not rules

The second edition of *The College Writer's Reference* continues to explain conventions of standard, written English as ways to facilitate efficient communication, not as arbitrary rules to be memorized and followed by rote. The text spends less time instructing students in grammatical terminology and more time showing students how to identify, analyze, and solve problems that can confuse readers.

Full coverage of electronic research writing and documentation methods

This edition of *The College Writer's Reference* now includes the most up-to-date strategies of using the Internet for research and documenting Internet sources correctly according to newly revised MLA and APA conventions. The chapters devoted to research guide writers through the many stages of the whole process, which is viewed here as yet another matter of making choices: from keeping a project log and learning how to find sources (including the proliferation of electronic choices), to conducting field research, to using and documenting sources. These chapters offer strategies for planning, organizing, and writing major research papers.

Help for those who speak English as a second language

The College Writer's Reference pays careful attention to the needs of second-language students. Graphically distinct boxes throughout the text provide information on everything from grammar, word idioms, and usage, to the how and why of rhetorical conventions.

Tips for writing with computers

The College Writer's Reference integrates up-to-date information on the role of computers in writing, insofar as any information on computers can be up-to-date. Word-processing tips offer students strategies for composing, revising, and editing on computer. This edition includes new ideas for gathering research information from the Internet and for testing the value and validity of the sources found there.

Unique design that facilitates quick reference

The four-color design of the book helps students locate information quickly, as they learn to identify the parts of the book, such as "grammar" and "mechanics," with their corresponding color bands. Thus, navigating the text becomes a visual as well as mental activity. The spiral binding allows the book to lie flat and fold back on itself for ease of use next to a computer.

Supplements

The following supplements accompany *The College Writer's Reference* to aid in teaching and learning:

- *Teaching Writing: A Resource for Instructors Using The College Writer's Reference* guides instructors on how to help students use the text to full advantage when writing and editing their papers, whether in class or on their own. This handy resource also includes teaching tips for the composition classroom, classroom activities, and writing assignments. (This resource is also available on disk and for downloading from America Online.)

- *Editing Activities to Accompany The College Writer's Reference* provides opportunities for students to apply and practice the editing strategies discussed in the text. (An answer key is available.)

- *Distance Education* illustrates the dynamics of writing instruction in the distance learning environment, explores professional opportunities enhanced by getting involved in distance education and distance learning techniques, and offers guidance on how to use the techniques described.

◆ *Classroom Strategies* shares classroom strategies that have worked for teachers of writing and encourages instructors to adapt the information to their individual classroom contexts and needs.

◆ *Portfolios* elaborates on the potential benefits and drawbacks of portfolio use and includes candid advice for teachers, administrators, and other educators who are weighing the possibility of using portfolios across classes, departments, or institutions.

◆ *Journals* offers advice on teaching students about journals—how they work and how students can use them to become more effective writers and capable thinkers.

◆ *Collaborative Learning* discusses how collaborative learning classrooms differ from traditional classrooms, how a collaborative learning environment can be encouraged and maintained, and how to use collaborative learning in the teaching of writing.

◆ *English as Second Language* considers how the adjustments made to help second-language learners can lead to effective teaching and learning for everyone in the classroom and addresses various strategies that can be employed in the teaching of English to non-native speakers.

◆ *Writing across the Curriculum* is written for college teachers in all disciplines and provides useful advice on writing across the curriculum—on teaching, on using writing as a tool for learning the subject being studied and as a strategy for improving the confidence and the ability of students to communicate effectively.

◆ *Windows V4.0 Writer's Helper* is based on the notion that software tools can contribute to sound, imaginative, and well-organized writing. It offers a collection of unique prewriting activities and revising tools to help students work through the writing process. Available in Windows® and Macintosh® versions, it includes 19 different *Prewriting Activities* and 18 different *Revising Tools*. NOTE: Each package contains the program disk and user's manual. Separate *Instructor's Manuals* are available for each version. Discount shrinkwrap packages are available to students when ordered with this text.

◆ *Webster's New World*™ *Dictionary, Third College edition,* or *Webster's New World*™ *Compact School and Office Dictionary* may be shrinkwrapped at a discounted price.

◆ *The Prentice Hall/Simon & Schuster Transparencies for Writers* is a set of 100 two- and four-color transparencies featuring exercises, examples, and suggestions for student writers that focus on all aspects of the writing process—from generating ideas and shaping an outline to preparing a final draft and revising, editing, and documenting the final paper. These transparencies also cover grammar, punctuation, and mechanics via overlays that show how sentence and paragraph errors can be corrected most effectively. These transparencies are free to adopters of this text when certain quantities of the text are purchased.

◆ *ABC News/Prentice Hall Video Library: Composition, Volume 2.* Through an exclusive agreement between ABC News and Prentice Hall, you can keep your classroom discussions lively and current with thematically arranged video clips from ABC News programs. Updated periodically, these clips serve as springboards for discussion, critical thinking, and writing. This video is free to adopters of this text when certain quantities of the text are purchased.

◆ *The Prentice Hall/New York Times "Themes of the Times" Program.* The *Themes of the Times* program, cosponsored by Prentice Hall and The New York Times, gives you and your students a newspaper supplement containing a recent collection of articles that provides students with timely examples of rhetorical principles and springboards for writing. The New York Times supplement is free upon adoption of this text and is available in student quantities.

◆ *The Prentice Hall Critical Thinking Audio Study Cassette* helps students develop critical thinking skills in 60 minutes—from asking the right questions to helpful tips on how to study, take effective notes, and become a more effective learner. This cassette is free to adopters of this text and can be shrinkwrapped to the qualifying text at a discount price.

Acknowledgments

As with any major project, many people worked to make this book happen. The following people were especially generous with knowledge, advice, support, and labor.

We would like to thank those instructors nationwide who agreed to share their insights on teaching writing, on using handbooks in general, and on improving our book in particular, among them Vivian R. Brown,

Laredo Community College; Christine Browning, University of Southern California; Hephzibah Roskelly, University of North Carolina at Greensboro; Laurie Sutherland, College of DuPage; and Kristin R. Woolever, Northeastern University.

We are grateful for the expertise and support of many people at Prentice Hall, namely, Phil Miller, President, Humanities and Social Sciences; Gina Sluss, Marketing Director; Anne Bonanno Nieglos, Art Director; Bonnie Biller, Senior Managing Editor; and Joan Foley, Production Editor.

Our text designers, Kenny Beck and Barbara Bert/North 7 Atelier, Ltd., have given form, order, and visual power to our ideas. Their design captures our message and makes it not only available but inviting.

We have saved special thanks for the sharpest Editor in Chief, Leah Jewell, whose critical commentary kept us honest and the book on track.

And finally, a word of thanks to friends and family members for their support.

Toby Fulwiler
Alan R. Hayakawa

The New York Times Program

The New York Times and Prentice Hall are sponsoring Themes of the Times, a program designed to enhance student access to current information of relevance in the classroom. Through this program, the core subject matter provided in the text is supplemented by a collection of time-sensitive articles from one of the world's most distinguished newspapers, *The New York Times*. These articles demonstrate the vital, ongoing connection between what is learned in the classroom and what is happening in the world around us.

To enjoy the wealth of information of The New York Times daily, a reduced subscription rate is available in deliverable areas. For information, call toll-free: 1-800-631-1222.

Prentice Hall and The New York Times are proud to cosponsor Themes of the Times. We hope it will make the reading of both textbooks and newspapers a more dynamic, involving process.

The ABC News / Prentice Hall Video Library: Composition

ABCNEWS Prentice Hall and ABC News have joined together to bring the most thoroughly integrated and comprehensive video libraries to the college market. These professional presentation packages offer both feature and documentary-style videos from a variety of ABC's award-winning news programs, including *World News Tonight, Nightline, 20/20, Primetime Live,* and others. Features in the **Composition Video Library** present current topics that can serve as springboards to discussion and writing.

THE
COLLEGE WRITER'S
REFERENCE

THE WRITING PROCESS

THE WRITING PROCESS

1 ◆ A WRITER'S QUESTIONS

Whether you know it or not, every time you write, you answer four questions: Why are you writing? To whom? Under what circumstances? And in what voice? These questions remain more or less the same whether you are writing at work or in school, in English or in other subjects across the curriculum. What makes a difference, however, is whether or not you are aware of these questions in the first place. Experienced writers usually don't ask each of these questions, as we did above, in so many words or at the start of every writing task. More likely, they begin already knowing how they intend to answer the first three questions—about purpose, audience, and situation—and return to these periodically as they draft, revise, and edit their texts. The fourth question, about voice, usually takes care of itself if writers have carefully addressed the first three. This chapter briefly examines the implications of these four questions, and the rest of *The College Writer's Reference* provides detailed strategies for answering them.

Purpose

1a

When you write a personal letter or journal entry, you know, consciously or not, the reason you are doing it and what you hope to accomplish—otherwise you wouldn't bother with it. When you write in response to a school assignment, however, your instructor determines the purpose, and you need to figure out, consciously and deliberately, what that purpose is. Regardless of who instigates it, thoughtful writing is purposeful writing. To have any chance at success, you need to know why you are writing.

For the moment, think about the broad range of purposes that writing serves. People write to *discover* what's on their minds, to pose or solve problems, and to vent frustrations. They write to *communicate* information to others about ideas, feelings, experiences, problems, questions, and answers. And sometimes they write to *create* literary artifacts by inventing new forms, poetic language, and make-believe worlds—for themselves and others to experience life in new ways. Look at each of these purposes more carefully.

Writing to discover

Writing helps you discover ideas, relationships, connections and patterns in your life. For serious writers, all writing is discovery writing. In college, writing can help you discover paper topics, develop those topics, expand and explain ideas, and connect seemingly unrelated material into coherent patterns.

topic and try to convince your audience that you are correct. The stand you take—your thesis—must be supported by evidence presented in a reasonable, believable manner. (For more on arguing positions, see Chapter 8.)

Writing to create

When your purpose is to create something, you pay special attention to the way your language looks and sounds—its form, shape, rhythm, images, and texture. While the term *creative writing* is usually associated with poetry, fiction, and drama, any text written with care, craft, and originality is potentially creative.

When you write to create, you pay less immediate attention to your audience and subject and more to the shape of the expression itself. Your goal is not to change the world or to transmit information about it; rather, you want to transform an experience or idea into something that will make your readers see the world from a different angle. You want the text—not just the information it contains—to affect your readers emotionally or aesthetically as well as intellectually.

Few college assignments will direct you to write creatively, but many papers could profit from imaginative approaches. Look especially for direction words such as *imagine, create, invent,* or *design.* Be careful, however, that your imaginative language supports rather than overshadows your communicative intention. (For more ideas about using creativity in college papers, see Chapter 9.)

Audience   1b

Whether a piece of writing is "good" is largely a question of how effectively it communicates with those who read it, the audience. To write effectively, you need to address your audience's needs. On one level, it helps simply to know that your audience is Professor Alvarez rather than your classmates or your mother. But on a deeper, more studied level, it helps to be aware of what your instructor knows, believes, and assumes, as well as why he or she made this particular assignment and what he or she expects it to accomplish.

All college papers are written for at least two audiences—the instructor and the person doing the writing. In addition, some assignments are written to be shared with classmates, the entire student body, or the world at large. Think of your different audiences as existing along a continuum, with those you know best at one end and those you know least at the other end.

Self ——— Peer ——— Instructor ——— Public

The better you know your readers' likes, dislikes, politics, interests, and assumptions, the easier the writing task should be.

The most common audience you write for in college, an instructor, is a difficult one. First, instructors create the assignments, which means they have ideas about what they want—and you need to figure out what they are. Second, they often know more about your subject than you do. And third, instructors from different disciplines as well as different instructors from the same discipline may have quite different criteria for what constitutes good writing. Writing successfully in one class is hard enough; writing successfully across the curriculum poses even more challenges. In spite of the difficulties of "reading" different college audiences, you will have a head start on the process if you understand the most fundamental reasons why most instructors assign papers: to witness your *knowledge, critical reasoning ability, creativity,* and *language skills.*

Knowledge

A good paper must demonstrate what you know and how well you know it. If, for instance, you argue for or against affirmative action policies, your instructor will look to see how much you know about recent civil rights history and current political debates. Are your facts accurate, your definitions correct, and your explanations clear? Are they presented in a believable manner? Is the information up to date? Were reputable sources consulted?

Critical reasoning

A good paper reveals your ability to reason logically and consistently, to support assertions, to organize information, and to be persuasive, whether you are writing a book review, a reflective essay, or a position paper. For example, in arguing for or against tighter gun control laws, you would offer reasons for your position and refute opposing arguments. Your reasoning ability shows in the clarity of your understanding, the justness of your claims, and the persuasiveness of your evidence.

Creativity

All good papers are original and creative in some way. When assignments are open-ended, it's a good idea to choose a topic that's challenging rather than simpleminded. When you present your information, approach it from a perspective that's original rather than commonplace. When you provide information to support assertions, reach for something unexpected instead of simply restating the predictable. And make your opening a surprise, your conclusion memorable.

Language skills

When reading your paper, instructors notice the language and clarity of your sentences; they see whether you have followed convention in your spelling, punctuation, and grammar and in your use of references. They also notice—sometimes unconsciously—what your writing looks like: its length, legibility, neatness, and accuracy and whether or not it's been proofread. Instructors' perceptions of your language skills often influence their attitudes toward the content of your papers.

Situation 1c

To "situate" or place yourself within a knowledgeable community is to write with authority and credibility about particular issues that this community cares about. Cutting across all disciplines and issues, however, are the overarching values of the academic community—the pursuit of *truth,* the need for *evidence,* and the importance of *balance.* When you write college papers, you need to remember that you are situated at all times within multiple language communities—that of your particular course and classroom, that of the discipline to which your instructor belongs, and that of the larger university community in which you, your classmates, and your instructor are participating. No college writer can learn the particular methods and conventions of all the academic disciplines, but all college writers can be aware of the central values subscribed to by the academic community at large. All college papers written with such understanding have a better chance of being successful.

Truth

Regardless of department or discipline, members of the university community are committed to the *pursuit of truth.* Instructors in each academic discipline—the sciences, social sciences, humanities, fine arts, business, and so on—pursue truth according to particular conventions, methods, and procedures. It is your job to learn and understand that knowledge and to represent it fairly in your papers and reports. To succeed in the academic world, you must pursue, if not catch, what is true and express it in language.

Evidence

Scholars in all disciplines use *credible evidence* to support the truths they find. Scientists make claims about the physical world and cite evidence to support those claims; art professors make similar claims about creative expression, and so on. As a college writer, it is wise to follow suit: make claims, assertions, or arguments that you believe to be true; then support those with the best evidence available. Always document the sources for this evidence. (For more on providing evidence, see Chapter 8; for more on documentation styles, see Chapters 47–49.)

Balance

It is difficult, even impossible, to prove that something is *absolutely* true. New authorities constantly call old conclusions into question. Consequently, those who write in the academic community make claims cautiously, with balanced, judicious language positioned somewhere between authority and doubt. Academic authors back up their claims with reasoning and evidence. As a college student, your own authority, like that of your instructors, will be based on how well you read, reason, and write. Present your inferences, assertions, and arguments in balanced language, being fair to opposing points of view.

1d Voice

Writing voices range from quietly assertive to tentative or insecure, from instructive to angry or aggressive, from serious to ironic or sarcastic, from clear to meandering or garbled. And each writer is capable of projecting all these voices at one time or another. On the one hand, each writer speaks with a collective voice derived from the social communities to which he or she belongs. On the other hand, each writer speaks with a unique voice derived from his or her particular blend of background and experience. Some voices create belief and inspire trust while others do not.

On one level, a written voice re-creates the sound of a person speaking on the page. Careful writers control, as much as they can, the sound of their words in their readers' minds. On another level, every writer's text conveys something of the person behind the words. This is a voice that needs to be heard—the voice on the page that represents a person's political, philosophical, and social values as well as his or her commitment to certain causes. To complicate matters further, what writers stand for may be revealed in the way they reason about things, whether in an orderly, scientific manner or more intuitively and emotionally.

At the same time, the choices an author makes regarding *purpose, audience,* and *situation* go a long way toward determining the voice he or she is likely to project. For example, if you are writing to explain your interpretation of a text in which you have carefully marked supportive passages, odds are that you will project a voice that is serious rather than sarcastic, objective as opposed to subjective, and confident, not timid. You might alter your voice depending on whether your instructor prefers formal or informal writing, has a sense of humor, or likes you. In other words, experienced writers make deliberate choices about the voice they project. If you understand the components of voice—tone, style, structure, value, and authority—you'll be better able to accomplish your goals for a piece of writing.

QUESTIONS FOR EXAMINING YOUR VOICE

1   Tone. Read drafts aloud and listen to the attitudes they convey. Consider how a member of your audience will envision you: What does this writer think of the subject matter? How does this writer feel about the audience being addressed? If the tone is not what you intended, how could you change it?

2   Style. What image of yourself do you create through your language? Is your language formal or informal? Complex or simple?

3   Structure. Create an outline of every draft. What does your structure say about your manner of thinking? Is your thinking careful and tight? Loose and flexible? Logical? Intuitive? Which do you want it to be?

4   Value. Do your beliefs show through when you speak on paper? Do you want them to?

5   Authority. Where does your writing voice sound especially knowledgeable and confident? Where does it sound tentative and unsure? What can you do to make it more consistently authoritative?

Tone

Tone is the attitude you adopt toward your subject matter and your audience: angry, joyous, sarcastic, puzzled, contemptuous, anxious, respectful, friendly, and so on. Writers control tone by adopting a particular perspective or point of view, selecting words carefully, structuring sentences, emphasizing some words and ideas over others, choosing certain patterns of inflection, and controlling the pace with pauses and other punctuation. Reread out loud everything you write and see if the tone matches your intentions.

Style

Style is the distinctive way you express yourself. It can change from situation to situation, and it will evolve over time as you grow and change. Style in writing is determined by the level of formality (formal, informal, or colloquial) and by the simplicity or complexity of your words, sentences, and paragraphs. Unless circumstances dictate otherwise, you should write in a style that is clear, simple, and direct, one that comes easily and sounds like a real human being speaking.

Structure

Structure is the organization of and relationships among the parts within your text: where you start and conclude, how things are ordered in between, and which ideas are grouped together. A structured pattern or logic governs all thoughtful writing, usually revealing something of the thought process that created it. A linear, logical structure presents you as a linear, logical thinker. A circular, intuitive structure presents you as creative and intuitive. Structure your discourse accordingly.

Value

When you state what you believe or give your opinion, you convey what you **value**—socially, politically, culturally and so on. Unless you deliberately mislead or lie, your personal beliefs will be somewhere in the foreground or background of everything you write. Learn when to feature your values and when not to. For example, personal values are expected in a personal essay but not in a lab report. When writing a paper, consider whether the purpose of the assignment calls for an implicit or explicit statement of your values. Examine drafts for opinions and judgments that reveal your values, and keep them or take them out as appropriate.

Authority

The conviction or **authority** with which you write is born of knowledge and implies self-confidence and control. Whether you write from research or personal experience, you can exert and project real authority only over material you know well. The more you know your subject, the more self-assured your voice will be, and the more readers will believe you. To gain authority in your writing, conduct thorough research and read sources of information carefully and critically.

ANSWERING A WRITER'S QUESTIONS

1 **Analyze the assignment.** Identify words that give directions and describe the subject. Does the assignment ask you to report, explain, define, describe, analyze, interpret, argue, compare/contrast, imagine, discuss, evaluate, or something else?

2 **Identify the audience.** Address your instructor, and be aware of the multiple ways in which he or she expects you to demonstrate your knowledge, reason, creativity, and use of language conventions.

3 **Place yourself in the academic community.** Recognize and adopt the conventions that are used. When you draft, pursue the goals of finding truth, providing evidence, and giving balance in everything you write.

4 **Make your paper speak for you.** Gain control of your writing voice by understanding the elements of tone, style, structure, values, and authority.

---

2 ◆ THE WRITING PROCESS

The process of writing serious academic papers from beginning to end can be complicated, frustrating, and exhilarating all at the same time. Once started, the thinking and rethinking, revising and editing won't stop until the paper is finished. Good papers begin sometimes as vague notions, at other times as specific intentions, as writers shape words into sentences, then paragraphs, then whole texts. In serious papers, revising is a given, as writers continue by asking questions, searching for answers, filling in gaps, shoring up arguments—sometimes even starting over. Thoughtful papers conclude with careful editing and line-by-line proofreading to guarantee clarity and correctness. If this messy process sounds familiar to you, you're not alone. Most writers wish it were simpler and easier, wish for formulas to follow, for guaranteed procedures, but good writing doesn't work that way.

This text assumes there are no formulas or procedures that will guarantee a good paper every time. No single technique or strategy works all the time or for everyone. Writing remains a complex, variable, many-faceted process that refuses to be reduced to a foolproof formula. However, some strategies work better than others for more people on more occasions.

The following chapters identify a set of discrete but overlapping and all too often nonsequential phases of the process of writing—planning, drafting, researching, revising, and editing. For discussion purposes, it's necessary to separate these phases of writing, but don't worry if they refuse to stay separate in practice. These phases are recursive; they move back and forth, over and under, around and back, refusing to stay in linear order. In other words, if you're a serious writer, you will go through all these phases again and again, but don't worry if they don't follow the sequence described here. Despite your best intentions, you sometimes edit when you are drafting, revise when editing, and draft as you research. What does matter, regardless of how you mix these phases, is that you know how to do them and take the time to do them well.

Planning   2a

Planning involves creating, discovering, locating, developing, organizing, and trying out ideas. Writers plan deliberately when they make notes, turn casual lists into organized outlines, write journal entries, compose rough drafts, and consult with others. They also plan less deliberately while they walk, jog, eat, read, browse in libraries, and converse with friends or when they wake up in the middle of the night with an idea. Planning also involves limiting options, making choices, locating the best strategies, and focusing energy in the most productive direction. Planning comes first—and it also comes second and third. No matter how careful your first plans, good writing necessitates that you make subsequent plans as you go through the process of deciding why you are writing, what you are writing, and for whom. (See Chapters 3–4 to help you find and develop topics for college papers.)

2b Drafting

At some point, all writers move beyond planning and actually start writing. The real secret to good writing is in learning to just sit down and begin. A first draft is concerned with ideas, with finding direction and clarifying concepts. Subsequent drafts—those at the revising and editing stages—are concerned with making the initial ideas clearer and more precise. While all of us hope that our first draft will be our final draft, it seldom is; give yourself the opportunity to create second and third drafts. (See Chapters 5–8 for suggestions for drafting particular kinds of college papers.)

2c Researching

Research writing commonly means two different things in college. On the one hand, serious writers conduct *informal* research every time their writing is based on new information rather than memory—personal essays, for example, benefit from additional factual information that substantiates and intensifies what the writer remembers. Every time you write an analysis or an interpretation of a text, you do research. You also do research when you track down the dates of historical events, conduct laboratory experiments, visit museums, consult books in a library, or interview people. In other words, whenever you write about unfamiliar subjects, you have two choices: bluff (make things up) or do research.

On the other hand, *formal* research writing within the college community is often tied closely to the search for knowledge within specific research communities called disciplines. In each discipline, such as English, history, sociology, or biology, students investigate certain kinds of knowledge and report the results in writing by following certain conventions of form and style. Writing such "research papers" calls for detailed knowledge of disciplinary conventions. (See Chapters 44–48 for guidance through the whole process of writing research papers.)

Revising   2d

Somewhere in the middle to later stages of composing, writers revise the drafts they have planned, drafted, and researched. **Revising** involves rewriting to make the purpose clearer, the argument stronger, the details sharper, the evidence more convincing, or the organization more logical. We discuss revising as a different process than editing. Revising means re-seeing the drafted paper and thinking again about its direction, focus, arguments, and evidence. It may involve cutting away material or adding new information. (See Chapter 9 to learn new strategies for revising any college paper.)

Editing   2e

Whether writers have written three drafts or five, they want the last one to be as nearly perfect as possible. **Editing**, in contrast to revising, means working with what is already there to sharpen, tighten, or clarify the language and to make sure that paragraphs and sentences express exactly what you intend. Writers pay careful attention to the language they have used, striving for the most punch possible. Many writers edit so that their writing sounds right to their own ear, in the hope that this improves communication with their intended readers. During the editing stage, check the clarity of ideas, the logic and flow of paragraphs, the precision and power of words, and the correctness and accuracy of facts, references, spelling, and punctuation. (See Chapter 10 for an overview of the editing process, which is discussed in detail in Parts II through V of the book.)

Writing with computers   2f

Computers have revolutionized the way writers work. Unlike typewriters, pens, or pencils, computers allow writers to change their writing easily before the words ever show up on paper. A writer does not have to commit to a final version before it is printed out; until then, the paper can be revised again and again without retyping everything. All word-processing programs work in much the same way: they can store each working session in a separate document or file.

Computers make it easy for you to move back and forth freely as you compose. If you are like most writers, you probably like to jump around from planning to drafting to researching and back again; computers facilitate this process by keeping everything fluid and endlessly changeable.

Following are ten ways that computers can help you in the process of writing.

1 **Planning.** Use the computer to invent and discover ideas. Write lists of topics or tentative outlines. The computer's ability to add, delete, and rearrange makes these planning and organizing strategies easy.

2 **Freewriting.** Freewrite rapidly on your computer when you're exploring ideas or simply stuck. Don't worry about spelling, punctuation, grammar, or style. Let your words trigger new thoughts and suggest new plans and directions. By saving these entries on disk, you can create a computer journal.

3 **Drafting.** Use the computer to compose initial ideas, taking advantage of the ease with which words, sentences, and paragraphs can be modified and moved around as your ideas and direction become clearer. It's also easy to lift whole passages from computer-written freewrites or journal writing and incorporate them directly into your draft.

4 **Researching.** Computers that are networked or equipped with modems allow you to gain access to library information or material on the Internet. Instead of traveling physically to locate books, periodicals, and special collections, you can search for material and print it at your desk.

5 **Revising.** Typing on a computer creates instant distance from your words and ideas, allowing you to view them more objectively. Whole paragraphs can be easily deleted, added, changed, and moved around— all useful activities when revising early drafts. You can add new research information or evidence in appropriate sections. Your computer will repaginate and reformat instantly.

6 **Editing.** Computers allow you to try out numerous possibilities when editing sentences and paragraphs. The search-and-replace function can make each sentence start a new line so you can judge it on its own merits. Periodically, print out a hard copy to review your text; changes you make on paper can then be incorporated easily on screen for a new printout.

7 **Referencing.** With a keystroke, you can consult online dictionaries, encyclopedias, thesauruses, grammar books, and style manuals to check and change your text.

8 **Proofreading.** In modern word-processing programs, built-in spelling and grammar checkers will identify words or sentence constructions that may be incorrect. Although the computer will mark these spots in your papers, it is you who will need to decide whether or not a change is in order. For example, if you use a sentence fragment deliberately, you will tell the program to ignore it. In addition, you must still proofread with your own eyes, since the computer will not flag omitted words or mistyped words that spell other words (*of/if* or *dinner/diner*).

9 **Formatting.** Many word-processing programs give you a choice of print

styles (font and size), graphic images (clip art, Internet images), and page layouts (one, two, or three columns) so you can produce professional-looking and visually exciting papers that have improved readability and aesthetic appeal.

10. **Saving.** When you write with a computer, it is easy to make backup copies of all your work. Serious writers save all versions of their papers on both a hard drive and floppy disks. You can always return to your backup copy if later revisions don't turn out well.

When English is your second language   2g

If English is not your native language, the most important thing you can do to improve your writing skills in English is to read, write, speak, and listen attentively to as much English as you can.

Besides learning new grammar and vocabulary, be prepared to adjust to the expectations and traditions of the American classroom. For example, American academic prose is often less formal than that in many other countries. Students who have learned to write in more formal systems may find instructors suggesting that they make their writing more lively or personal. Also, while U.S. schools increasingly treat writing as a multiple-draft process, instructors in many other countries may expect a piece of writing to be finished when it is handed in.

Throughout this book are boxes that provide information of particular interest to nonnative speakers. The letters *ESL* in the table of contents identify each section of the book that includes one of these specially marked boxes. An ESL index is provided at the back of the book to help you locate these topics.

USING YOUR NATIVE LANGUAGE WHEN COMPOSING IN ENGLISH   ESL

You may want to compose in both your native language and English when working on a writing assignment. For example, you might brainstorm, make notes, or create outlines in your native language, or you could use native language words or phrases when you're not sure of the English equivalents. Using your native language this way may help you avoid writer's block and develop fluency in English. Periodically you should evaluate the effectiveness of your composing strategies. For instance, if you find that using a native language–English dictionary often results in unidiomatic constructions, you may want to become more familiar with a good dictionary of standard American English.

3 ◆ INVENTING AND DISCOVERING

You can't write if you don't have ideas. Experienced writers, however, know that you don't have to *start* with ideas, that ideas will come if you know where and how to look for them. In fact, one of the simplest ways of finding ideas is simply to start writing, even when you think you have nothing to say, and let the writing force ideas out. Once that happens, you're started, and you can accept, reject, or modify those ideas. But if just writing doesn't bring forth the muse, writers must invent and discover ways to make her show up.

Writers invent when they create new ideas. Writers discover when they relocate forgotten ideas or learn by reading or listening to others. Writers invent and discover in virtually all phases of the writing process: when limiting and focusing assignments, when finding topics and approaching topics, when developing answers to questions and solutions to problems, and when figuring out openings and conclusions, arranging arguments, and placing supporting examples. This chapter outlines six specific strategies to help you invent or discover ideas when you need them: *brainstorming, freewriting, looping, asking reporter's questions, outlining,* and *clustering.*

3a   Brainstorming

Brainstorming is nothing more than systematic list making. Ask yourself a question, and then list all possible answers that come to mind. Write these down fast, and look for more answers. Sometimes it helps to set goals for yourself: *What are seven possible topics for my paper on pollution?* Try leaving the question open-ended and see what happens: *What are all the sources of lake pollution that I've heard about?* Each item in your list becomes a possible direction for your paper.

Let one idea on your list lead to the next. For example, in making a shopping list, you do a form of brainstorming: you write *eggs* and it reminds you of *bacon* or *orange juice.* To brainstorm, generate as long a list as possible, and force yourself to find and record even vague, half-formed ideas in concrete language. Then examine your list and decide which items are worth pursuing.

Whenever they're stuck in any phase of their writing process, writers brainstorm by making lists, asking questions, and posing answers. The following exercise helps push vague subjects into shaped topics.

1 List as many topics as you can in three minutes. Circle the three that interest you most and write a paragraph about each.
2 Ask two questions about each paragraph. Find two answers to each question.
3 Select the paragraph that now interests you most, and list three different ways to start this paper.

Freewriting   **3b**

Freewriting is writing quickly without rules. When you freewrite, you deliberately free-associate, allowing one word to trigger the next, one idea to lead to
another. You attempt to discover ideas by writing intensely, nonstop and without censoring, drawing thoughts from wherever in your memory they may reside. We don't exactly understand why freewriting works, but it does. The following suggestions will help.

1 Write as fast as you can for a fixed period of time, say five or ten minutes, toward whatever problem you need to solve.
2 Don't allow yourself to stop writing or typing until the time is up.
3 Don't worry about what your freewriting looks like or how it's
   organized — your only audience is yourself.
4 If you can't think of what else to write, write about being stuck — a better idea will come along soon.

   Don't worry if you digress, misspell a word, or write something silly. If
you catch a fleeting thought that's especially interesting or think of something
you've never thought of before, then the freewriting has worked. The following five-minute freewrite started John on a research topic about a local vendor.

> I can't think of anything special just now, nothing really comes to
> mind, well maybe something about the downtown mall would be good be-
> cause I wouldn't mind spending time down there. Something about the
> mall . . . maybe the street vendors, the hot dog guy or the pretzel guy
> or that woman selling T and sweatshirts, they're always down there, even
> in lousy weather — do they like it that much? Do they need the money
> that bad? Why do people become street vendors — like maybe they gradu-
> ated from college and couldn't get jobs? Or were these guys who never
> wanted anything to do with college? Pretty interesting.

FREEWRITING AS A WAY TO DEVELOP FLUENCY   ◆ ESL

Writing in a second language can be frustrating when you are trying to
pay attention to ideas, sentence structures, word choices, and so on.
Many ESL writers have discovered that freewriting helps tremendously
with this problem. If you haven't tried freewriting before, you might find
it hard at first not to stop and carefully check each sentence, but with
continued practice this activity should help you to postpone editing and
improve your fluency in English.

3c Looping

Looping is an extended variation of freewriting in which you do a series of freewrites, each one focusing more closely on the issue becoming foremost in your mind. Loop writing focuses freewriting; it zooms in on an as yet unspecified target. Your goal is to discover that target. To loop, follow this procedure.

1 Freewrite for ten minutes to discover a fresh topic or to advance the one you are working on.
2 Review your freewrite and select one sentence that you want to continue developing. Copy this sentence, and freewrite for another ten minutes. (John selected *Why do people become street vendors?* and started another freewrite.)
3 Repeat step 2 for each successive freewrite to continue looping.

3d Asking a reporter's questions

Writers who train themselves to ask questions are also training themselves to find information. Reporters train themselves to ask six basic questions: *Who? What? Where? When? Why?* and *How?* Using these questions will help you discover information. To initiate paper topics about issues, events, or personal experience, ask yourself the reporter's questions.

Who was involved?

What happened?

Where did this happen?

When did it happen?

Why did it happen?

How did it happen?

3e Making outlines

Essentially, **outlines** are organized lists. In fact, outlines grow out of lists as writers determine which ideas go first and which later, which are equally important and which need to be subordinated. Sometimes an informal outline, using indentations to indicate the relationships, is all you need.

When one student set out to write a research essay on the effect of acid rain on the New England environment, she first brainstormed a list of areas that such an essay might cover:

What is acid rain?

What are its effects on the environment?

What causes it?

How can it be stopped?

After a substantial amount of preliminary research, this student had so much information that she turned to a formal outline to help her organize her paper and guide her writing process.

Formal outlines follow a few guidelines to establish hierarchy and logic. Major headings for large topics are made with Roman numerals. Subordinate or supporting ideas are indented and identified with capital letters. Ideas subordinate to these levels are indented further and identified by Arabic numbers. Smaller ideas still are indented further and identified with lowercase letters. Every level should present at least two ideas since an idea cannot be divided only once.

- Every Roman numeral I has at least a II.

- Every capital letter *A* has at least a *B*.

- Every number 1 has at least a number 2.

- Every lowercase letter *a* has a *b*.

Keep ideas that are paired in the same grammatical form, such as nouns or whole sentences.

In the following example, the four main points are Roman numerals; the supporting ideas are capital letters; the smaller details, Arabic numbers; and so on.

I.   Definition of acid rain
II.   Causes of acid rain
    A.   Coal-burning power plants
    B.   Automobile pollution
    C.   Military pollution
III. Effects of acid rain
    A.   Deforestation in New England
       1.   The White Mountains study

2.   Maple trees dying in Vermont
    a.   Aerial survey of 1987
    b.   Satellite evidence
    c.   Decline in maple syrup production
B.   Dead lakes
IV.   Solutions to the acid rain problem

The effort to make an outline not only helps organize the paper; it also shows the writer what she doesn't know and where her supporting information is weak. Inventing an outline helps you discover your paper's true focus.

3f   Clustering

Clustering is a method of listing ideas in a nonlinear way to reveal the relationships among them. Clustering is useful both for inventing and discovering a topic and for exploring a topic after you have done preliminary research. Like outlining, the act of clustering helps you both invent and organize at the same time. To create a clustering diagram, follow this procedure.

1 Write a word or phrase that seems to focus on what you want to write about. For example, write *acid rain* on a page and circle it.

2 Connect supporting ideas related to your circled phrase by drawing a line from the phrase to the related concepts. Circle and connect each aspect of *acid rain* back to the central idea.

3 Start a new cluster of related ideas around each supporting idea until you have mapped the relationships and dimensions of your paper.

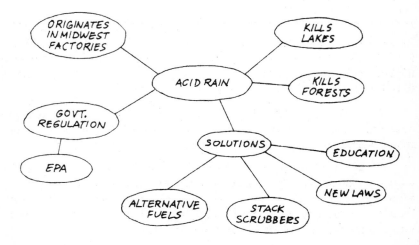

SUGGESTIONS FOR INVENTION AND DISCOVERY

1   Brainstorm a list of five possible topics to write about for your next paper assignment. [See 3a.]
2   Freewrite for ten minutes about the most interesting topic on your list. [See 3b.]
3   Loop back in your freewriting, selecting the most interesting or useful point, and freewrite again with that point as the focus [See 3c.]
4   Ask the reporter's questions about the topic, look at your answers, and determine your next step. [See 3d.]
5   Cluster ideas about your topic until it is developed as far as possible. [See 3f.]
6   Make an outline of a possible structure for your paper. [See 3e.]

---

4 ◆ JOURNAL WRITING

Journals allow people to talk to themselves without feeling silly. They help college students figure out and reflect on what is happening in their personal and academic lives. Journal writing can focus narrowly on the subject matter of a single discipline or speculate broadly on the whole range of academic experience. Personal journals allow writers to explore their private thoughts and feelings about anything that matters.

Understanding journals   4a

In simplest terms, journals are daily records of people's lives (*jour* is French for "day"), similar to diaries, daybooks, or logs. Record whatever snippets of life you find interesting and potentially useful when you sit down to write. Certain characteristics, however, remain true for most journals.

Sequence   Journals capture thoughts sequentially, from one day to the next. By dating each entry you can create an ongoing record of your constancy, change, or growth over the course of a semester or a project.

Audience   Journals are written to help writers rather than readers. A journal is a place to explore what's important to you, not to communicate information or ideas to someone else. By providing a place to share your thoughts and hear reactions, however, an assigned journal may initiate an informal conversation between you and your instructor.

Language   Your journal-writing style is whatever you want it to be. Use your most comfortable voice, and concentrate on ideas rather than on grammar, spelling, or punctuation.

Freedom   Journals are discovery and practice books in which you are free to try out new ideas. Nothing is "wrong" in a journal, so you cannot be penalized. Explore whatever you choose: try to put new concepts into your own words, explore new lines of reasoning, or vent your frustrations. Don't worry about completing every thought; you can always come back to any topic.

4b   Academic journals

Academic journals might be described as a cross between private diaries, written solely for the writer, and class notebooks, which record an instructor's words. Like diaries, journals are written in the first person about ideas important to the writer; and like class notebooks, they focus on a college subject.

Diary————> *Academic journal* <———— *Class notebook*

A well-kept journal will include your thoughts, reactions, reflections, and questions about classes and ideas, written in informal language—and it will be the best possible record of your educational experience.

Journals in the writing class

Journals are often assigned in writing classes, both to help student writers discover, explore, advance, and critique their writing projects and to help instructors informally assess their students' development as writers.

Part of the content of a writing course is the business of learning to write. Use your journal to document how your writing is going and what you need to do next to improve it. Learn to assess your writing attitudes and actions, and to record the plans, strategies, and situations that promote your best writing.

Also use your journal to find paper topics, to try out introductions and arguments, to record relevant research and observations, to assess how a paper is turning out, and to make plans for what to do next. In the following journal entry, John tells himself what to do in the next draft of a paper describing his coaching of an eighth-grade girls' soccer team.

9/16 I'm going to try to use more dialogue in my paper. That is what I really think I was missing. The second draft is very dull. As

I read it, it has no life. I should have used more detail. I'll try more dialogue, lots more, in draft 3. I'll have it take place at one of my practices, giving a vivid description of what kids were like. I have SO MUCH MATERIAL. But I have a hard time deciding what seems more interesting.

John's entry is an excellent example of a writer critically evaluating himself and, on the basis of that evaluation, making plans to change something.

Also use your journal to record regularly what you've learned about writing through class discussions, through reading other student papers, and through reviewing your own writing. Near the end of John's writing course, he reflected in his journal about what he'd learned so far.

11/29 I've learned to be very critical of my own work, to look at it again and again, looking for big and little problems. I've also learned from my writing group that other people's comments are extremely helpful—so now I make sure I show my early drafts to Kelly before I write the final draft. I guess I've always known this, but now I actually do it.

Journals across the curriculum

Journals are good tools for learning any subject. Use your journal to clarify course goals, pose and solve problems, keep track of readings, raise questions to ask in class, practice for exams, and explore paper topics. Julie, who kept a journal about all the authors she studied in her American literature course, noticed a disturbing pattern and tried to evaluate it. She used the act of journal writing to process an idea, interpret that idea, and test her hypothesis. Writing to learn means trusting that as you write, ideas will come.

5/4 So far, the two authors we have read have led tragic, unhappy lives. I wonder if this is a coincidence or if it has something to do with the personality of successful writers. Actually, of all people, writers need a lot of time alone, by themselves, thinking and writing, away from other people, including, probably, close family members. The more I think about it, writers would be difficult to live with, that's it—they spend so much time alone and become hard to live with.

Try putting your instructor's question into your own language and see if that leads you closer to an answer. If you are asked to keep journals for several classes at one time, consider using a loose-leaf notebook with dividers for each class to cut down the number of notebooks you carry. You can hand in relevant entries for each class while keeping your journals active.

Personal writing

Try making connections between college knowledge and personal knowledge. For example, by recording personal reflections in a literature or history journal, you may begin to identify with and perhaps make sense of an otherwise distant or confusing past. Or you can use your journal to develop a wider awareness of the world, to examine your social and political climate, and to reflect on the everyday happenings in the news. In the following example, Jennifer uses her journal to reflect on sexist language.

> 3/8 Sexist language is everywhere. So much so that people don't even realize what they are saying is sexist. My teacher last year told all the "mothers-to-be" to be sure to read to their children. What about the fathers? Sexist language is dangerous because it so easily undermines women's morale and self-image. I try my hardest not to use sexist language, but even I find myself falling into old stereotypes.

In personal journals, writers explore feelings about college, declaring a major, getting along with a roommate, receiving a low grade on a paper, going to a party, or meeting a new friend. If you find yourself writing mostly about personal experiences in your academic journal, maybe you should start a separate personal journal that you keep strictly for yourself.

ESL ▷ **JOURNALS FOR SECOND-LANGUAGE WRITING**

When you are writing in a language other than your native language, journals can be especially useful. Since you don't have to be concerned with correctness, you can work on developing fluency. A journal is a good opportunity for experimenting with language; you may want to try out new vocabulary or use different kinds of sentence structures.

For an academic journal, your instructor will most likely expect you to do more than summarize assigned reading. Consider a double-entry journal. Summarize what you have read in one column, and then comment on or raise questions about the reading in the column next to it.

To develop your English vocabulary, use a journal to keep an ongoing list of new words. This list can include both vocabulary you learn in your classes and words or idioms you hear outside of class.

Journal-writing activities   **4c**

Planning

A journal can help you plan any project by providing a place to talk it
over with yourself. Whether you need to write a research paper, a personal essay, or a take-home examination, make journal notes on how to approach it,
where to start, or who else to consult before actually beginning a draft. Here is
an entry from Peter's journal kept for his first-year writing class.

> 10/12 Well, I switched my research topic to something I'm actu-
> ally interested in, a handicapped children's rehabilitation program right
> here on campus. My younger brother was born deaf, and our whole fam-
> ily has pitched in to help him—but I've never really studied what a col-
> lege program could do to help. The basis of my research will be inter-
> views with people who run the program—I have my first appointment
> tomorrow with Professor Stanford.

Sometimes planning means evaluating what's wrong and exploring new
directions. Journals can be powerful problem-solving tools.

KEEPING A JOURNAL

1   Keep it flexible. Buy a loose-leaf notebook that will allow you to
add, subtract, and rearrange entries, so you can edit your journal before sharing it with an instructor.
2   Organize. Add dividers and set aside space to write about different subjects, some personal, some academic.
3   Make it fun. Write with a favorite pen; sketch ideas; experiment
with voice and style.
4   Make it a ritual. Write at the same time or same place each
day, whether you think you have anything to say or not. If you start
writing, the ideas will come.
5   Leave blank space. Start each entry on a new page. Leave
plenty of white space so new thoughts can emerge without competing
with previous ones. Later, use the blank space for notes or clippings.
6   Date each entry. Record the date and other information of interest (time, place, weather, etc.). Your journal is a personal historical
document, and such information may be of interest in the future.
7   Write to yourself. Write in your natural voice, your letter-writing
voice. Don't worry about style, spelling, or punctuation.
8   Carry it everywhere. Tote your journal in a book bag or back-
pack, in school and out, and stop during the day to capture the unique
events of your life.

Recording growth

Sometimes it's hard to see how much you've learned until you reread your journal at the end of a term and notice where you began and where you ended. Your writing may have been casual and fast, your thinking tentative, your assessments or conclusions uncertain. But your journal gives you a record of who you were, what you thought, and how you've changed. Reread your journal periodically and record what you discover, as Jeff does below.

> 11/21 The journal to me has been like a one-man debate, where I could write thoughts down and then later read them. This seemed to help clarify many of my ideas. To be honest there is probably fifty percent of the journal that is nothing but B.S. and ramblings to fulfill assignments, but that still leaves fifty percent that I think is of importance. The journal is also a time capsule. I want to put it away and not look at it for ten or twenty years and let it recall for me this period of my life.

5 ◆ RECOUNTING EXPERIENCE

All of us have stories to tell. We tell stories to inform and entertain others, to leave behind permanent records of our lives, and to know and understand ourselves better. And all narratives are made up of the same elements: *Who* did this happen to? *What* happened? *Where* did it happen? *When? Why?* and *How?* To recount a personal experience, a writer must weave these elements together into a coherent whole.

5a   Finding a topic (what?)

Topics for good stories know no limits. You already have a lifetime of experiences to choose from. Each of your experiences is a potential story that helps explain who you are, what you believe, and how you act today. In choosing a topic, your first two questions should be *Which experience do I want to write about?* and *Can I make it interesting for others to read?* The following are three possible writing topics.

Winning and losing

Winning something—a race, a contest, a game, an argument—can be a good subject since it allows you to explore a unique situation or celebrate a special talent. Losing is also a good subject since it happens to us more often. When one person wins a race or one team a championship, dozens do not, so there is a large, empathetic audience who will understand and identify with a narrative about a loss or struggle. Why something doesn't work out is often fertile territory for fresher, deeper original stories.

Milestones

An interesting but also difficult experience to write about is one that you already recognize as a turning point in your life, whether it's performing before a live audience for the first time, traveling abroad, or publishing a first story. When you write about milestones, try to be more descriptive than celebratory, pointing out the physical details of the experience to put your reader at the scene rather than generalizing and explaining things that are obvious.

Daily life

Commonplace experiences make strong subjects for personal narratives precisely because everyday experiences are often overlooked. Describe practicing for rather than winning the big game, cleaning up after rather than attending the prom, or clerking at the supermarket when nothing special happened. Work experiences are especially fruitful subjects since you know the inside details and routines that the rest of us can only guess about.

Delineating character (who?)   5b

When characters in a good story are believable and interesting, they come alive. In personal experience writing, the main character is yourself, so give your readers a good sense of who you are. You can accomplish this through the voice in which you speak, the actions you portray, and the insights you share.

Voice

When you recount an experience, your language reveals the kind of person you are—playful, serious, rigid, loose, stuffy, honest, warm, or whatever. In the following excerpt, Beth's casual inside-the-head voice relates her experience playing oboe during a two-hour Saturday morning orchestra rehearsal.

> I love that section. It sounds so cool when Sarah and I play together like that. Now I can put my reed back in the water and sit back and listen. I probably should be counting the rests. Counting would mean I'd have to pay attention and that's no fun. I'd rather look around and watch everyone else sweat.

Action

Readers learn something about the kind of person you are from your actions. While the term *action* usually suggests movement of some kind, action can also be very quiet, as Mary demonstrates in relating her experience as a summer camp counselor for emotionally disturbed children.

> Josh looked so peaceful and sweet asleep that it was hard to imagine how difficult he had been all afternoon. He asked me to rub his head so he could fall asleep. I remember that first night hoping that he liked me—at least a little bit. I was so happy that I could give him a week of the love and happiness he couldn't get at home.

Insight

One of the best ways to reveal who you are is to show yourself gaining a new insight—a new self-awareness or a new way of seeing the world. While insights can occur for unexplainable reasons, they are most likely to occur when you encounter new ideas or have experiences that change you in some way. Jeff developed a new self-awareness when he participated in Outward Bound, a monthlong program that teaches wilderness survival skills.

> Day 13. After three days of not seeing one single person, I know the three basic necessities of life. Sorry, Dad, they are not stocks, bonds, and spreadsheets. And no, Mom, they're not *General Hospital, Days of Our Lives,* and *All My Children.* All I have been doing is melting snow for drinking water, rationing my food so it will last, and splitting dead trees for firewood.

5c Establishing perspective (how?)

Perspective addresses how close—in time, distance, or spirit—you are to the experience. Do you write as if it happened long ago or just yesterday? Do you summarize what happened or put readers at the scene? Do you explain the experience or leave it mysterious? Point of view and verb tense are two means of controlling perspective.

Point of view

Using the first-person perspective puts the narrator right in the story itself, as a participant (*I camped out*). The third person (*he* or *she camped out*) establishes a distinction between the person narrating the events and the person experiencing them and thus tends to depersonalize the story.

Tense

Verb tense establishes the time when the story happened or is happening. The tense used to relate most of the events in a story is called the **governing tense.** Personal experience stories are usually set in either the past tense (see Mary's in 5b) or present tense (see Beth's in 5b).

Describing setting (where?)   5d

Experiences always happen in a particular place, and good stories describe these settings. To convincingly describe a physical setting, re-create the sights, sounds, smells, and physical sensations that allow readers to experience it for themselves. Try to include evocative, unusual details that let your readers be there with you. In the following example, notice how many sight words Heather uses to describe the farm where she spent the summer picking strawberries.

> The sun is just barely rising over the treetops, and there is still dew covering the ground. In the strawberry patch, the deep green leaves are filled with water droplets, and the strawberries are big and red and ready to be picked. The patch is located in a field off the road near a small forest of Christmas trees. The white house, the red barn, and a checkerboard of fields can be seen in the distance. It is 5:30 a.m. and the day has begun.

Ordering events (when?)   5e

In every story, events are ordered one way or another. While you cannot alter the events that happened in your experience, as a writer you need to decide which events to portray and in what order to present them.

The most common way to sequence events is **chronological order,** with events presented in the order in which they happened. Chronological order can be straightforward, following a day from morning to night or an event over several weeks or months. Chronology can also be broken up, so that readers are introduced to an event in the present and then flash back to events that happen earlier. For example, Jeff's Outward Bound paper could start with his last day of solo camping and then flash back to his arrival. Such a sequence has the advantage of stimulating readers' interest by opening with a point of exceptional drama or insight.

Developing a theme (why?)   5f

Perhaps the most important element in a story is its meaning for both writer and reader. Why was this story worth telling in the first place? Unlike argument or informational writing, the theme of a personal essay or story is sel-

---

CHECKLIST FOR PAPERS OF PERSONAL EXPERIENCE

1 Who is telling the story? What does the reader need to know about the narrator?
2 What is the story about? A major event? A minor event?
3 Where does the story take place? Do details reveal the setting?
4 When does the action take place: Hour? Day? Month? Year? Is time important?
5 Why is this story worth recounting to somebody else?
6 How is the story told: First person? Third person? Past tense? Present tense?
7 Is the dialogue helpful? Does it sound like real people talking?
8 Is it necessary to tell the reader how to react to the story? Should it be?
9 Is the story best told through straight chronology or flashbacks? Why?

---

dom explicitly stated in the first paragraph. Instead, storytellers may create a meaning that is not directly stated anywhere or that becomes clear only at the end of the narrative. To make sure your theme emerges by the end of your recounted story, be sure to reread and revise so that all elements and incidents are purposeful. If several events contribute toward the theme of your paper, relate the most important or most dramatic one last.

5g Shaping the whole paper

The shape of your final essay depends on the story you want to tell. To tell a story that happens in the span of a few hours, a dramatic present-tense voice, fictive though it is, may be the best. To tell a story in a more reflective way, a first-person, past-tense voice makes the most sense.

Read through the complete final draft of Karen's essay recounting her experience in the Eastern Massachusetts basketball tournament. Note that she elects to play creatively with both time and perspective in telling her story. First, she opens her story by recounting the last six minutes of the game as told by the play-by-play announcer in the broadcast booth, letting us see the game from the announcer's imagined perspective. Second, she recounts the same six minutes from her own perspective on the floor, including occasional snatches of the announcer's voice. As you read this account, notice how she characterizes herself through her voice and actions, uses present tense to create suspense, and lets the theme emerge indirectly only in the last paragraph.

Three-Pointer in the Boston Garden

2:15 Well folks, it looks as if Belmont has given up; the coach is preparing to send in his subs. It has been a rough game for Belmont. They stayed in it during the first quarter, but Walpole has run away with it since then. Down by twenty with only six minutes left, Belmont's first sub is now approaching the table.

Meghan Sullivan with the ball goes coast to coast and lays it in for two. She has sparked Walpole from the start. The fans have livened up a bit, but oddly enough they aren't Walpole's fans, they're Belmont's.

"KAREN IS SMALL, SHE'S NOT TALL, WE LOVE KAREN!"

Meanwhile, Belmont's number eleven, 5'1", Karen Santosuosso, replaces Michelle Hayes. With three minutes left, Belmont's Kristin Sullivan brings up the ball, spin-dribbles--but the ball is stripped away by Meghan Sullivan, who takes it downcourt. She throws on the fly and hits a three-pointer! That girl has truly amazing talent.

Belmont with the ball. Santosuosso brings it up, passes to Jones, Jones shoots and hits it! Belmont may be out of the game, folks, but these reserves are having the time of their lives.

Walpole brings it up. Called for traveling.

Both Belmont and Walpole are now emptying their benches. As she sits down, Meghan Sullivan receives a standing ovation. An honor roll student and all-star athlete, she'll be attending Holy Cross this fall. What a night she had, eighteen points.

One and a half minutes left, D'Andrea inbounds to Santosuosso, who brings it up. Walpole sitting back in a twenty-one zone, Karen, over half court, stops, pops, swish. Santosuosso for three! The Belmont fans are going wild--

"KAREN IS SMALL, SHE'S NOT TALL, WE LOVE KAREN!"

As the clock winds down, fifteen seconds left, Walpole has started celebrating. The Belmont bench is quiet, but they have nothing to be ashamed of. Smith misses the second free throw, Hathaway on the rebound, gives it off to

Keohane--and that will do it, folks. Walpole is the Eastern Massachusetts women's basketball champion.

2:15 Where are they? Oh, there they are, Mom's waving and Dad has the camera. It's awesome, they come to every game, even to watch me bench.

"KAREN IS SMALL, SHE'S NOT TALL, WE LOVE KAREN!"

Oh, God, I'm so embarrassed, complete silence and those guys start yelling again. I can't believe them. Nothing is happening and no one else is cheering. . . . Well, at least maybe coach hears them now--not that it will make any difference. With six minutes to go, we're still down by eighteen. No matter how badly the starters play, he won't let the subs play. My senior year, six minutes left in the Boston Garden--in my career as the shortest player in the history of Belmont High--and he hasn't played me yet.

At least my friends are on my side--they're all sitting in the bleachers on the Walpole side with their faces painted maroon and blue and wearing Belmont clothes. I want to wave to them again. Oh no, he caught me waving. No big deal, three months ago I would have minded, but what difference does it make now?

Meghan Sullivan with the ball goes coast to coast and lays it in for two. She has sparked Walpole from the start.

"Girls, you have got to keep your heads into the game. Don't let them get you down. You have worked so hard all season, and you are as good as they are. Look at our record, 18-2-0, there's no reason you can't play with them."

"Coach, they're killing us. They are making us look like fools. We're down by eighteen with six minutes left. It's hopeless."

"I don't want to hear any of you talk like that. You have worked too hard to get to this point only to give up now. Remember every sweat-dripping, suicide-sprinting, drill-conditioning, nine o'clock Saturday morning practice!"

"All right girls, now get out there, play hard, and have fun."

"KAREN IS SMALL, SHE'S NOT TALL, WE LOVE KAREN!"

I can't believe those guys, I love them. My own personal fan club, and they're even audible in the Boston Garden. Those guys won't stop until he plays me. Five and a half minutes left, I wonder if he has the guts. . . .

"Karen, come here. Go in for Michelle."

Am I imagining this? There's a whole five minutes left and he's letting me play--but I'll take it!

There goes Sullivan again, burning up the court, right by all of us and she hits the one on the fly. <u>She</u> is truly awesome!

Kristin's got two defenders on her . . . "Kristin, I'm open." So, she won't pass and she misses her shot clean, bricked it off the backboard, what a heave.

Walpole brings it up. Called for traveling.

"Karen, coach wants you to bring it up."

If I don't do this now, I'll hate myself tomorrow. If I miss, big deal, I tried. I have to try it. Just think of Dad . . . think of the guys. Over half court, approaching the key, they aren't challenging me. Stop, pop, and there it goes. Oh please, please go in, please . . .

Karen, over half court, stops, pops, swish. Santosuosso for three!

Yes! I did it. I can't believe . . . Oh my, oh my . . . I did it! Where's Dad? I can't find him, where is he? I can't believe I'm crying. There he is, Dad! And Mom's jumping up and down--we must look like twins dancing around, only she's in the stands and I'm on the court.

"KAREN IS SMALL, SHE'S NOT TALL, WE LOVE KAREN!"

As the clock winds down, fifteen seconds left, Walpole has started celebrating. The Belmont bench is quiet, but they have nothing to be ashamed of.

Walpole is the Eastern Massachusetts women's basketball champion.

It's over now, and I've stopped crying, and I'm very happy. In the end I have to thank--not my coach, not my team--but Walpole, for beating us so badly that I got to play. I can't get over it. I played. And my dream came true, I hit a three-pointer in the Boston Garden.

6 ◆ EXPLAINING THINGS

To explain something is to make it understandable to someone else. Explanation, perhaps the most fundamental act of communication, is embedded in many types of writing, including personal experience (Chapter 5), interpretation (Chapter 7), and argument (Chapter 8). In pure explanatory writing, however, the main purpose is to help readers understand something. Such writing can range from a news article on baseball card collecting to a textbook on the French Revolution to a recipe for making chili.

6a Writing to explain

Explanatory writing is defined not so much by its subject (which can be almost anything) as by the way the subject is treated. First, explanatory writing commonly uses an objective perspective; that is, it emphasizes the thing explained rather than the writer's beliefs and feelings. Second, explanatory writing focuses on the reader's need for information rather than the writer's desire for self-expression. Third, explanatory writing is usually systematic and orderly, having a stated thesis or goal, clear explanatory strategies, and a logical organizational structure. Explanatory writing is objective, reader-focused, and systematic because this writing style simplifies an audience's task of reading to understand.

In writing classes, explanation usually takes the form of research essays and reports that inform rather than argue, interpret, or reflect. An assignment may ask you to describe how something works or to explain the cause and effect of a particular phenomenon. To explain anything successfully, you will need to decide on a topic, have a clear sense of your audience, locate information about your topic, develop a working thesis, use clear explanatory strategies, organize predictably, and focus on explaining something rather than expressing your feelings and opinions.

6b Finding a topic

It's easier to explain a specific topic than a broad one. For example, general subjects such as mountains, automobiles, or stereo systems are so broad that it's hard to know where to begin. However, a specific aspect of stereo systems, such as compact discs, will be easier; within the subject of CDs, there are probably several topics (cost, sound quality, manufacturing process, marketing).

Effective explanations have details, are well developed, include examples, and focus on a central question: *Why are CDs better than tape recordings?* or *Why do CDs cost more than records?* Of course, there may be other questions to be answered along the way (*How do CDs work? How are CDs made?*), but these are secondary.

Developing a thesis   6c

Explanations are easier to follow if their purpose is stated explicitly near the beginning of the paper rather than left implicit or stated at the end. This declaration of purpose is called a **thesis**—a statement that lets readers know what to expect and guides their understanding of the information presented. In explanatory writing, the thesis states the answer to the paper's central question.

QUESTION   Why do CDs cost so much?

THESIS   CDs cost more than records because the laser technology required to manufacture CDs is so expensive.

Throughout the writing process, keep in mind that your first thesis is a *working* thesis. It should remain flexible and subject to change until you are sure what you want to say; its primary function is to guide further research and help keep your paper focused.

Strategies for explaining   6d

Standard explanatory strategies include defining, describing, classifying and dividing, analyzing causes and effects, and comparing and contrasting. Select the strategy or strategies that best serve your purpose, realizing that other strategies may be needed along the way. For example, it is difficult to describe a complex process that has several parts or happens over an extended period of time without first dividing it into steps. It is difficult to compare and contrast without first describing or defining the things being compared.

The explanatory strategy is determined by the central question.

QUESTION	EXPLANATORY STRATEGY
What is it?	Definition
What does it mean?	Definition

QUESTION	EXPLANATORY STRATEGY
What are its characteristics?	Description
How does it work?	Process description
How is it related to other things?	Comparison and contrast
How is it put together?	Classification and division
To what group does it belong?	Classification and division
Why did it happen?	Cause-and-effect analysis
What are the consequences?	Cause-and-effect analysis

Definition

To **define** something is to identify it, to set it apart so that it can be distinguished from similar things. In order to make points clearly and with authority, writers need to define all terms unfamiliar to their readers.

Usually, defining something is a brief, preliminary step accomplished before moving on to a more important part of the explanation. When you need to define something complex or difficult or when your primary explanatory strategy is definition, you will need an extended definition consisting of a paragraph or more. This was the case with Mark's paper explaining computers. After defining the central processor unit (CPU), he defined computer memory.

Computer storage space is measured in units called kilobytes (K). Each K equals 1024 bytes or approximately 1000 single typewriter characters. So 1K equals about 180 English words, or a little less than half of a single-spaced typed page, or three minutes of fast typing. The first Apple Macintosh computer had 128K of built-in memory.

Personal computers generally have their memories measured in megabytes (MB). Each MB equals 1,048,567 bytes (or 1000K), which translates into approximately 400 pages of single-spaced type. A new personal computer today may have 32MB of built-in storage space.

Description

To **describe** a person, place, or thing is to create a verbal image so that your readers can see what you see, hear what you hear, and taste, smell, and feel what you taste, smell, and feel. Your goal is to make the image real enough for readers to experience it for themselves. However, descriptive details need to be purposeful. Heed the advice of Russian writer Anton Chekhov: "If a gun is hanging on the wall in the first chapter, it must, without fail, fire in the second or third chapter. If it doesn't fire, it mustn't hang either."

To describe how a process works is more complicated than giving a simple physical description, for in addition to showing objects at rest, you need to divide the process into discrete steps and present the steps in a logical order.

For some processes this is easy (making chili, giving highway directions). For others it is more difficult, either because many steps are all happening at once or because it is hard to decide which steps come before others (manufacturing a car, writing a research paper).

In either case, show the steps in a logical sequence that will be easy for readers to understand. To orient your readers, you may also want to number the steps by using transition words such as *first, second,* and *third.* In the following example, taken from an early draft of his paper, Keith describes the process of manufacturing compact disks.

> CDs start out as a refrigerator-sized box full of little plastic beads that you could sift through your hands. They are fed into a giant tapered corkscrew — a blown-up version of an old-fashioned meat grinder. As the beads pass down the corkscrew, they are slowly melted by the heated walls.
>
> At the bottom of their descent is a master recording plate onto which the molten plastic is pressed. The plastic now resembles a vinyl record, except that the disc is transparent. The master now imprints pits, rather than grooves, around the disk; the surface resembles a ball of Play-Doh after being thrown against a stucco wall — magnified 5000 times.

Comparison and contrast

To **compare** two things is to find similarities between them; to **contrast** is to find differences. Comparing and contrasting one thing to another clarifies both the similarities and differences between the two things. College assignments frequently ask you to compare and contrast two things such as authors, books, presidents, governments, cultures, centuries, philosophies, or inventions.

The two things compared and contrasted should usually be reasonably similar. Compare and contrast the same elements or features of each thing; for example, if you describe the digestive system of one frog species, describe the digestive system of the frog species with which you are comparing it.

There are three common ways to present a comparison-and-contrast analysis.

1 A **point-to-point** strategy examines one feature at a time for both similarities and differences.
2 A **whole-to-whole** strategy describes one object as a whole and then presents the other object as a whole; it concludes by highlighting important similarities or differences.
3 A **similarity-and-difference** strategy presents all the similarities and then all the differences between the two things, or vice versa.

Use a point-to-point or similarity-and-difference analysis for long explanations of complex things; use a whole-to-whole analysis for simple objects that readers can easily comprehend.

In the following whole-to-whole example, Keith compares and contrasts how records and CDs transmit the information that eventually becomes music.

> On a record, the stylus (needle) sits in a spiral groove and reads the depth and width of the groove, from which it receives its audio signal. However, the depth of the groove is constantly changing by fractions of millimeters because of specks of dust and the wear caused by the needle, which reads not only the music but also the dust and wear, passing along all the sound as "music."
>
> In a CD player, however, a laser sends out a beam of light, which bounces off an object, like radar, and returns with a message, which becomes the music. The CD player doesn't read an ever-changing and dirty groove. Instead, it reads either a "yes" or a "no"--a pit or no pit-- from the disc. On one CD there are hundreds of thousands of tiny pits. . . . The laser in your CD player reads the distance to the disc to determine whether there's a pit, which will be farther away, or not.

As Keith's example shows, most comparison-and-contrast explanations give equal space to each of the two things. Analogies ("like radar") are effective because they explain something new by comparing it to something familiar.

Classification and division

People generally understand short things better than long ones, simple things more easily than complex ones. To help readers understand a complex topic, writers often classify and divide the pieces into a manageable context.

To **classify** something, put it into a category or class with other things that are like it: *Like whales and dolphins, sea lions are aquatic mammals.*

To **divide** something, break it into smaller parts or subcategories: *An insect's body is composed of a head, a thorax, and an abdomen.*

Many complex systems need both classification and division to be clear. To explain a stereo system, for example, you might divide the whole into headphones, record player, graphic equalizers, tape deck, CD player, preamplifiers, amplifiers, radio, and speakers. Then you might classify all these parts into a few categories.

INPUTS	radio, record player, tape deck, CD player
PROCESSORS	preamplifiers, amplifiers, graphic equalizers
OUTPUTS	speakers, headphones

Combining classification and division is particularly important when your division results in a large number of parts or subcategories. Most readers have a difficult time remembering more than six or seven things, so organize a long list into a few logical groups, as in the preceding example.

Cause and effect

Nothing happens all by itself. Instead, one thing happens because something else happened; then it, in turn, makes something else happen. You sleep because you're tired, and once you've slept, you wake up because you're rested. In other words, you already know about cause and effect because it is a regular part of life. A **cause** is something that makes something else happen; an **effect** is the thing that happens.

When you write a cause-and-effect analysis, usually you know what the effect is and you're trying to explain what caused it: *Why do CDs cost more than records?* The thesis for an explanation analyzing causes should always include the word *because* either implicitly or explicitly: *CDs cost more than records because manufacturing costs are higher for CDs.*

Organizing logically   6e

Since the information in an explanatory paper will be new and therefore challenging to readers, a strong, easy-to-follow organization is crucial. If you give your readers a good sense of where you're taking them, they will be more willing to follow you. To return to the previous example, if you wanted to explain how a CD system works, you could start your paper with a description of putting a CD on a player and end with the music coming out of the speakers, explaining what happens at each step along the way. Or you could describe the system technically, starting with the power source and working toward the speakers. Or you could describe it historically, starting with components invented first and working toward those developed most recently.

Staying neutral   6f

Explanatory writing is clearer when the ideas and information are presented without obvious bias, in a neutral or fairly objective tone that concentrates on the thing explained (the object) rather than the writer's beliefs and feelings. A neutral perspective allows you to get information to readers as quickly and efficiently as possible without you, the writer, getting in the way.

To adopt an objective stance, write from the third-person point of view, using the pronouns *he, she,* and *it.* Keep yourself in the background, unless you have a good reason not to—such as explaining your personal experience with the subject. In some instances, adopting the second-person *you* adds a friendly, familiar tone that keeps readers interested (as we've tried to do in this handbook).

And be fair. Present *all* the relevant information, both things you like about the topic and things you dislike. Avoid emotional or biased language. Remember, your goal is not to win an argument but to convey information.

6g   Shaping the whole paper

For an essay on the high cost of CDs, Keith narrowed his focus to one sound medium, CDs, and to one feature of that medium, the high cost. His thesis, that CDs cost more than records because their manufacturing costs are higher, evolves throughout the essay and is explicitly stated at the end. It is clearly implied from his opening paragraph. His organization is simple and easy to follow. First, the whole essay is framed by a description of someone in a record store wondering why CDs cost more than records. Second, within this frame is a point-by-point comparison of the operational and manufacturing processes of records and CDs. Keith's voice throughout is that of a knowledgeable tour guide. Although his personality is clear, his biases do not affect the report.

Although the primary explanatory strategy in Keith's essay is cause and effect, he uses most of the other strategies discussed in this chapter as well: definition, process description, and comparison and contrast. His essay is most remarkable for its effective use of analogy. At various points, he asks his readers to think of radar, the game of telephone, jimmies on an ice cream cone, corkscrews, meat grinders, player pianos, and Play-Doh.

```
              CDs: What's the Big Difference?

        The little package in your left hand says
   $14.95. The larger package in your right hand says
   $7.95. The question is, do you want to hear James
   Taylor in true stereo quality or not? Since you
   don't want to settle for second best, you nestle
   the larger LP back between some Disney classics
   and head to the counter with your new JT compact
   disc. Wandering out of the store you wonder what,
   besides costing $7 more, was the difference
   between this little CD and that LP record.
```

The purpose of your stereo system is to interpret recordings and reproduce them faithfully. Of course, nothing's perfect, so your music always has that quaint amount of background fuzz that never goes away. The fuzz is due to your stereo's misinterpretation of the signal from the magnetic tape or vinyl record.

On a record, the stylus (needle) sits in a spiral groove and reads the depth and width of the groove, from which it receives its audio signal. However, the depth of the groove is constantly changing by fractions of millimeters because of specks of dust and wear caused by the needle, which reads not only the music but also the dust and wear, passing along all the sound as "music."

In a CD player, however, a laser sends out a beam of light, which bounces off an object, like radar, and returns with a message, which becomes the music. The CD player doesn't read an ever-changing and dirty groove. Instead, it reads either a "yes" or a "no"--a pit or no pit--from the disc. On one CD there are hundreds of thousands of tiny pits that resemble those of a player piano scroll, telling the piano which keys to hit. The laser in your CD player reads the distance to the disc to determine whether there's a pit, which will be farther away, or not.

What's the difference, you ask, in receiving music from grooves versus pits? Do you remember playing the "telephone game" in fifth grade? You know, the one where someone on one side of class whispers something in your ear and it gets passed along until it gets to the last person, who says what he or she was told? This is much the way in which your stereo works: the LP or CD is like the first person and your speakers are like the last. In the case of the record, I whisper some line in your ear and you pass it on, but by the time it reaches the last person, it's been twisted and has a few more words attached. In the case of the CD, I whisper either a "yes" or a "no," and by the time it reaches the last person it should be exactly the same--this is where the term "digital" comes from, meaning either there is a signal ("yes") or there isn't one ("no"). How much can you screw up a yes or a no?

Although a vinyl record would be nearly finished at this point, there's still important work to be done on the CD. From here the disc is metallized, a process that deposits a thin film of metal, usually aluminum, on the surface; you see it as a rainbow under a light. Since light won't bounce back from transparent plastic, the coating acts as a mirror to bounce back the laser beam.

The disc is mirrored by a spray-painting process called "sputtering" that must be extremely precise. You couldn't just dip the thing because then the pits would fill in or melt. The clear disc is inserted into a chamber and placed opposite a piece of pure aluminum called a "target," which is bombarded with electricity, causing the aluminum atoms to jump off and embed themselves into the surface of the disc, like jimmies on an ice cream cone. Then the disc is "spin-coated" with a fine film of resin, which becomes the outer coating on the CD.

Once the resin is cured by a brief exposure to ultraviolet light, your CD is pretty much idiot-proof. As long as you don't interrupt the light path in the film, your CD will perform perfectly, even with small scratches, so long as they don't diffract the laser beam—and even then you may be able to rub them smooth with a finger. Never does anything come in contact with the recorded surface.

The CD is finished when it is stamped with the appropriate logo and allowed to dry. All these steps take a mere seven seconds to produce one CD, and the materials cost no more than a pack of gum, but the cost of buying and operating one CD-producing machine is close to that of running a small team of Formula 1 racing cars.

So next time you walk into Musicland, you will know what you are paying for. A CD may be expensive, but the sound is superior and the disc will last forever.

7 ◆ INTERPRETING TEXTS

When most of us encounter a new story, essay, play, or poem, we try to make sense of it by analyzing it, comparing it to familiar things, examining our reactions to it, and trying to explain why it affects us the way it does. In other words, we **interpret** texts in order to understand them and assess their importance in our lives.

Our initial reactions to a new text of any kind are often a jumble of impressionistic thoughts, feelings, and memories—seldom are they fully realized interpretations. To write an interpretive essay, you must take the time to analyze this jumble and develop a reasonable, systematic understanding of what the text means and why. Since most texts have more than one possible meaning and are open to more than one interpretation, an interpretive essay argues that one specific meaning and one particular interpretation is especially good and worthy of attention.

Writing interpretive essays   7a

In the humanities and social sciences, instructors commonly assign critical and analytical essays about course readings which ask for interpretation. If given a choice, the best texts to select for an interpretive assignment are those which are most questionable and problematic—texts whose meaning seems to you somewhat slippery and elusive—since these give you, the interpreter, the most room to argue one meaning against another. Whether given a choice or not, your job remains the same: to make the best possible case that your interpretation is reasonable and deserves attention.

A fully developed interpretation incorporates several rhetorical strategies to make its case. It *explains* what the text says, in and of itself, as reasonably as possible. It also *argues* for a particular interpretation of the text's meaning—what the text implies or suggests about something beyond itself—and, like any argument, an interpretive essay should be as persuasive as possible, though it can never be an absolute proof. And it may also *evaluate* the importance or quality of the text being interpreted.

A typical assignment may ask for an interpretation of a poem, story, essay, or historical document—a complex task that draws on all of your reasoning and writing skills. You may have to *describe* people and situations, *retell* events, and *define* key terms. You may need to *analyze* passages and *explain* how they function in the text, perhaps by *comparing* or *contrasting* one part of the text to another—or this text to other texts. Finally, you will *argue* for one meaning rather than another by stating a thesis and defending it with sound *reasoning* and convinced *evidence*. (See Chapter 6 for more on explanatory strategies; see Chapter 8 for more on argument strategies.)

This chapter offers a methodical approach to developing an interpretive essay on one specific text, the poem "We Real Cool" by Gwendolyn Brooks, a short text rich with numerous interpretive possibilities. We believe our approach to interpreting this single poem also applies to interpreting many other kinds of texts. Please read "We Real Cool" and follow along as we examine some interpretations of its meaning.

We Real Cool

THE POOL PLAYERS.
SEVEN AT THE GOLDEN SHOVEL.

We real cool. We
Left school. We

Lurk late. We
Strike straight. We

Sing sin. We
Thin gin. We

Jazz June. We
Die soon.

7b   Exploring a text

Interpreting a text requires understanding. Plan to read the text more than once. The first time, read the text to understand it on a literal level: Who are the characters involved? Where are they? What happens? How does the situation end? As you read, mark passages that interest you, passages that seem important or are difficult to understand. Now read the text a second time, more slowly, making notes in the margin or writing in your journal about passages that are interesting, questionable, or problematic. As you do this, look for answers to your previous concerns, rereading as many times as necessary to further your understanding. Using the poem "We Real Cool" as an example, we will explore ways of interpreting a short poetic text as well as general guidelines that are applicable to interpreting most prose texts.

7c   Finding a topic

A good topic for an interpretive essay must involve an interesting question that has more than one possible answer. Without the possibility of more than one answer, there is no need to argue for one interpretation over another. If your question isn't interesting, both you and your reader will be bored. Here are some suggestions for finding and exploring topics.

1 **Identify.** Ask, What genre is this text—poem, play, story, or essay? What is its title? Who is the author? When was it published? Tell your reader: *"We Real Cool" is a poem by Gwendolyn Brooks published in 1963.*

2 **Annotate.** Locate ideas, problems, or puzzles, both small and large, that interest or puzzle you. Good topics for analyzing any genre of text arise from material in which the meaning is not obviously stated: *In "We Real Cool," what is the setting? Who is speaking? How many characters are there? What does "Jazz June" mean? Why do the characters "die soon"?*

3 **Notice patterns.** Look for repeated words, ideas, or images that serve as clues to the author's main ideas. In both factual and poetic texts, repetition is a means by which writers call attention to their central ideas and indicate that they are important to the meaning of the text: *In "We Real Cool," why does each line except the last one end with "We"?*

4 **Examine structure.** Analyze how the text is put together or organized. Authors arrange ideas and information to help readers understand the point they want to make. Whether book chapter or short story, organization is a major clue to meaning. Ask why the author made the choices he or she did: *Brooks creates rhythm in "We Real Cool" through a series of four rhymed pairs: "cool/school," "late/straight," "sin/gin," and "June/soon." What effect does this have?*

5 **Consider context.** Compare or contrast the text with other things you know about culture, history, or similar texts. Bring to bear all of your knowledge to situate the work in a context that sheds light on possible meaning. If comparing to other texts, use two works by the same author or a similar work by a different author: *"We Real Cool," written over thirty years ago, has characteristics similar to the lyrics and rhythm of a rap tune. Is Brooks's message similar to that of rap artists? If not, how does her message differ?*

Developing an interpretation   **7d**

An interpretation starts by asking questions but concludes by presenting answers. Your essay will argue that a text means one thing rather than another and will explain why. The following suggestions may help.

Choose a perspective

Many college assignments ask you to interpret a text *objectively*—to focus on the object (text) under study instead of the subject (yourself) doing the study. When adopting an objective stance, write from the third-person point of view. Keep yourself and references to yourself to a minimum, and use language that is emotionally neutral and unbiased: *Possible themes to explore in "We Real Cool" could be companionship, mischief, or the love of revelry.*

Some college assignments, however, call for a *subjective* stance, encouraging you to acknowledge your own personal history as a reader. Instead of keeping your opinions or emotions out of the paper, you incorporate them as they suit your purpose. In the subjective stance, write from the first-person point of view and refer to personal experience to support the theme you are developing: *"We Real Cool" . . . reminds me of the gang in high school who used to skip classes and come back smelling of cigarette smoke and cheap liquor—not that I knew it was cheap back then.*

State your thesis

To write an interpretation from any point of view, you need to locate, identify, and understand what you consider to be the text's central meaning. It is customary to state this central meaning as a thesis directly in the first paragraph. Your thesis is a clear, concise statement of your interpretation, explaining to readers your argument for what the text means. They expect your thesis to be advanced and supported with sound reason and good evidence: *"We Real Cool" explores the meaning of the word "cool" in the actions and attitudes of a group of young, urban black males, known in the poem as "the pool players."*

If you write from a subjective perspective instead of stating a thesis outright, you commonly develop your essay around a *theme* that holds your interpretation together—though sometimes the theme is implied rather than stated. Your first paragraph often signals a subjective interpretation by using the first-person point of view and featuring personal ideas, opinions, or values. In this personal or reader-response essay, readers expect a more speculative, less argumentative interpretation that is supported by memories, experiences, or associations in addition to textual evidence: *Brooks's pool players "Die soon," so we never know where else their adventurous spirits might have taken them. In the end, this poem just makes me sad.*

Provide support

An interpretive thesis should be tightly focused so that you can support your argument with evidence from the text itself. Refer to your underlinings, highlightings, margin notes, and journal entries to bring specific textual references into your paper to serve as evidence, or proof, that your own reading of the text is a valid one.

When you draw on the text itself or bring in additional sources to support your view, you will have to decide when to summarize, when to paraphrase, and when to quote directly. In general, **summarize** larger ideas in your own language to conserve space; **paraphrase** more specific ideas also in your own words; and **quote** directly to feature especially colorful or precise language: *The companionship seen in the urgent repetition of the word "We" becomes the coercive force of a street gang, until the poem ends with what seems to be their mass suicide, as suggested by the ending—"We / die soon."*

If you bring in outside information for support, comparison, or contrast, document carefully where it came from. (For more information on using and documenting sources, see Chapter 46.)

If you write from a subjective perspective, it's a good idea to identify or quote specific textual passages that trigger memories, associations, or personal ideas. The more specific your examples, the better. For example, one reader explains her reason for *not* hanging around pool halls: *I was*

GUIDELINES FOR WRITING INTERPRETIVE ESSAYS

1   Identify text. No matter what kind of interpretation you choose to write, personal or analytical, tell your audience the specifics about the text: name its title and author and the place and date of publication.

2   Position yourself. Early in the essay, let your reader know what approach you are taking. If analytical, make that clear by writing your first paragraph in carefully nonopinionated prose; if personal, make that clear by writing in the first person and advancing your own experience as part of your authority.

3   State your thesis. You may state the main point your essay makes on the first page (common in analytical essays), or you may delay it, inviting readers to witness how you arrived at it. In either case, state your thesis clearly, so that after they have finished reading your paper, they know where you stand.

4   Support your thesis. If you take an analytical approach, provide evidence for your assertions from lines in the text as well as other relevant cultural information. If you take a personal approach, provide evidence from text itself, but also include your own experience as a form of evidence to support your position.

5   Document assertions. Give credit for ideas that are not your own or passages of text that you quote or paraphrase.

6   Apply the writing process. Interpretive essays need to be careful and tight. One idea needs to lead clearly to the next until a final position is stated. In writing this essay, make time to reread your first draft critically, organize it logically, provide more evidence as needed, and edit for clarity.

---

always afraid . . . of the consequences, so I practiced piano, did my algebra, and stayed put.

7e Shaping the whole paper

This chapter concludes with two short interpretive papers on Brooks's poem. One is an objective critical essay written to keep the focus on the argument of the poem, not on the writer's own opinion; he has an opinion, of course, but keeps it in the background. The other interpretation is written in a genre we might call a personal essay or reader-response paper—the essay is triggered by the poem but is admittedly as much about the writer as the poem. Such essays are deliberately subjective and treat the writer's experience and values as important as the text under discussion.

Objective response to the poem "We Real Cool"

Kelly writes a brief objective interpretation of "We Real Cool," keeping himself in the background and writing from the third-person point of view. He presents his thesis early and supports it with frequent quotations from the text.

```
     The three interrelated themes in "We Real
Cool" are companionship, mischief, and revelry.
The speakers in the poem, referred to as "We," are
teenagers who have dropped out of school, and
these three qualities are inseparable elements of
adolescent hedonism.
     For teenagers, fitting in or conforming to a
group identity is more important than developing
an individual identity. This need for companion-
ship is suggested in the poem's subtitle, "Seven
at the Golden Shovel"; the Golden Shovel proves to
be their regular hangout. It is also supported by
the plural point of view, "We," repeated at the
end of each line.
     Mischief is what these dropouts do instead of
attending school. They "Lurk late," "Strike
straight," "Sing sin," drink "Thin gin," and move
to their own music, "Jazz June"--actions frowned
upon by society and deliberately harmful to other
people. This is a bunch of kids to watch out for.
If you see them coming, cross the street.
```

> However, this gang is also out to celebrate
> the high moments that life gives them--references
> to feeling cool, singing, and drinking gin all sup-
> port this. To themselves, they are not so bad, not
> dangerous, maybe even happy and full of life. But,
> as their language tells us, they are young and not
> well educated and see little hope in the adult fu-
> ture--the simple one-syllable words reinforce this
> singleminded, simplistic view of a short life.
>   The poem's last line calls their bluff and
> suggests that their pleasures--companionship, mis-
> chief, and revelry--are brief and doomed. Brooks
> declares the fate of misfits who violate social
> norms in the last and shortest line of the poem:
> they "Die soon."

Subjective response to the poem "We Real Cool"

In the following essay, Mitzi writes about her personal reaction to Brooks's poem, describing how it reminds her of her own high school experience. Mitzi does not state a thesis, but the theme of sadness opens and closes the essay, providing the necessary coherence. Although she quotes the text several times, her primary supportive examples come from her own memories.

> "We Real Cool" is a sad poem. It reminds me
> of the gang in high school who used to skip
> classes and come back smelling of cigarette smoke
> and cheap liquor--not that I knew it was cheap
> back then. I think everybody who ever went to a
> public high school knows these guys--at least,
> most of them were boys--who eventually "left
> school" altogether and failed to graduate. They
> dressed a little differently from the rest of us--
> baggier pants, heavier boots, dirtier shirts, and
> too-long hair, never washed. And if there were
> girls--too much makeup or none at all.
>   They had their fun, however, because they
> stayed in their group. They came late to
> assemblies, slouched in their seats, made wise-
> cracks, and often ended up in detention after
> school or on Saturday morning.

And no matter how straight-laced and clean-cut the rest of us were, we always felt just a twinge of envy toward these careless, jaunty rebels who refused to follow rules, who didn't care if they got detentions, who didn't do homework, and whose parents didn't care if they stayed out all night. I didn't admit it very often--at least not to my friends--but some part of me wanted to have their pool hall and adventures, the adult freedoms they claimed for themselves. However, I was always afraid--chicken, they would have said--of the consequences, so I practiced piano, did my algebra, and stayed put.

Then I think of the poem's last line and know why I obeyed my parents (well, most of the time), listened to my teachers (at least some of them), and stayed put (if you don't count senior cut day). These "cool" ones paid for their rebellion in drug overdoses, jail terms, police shootouts, and short lives. Brooks's pool players "Die soon," so we never know where else their adventurous spirits might have taken them. In the end, this poem just makes me sad.

8 ◆ ARGUING POSITIONS

Argument is deeply rooted in the American political and social system; free and open debate is the essence of the democratic process. Argument is also at the heart of the academic process. Scholars investigate scientific, social, and cultural issues, hoping through the give-and-take of debate to find reasonable answers to complex questions.

Argument in the academic world is less about winning or losing than about changing minds or altering perceptions. Argument as rational disagreement—not quarrels, fights, or contests—most often occurs on issues of genuine uncertainty about what is right, best, or most reasonable. A **position paper** sets forth an arguable position on an issue about which there is some debate; if there's no debate, there's no argument. College assignments commonly ask you to argue one side of an issue and defend your argument against attacks from skeptics. This chapter explains the elements that constitute a basic position paper: an arguable issue, a claim and counterclaim, a thesis, and evidence.

Selecting an issue   8a

An **issue** is a controversy, something that can be argued about. For instance, mountain bikes and cultural diversity are things or concepts, not in themselves issues. However, they become the foundation for issues when questions are raised about them and controversy ensues.

ISSUE Do American colleges adequately represent the cultural diversity of the United States?

ISSUE Should mountain bikes be allowed on wilderness hiking trails?

These questions are issues because reasonable people could answer them in different ways; they can be argued about because more than one answer is plausible, possible, or realistic.

State a position

Virtually all issues can be formulated, at least initially, as yes/no questions about which you will take one position or the other: pro (if the answer is yes) or con (if the answer is no).

ISSUE Should American college faculty represent the cultural diversity of the United States?

PRO Yes; minority students learn better from instructors who understand their culture.

CON No; for learning to occur, the quality of teaching is all that matters.

A good issue around which to write a position paper will meet the following criteria.

1 There is real controversy and uncertainty.
2 There are at least two distinct and arguable positions.
3 Resources are available to support both sides.

Consider both national and local issues. The advantages of national issues are that you are likely to see them explained and argued in national news media and that you can count on your audience's having some familiarity with them. The advantage of local issues is that you can often visit a place where the controversy occurs, interview people who are affected by it, and find generous coverage in local news media. The disadvantage is that not all of your audience may be familiar with the issue.

8b Analyzing an issue

To **analyze** an issue, you need to conduct enough research to explain it and identify the arguments of each side. Treat each side fairly, framing the opposition as positively as you frame your position, and have an honest debate with yourself. Doing so may even cause you to switch sides—one of the best indications of open-minded research. Furthermore, empathy for the opposition leads to making qualified assertions and heads off overly simplistic right-versus-wrong arguments.

Establish context

Provide full context for the issue you are writing about, as if readers know virtually nothing about it. Providing **context** means answering these questions: What is this issue about? Where did the controversy begin? How long has it been debated? Who are the people involved? What is at stake? It helps to use a neutral tone, as suggested in the following example about mountain bikes on wilderness trails.

> With all these new riders, there is a need for places to ride, and this is where the wilderness trail controversy begins. The mountain bike is designed to be ridden on dirt trails, logging roads, and fire trails in backwoods country. However, other trail users who have been around much longer than mountain bikers prefer to enjoy the woods at a slow, leisurely pace. They find the rapid and sometimes noisy two-wheel in-truders unacceptable.

State claims and counterclaims

Claims are statements or assertions that something is true or should be done. In arguing one side of an issue, you make one or more claims in the hope of convincing an audience to believe you. **Counterclaims** are statements that oppose or refute claims. You need to examine an opponent's counter-claim carefully in order to refute it or, if you agree with the counterclaim, to argue that your claim is more important to making a decision.

Annotate references

Use note cards or computer files to make an alphabetical list of the references you consulted during research, briefly identifying each according to the kind of information it contains. The same article may present claims from both sides as well as provide context. Following are three of Issa's annotated references.

```
  Buchanan, Rob. "Birth of the Gearhead Nation."
       Rolling Stone 9 July 1992: 80-85. Marin Co.,
       CA, movement advocates more trails open to
       mountain bike use. Includes history. (pro)

  "Fearing for Desert, A City Restricts Mountain
       Bikes." New York Times 4 June 1995, A24.
       Controversy in Moab, Utah, over conservation
       damage by mountain bikes. (con)

  Schwartz, David, M. "Over Hill, Over Dale on a
       Bicycle Built for . . . Goo." Smithsonian
       25.3 (June 1992): 74-84. Discusses the hiker
       vs. biker issue, promotes peaceful co-exis-
       tence, includes history. (pro/con)
```

Take a position

Once you have considered the two positions fairly, weigh which side is the stronger. Select the position that you find most convincing, and then write out the reasons that support this position, most compelling reasons last. This will be the position to start with, not necessarily to stick with. Even though it's tentative, a working thesis focuses your initial efforts in one direction and helps you articulate claims and assemble evidence to support it.

WORKING THESIS   Hikers and mountain bikers should cooperate and support each other in using, preserving, and maintaining wilderness trails.

Your working thesis should be manageable and specific, and it should propose a plan of action.

Developing an argument   8c

Your **argument** is the case you will make for your position; it is the means by which you will try to persuade your readers that your position is correct. Good arguments need solid and credible evidence and clear and logical reasoning.

FALSE ARGUMENTS (FALLACIES)

The following false arguments are often made when a writer does not have enough evidence to support his or her claims. Learn to recognize and avoid them.

1   Bandwagon. Encourages people to accept a position simply because others already have: *More than three-fourths of Americans have already begun to recycle paper and plastics—shouldn't you recycle too?* (Those other people could have made bad decisions.)

2   Begging the question. Treats a questionable statement as if it had already been accepted: *If the United States is to maintain its position as the foremost military power on the planet, defense spending must be increased.* (Many people question whether the United States should try to maintain its military supremacy.)

3   Does not follow (non sequitur). Presents a conclusion that does not logically follow from its premises: *Catharine MacKinnon has been an ardent supporter of women's rights, so she would be a good senator.* (The fact that MacKinnon supports women's rights does not mean that she has, or does not have, the skills to be a good senator.)

4   False analogy. Uses analogy to show that two things are alike for the purpose of the argument when, actually, they are different: *Just as the lioness is the one to protect her cubs, so do women bear the responsibility of caring for their children.* (Lions and humans are not alike.)

5   False cause (post hoc). Assumes that if one event happened after another, the earlier event must have caused the later one: *Federal spending on schools should be decreased: the last time the government decreased education spending, SAT scores went up.* (There is no clear connection between education spending and SAT scores.)

6   Oversimplification. Reduces a complex system of causes and effects to an inaccurate generalization: *Ronald Reagan's election in 1980 led to a far more stable economy in the 1980s.* (Reagan's election may have been one factor in the economy of the 1980s, but there were no doubt many other forces at work.)

Assemble evidence

Evidence can come from a variety of sources: *facts, examples, inferences, expert opinion,* and *personal experience* all provide believable evidence.

Facts, examples, and inferences   **Facts** are verifiable and agreed upon by everyone involved, regardless of personal beliefs or values. It is a fact that water boils at 212 degrees Fahrenheit. Facts are often numerical or statistical and are recorded where anybody can look them up—in a dictionary, almanac, public report, or college catalog, for example. Not all facts are of the type found in an almanac: In Kenya, anthropologist Mary Leakey found a skull that she later concluded belonged to a 25 million-year-old common ancestor of apes and humans. The find is a fact. If you think your audience might doubt it, you can document where you learned about it. That Leakey reached that particular conclusion is also a fact, but the conclusion itself is her expert opinion or interpretation of the fact.

Examples can be used to illustrate a claim or clarify an issue. To demonstrate that many wilderness trails have been closed to mountain biking, you mention this example: *The New Jersey trails at South Mountain, Eagle Rock, and Mills Park have all been closed to mountain bikes.*

Inferences are generalizations based on the accumulation of a certain number of facts and examples. For example, if you check ten national wilderness trails in ten states and find they are all closed to mountain biking, you might infer that a national policy bans mountain bikes in wilderness areas; but such an inference is not a fact, since you have not checked the other forty states or contacted the government agency that sets such policies.

Expert opinion   Expert opinion makes powerful evidence. When a forest ranger testifies about trail damage caused by mountain bikes or lug-soled hiking boots, his training and experience make him an expert. A casual hiker making the same observation is less believable.

Personal experience   A useful kind of evidence is testimony based on personal experience. When you have experienced something firsthand, such as hiking or biking on wilderness trails, your knowledge cannot easily be discounted.

Demonstrate reasoning

To build an effective argument, consider the audience you must persuade. The more you know about the audience you're trying to sway, the easier it will be to present your case. In writing about the mountain bike controversy, for example, ask yourself (1) Who will read this paper? (2) Where do I think the readers stand on the issue? and (3) What evidence would they consider convincing?

Remember that inferences based on a single piece of evidence may often be wrong. Find out more before you make simple assumptions. And sometimes audience analysis doesn't work very well when an instructor assumes a deliberately skeptical role in reading a set of papers. It's best to assume you will have a critical reader and to use the best logic and evidence available.

8d Organizing the Paper

To organize your paper, you need to know what is the main point of your argument. It's time to consider the working thesis that's been guiding your research: confirm it, or modify it, or scrap it altogether and assert a different one. Try to articulate this thesis in a single sentence as the answer to the yes/no question.

THESIS   Wilderness trails should be open to both mountain bikers and hikers.

THESIS   Wilderness trails should be closed to mountain bikers.

Your next decision is where in this paper you should reveal your thesis to the reader. Will you state it openly up front or strategically delay it until later? Neither strategy is right or wrong, but each has a different effect on your reader.

Thesis-first organization

When you lead with a thesis, you tell readers from the beginning where you stand on the issue. The remainder of the essay supports your claim and defends it against counterclaims. Following is one good way to organize a thesis-first argument.

1 **Introduce and explain the issue.** Make sure there are at least two debatable sides. Pose the question that you see arising from this issue; if you can frame it as a yes/no, for/against construction, both you and your reader will have the advantage throughout your answer of knowing where you stand.
2 **Assert your thesis early.** Your thesis states the answer to the question you have posed and establishes the position from which you will argue. Think of your thesis as the major claim the paper will make.
3 **Explain the opposition's counterclaims** before elaborating on your own claims; doing so gives you something to refute. Squeezing the counterclaims between the thesis (2) and the evidence (5) reserves the strongest places—the opening and closing—for your position.
4 **Refute the counterclaims.** Point out weak spots in the opposition's argument. Use your opponent's language to show you have read closely but still find problems with the claim.
5 **Support your claims with evidence.** Spell out your own claims clearly and precisely, enumerating them or being sure to give each its own full-

paragraph explanation, and citing supporting evidence. This section will constitute the longest and most carefully documented part of your essay.

6 **Restate your position in your conclusion.** Synthesize your accumulated evidence into a broad general position, and restate your original thesis in slightly different language.

Delayed-thesis organization

Using the delayed-thesis type of organization, you introduce the issue and discuss the arguments for and against your position but do not obviously take a side until late in the essay. Near the end of the paper, you explain that after carefully investigating both pros and cons, you have now arrived at the most reasonable position. Concluding with your own position gives it more emphasis.

1 **Introduce the issue and pose a question.** Both thesis-first and delayed-thesis papers begin by establishing context and posing a question.

2 **Summarize the claims for one position.** Before stating which side you support, explain how the opposition views the issue.

3 **Refute these claims.** Still not stating your own position, point out your difficulties with believing this side. (You can actually strengthen your position by admitting that some claims might be true.)

4 **Summarize the counterclaims.** You are supporting these claims, so they should occupy the most emphatic position in your essay, coming last.

5 **Support your counterclaims.** Now give your best evidence; this should be the longest and most carefully documented part of the paper.

6 **State your thesis in your conclusion.** Your rhetorical stance or strategy is this: You have listened carefully to both the claims and counterclaims, and after giving each side a fair hearing, you have arrived at the most reasonable conclusion.

Shaping the whole paper   8e

In the following paper, Issa explores whether or not mountain bikers should be allowed to share wilderness trails with hikers. In the first part of the paper, he establishes the context and background of the conflict. Then he introduces the question his paper will address: *Is any resolution in sight?* Note his substantial use of sources, including the Internet and interviews, cited in the MLA documentation style. Issa uses the delayed-thesis strategy, airing both sides of the argument before revealing his solution, a compromise position: *Educated mountain biking, like hiking and horseback riding, respects the environment and promotes peace and conservation.*

On the Trail: Can the Hikers Share with the Bikers?

The narrow, hard-packed dirt trail winding up the mountain under the spreading oaks and maples doesn't look like the source of a major environmental conflict, but it is. On the one side are hikers, environmentalists, and horseback riders who have traditionally used these wilderness trails. On the other side, looking back, are the mountain bike riders sitting atop their modern steeds who want to use them too. But the hikers don't want the bikers, so trouble is brewing.

The debate over mountain bike use has gained momentum recently because of the increased popularity of this form of bicycling. Technology has made it easier for everyone to ride these go-anywhere bikes. These high-tech wonders incorporate exotic components including quick gear-shifting derailleurs, good brakes, and a comfortable upright seating position—and they can cost up to $2000 each (Kelly 104). Mountain bikes have turned what were once grueling hill climbs into casual trips, and more people are taking notice.

Mountain bikes have taken over the bicycle industry, and with more bikes come more people wanting to ride in the mountains. The first mass-produced mountain bikes date to 1981, when 500 Japanese "Stumpjumpers" were sold. By 1983 annual sales reached 200,000; today the figure is 8.5 million. In fact, mountain biking is second only to in-line skating as the fastest-growing sport in the nation. "For a sport to go from zero to warp speed so quickly is unprecedented," says Brian Stickel, director of competition for the National Off Road Bicycle Association (Schwartz 75).

With all these new riders, there is a need for places to ride, and this is where the wilderness trail controversy begins. The mountain bike is designed to be ridden on dirt trails, logging roads, and fire trails in backwoods country. However, other trail users who have been around much longer than mountain bikers prefer to enjoy the woods at a slow, leisurely pace. They find the rapid and sometimes noisy two-wheel intruders unacceptable: "To traditional trail users, the new breed of bicycle [is] alien and dangerous, esthetically offensive and physically menacing" (Schwartz 74).

"The problem arises when people want to use an area of public land for their own personal purpose," Carl Newton, forestry professor at the University of Vermont, said in an interview. "Eventually, after everyone has taken their small bit of the area, the results can be devastating. People believe that because they pay taxes for the land, they can use it as they please. This makes sense to the individual, but not to the whole community." Newton is both a hiker and a mountain biker (Newton).

When mountain bikes first came on the scene, hikers and environmentalists convinced state and local officials to ban the bikes from wilderness trails (Buchanan 81; Kelly 104). The result was the closing of many trails to mountain bike use. "Many state park systems have banned bicycles from narrow trails. National Parks prohibit them, in most cases, from leaving the pavement" (Schwartz 81). These trail closings have separated the outdoor community into the hikers and the bikers. Each group is well organized, and each group believes it is right. Is any resolution in sight?

The arrival of mountain bikes during the 1980s was resisted by established hiker groups, such as the Sierra Club, which won debate after debate in favor of closing wilderness trails to mountain bike activities. The younger and less well organized biking groups proposed compromise, offering to help repair and maintain trails in return for riding rights, but their offers were ignored. "Peace was not given a chance. Foes of the bicycle onslaught, older and better connected, won most of the battles, and signs picturing a bicycle crossed with a red slash began to appear on trail heads all over the country" (Schwartz 74).

In Milburn, New Jersey, trails at South Mountain, Eagle Rock, and Mills Park have all been closed. Anyone caught riding a bike on the trails can be arrested and fined up to $100. Local riders offered an amendment calling for trails to be open Thursday through Sunday, with the riders helping maintain the trails on the other days. The amendment was rejected. According to hiker Donald Meserlain, the bikes "ruin the tranquility of the woodlands and drive out hikers, bird watchers, and strollers. It's like weeds taking over the grass. Pretty soon we'll have all weeds" (Hanley B4).

Until more public lands are opened to trail riding, mountain bikers must pay fees to ride on private land, a situation beneficial to ski resorts in the off season: "Ski areas are happy to open trails to cyclists for a little summer and fall income" (Sneyd).

However, the real solution to the conflict between hikers and bikers is education, not separation. In response to the bad publicity and many trail closings, mountain bikers have banded together at local and national levels to educate both their own member bike riders and the nonriding public about the potential alliance between these two groups (Buchanan 81).

The largest group, the International Mountain Bike Association (IMBA), sponsors supervised rides and trail conservation classes and stresses that mountain bikers are friends, not enemies, of the natural environment. "The IMBA wants to change the attitude of both the young gonzo rider bombing downhill on knobby tires, and the mature outdoorsman bristling at the thought of tire tracks where boot soles alone did tread" (Schwartz 76). IMBA published guidelines it hopes all mountain bikers will learn to follow:

1. Ride on open trails only.
2. Leave no trace.
3. Control your bicycle.
4. Always yield trail.
5. Never spook animals.
6. Plan ahead. (JTYL)

The New England Mountain Bike Association (NEMBA), one of the largest East Coast organizations, publishes a home page on the Internet outlining goals: "NEMBA is a not-for-profit organization dedicated to promoting land access, maintaining trails that are open to mountain bicyclists, and educating riders to use those trails sensitively and responsibly. We are also devoted to having fun" (Koellner).

Educated mountain biking, like hiking and horseback riding, respects the environment and promotes peace and conservation, not noise and destruction. Making this case has begun to pay off, and the battle over who walks and who rides the trails should now shift in favor of peaceful coexistence. "Buoyed by studies showing that bicycle tires cause no more erosion or trail damage than the boots of hikers, and far less than horses' hooves, mountain bike advocates are starting to find receptive ears among environmental organizations" (Schwartz 78).

The Wilderness Club now officially supports limited use of mountain bikes, while the Sierra Club also supports careful use of trails by riders so long as no damage to the land results and riders ride responsibly on the path. "In pursuit of happy trails, bicycling organizations around the country are bending backward over their chain stays to dispel the hell-on-wheels view of them" (Schwartz 83).

Education and compromise are the sensible solutions to the hiker/biker standoff. Increased public awareness as well as increasingly responsible riding will open still more wilderness trails to bikers in the future. It's clear that mountain bikers don't want to destroy trails any more than hikers do. The surest way to preserve America's wilderness areas is to establish strong cooperative bonds among the hikers and bikers, as well as those who fish, hunt, camp, canoe, and bird-watch, and to encourage all to maintain the trails and respect the environment.

Works Cited

Buchanan, Rob. "Birth of the Gearhead Nation."
Rolling Stone 9 July 1992: 80–85.

Hanley, Robert. "Essex County Mountain Bike
Troubles." New York Times 30 May 1995: B4.

JTYL (editor). Western New York Mountain Bike
Association Home Page. Western New York
Mountain Bike Association. 12 Nov. 1996
<http://128.205.166.43/public/wnymba/wnymba.
html>.

Kelly, Charles. "Evolution of an Issue."
Bicycling 31 (May 1990): 104–105.

Koellner, Ken (editor). <u>New England Mountain Bike
Association Home Page</u>. 19 August 1995. New
England Mountain Bike Association. 12 Nov.
1996 <http://www.ultranet.com/~kvk/nemba.
html>.

Newton, Carlton. Personal interview. 13 Nov. 1996.

Schwartz, David M. "Over Hill, Over Dale on a Bicycle Built for . . . Goo." <u>Smithsonian</u> 25.3
(June 1992): 74-84.

Sneyd, Ross. "Mount Snow Teaching Mountain
Biking." <u>Burlington Free Press</u> 4 Oct. 1992:
E1.

9 ◆ REVISING

Inexperienced writers sometimes see revising as an alien activity that neither makes sense nor comes easily. Experienced writers, however, know that revising is the very essence of writing, the primary way of developing thoughts and preparing them to be shared with others.

Revising is not the same as editing. Revision is conceptual work, in which you reread, rethink, and reconstruct your thoughts until they match those in your mind. Revising means re-seeing your topic, thesis, argument, evidence, organization, and conclusion and making major changes that affect the content, direction, and meaning of your paper.

9a General revising strategies

While there is no one best way to revise, the following strategies have proved helpful to experienced writers.

1 **Plan to revise.** You cannot revise a paper you haven't yet written. Finish drafting your paper *before* the night before it is due.
2 **Establish distance.** Let your draft sit at least overnight. When you return to it the next day, you'll see more clearly what works well, what doesn't, and where your writing can be improved.

3 **Ask, "So what?"** Writing should teach readers something. Reread your paper and ask what can be learned from it. If you're not sure, it's time to revise.

4 **State the theme or thesis.** Most papers make assertions early on that say, in effect, "Here's what this paper is about." If yours does not, revise.

5 **Evaluate evidence.** To convince readers that your claims or assertions are good ones, double-check your facts and examples.

   ◆ **What evidence supports my thesis or advances my theme?**

   ◆ **What objections can be raised about this evidence?**

   ◆ **What additional evidence will answer these objections?**

6 **Reconsider everything.** When you return to your draft, reconsider the whole text. If you change the information on one page, it may change ideas on another. If a classmate or instructor suggests improvements on certain pages, don't assume the others are perfect.

7 **Make a paragraph outline.** A paragraph outline creates a map to check for logical organization.

   ◆ **Number each paragraph.**

   ◆ **Describe briefly the topic of each paragraph.**

   ◆ **Keep all related paragraphs together.**

   ◆ **Reorganize so that your paper has a beginning, middle, and end.**

8 **Play with titles.** Titles tell readers whether they want to read your essay. Changing a title can also give you, the writer, a new sense of direction. So, use titles as prompts to revision. Here are some ideas for finding good titles.

   ◆ **Use one good sentence from your paper.**

   ◆ **Ask a question that your paper answers.**

   ◆ **Use a strong sensory word or image from your paper.**

   ◆ **Locate a famous quotation that relates to your paper.**

   ◆ **Write a one-word title (a two-word title, a three-word title).**

9 **Listen for your voice.** Read your paper out loud. Does it sound like you—your ideas, your commitments, your style? If not, revise so that it does.

10 **Seek response.** Share your early drafts with an audience you trust and ask for a response about the strength of your claim, the credibility of your evidence, the clarity of your conclusion, and so on. The fresh eyes

of other readers can usually spot things in your writing that you can no longer see for yourself.

11 **Let go.** No matter how well an idea is expressed, if it no longer matches your paper's purpose, get rid of it or revise it until it does. When writers let go of early drafts, they trust that the power, creativity, and authority they found for their first draft will return for the second draft (and third).

12 **Start over.** Instead of always returning to the language of your original text, start over and let fresh language point you in new directions. Starting over may generate better writing as you delete dead ends and false starts.

9b Focused revising strategies

Sometimes you can bring new life to a paper by challenging yourself to see it in an entirely new way. Four specific suggestions for creatively refocusing your work are (1) limit your focus or scope, (2) add new material, (3) switch perspective, and (4) transform into another genre. These moves can be done as experiments at one sitting or as a sequence of drafts over several days or weeks.

Limit

Early drafts of papers are often too broad and cover too much ground in too few pages. Rather than continue writing many more pages, consider limiting your topic. How much of it should you cover? Ask these limiting questions: What are the parts of my paper? How many different parts are there? What are the subsections of each part? What is a specific example of each part? Could I write a complete paper about any of these smaller units?

Instead of writing a personal essay covering the two months last summer when you worked at McDonald's, for example, limit your draft to one specific day, afternoon, or hour, and tell that story with specific details so your readers can hear the hamburgers sizzle. Instead of writing a research paper about gun control as a national problem, limit your study to gun control in your own neighborhood, using local people and newspapers as resources.

When you limit your topic from something general to something specific, from something national to something local, you can find a lot of interesting and detailed information. When you select a specific and local issue, you have the opportunity to visit a place and talk to real people.

The following suggestions will help you limit a second draft.

1 **Limit ideas.** Focus on one idea covered in a single paragraph or sentence of your first draft. Develop that single idea into your whole next paper.

2 **Limit time.** Focus on "real time" so that what you describe could really happen in the amount of time it takes to read your paper.

3 **Limit place.** Focus on a single setting in which something happens or somebody speaks. Write as if you were a video camera recording in words everything you witness.

Add

Drafts get stale when writers keep revising over the same ground. Make a resolution to add new information each time you revise. For example, when you limit your topic to something local, it's easy to add material you discover through field research. A paper is more fun to write when the research process includes living as well as textual sources.

In a personal experience paper, for example, add dialogue between yourself and a customer or a co-worker and let readers hear other voices in your paper. In a research paper on gun control, add interviews with local police officers, members of the National Rifle Association, politicians, and priests or rabbis to better explain your case for or against gun control. Take notes or use a tape recorder to ensure accuracy.

Whatever your new sources of information, take careful notes. Include details that appeal to the senses of sight, sound, touch, smell, and taste. When using quotations from an interview, be faithful to the spirit of the occasion and the character of the person talking.

The following suggestions will help you add new material to later drafts.

1 **Add local people.** Find a local person who knows something about your topic and include his or her testimony in your paper.

2 **Add re-created dialogue or interior monologue.** Close your eyes and visualize the experience from your memory, and make your re-created words faithful to the spirit of the occasion.

3 **Add text research.** Use books, periodicals, or Internet sources to teach readers more than you knew when you started researching your topic.

Switch

Writers sometimes lock themselves into one way of seeing a topic. They write draft after draft from the same perspective and in the same point of view, in the same tense, tone, and style. A good way to revitalize a later draft is to change one of these mechanical elements and see the effect on the conceptual elements. For example, in retelling a personal experience, instead of always writing in the past tense—which is normal—switch to present tense: instead of *I walked,* write *I walk.* In writing about your experience as an intern at the local hospital, switch from first-person point of view and past tense to third-person point of view and present tense. Signal tense changes within the same piece of writing by giving clear typographical signals (subheadings, indentations, type changes, or white space) or by including careful transitional phrases. Notice how you re-see the experience as well as how readers respond to it. The present tense places you and your readers at the scene so that you both witness it. Instead of summary and generality, readers experience drama and life.

Consider switching other elements of your composing to force yourself to see your topic in a new light. If you have been writing in the first person, switch to third person. If you've been writing in an academic voice, switch to a personal voice. If you've been writing in term-paper style, switch to letter or journal style, and vice versa. If you have been writing an argument paper in support of legalizing marijuana or euthanasia, write a draft in which you argue convincingly against legalizing it.

You don't need to stay "switched" in any of these cases for your final draft, but the change will be mentally challenging and lead to new insights. The following suggestions may help you switch effectively.

1 **Switch point of view, verb tense, style, or voice.** Look at your ideas from a different perspective.
2 **Switch audience.** Write a draft to your younger brother, your mother, or the local newspaper and notice how change in audience results in change in style, tone, or voice.
3 **Switch from exposition to narrative.** Instead of reporting the results of research, write a research draft detailing how you went about your search for information, telling who you talked to and when, where you went next and with what results.

Transform

College writers often write in the same academic forms over and over: a critical essay for literature class, a personal narrative for writing class, a position paper for political science, a term paper for history, and so on. For your next draft, experiment with a new form or genre for reporting information or telling a story.

For example, instead of writing a traditional comparison-and-contrast paper about Edgar Allan Poe and Stephen King, transform a draft into a dialogue between King and Poe sitting in a coffee house. Instead of writing a position paper on alcohol abuse or gun control, transform your research into a script for *60 Minutes,* complete with interviewer, interviewee, settings, and camera angles.

No matter what your new form or genre, be consistent with its conventions. Note that although you may use the techniques of fiction and drama, your facts, events, dialogue, and feelings should remain true to the experience. If you write a paper on personal organizers as if it were an article for *Consumer Reports,* follow the magazine's style and conventions all the way through.

Remember that you will not know the full effect of a new form until you actually create one. Even if you don't like the final results of these experimental drafts, the new ideas generated by experimenting will usually find their way into your final paper. The more you experiment, the more you will grow as a writer. The following suggestions provide ideas for when to transform to what.

1 **Transform for a good reason.** Use a form that complements and enhances the content of the paper.
2 **When you have time to experiment, transform from one genre to another.** If the new form doesn't work, you still have the time to write conventionally.
3 **Just do it.** Don't *imagine* what the new form will do to your ideas — write in it long enough to see what the possibilities are.

When you try a switching or transforming experiment, make sure you treat the content of the paper just as seriously as if you wrote in a more conventional mode. To be safe, check with your instructor before turning in your final draft.

FOCUSED REVISION

Try any or all of these revision moves on different drafts of a multiple-draft paper assignment.

LIMIT
Writing from memory: Limit time, place, and action.
Writing from research: Limit scope and focus.

ADD
Writing from memory: Add dialogue, description, and details.
Writing from research: Add interviews, observations, and information.

SWITCH
Writing from memory: Switch tense and point of view.
Writing from research: Switch voice and audience.

TRANSFORM
Writing from memory: Transform to journals, letters, and drama.
Writing from research: Transform to articles, chapters, and scripts.

9c   Tools for revising

Revising is easier when you use the tools and techniques necessary to keep the process under control. Use the following tools to your advantage.

1 **Revision notebook.** Make a point of writing about revision in your journal or class notebook. Record notes about books, authors, and articles related to your project. Capture ideas about theme, direction, and purpose. Writing informally about your revision plans will almost certainly advance your project.

2 **Computer.** Word-processing programs help you revise in three important ways. First, by typing instead of handwriting your ideas, you create a distance that allows you to see clearly where to revise. Second, the computer lets you easily change your text before you print out a hard copy—saving time, energy, and paper. Third, the computer allows you to move blocks of text—sentences, paragraphs, pages—from one place to another, an essential act in revising form and organization.

3 **Due dates.** Create self-imposed due dates and complete several early drafts. Write the instructor's due date on your calendar; then subtract two weeks for your first draft. Try a radical revision a week before the final due date, and then complete a final draft. Early due dates give you time to both revise and edit your final paper so you will do your best work.

10 ◆ EDITING

In the editing stage of the writing process, writers read their drafts for clarity, correctness, precision, and style. Editing is more than just putting the finishing touches on your paper, the way a carpenter puts a final coat of paint or varnish on a new cabinet. Of course you want to make your work as polished and as close to perfect as you can. But editing also presents your last chance to see that your paper communicates your intended meaning to your target audience as clearly, directly, and forcefully—that is, as effectively—as possible.

Your task when editing is to anticipate how readers will understand your writing. Anticipate their questions; identify any lingering questions of your own, and resolve them by clarifying passages. Remove errors and ambiguities that may distract or confuse. Aim to please yourself by creating a paper that clearly reflects your ideas and beliefs in your own particular voice.

Strategies for editing   10a

There are as many ways to edit a paper as there are to draft one. Nevertheless, most writers find it best to tackle larger concerns before taking on individual sentences and words. The following suggestions are practiced, not necessarily in this order, by experienced readers before they send in a paper for grading or send one out for publishing.

1 **Read for sense.** Where is your paper strong and where is it weak? If you were reading this paper for the first time, would you grasp its purpose? Is its main idea clear? Do the points support the main idea? Are the facts correct and the examples suitable?

2 **Read for style and tone.** Is the language appropriately formal or informal for the audience? Look at the words that judge or describe. Look for overstatement or exclamation. Is the tone what you want?

3 **Reread for paragraph unity.** Pause at the end of each paragraph and ask: Does it have a main idea or a topic sentence? Should it? Is the purpose clear? Does each paragraph follow with some logic from the previous one? Does each lead inevitably to the next one?

4 **Reread the opening and closing paragraphs.** These are the most emphatic points in any paper. What in the opening paragraph catches readers' attention and invites them to read further? Does the final paragraph conclude with a sense of being final and finished?

5 **Reread for sound and rhythm.** Does your language sound as if a real live human being is speaking? Reading your paper aloud can help highlight problems. If any phrases or sentences sound clumsy or awkward as you voice them, can you simplify them?

Editing for specific purposes   10b

The process of analyzing and improving your entire paper can be overwhelming. Therefore, we have divided the editing process into steps and arranged them from large-scale concerns to finer points. Each of the following steps is discussed in a separate section in this handbook.

Editing for effectiveness   Is your writing as readable as possible? Are your openings and conclusions clearly and forcefully worded? Do the rhythm and structure of the sentences support your meaning by emphasizing the important points? Is each word the best possible word? (See Chapters 12 – 20.)

Editing grammar   Is every sentence logical and complete? Do the verbs and pronouns help clarify your meaning? Are modifiers correctly placed? (See Chapters 21 – 29.)

10c EDIT

Editing punctuation   Have you used punctuation marks—end punctuation, commas, semicolons, colons, and so on—correctly? (See Chapters 30–36.)

Editing mechanics   Is every word spelled correctly? Are words capitalized, abbreviated, or italicized according to standard practice? Do the numerals conform to convention? Are your papers formatted according to convention? (See Chapters 37–43.)

10c Editing with peers

To sharpen your editorial eye, consider exchanging work with a classmate or a friend. This gives both of you an opportunity to hear and see an outside response to your papers. Often, fresh eyes notice what you might have missed. Note anything that slows the progress of your understanding of your friend's paper—a sentence that seems too long, a misspelled word, an illogical sequence of ideas. Take turns discussing each other's work, and allow yourself time to make any final changes. The following suggestions will help you and your peers edit each other's work.

◆   Follow the Golden Rule. Comment on others' papers as you hope they will comment on yours: be both critically helpful and kind.

◆   Comment on the language you find in the written text, not on the values or personality of the author.

◆   Be specific and tell the author exactly where a word, sentence, or paragraph causes difficulty.

ESL ▷ EDITING OTHER STUDENTS' WRITING

As a nonnative speaker of English, you may question your ability to edit your classmates' writing. Nevertheless, trust your own reactions. Since you may be a part of the audience your classmate wants to reach, your point of view is useful. As a reader you can offer helpful feedback about clarity of purpose, variety of sentence structure, words or phrases that seem unfamiliar, and many other elements of an essay that are discussed in this chapter.

SUGGESTIONS FOR EDITING

1   Read each draft out loud. Your ear is usually a trustworthy guide for finding awkward sentence constructions, grammatical mistakes, and inappropriate tone.

2   "Simplify. Simplify. Simplify," wrote Henry David Thoreau in *Walden*, about living and writing. Edit your work to simplify words, sentences, paragraphs, whole papers so that you make your points as economically and forcefully as possible.

3   Delete unnecessary words. Omit words that do not contribute to your meaning. Many sentences can be improved by cutting needless words and not rewriting anything.

4   Edit with a word processor. The advantage of infinitely changeable electronic type is that you can play with phrases, sentences, metaphors, titles, rhythms, and formats until they please you, making your job more fun and less of a chore.

5   Proofread line by line. Using a ruler to mask the coming lines, proofread your paper after any computer programs have automatically checked your grammar or spelling. You may still find missing words, misused punctuation, and even unintended words when the spelling checker fails to recognize a spelling mistake (*two* instead of *too*, etc.).

◆   When you find many errors in a classmate's paper, mention the larger ones first so that you don't overwhelm the writer with too much to do all at once.

◆   When conceptual or stylistic issues are under discussion, write margin notes. When matters of mechanics are under discussion, use conventional editing symbols (see the last page of *The College Writer's Reference*).

11 ◆ PORTFOLIOS AND PUBLISHING

The final product of careful writing is publication for an audience other than the author. This chapter explores three common avenues of presenting finished work to instructors, classmates, and the wider world of the Web.

11a Preparing writing portfolios

Writing portfolios are collections of writing contained within a single binder or folder. A **course portfolio** presents a record of your cumulative work over a term and is used to assign a grade. A **story portfolio** presents a condensed, edited story of your writing progress in narrative form. A **professional portfolio** is often requested by prospective employers in education, journalism, and other fields in which writing is important.

Course portfolios

The most common type of portfolio assigned in a writing course contains your cumulative work collected over the term plus a cover letter in which you explain the nature and value of these papers. Sometimes you will be asked to assign yourself a grade based on your own assessment. The following suggestions may help you in preparing a course portfolio.

- ◆ **Make your portfolio speak for you.** Judgment depends on whether your work is careful, clean, and complete or careless, messy, and incomplete.

- ◆ **Include exactly what is asked for.** Sometimes you can include more than you are asked for, but do not include less.

- ◆ **Add supplemental material judiciously.** Course portfolios are usually flexible. If you believe that supplemental writing (journals, notes, letters, and sketches) will present you in a better light, add that to the required material.

- ◆ **Include perfect final drafts.** Final drafts should be carefully proofread and printed double spaced on one side only of high-quality paper.

- ◆ **Demonstrate growth.** Demonstrate how a finished paper came into being by including all drafts and instructor comments leading up to the final draft.

- ◆ **Attach a table of contents.** For portfolios containing more than three papers, attach a separate table of contents.

- ◆ **Order chronologically or thematically.** Arrange your work systematically in a lightweight three-ring binder so readers can follow the work easily.

- ◆ **Write a cover letter.** This letter serves as (1) an introduction describing and explaining the portfolio's contents and (2) an assessment of the work therein.

Following is an excerpt of a final portfolio cover letter.

> As I look back through all the papers I've written this semester, I
> see how far my writing has come. At first I thought it was stupid to
> write so many different drafts of the same paper, as if I would beat the
> topic to death. But now I realize that these different papers on the
> same topic all went in different directions. This happened to some de-
> gree in the first paper, but I especially remember in my research project,
> when I interviewed the director of the homeless shelter, I really got ex-
> cited about the work they did there, and I really got involved in the
> other drafts of that paper. I have learned to shorten my papers by
> editing and cutting out needless words. I use more descriptive adjec-
> tives now when I'm describing a setting and try to use action verbs in-
> stead of "to be" verbs in all of my papers. I am writing more consciously
> now—I think that's the most important thing I learned this semester.

Story portfolios

A story portfolio is a shorter, more selectively composed production
than a course portfolio. Instead of including a cover letter and all papers and
drafts written during the term, a story portfolio presents in narrative form the
evolution of your most important work over the course of the term. Include
excerpts rather than whole papers to illustrate points in your development as
a writer. Include informal texts—early drafts of papers, journal entries,
freewriting, instructors' and classmates' comments—when they advance your

---

SUGGESTIONS FOR ASSEMBLING COURSE PORTFOLIOS

1   Collect, date, and save all papers written during the course.

2   Arrange all papers chronologically or thematically, depending on
the assignment.

3   Include supplemental writing such as journal excerpts, letters,
class exercises, or quizzes, arranged chronologically, thematically, or
in an appendix.

4   Compose a cover letter that considers the strengths and weak-
nesses of each individual paper as well as the combined collection.
Provide a summary statement of your current standing as a writer as
your portfolio represents you.

5   Attach a table of contents, write explanatory memos to explain
unusual materials, and make sure the portfolio meets the minimum
specifications of the assignment.

story. The best story portfolios commonly reveal a theme or a set of issues that runs from week to week or paper to paper throughout the semester. Following are selected pages from Karen's story portfolio.

When I entered English I, I was not a confident writer and only felt comfortable writing factual reports for school assignments. Those were pretty straightforward, and personal opinion was not involved. But over the course of the semester I've learned that I enjoy including my own voice in my writing. The first day of class I wrote this in my journal:

> 8/31 Writing has always been hard for me. I don't have a lot of experience writing papers except for straightforward things like science reports. I never did very well in English classes, usually getting B's and C's on my papers.

Our first assignment was to write a paper about a personal experience that was important to us. At first, I couldn't think where to start, but when we brainstormed topics in class, I got some good ideas. Three of the topics listed on the board were ones I could write about.

— Excelling at a particular sport (basketball)
— High school graduation
— One day in the life of a waitress

I decided to write about our basketball season last year, especially the last game that we lost. Here is a paragraph from my first draft.

> We lost badly to Walpole in what turned out to be our final game. I sat on the bench most of the time.

As I see now, that draft was all telling and summary—I didn't show anything happening that was interesting or alive. But in a later draft I used dialogue and wrote from the announcer's point of view, and the result was fun to write and, my group said, fun to read.

> Well folks, it looks as if Belmont has given up; the coach is preparing to send in his subs. It has been a rough game for Belmont. They stayed in it during the first quarter, but Walpole has run away with it since then. Down by twenty with only six minutes left, Belmont's first sub is now approaching the table.

Story portfolios are small research-writing projects in themselves. Successful ones will exhibit all the characteristics of a well-written research paper, including the careful use of sources and numerous, various, and lively quotations properly identified.

SUGGESTIONS FOR ASSEMBLING STORY PORTFOLIOS

1   Assemble both formal and informal writing samples in chronological order, from beginning to end of the term.

2   Reread informal writing and highlight significant passages.

3   Reread formal writing and highlight significant passages. Note especially a particular passage that evolved over several drafts in the same paper, showing how you learned to revise.

4   Arrange all highlighted passages in order and write a story that shows (a) how one passage connects to another and (b) the significance of each passage.

5   Identify common themes, ideas, or concerns and write a reflective conclusion.

Publishing class books   11b

Publishing a class book is a natural end to any class in which interesting writing has taken place. A **class book** is an edited, bound collection of student writing, usually featuring some work from each student in the class. Compiling and editing such a book is commonly assigned to class volunteers, who are given significant authority in designing and producing the book. If you volunteer to edit such a book, these guidelines will help.

1 **Establish manuscript guidelines.** Discuss with the class what each submitted paper should look like: consider single or double-spaced typing, type face, font size, margins, justification, and title and author names.

2 **Set page limits.** Printing charges are usually made on a per-page basis.

3 **Set deadlines.** Arrange for books to be delivered to class or picked up by students in time for a discussion of their contents.

4 **Ask for camera-ready copy.** To simplify and speed the publishing process, have each student prepare her own manuscript in final form to submit to editors.

5 **Organize the essays.** Arrange collected essays according to some logic — theme, content, quality, or last names of the authors.

6 **Write an introduction.** Explain to readers the nature of the reading experience to follow. Introductions vary in length from a paragraph to several pages.

7 **Prepare a table of contents.** Include essay titles, authors' names, and page numbers.

8 **Ask the instructor to write an afterword.** Instructors may write about the assignment objectives, their impressions of the essays, or their reactions to the class, or they may add another perspective relevant to the book.

9 **Collect biographies of student writers.** Conclude with short (50–100 words) serious or semiserious or comical biographies of the student writers.

10 **Design a cover.** Plan the cover or commission a classmate to do so. (Color cardboard covers cost extra but are usually worth the expense.)

11 **Arrange for publication.** Contact local print shops to explore production costs and a timetable for producing a copy for every student in the class.

12 **Divide editorial responsibilities.** Class books are best done by editorial teams consisting of two or more students who arrange among themselves the various duties described above.

SUGGESTIONS FOR DISCUSSING CLASS BOOKS

The following questions will generate critical discussions of class books.

◆ Which are your favorite titles, and why?
◆ What essay (other than your own) is your favorite, and why?
◆ What ideas or techniques did you learn from classmates' essays?
◆ In your own essay, what are your favorite passages?
◆ What would you like to change in your essay?
◆ Which essays present graphics most effectively? How are they used?

11c   Publishing on the World Wide Web

Academic writing can now be placed on the World Wide Web, where text, illustrations, and graphics are presented together, along with electronic "links" to related pages or articles. When you publish on the Web, your ideas are made available to networked computers around the world. Thus you can quickly and inexpensively reach a potentially vast audience. Modern word-processing programs such as *Word* for either IBM-compatible or Apple Macintosh computers include commands that facilitate constructing Web pages. When setting up a Web page, consider the quantity and quality of hyperlinks, images, and sound effects. To learn the specifics of publishing a Web page at your school, consult your instructor or the director of campus computing.

EDITING FOR EFFECTIVENESS

EDITING FOR EFFECTIVENESS

The goal of editing, like that of revising, is to improve communication. As you draft and revise, you focus primarily on what you intend to communicate. As you edit, you imagine the reactions of your intended audience, anticipating how you will be understood. Editing for effectiveness involves reshaping paragraphs so that they flow from point to point, revising sentences to clarify your ideas, and finding better words to express your thoughts precisely.

Each editing action involves three steps.

◆ Recognize the problem.

◆ Generate possible solutions.

◆ Pick the solution that best fits the situation at hand.

When you begin to edit your work, consider these questions. Refer to the chapter in parentheses for tips on how to create and choose alternatives.

◆ Does my introduction catch the reader's attention? (Chapter 12)

◆ Does my conclusion produce the effect I intended? (Chapter 12)

◆ Is my main point (or thesis) clearly stated? (Chapter 12)

◆ Does one paragraph flow logically to the next? (Chapter 13)

◆ Do I vary the structure of my sentences? (Chapter 14)

◆ Are my sentences clear, direct, and interesting? (Chapters 15–16)

◆ Do I use language appropriately? (Chapters 17–19)

12 ◆ OPENINGS AND CONCLUSIONS

The first words of your paper may be the most important. Your **opening** must engage your readers, introduce your topic and your thesis or main idea, and provide an idea of what you intend to say.

Your **conclusion** is equally important because what it says will linger in the reader's mind. Here you tie together everything you have covered into a tidy package. Without strong openings and conclusions, your ideas can be lost.

Expect to work and rework your openings and conclusions. Many writers find it impossible to create polished openings during the drafting or revising stages. Instead, they draft rough passages with the idea of finishing them later. Whenever you're ready to work on your openings and conclusions, consider the following strategies.

12a Engaging openings

You want to catch the reader's interest, but how much space can you afford to spend doing so? In an essay of two or three pages, *one paragraph* is the standard length for an opening in most college writing. In longer papers, you may want to use *two paragraphs,* the first paragraph for an attention-grabbing quotation, anecdote, or fact and the second for commenting on it and introducing your thesis.

Whether the opening is one paragraph or two, readers should be able to recognize both your **subject**—the general area you are writing about—and your **topic**, or specific focus. They should also grasp your main idea, the central point of your paper. In argument and research writing, this is called a **thesis**, an explicit statement that usually appears in the opening. In personal experience and reflective writing, the main idea instead can be an implicit theme.

Several techniques can make openings more engaging.

General-to-specific pattern

Many opening paragraphs in college papers start with a broad general statement, narrow the focus, and end by stating the thesis.

> Anxiety, stress, and tension exist in us all. At worst, too much stress can cost us our lives. At the very least, it jeopardizes our health. The most effective way to control stress and live more comfortable lives is to use techniques for relaxation.

Striking assertion

You may want to open with a statement so improbable, eye-opening, or far-reaching that the reader will demand to see proof. After grabbing his reader's attention, this writer directly states his thesis.

> John Milton was a failure. In writing *Paradise Lost,* his stated aim was to "justify the ways of God to men." Inevitably, he fell short of accomplishing that and only wrote a monumental poem. Beethoven, whose music was conceived to transcend Fate, was a failure, as was Socrates, whose ambition was to make people happy by making them reasonable and just. The inescapable conclusion seems

to be that the surest, noblest way to fail is to set one's own standards titanically high.

Lawrence Shanies, *"The Sweet Smell of
Success Isn't All That Sweet"*

Anecdote

Try telling a brief story about someone or something that introduces the topic and illustrates the thesis.

> Once I met a woman who grew up in the small North Carolina town to which Chang and Eng, the original Siamese twins, retired after their circus careers. When I asked her how the town reacted to the twins marrying local girls and setting up adjacent households, she laughed and said: "Honey, that was *nothing* compared to what happened *before* the twins got there." Get the good gossip on any little mountain town, scratch the surface and you'll find a snake pit!

Francine Prose, *"Gossip"*

By the end of this opening, you are well aware of the author's implicit thesis, that gossip is an inescapable part of community life.

STRONGER OPENINGS

Examine your opening paragraphs for unnecessary words, overgeneralizations, or clichés that may distract your readers. The following advice will help you strengthen your openings.

◆ **Be direct.** Get to the point without rambling. Phrases like *it is a fact that, it appears that,* and *it has come to my attention that* keep the reader from engaging with your essay. During editing, pare away loose or empty phrases and clauses that don't serve your writing goals.

◆ **Sharpen your focus.** Opening statements that are too broad or obvious may fail to engage readers. Opening statements can be general, but they should also help readers know immediately what you are talking about. When editing, limit generalizations carefully, and use the strongest as a springboard to your thesis.

◆ **Emphasize the main idea.** Your opening should quickly establish your main idea. Anything that leads away from this idea confuses readers about the goals of your paper. When editing, place your thesis statement in a prominent position in the paragraph, and include only those points that appear later as crucial supporting details.

Interesting detail, statistic, or quotation

With this technique, you plunge readers into an unfamiliar situation to pique their curiosity.

> "Mrs. Tolstoy is your basic L.O.L. in N.A.D., admitted for a soft rule-out M.I.," the intern announces. I scribble that on my patient list. In other words, Mrs. Tolstoy is a Little Old Lady in No Apparent Distress who is in the hospital to make sure she hasn't had a heart attack (rule out a myocardial infarction). And we think it's unlikely that she has had a heart attack (a *soft* rule-out).
>
> If I had learned nothing else during my first three months of working in the hospital as a medical student, I learned endless jargon and abbreviations.
>
> Perri Klass, *"She's Your Basic L.O.L. in N.A.D."*

The unfamiliar jargon in the quotation attracts the reader's attention. Klass quickly explains it and, in her second paragraph, identifies jargon itself as the topic of her essay.

Provocative question

If you want to tease your readers, introduce your thesis as a question. After a few sentences of background information, pose the question that your thesis will later answer.

 CROSS-CULTURAL DIFFERENCES IN ESSAY OPENINGS

Writing instruction in your native language may have emphasized different approaches to openings than those presented here. For example, you may have learned to be indirect rather than direct, to start with a proverb, or to quote a recognized authority. To gain a better understanding of composing in English:

♦ Discuss with your instructor or your classmates what you have learned elsewhere about writing openings. Try to identify the differences between the way people write in your native language and the way they write in English.

♦ Ask a friend or classmate to read and respond to the openings in your drafts before you turn in your final papers.

♦ Examine the way openings are developed in published works and in your classmates' papers. You may see, for example, how using a proverb or a familiar story in an opening is appropriate on some occasions but not others.

Many children spend more than five hours a day watching television when they could be reading or playing outside. What effect does television have on these kids? At what levels do those effects appear? In other words, how much TV is too much?

Satisfying conclusions   12b

An effective conclusion leaves readers satisfied with the discussion and gives them something to think about. It also reminds readers of your main idea or thesis. You can develop a statement or restatement of the main idea in one of several ways. (If you have not yet explicitly stated your main idea, do so now.)

Rhetorical question

A rhetorical question is asked only for effect. It is meant not to be answered but to persuade the reader to agree with you.

> Drug violence will continue as long as citizens tolerate the easy availability of guns on the streets; as long as the public shells out money for violence glorified in television and film; as long as drug users, deprived of effective treatment, pour money into disadvantaged neighborhoods. How can society sit by and do nothing?

Summary

A concise summary of the important points in a paper usually concludes with an assertion based on them.

> The tasks are urgent and difficult. Realistically, we know we cannot abolish crime. But we can abolish—as a nation, not just state by state—capital punishment. We can accept the fact that prisoners, convicted criminals, are hostages to our own human failures to develop and support a decent way of living. And we can accept the fact that we are responsible to them, as to all living beings, for the protection of society, and especially responsible for those among us who need protection for the sake of society.
>
> Margaret Mead, *"A Life for a Life"*

Call to action

In argument papers, you use your powers of persuasion to make your case. The conclusion is one place to mobilize readers to action.

> Until the SAT is reformed or abolished, those students who score low on the test will suffer. They will have a hard time getting into many

colleges, even though they may have what it takes to succeed. The emphasis on the test distracts high school students from things that are also important to admission decisions, such as writing ability, grades, course load, and extracurricular activities. *It is time for those who care about justice to see that this system is fixed.*

Speculation

You might close your paper with some speculation about what the future will be if the action you propose is—or is not—taken. This can have a powerful impact on your readers.

> Someday, perhaps, a democratic account of the physiology of sex will be written, an account that will stress both the functional and organic aspects of reproduction.
>
> Ruth Herschberger, *Adam's Rib*

STRONGER CONCLUSIONS

An effective conclusion summarizes, but it should do something more. This is your last chance to speak to your readers. What do you most want them to remember? When editing, focus on the single most important idea and try to take it a step further.

◆ **Be direct.** Wordiness can undermine the authority of your final sentences and weaken your message. In editing, make sure you have used **transitional phrases**—*in conclusion, all in all,* or *to sum up*—sparingly; your readers should recognize your conclusion without them. Most **qualifying phrases**—*I think* or *I believe,* for example—are also unnecessary because readers assume the ideas in your paper are your own. Use such phrases only when you need to distinguish your conclusions from someone else's.

◆ **Check your focus.** Take care not to *limit* the scope of your conclusion too much. When editing, check to see that your concluding statements or questions are general enough to fulfill the promises you have made in your thesis, even though your examples may have been specific.

◆ **Limit your claims.** Make sure that your conclusion is not too *broad.* As you edit, check that you have not asked or answered a question your paper didn't cover and that you have not added new material or wandered into wide-ranging speculation.

13 ◆ PARAGRAPHS

Good paragraphing helps readers follow an author's ideas throughout a piece of writing. When a new paragraph begins, readers expect a new idea to begin. They expect that within a paragraph, each sentence will help develop a single main idea—that the paragraph will be **unified.** They expect that the paragraph will present its ideas in a logical order—that it will be **organized.** And they expect that each sentence will relate clearly to the sentences around it— that it will be **coherent.**

Most writers start new paragraphs intuitively at places where they leave one thought and begin to develop another. As you edit, review and improve your paragraphing decisions.

Unified paragraphs 13a

To edit for paragraph unity, first determine the paragraph's main idea, or **topic.** In college writing, that idea often is stated in a **topic sentence.** In some kinds of writing, such as personal experience, it may be implied rather than explicitly stated. In either case, words or sentences that do not support or clarify the main idea should be deleted or moved.

In the following passage, the writer identified the first sentence as her topic sentence. When she read the other sentences, she realized that her fourth sentence did not illustrate the topic sentence, so she moved it to the next paragraph, where it fit better.

◆   For various reasons, some unhappy couples remain married. Some are forbidden to divorce by religion, others by social custom. Still others stay together "for the sake of the children." In recent years, psychologists and sociologists have studied families to determine whether more harm is done to children by divorce or by parents who stay together despite conflict. ~~But by staying together, such parents feel~~ believing they are sparing their children the pain of divorce.

In his study of family conflict, Robert S. Weiss found that children in such families were often happiest "when Daddy is at work."

13b   Well-organized paragraphs

Ideas presented in no apparent order can confuse readers. In organizing paragraphs, you must decide where to put the topic sentence and what pattern of organization to use. The order you create depends on what you are trying to do.

If you are giving examples, you might describe what they have in common and then list them (a general-to-specific pattern). If you are arguing from evidence, you might cite your evidence and then tell readers what you think it means (a specific-to-general pattern.) (See also Chapter 15, "Sentence Emphasis and Variety," for tips on how to get the most impact out of the beginnings and ends of paragraphs and sentences.)

◆ **WP TIPS** (1) Insert returns so that each sentence begins on a new line. Then rearrange sentences until you find the best organization. (2) Use the copy function to make several copies of the same paragraph; then create several different organizations and compare them. Choose the one that works best in your situation.

Standard patterns of organization

General to specific
This common paragraph pattern begins with a general statement of the main idea. Subsequent sentences contain examples that support, explain, and expand that statement.

> *The evolution of the horse can be inferred from fossil evidence of related animals with progressively more sophisticated leg structure.* The earliest horse, *eohippus,* ran on four toes like many mammals. A later species, *mesohippus,* or middle horse, ran on three toes. The modern horse runs on one toe; its hoof is the toenail of the digit that corresponds to a middle finger. Vestiges of the second and fourth toes can be found above the hoof.

GENERAL
STATEMENT

SPECIFIC
EXAMPLES

Specific to general
This pattern begins with a series of details or examples and culminates in a general statement. Placing your general statement, or topic sentence, at the end of the paragraph allows you to build toward and emphasize your conclusion.

> As early horse species changed, so did their environment, from forest to open grasslands. The

SPECIFIC
EXAMPLES

tougher hooves were better on hard ground. Longer legs provided speed where there was nowhere to hide. Along with the changes in the feet came changes in teeth to shift from chewing leaves to grinding grasses and grain. *The fossil record shows the horse's ancestors adapting to their changing habitat.*

GENERAL
STATEMENT

Chronological order

Events are sometimes best presented in the order in which they happened. The topic sentence, or general statement, can appear at the beginning or the end of the paragraph.

Before the arrival of Europeans, Haiti was populated by the Arawak tribes. Within fifty years after Columbus set foot on the island in 1492, the Arawaks had nearly died out, victims of disease and enslavement. The Spanish colonists imported blacks from Africa to replace the natives as slaves on their plantations. Late in the seventeenth century, the island was ceded to France but was the subject of dispute among England, Spain, and France for decades before achieving independence. *The population of Haiti today, predominantly black and French-speaking, reflects that history.*

EVENT 1
EVENT 2

EVENT 3

EVENT 4

GENERAL
STATEMENT

Consider using reverse chronological order—moving backward from the most recent events to the most distant. This can be an effective way to reflect on the past.

Climactic order

To draw readers in and build toward a conclusion, begin with a general statement, present specific details in order of increasing importance, and end with a dramatic statement or prediction.

Consider the potential effect of just a small increase in the earth's atmospheric temperature. A rise of only a few degrees would melt the polar ice caps. Rainfall patterns would change. Some deserts might bloom, but lands now fertile might turn to desert. Many hot climates could become uninhabitable. *If the sea level rose only a few feet, dozens of coastal cities would be destroyed, and life as we know it would be changed utterly.*

GENERAL
STATEMENT

SPECIFICS OF
INCREASING
IMPORTANCE

CLIMAX

Spatial order

The details in a descriptive paragraph can be ordered so that the mind's eye moves from one concrete object to another. The topic sentence, here a general statement summarizing and interpreting the details, can appear at the beginning or the end.

Above the mantelpiece hung an ancient wheel-lock musket that gave every indication of being in working order. A small collection of pewter, most of it dating from the colonial period, was arrayed across the mantel. To the left of the hearth stood a collection of wrought-iron fireplace tools. At the right, a brass hopper held several cut limbs of an apple tree. On an iron hook in the fireplace hung a copper kettle, blackened with age and smoke. *The fireplace looked as if it had changed little since the Revolution.*

SPECIFICS ARRANGED SPATIALLY

GENERAL STATEMENT

13c Coherent paragraphs

Paragraphs are coherent—literally, they "stick together"—when each sentence relates appropriately to the surrounding ones. Your writing will be more coherent if you join choppy paragraphs by using transitional expressions, shorten overly long paragraphs, and deliberately repeat key words.

Transitional expressions

Many words and phrases can indicate that one idea expands, exemplifies, qualifies, specifies, summarizes, implies, causes, or results from another. Other terms can compare or contrast ideas or show relationships in time and space. **Transitions** smooth out shifts in ideas. Without its transitional expressions, the following paragraph would be a string of seemingly unrelated facts.

Newspaper and magazine publishing is not usually regarded as cyclic, *but* the recent recession cut deeply into advertising revenue. As the economy gathers steam, classified-ad buyers should return, *although* display advertising will lag. *Meanwhile,* publications that have already sharply cut their costs should see profits taking a strong upturn as advertisers return. *For them,* the coming year looks rosy.

The changes you make when restructuring paragraphs for unity, organization, or length often mean adding new transitional expressions. In this paper on divorce, the writer added two new transitional sentences.

◆   During a divorce, parents have the ability to shield a child from potential harm. Many couples who stay together believe that the two-parent structure is crucial to the child's well-being. This, however, appears not to be the case. A child's security is based on his or her relationship with each parent individually, according to studies by Judith Wallerstein, who found that a stable, caring relationship between a child and each parent is the most significant ingredient in a child's emotional health. Maintaining even one stable relationship appears to reduce the effect of divorce on a child's emotions. The issue during a divorce, then, is how well a child can maintain at least one secure relationship. During the early stages of a breakup, both parents are often distracted by other issues. The child may suffer as a result.

Revising paragraph length

A very long paragraph may strain readers' attention. A string of very short paragraphs, on the other hand, can seem choppy and make ideas appear disconnected. Look for places where several small paragraphs develop what is really one idea, and join them together.

    ◆ **WP TIP** To try out different paragraphing solutions, use the copy function to make several copies of a passage. Break the paragraphs into smaller units or even individual sentences. Then build the passage back up in different ways, and see which solution works best.

Deliberate repetition

Words or phrases, repeated sparingly, link sentences and help your ideas stick together. Deliberately repeating key words keeps the writing focused, making it easier for readers to follow your thoughts. Notice how the key words, in italics, echo the topic of this paragraph.

    The *controversy* over the proposed Northgate Mall has continued for at least five years. The *dispute* has divided the city into two camps. A small group seems *opposed* to the mall, but its members are vocal and energetic. The *opponents* maintain that the mall would rob trade from existing businesses downtown and contribute to traffic congestion. *Proponents* say that the growth it would bring would be easily manageable.

TRANSITIONAL EXPRESSIONS

TO EXPAND
also, and, besides, finally, further, in addition, moreover, then

TO EXEMPLIFY
as an illustration, for example, for instance, in fact, specifically, thus

TO QUALIFY
but, certainly, however, to be sure

TO SUMMARIZE OR CONCLUDE
and so, finally, in conclusion, in short, in sum, therefore, this shows, thus we see

TO SHOW LOGICAL RELATIONSHIPS
as a result, because, by implication, for this reason, if, since, so, thus, therefore, this shows that

TO COMPARE
also, as well, likewise, similarly

TO CONTRAST
although, but, despite, even though, nevertheless, on the other hand, yet

TO SHOW RELATIONSHIPS IN TIME
after, before, between, earlier, formerly, later, longer than, meanwhile, since

TO SHOW RELATIONSHIPS IN SPACE
above, adjacent to, behind, below, beyond, in front of, nearby, next to, north (south, east, west) of, opposite to, over, through, within

---

Substituting similar words (*dispute* for *controversy*) prevents the repetition from becoming monotonous.

A deliberate repetition can also create a rhythmic effect.

◆   ~~When~~ she read to me, I ~~could see~~ faraway islands fringed with coconut palms. ~~With~~ Jim Hawkins, I shivered in the apple barrel while the

She read to me, and
pirates plotted. I ran with Maori warriors to raid the villages of neighboring

tribes. I heard Ahab's peg leg thumping on the deck overhead, and I marveled

at the whiteness of the whale.

Make sure that any element you repeat deserves the emphasis you give it and that any rhythmic effect you create is appropriate to your subject and your audience.

SUGGESTIONS FOR USING TRANSITIONAL EXPRESSIONS

Here are some guidelines for deciding when to use a transitional expression.

1 Use transitions to warn readers of shifts in thought that they may not expect. For example, a contrast or contradiction is often unexpected and needs a transition.

> The film's plot is very predictable, and the characters are not especially likable. *Nevertheless,* the movie is worth seeing.

Other relationships, such as those in time and space, are often obvious from the context and do not need a transitional phrase.

> The main character of the film moves to Brazil. He *then* finds a job in a large corporation and settles into a routine.

> *The* then *in the second sentence signals the passage of time, but the reader can infer the sequence from the context without it.*

2 If you use a series of transitional expressions to mark a sequence or to list points, make them parallel in form. For example, use *first, second,* and *last* to introduce three points, but not *first, in the second place,* and *the last.*

3 Avoid beginning a series of sentences with one-word transitions. Consider omitting some transitions, or put some of the transitional expressions in the middle of sentences.

> Keeping a journal is helpful, in addition, because . . .

4 Incorporate a variety of transitional expressions. Instead of always using *first, second,* and *third* to list sequences, for example, vary the fare with *for example, also,* and *finally.*

14 ◆SENTENCE STRUCTURE

The way you structure a sentence can help readers understand how it relates to the sentences around it. Using sentence structure purposefully—in particular the strategies of **coordination, subordination,** and **parallelism**—can help you write more clearly.

14a   Coordination to relate equal ideas

A **compound sentence** contains two or more independent clauses that could stand by themselves as full sentences. Putting two or more ideas together in a compound sentence gives them equal emphasis.

Coordinating conjunctions

The most common method of joining independent clauses uses a **coordinating conjunction**—*and, or, nor, for, but, yet, so*—and a comma. Each coordinating conjunction expresses a different relationship, so be sure to choose the right one for the meaning you intend.

- ◆   Incoming students must pass a placement examination to meet the foreign language requirement. *, or they* ~~Those who fail the test~~ must register for an introductory language course.

Correlative conjunctions

Another way to coordinate two independent clauses is by using a pair of **correlative conjunctions** such as *both . . . and, either . . . or,* or *not only . . . but also.*

- ◆   *not only* Lavar won high honors in mathematics and physics. *, but he* ~~He~~ was also recognized for his achievement in biology.

Conjunctive Adverbs

A **conjunctive adverb** such as *however, moreover,* or *nevertheless* used with a semicolon can also join two independent clauses.

- ◆   An Advanced Placement Test score will be accepted. *; however,* ~~However,~~ the test must have been taken within the last year.

COORDINATING CONJUNCTIONS, CORRELATIVE CONJUNCTIONS, AND CONJUNCTIVE ADVERBS

RELATIONSHIP	COORDINATING CONJUNCTIONS
addition	*and*
contrast	*but, yet*
choice	*or, nor*
effect	*so*
causation	*for*

RELATIONSHIP	CORRELATIVE CONJUNCTIONS
addition	*both . . . and*
	not only . . . but also
choice	*either . . . or*
substitution	*not . . . but*
negation	*neither . . . nor*

RELATIONSHIP	CONJUNCTIVE ADVERBS
addition	*also, besides, furthermore, moreover*
contrast	*however, instead, nevertheless, otherwise*
comparison	*likewise, similarly*
effect	*accordingly, consequently, therefore, thus*
sequence	*finally, meanwhile, next, then*
emphasis	*certainly, indeed*

Effective coordination   14b

Skillful coordination can connect ideas and enhance readability. When you edit, look for places where your use of coordination sends a confusing message to your readers.

Illogical coordination

Because coordination implies equal relationships, avoid using coordination where the meaning of the two sentences is not related closely enough to warrant joining them.

I made eggs for breakfast, and I missed the bus.

Is a cause-and-effect relationship intended? The conjunction and *does not make this clear.*

Faulty coordination can connect ideas in a way that is not only confusing but inaccurate.

◆   The project was a huge undertaking/ y̶e̶t̶ I was exhausted at the end. *so*

The conjunction yet *implies contrast, but that is not what the sentence means. The conjunction* so *states the proper cause-and-effect relationship.*

When the relationship between two ideas is apparent, a semicolon alone can join two independent clauses.

◆   Taking an introductory language course will fulfill the foreign language requirement/ T̶h̶e̶ courses are offered during the fall semester. *; the*

Overused coordination

Too much coordination begins to sound like baby talk. How much is too much? If a sentence with several coordinate structures seems weak, decide which elements belong together and which should stand alone. The following paragraph, for example, could be edited like this:

◆   Coordination can be overdone, a̶n̶d̶ ̶w̶h̶e̶n̶ it is used too much, it begins to *. When*
sound repetitive, a̶n̶d̶ ̶r̶e̶a̶d̶e̶r̶s̶ may begin to imagine the voice of a child *. Readers*
speaking in sentences that go on and on, strung together with *and,* a̶n̶d̶ ̶s̶o̶o̶n̶ *; soon*
they may get confused or bored, s̶o̶ ̶a̶s̶ a writer you should try to prevent that. *. As*

◆ **WP TIP** Use the search-and-replace function to highlight each instance of the conjunctions *and, but,* and *or.* This tells you how often you have used coordination so that you can consider its effectiveness case by case.

14c   Subordination to emphasize main ideas

Joining sentences or parts of sentences through subordination implies that some ideas are less important than others. Subordinating certain ideas in turn emphasizes the remaining ideas. When editing, if you find two related sentences with one more important than the other, put the less important sentence into a subordinate structure.

NO SUBORDINATION	John Playford was an English musician. He collected seventeenth-century music and descriptions of popular dances in a book called *The English Dancing Master*.
SUBORDINATION	John Playford was an English musician who collected seventeenth-century music and descriptions of popular dances in a book called *The English Dancing Master*. *Emphasizes the identification of Playford.*
SUBORDINATION	John Playford, an English musician, collected seventeenth-century music and descriptions of popular dances in a book called *The English Dancing Master*. *Emphasizes what Playford did.*

A subordinate element may appear as a clause, a phrase, or a single word. The less important the element is grammatically, the less attention the reader pays to it.

NO SUBORDINATION	The campaign manager wrote a plan. It seemed to cover every major contingency.
CLAUSE	The plan *that the campaign manager wrote* seemed to cover every major contingency.
PHRASE	The plan *written by the campaign manager* seemed to cover every major contingency.
WORD	The *campaign manager's* plan seemed to cover every major contingency.

A **dependent** or **subordinate clause,** one that contains a subject and a verb but cannot stand alone as a full sentence, is usually introduced by a **relative pronoun** such as *who, whom, which, what,* or *that* or a **subordinating conjunction** such as *although, because, if, since, whether,* or *while.*

Relative pronouns

Common relative pronouns include *that, what, which, who,* and *whom.* The clauses they introduce usually modify nouns or pronouns, so they are called **adjective clauses.** (See 24h.)

◆ The gap between rich and poor has caused great concern among social thinkers. ~~The gap has been widening for over twenty years.~~

, which has been widening for twenty years,

You can also subordinate a sentence by using it as a subject or as an object. Such **noun clauses** can be introduced by *why, what, that, where, whether,* or *how.*

◆   ~~There are a few basic facts~~ about AIDS ~~we know today. They are~~ the result

  of years of painstaking research.

(handwritten additions: "What we know today" above "There are a few basic facts"; "is" above; "They are")

SUBORDINATING CONJUNCTIONS

RELATIONSHIP	SUBORDINATING CONJUNCTIONS
cause/effect	*as, because, since, so, so that, in order that*
condition	*if, even if, if only, unless*
contrast	*although, even though, though*
comparison	*as if, as though, than, whereas, while*
choice	*rather than, than, whether*
sequence	*after, as, as long as, as soon as, before, once, since, until, when, whenever, while*
space	*where, wherever, whence*

Subordinating conjunctions

Using a subordinating conjunction makes the dependent clause an **adverb clause.**

◆   The campaign plan has a chance of success. ~~It needs~~ careful execution by

  many people.

(handwritten addition: "if it receives" above "It needs")

  Clause introduced by if *modifies* has.

14d   Effective subordination

Choose the subordination strategy that best expresses the relationship you intend between two ideas.

Illogical subordination

Subordinating the wrong element in a sentence changes the meaning of what you want to say. Watch for illogical subordination that may confuse readers.

USING SUBORDINATING CONJUNCTIONS

1 When you use *whereas, while, although, though,* or *even though* in a dependent clause to contrast or concede something, do not use *but* before the independent clause.

◆ *Although* a smile shows happiness in most cultures, ~~but~~ in some it may be a sign of embarrassment.

2 When you use *because* or *since* in a dependent clause to describe a reason or cause, do not use *so* in the independent clause.

◆ *Because* Rudolf Nureyev defected from Russia, ~~so~~ for many years he could not return to dance in his native country.

3 *Because* and *because of* are not interchangeable. *Because* is a subordinating conjunction. Use it when your subordinate idea is expressed as a clause, with a subject and a verb.

subject verb

◆ *Because* snow peas die in hot weather, you should plant them in early spring.

Because of is a two-word preposition. Use it when your subordinate idea is expressed as a *phrase,* with no verb.

phrase

◆ *Because of* the hot weather, the snow peas did not grow well.

4 Used by itself, *even* is not a subordinating conjunction. *Even though* is a subordinating conjunction meaning "despite the fact that."

though
◆ Even I don't play well, I still enjoy taking piano lessons.
     ^

Even if is a subordinating conjunction meaning "whether or not."

if
◆ Even it rains tomorrow, the race will be held.
    ^

INDEPENDENT SENTENCES	Scientists have carefully examined this theory. Some have criticized it.
INCORRECT SUBORDINATION	Some scientists who have criticized this theory have carefully examined it.

This inadvertently implies that some opponents have not been so careful.

CORRECT SUBORDINATION Some of the scientists who have carefully examined this theory have criticized it.

Look also for subordination that suggests causal relationships you do not intend.

◆   The nation was plunged into a deep recession ~~when~~ *that began shortly after* Ronald Reagan took office in 1981.

The writer did not mean to imply that Reagan's election caused the recession.

Overused subordination

If you believe you have subordinated too much, first find the ideas that are most closely related and leave the subordination you have there. Then edit the more distantly related ideas into independent sentences.

◆   Sometimes you may create passages that rely too much on subordination, *This makes* ~~which can make~~ them sound insipid ~~because every~~ *. Every* point seems to be qualified, while nothing is said directly.

  ◆ **WP TIP** To find excessive subordination, use the search-and-replace function to highlight common subordinating conjunctions and relative pronouns—see 14c and 25c for lists. This shows you how often you have used subordination so that you can reconsider each case.

14e   Sentence flow

If every idea goes in a separate simple sentence, your writing will be choppy and disjointed. Carefully choosing subordination or coordination can make your ideas flow better.

Coordination to combine sentences

Use coordination to connect equally important ideas and to give your sentences weight and balance.

◆   To generate electricity, utilities burn tremendous quantities of coal. ~~An-~~ *and*

~~other fuel widely used is~~ oil. ~~Many~~ *, but many* utilities also operate hydroelectric dams.

Subordination to combine sentences

Use subordination to emphasize central ideas.

◆   *Although they are quite different restaurants,* Zoë and Match have both become popular within the past year. ~~They are quite different restaurants.~~ To succeed in New York, a restaurant should not emulate a certain style. ~~It must set~~ *Customers will respond best if it sets* its own style and ~~excel~~ *excels* at it. ~~Custom-ers will respond best to that.~~ Zoë and Match accomplish this goal. ~~They~~ *, even though they* do it in different ways.

Parallel structures   **14f**

Writers use **parallelism**—the repetition of a grammatical structure—to emphasize a similarity among ideas. The elements of a parallel structure are balanced grammatically: words paired with words, phrases with phrases, clauses with clauses.

WORDS   We saw the frogs swimming, jumping, and splashing.

PHRASES   Of the people, by the people, for the people.

CLAUSES   Where there's smoke, there's fire.

◆ **WP TIP** Search for and highlight common coordinating conjunctions—*and, but, or.* These words may alert you to constructions that should be parallel.

Compound elements

Compound elements can be joined by a coordinating conjunction (*and, but, or, nor, so, for,* or *yet*). Such elements should be grammatically parallel so they won't confuse readers.

◆   They spent their time praying and ~~work~~ *working* with the poor.

Compound elements can also be joined by correlative conjunctions (*either . . . or, neither . . . nor, not only . . . but also, both . . . and, whether . . . or*).

◆   Wind-generated electric power is not only difficult to capture, but also *expensive to store.* ~~it must be stored at great expense.~~

Comparisons

When you use *than* or *as* in comparisons, set up equivalent alternatives that are parallel in grammatical form.

◆   Laura likes painting as much as ~~to read.~~ *reading.*

◆   He always believed that effective communication was more a matter of thinking clearly than ~~to try to write~~ *writing* well.

Lists

Elements presented in a series or list joined with *and* or *or* are also parallel in grammatical form.

◆   Her favorite activities were painting, walking, and ~~she liked to visit~~ *visiting* museums.

14g   Effective parallelism

Few devices achieve greater power, gravity, and impact than the formal, rhythmic, and forceful words of a well-constructed parallel. Use parallel structures to highlight a comparison or to emphasize a main point.

◆   With local leaders afraid of the "no growth" label, the quality of local decision making has clearly declined. The question facing towns like Abilene is ~~whether they will do enough planning to avoid uncontrolled develop-~~ *not whether they will plan to have no growth but whether they will face growth with no plan.* ~~ment.~~

The addition of not whether . . . but whether *and* no growth . . . no plan *makes the conclusion more resonant.*

Many writers repeat parallel structures to create a rhythmic effect. (For more on using rhythm in your writing, see 15b.)

To die, to sleep. To sleep, perchance to dream.

William Shakespeare, *Hamlet*

Good parallelism helps make comparisons clear. Edit ambiguous parallel structures in which the elements are not similar in form.

Also watch for words omitted from parallel structures: prepositions *(to, for, at)*, subordinating conjunctions *(although, since, because)*, and relative pronouns *(who, which, what).*

◆ **The researchers tried to ensure that interviewees were representative of the**
   that
   campus population and their opinions reflected those of the whole student
   body.

   Without the additional that, *it is unclear whether the clause beginning with* their opinions *refers to the researchers or the interviewees.*

15 ◆ SENTENCE EMPHASIS AND VARIETY

Effective writing focuses the reader's attention by putting emphasis, or special stress, on words that express important ideas.

Sentence emphasis   15a

One way to create emphasis is to vary the structures and rhythms of your sentences, giving distinctive treatment to the idea to which you want to attract attention.

You can also emphasize an idea by placing it at the beginning or end of a sentence. The first words get the reader's purest attention. The last words linger in the reader's mind and provoke further thought. When you edit, look for ways to use these emphatic first and final positions. (For sentence positions within paragraphs, see 13b.)

15b EMP VAR

> **OLD AND NEW INFORMATION IN SENTENCES**
>
> As you edit, think about how you want to emphasize the information given to your readers. Information that readers already know—"old" information—is usually presented before new information is introduced. This not only helps readers see the connection between the two but emphasizes the new information by placing it last.
>
> Most artificial colorings are synthetic chemicals.
>
> old information   new information
>
> These colorings are suspected of causing hyperactivity in children.

15b Varying sentence length

Both short and long sentences have their uses, given the purpose and intended audience of a paper. Mixing them provides variety as well as emphasis, especially if you break a pattern of short or long sentences with a sentence of different length.

When you edit, be aware of sentence lengths, and think about your readers' needs. Use long sentences to clarify relationships between ideas, and use shorter sentences to strengthen a point or to break up a monotonous pattern.

◆ **WP TIPS** (1) Use the count function to tally up how many words each sentence in your paper contains and how many sentences of various lengths you have written. (2) Use the search-and-replace function to start each sentence on a new line: set the computer to search for periods and replace each one with a period and a return. This lets you see where you have used long and short sentences.

Short sentences

Short sentences sound honest and direct. They have power. In a series of short sentences, each idea stands alone and asks for the reader's full attention. In a passage of long sentences, changing to a sharply worded, simple sentence will break the rhythm and stress a key point. Try it. It works.

To achieve a dramatic effect, try also condensing your ideas into as few words as possible, as this author does in the first three sentences.

Imagine it. You are chained to a radiator in a bare, dank room. You never see the sun. When your captors fear that a noise in the night is an impending rescue attempt, you are slammed up against the wall, the barrel of a gun pressed against your temple. Each day you have 15 minutes to shower, brush your teeth, and wash your underwear in the bathroom sink. Your bed is a mat on the floor.

Scott Macleod, *"The Lost Life of Terry Anderson"*

An extended pattern of short, simple sentences, however, may create a choppy effect. Adding a longer sentence in the right place — such as the fourth sentence above — can add contrast and balance the passage.

Long sentences

Most academic writing requires that you fully develop your ideas and establish relationships among them. Long sentences can help you show the relative importance of ideas and the connections between them. Coordination and subordination are valuable tools for long sentences. (See 14a – 14d.)

In this sample, turning short sentences into longer ones not only smooths the paragraph; it also strengthens emphasis.

◆   Athletes must decide how they want to perfect their physical condi-

tion. The first choice is to do it the old-fashioned way. ~~This means~~ *by* eating

right, running, and lifting. This alternative requires hard work and consid-

erable discipline. The second alternative is to use steroids. ~~These~~ : *that* drugs help

athletes become strong and fast in a short period of time. / *with little effort.* Obviously many

athletes will resort to this second method. ~~This is because they do not have~~

~~to exert much effort.~~ The trade-off, though, may be serious health prob-

lems in a few years.

Don't overdo long sentences. A sentence shouldn't cover more territory than a reader can span in a single stride.

Varying sentence types   **15c**

Sentences can vary by **grammatical type,** by **rhetorical type,** or by **functional type.** Because readers pay special attention to an atypical sentence — a ques-

---

GRAMMATICAL SENTENCE TYPES

A **simple sentence** has a single independent clause.

> Pollution is a growing problem.

A **compound sentence** has two or more independent clauses joined either by a comma and a coordinating conjunction or by a semicolon.

> Pollution is a problem, and it affects every aspect of our lives.
> Recycling will help; it conserves energy and saves on landfill space.

A **complex sentence** has one independent clause and one or more dependent clauses.

> Because the problem continues to grow, our legislature must act before it is too late.

A **compound-complex sentence** has at least two independent clauses and one or more dependent clauses.

> Pollution can be prevented, and we must take action to stop it, because there is no other way to survive on this planet.

---

tion or a command, for instance—varying sentence types helps you create emphasis within a passage.

Grammatical sentence types

Long sentences are usually **compound, complex,** or **compound-complex.** Short sentences are usually **simple.** Each grammatical sentence type has its own typical pattern and rhythm quite apart from its length (see 29c), and varying these makes your prose more emphatic and readable.

Rhetorical sentence types and word order

Should you put the main point first within a sentence and the less important information later? Or should you first establish the context and then deliver the main message? Such questions refer to rhetorical sentence types.

When you place the main idea first, you create a **cumulative sentence.**

> *Othello smothers* the delicate Desdemona in a fit of anguished passion and boiling fury.

> *He kills* the person he loves most because he has trusted the lies of the vicious Iago.

When you save the punch for the end, you create a **periodic sentence.**

In a fit of anguished passion and boiling fury, *Othello smothers* the delicate Desdemona.

Because he has trusted the lies of the vicious Iago, *he kills* the person he loves most.

Cumulative sentences are common in academic writing because they allow you to make a point, then support it. But relying exclusively on either type can be monotonous. When you edit, look for places where switching types can break the pattern.

INVERTING SUBJECTS AND VERBS

ESL

When any of the following structures is placed at the front of a sentence, the subject goes after the first auxiliary (a form of *have* or *be* or a model such as *could*) of the independent clause. If there is no auxiliary, the subject goes after the main verb.

ADVERB OF EXTENT OR DEGREE	*So antagonizing* had the speaker been that members of the audience walked out.
NEGATIVE ADVERB OF FREQUENCY	*Seldom* has a verdict created such an outrage among citizens. (Others: *ever, hardly, only once, rarely, scarcely*)
OTHER NEGATIVE ADVERBS OR ADVERB PHRASES	*Under no circumstances* should funding for this program be cut. (Others: *in no case, in no way, not until* + [time], *not since* + [time])
CONDITIONAL CLAUSES	*Only if we take measures now* will we rescue our city from urban blight.

When the following structures are at the front of a sentence, the subject goes after both the auxiliary (if there is one) and the main verb of the independent clause.

ADVERB OF POSITION	*Near the campsite* appeared a doe and two fawns.
COMPARATIVES	*More intriguing than the main plot of the novel* are several of the subplots.
PARTICIPLES WITH MODIFIERS	*Lying on my desk* should be a large sealed envelope.

Functional sentence types

Most writing relies primarily on declarative sentences, sentences that make statements. But an occasional question, exclamation, or command can call the reader's attention to a significant point. (See also 15a.)

DECLARATIVE The number of violent crimes committed by strangers has gone down in the past ten years.

QUESTION So why has the public's fear of crime gone up?

EXCLAMATION The news media manipulate us all!

COMMAND Write to the program director of your local TV station and protest.

15d Varying sentence openings

By varying sentence openings, you can change the pace of a passage. Consider repositioning modifiers, dependent clauses, and transitional expressions so that some sentences begin with elements other than the subject. Remember, however, that any element you move to the beginning of a sentence receives more attention there than elsewhere, so the emphasis of the sentence changes.

◆ Increasingly, doctors rely
  ∧Doctors rely increasingly on advanced diagnostic equipment.

◆ Until researchers learned to translate its hieroglyphs, much
  ∧Much of ancient Mayan culture remained a mystery. until researchers
  learned to translate its hieroglyphs.

◆ Although most   , they
  ∧Most teenagers are aware of the dangers of smoking./ They don't always
  realize the addictive power of nicotine.

Another way to get important information into a sentence early is to invert the expected word order. As you edit, consider using inverted word order for a strong special effect.

STANDARD The land onto which they wandered was hard and barren.

INVERTED Hard and barren was the land onto which they wandered.

16 ◆ SENTENCE VITALITY

Which of these passages better encourages you to read further?

> The sky and the sunrise are reflected by the snow. There is a road in front of me that goes down the slope toward the stone formations.

> The snow-covered ground glimmers with a dull blue light, reflecting the sky and the approaching sunrise. Leading away from me the narrow dirt road, an alluring and primitive path into nowhere, meanders down the slope and toward the heart of the labyrinth of naked stone.
>
> Edward Abbey, *Desert Solitaire*

What makes the second passage more vivid and powerful than the first? Why is it more vital? The first uses **general, abstract nouns** and few modifiers: *sunrise, road, stone formations.* The second uses **specific, concrete nouns** and modifiers that create tangible images: *dull blue light, alluring and primitive path, labyrinth of naked stone.* The first uses all-purpose **static verbs:** *is, goes.* The second uses **strong verbs** evoking actions that can be visualized: *glimmers, leading, meanders.* Finally, while the verb *are reflected* in the first passage is passive, the verbs in the second passage all use the active voice.

To improve the vitality of your writing, think of each sentence as a story. Like any story, each sentence has actors—usually nouns—and actions— usually verbs. When each actor and each action is vivid and tangible, the story unfolds before the reader's eyes. When editing, use the following techniques to give your sentences immediacy and energy.

Concrete, specific nouns and modifiers   16a

Compare the mental pictures you get from the phrases *an old blue car* and *a rusted baby-blue '59 Buick.* The first phrase evokes any number of cars, the second, a specific car. If a sentence is to tell a story, your first task is to identify the "characters" in it so that readers can recognize them.

As you edit, examine the language you use to describe your characters. Is your language abstract or concrete? **Abstract** words refer to ideas and concepts that cannot be perceived by the senses: *transportation, wealth, childhood, nutrition.* **Concrete** words name things that can be seen, felt, heard, tasted, or smelled: *cars, dime, child, broccoli.*

Next, is your language general or specific? **General** words refer to categories and groups: *pets, stores, teachers.* **Specific** words identify individual objects or people: *Rover, Murphy's Drugs, my biology professor, Pauline Clay.*

ABSTRACT	**CONCRETE**
wealth	
paper money	
currency	
U.S. dollars	$20 bill

GENERAL	**SPECIFIC**
performers	
jazz musicians	
vocalists	Billie Holiday

Concrete, specific nouns

We would be unable to think, speak, or write about *truth, insurance, constitutionality,* or *political risk* without the terms that name these abstract ideas. Although such terms allow you to express abstract ideas or to draw conclusions, writing that relies exclusively on abstractions may seem like nothing but hot air. To revitalize such passages during editing, keep looking for places where you can renew readers' connection to direct experience.

♦ Campus radicalism increased in the 1960s. Protests and antiwar demonstrations were common. _like the one at Kent State University in Ohio_

♦ Repeated deception by politicians contributed to widespread public cynicism. _—such as Nixon's "secret plan" to end the war and the clandestine invasion of Laos—_

Concrete, specific modifiers

Choose **modifiers** (words and phrases that describe nouns and verbs) that are specific and concrete. If sentences are stories, adjectives and adverbs provide the descriptive details in them. As much as nouns, they give life to your writing. Some descriptive modifiers—*pretty, dull, dumb, nice, beautiful, good, bad, young, old, great, fantastic, terrible, awful*—have become empty through overuse. The intensifier *very* can be one of the worst offenders.

♦ Madeline was a ~~pretty~~ girl with ~~nice~~ brown eyes. _fair-skinned_ _laughing_

♦ The city housing manager pointed out a row of ~~old~~ wooden houses. _peeling and crumbling_

USING ARTICLES WITH NOUNS

ESL

Whether to use *a, an,* or *the* before a noun depends on the type of noun and the context in which it is used. Nouns are either count nouns or noncount nouns. **Count nouns,** which name things that can be counted, can be singular (*island, child, ratio*) or plural (*islands, children, ratios*). **Noncount nouns,** naming things that generally cannot be counted or quantified, usually cannot be made plural (*information, homework, justice, success*).

1   You must use an article before a singular count noun unless the noun has a quantifier (*one*) or a possessive (*my, her*) before it.

   an island   the child   a ratio

Exceptions to this rule are singular proper nouns, which in most cases do not require an article.

   Italy   Pearl Street   Lake Erie

2   Use *a* or *an* with a singular count noun when you have not specified one particular thing or individual.

   There is *a problem* with this approach.

   Readers don't know what the problem is yet.

   We all appreciate *an understanding friend.*

   Any understanding friend, *not a particular one.*

3   Use *the* with a singular count noun in the following cases.

   ◆   The noun has already been mentioned.

   There is a problem with this approach. *The problem* is a subtle one.

   ◆   The noun is made specific by elements that follow it.

   The problem that I see with this approach is a subtle one.

   The modifying clause that I see with this approach *makes it clear that the writer is referring to one specific problem*

   ◆   The noun is made specific by the context.

   I entered a large lecture hall. *The teacher* was standing behind a lectern. *The blackboard* seemed very far away.

   In a lecture hall, there is likely to be only one teacher and only one blackboard.

◆ The noun names a unique person, place, or thing.

> *The moon* was still hovering on the horizon.
>
> *There is only one moon and only one horizon.*

4   Use *the* with plural count nouns in the following cases.

◆ The noun is made specific by elements that follow it.

> *The novels* that I like best focus on characters rather than on events.
>
> *The modifying clause* that I like best *makes it clear that the writer is referring to a specific set of novels.*

◆ The noun is made specific by the context.

> We saw a play tonight. *The actors* were from London.
>
> *The context makes it clear that the writer is referring specifically to the actors in tonight's play.*

◆ The noun is a proper noun referring to a country or a set of lakes, mountain ranges, or islands.

> the United States   the Rocky Mountains
> the Great Lakes   the Bahamas

5   Use *some* (*any* in negative sentences) or no article with noncount nouns if the noun is not specific.

> They asked for *some information* at the tourist center.
>
> There isn't *any homework* for tomorrow.
>
> The citizens are demanding *justice.*

6   Use *the* with noncount nouns if the noun is specific because it has been previously mentioned, it is clear from the context, or it has modifiers.

> We ordered some new skiing equipment. After *the equipment* arrived, we decided we didn't need it.
>
> As class came to an end, she passed out *the homework.*
>
> *The justice of this verdict* is questionable.

16b   Strong verbs

Once you have identified the actors in your sentence, you must describe their actions in equally vivid language.

Replace static verbs with action verbs

Verbs drive sentences the way an engine powers a car. **Action verbs**—verbs that denote specific actions—add horsepower to your writing. **Static verbs**—ones that show a state of being, like *be, appear, become, seem, exist*—can leave your sentences underpowered. As you edit, replace static verbs with action verbs when you can.

◆ The outer suburbs of Los Angeles ~~are in~~ the hills beyond the San Fernando *(sprawl onto)* Valley.

◆ This problem will soon ~~become evident.~~ *(erupt.)*

A form of *be* preceding a phrase or a clause often signals a stronger verb coming up. Make this verb the main verb of the sentence.

◆ The most effective writers ~~are those who~~ write as though they were simply talking.

You can also find stronger verbs hidden in parts of sentences where you have used expletive constructions: *there are, there is,* and *it is.* Usually you can turn the verb of the clause into the main verb of the sentence.

◆ ~~There are~~ Many people ~~who~~ believe that Elvis Presley is still alive, even though ~~it is~~ only the tabloids ~~that~~ take such "news" seriously.

Avoid weak action verbs

Not all verbs that describe action spark clear images. Overuse has exhausted the image-making power of verbs such as *do, get, go, have, make,* and *think.* As you edit, watch for these weak action verbs and substitute stronger verbs where possible.

◆ He ~~makes~~ good sourdough bread. *(bakes)*

◆ She ~~has a wonderful singing voice.~~ *(sings wonderfully.)*

Often a verb that relies on other words for its descriptive power can be replaced with a more effective one.

◆ He ~~walked quickly~~ from the room. *(scurried)*

Change nouns back to verbs

Many English verbs have been changed into useful nouns with the help of a suffix — *announce/announcement* or *tempt/temptation,* for example. The use of nouns made from verbs, however, often buries the real action of a sentence, and these nouns usually require a static verb — *have, do, make,* or *be.* As you edit, you may have to dig up the buried verbs to resurrect your point.

◆   Few biographies of FDR have ~~given a satisfactory explanation of~~ the
the disastrous Yalta conference.

satisfactorily explained

Some nouns and verbs have the same form: *cause, dance, march, tie, love, hate.* If you use them as nouns, then you also need a verb. You needn't *perform a dance* when you can simply *dance* or *hold a march* when you can simply *march.*

16c   Active or passive voice?

When a verb is in the **active voice,** the person or thing performing the action is the subject.

actor	active-voice verb	direct object, recipient of action
Juana	**collects**	**the tickets.**

CHANGING NOUNS TO VERBS

To enliven your writing, replace these common expressions with the action verbs buried within them.

EXPRESSION	BURIED VERB
put forth a proposal	propose
hold a discussion	discuss
formulate a plan	plan
reach a decision	decide
arrive at a conclusion	conclude
hammer out an agreement	agree
hold a meeting	meet
call a strike	strike
make a choice	choose

VERBS THAT CAN'T BE PASSIVE   ESL

Not all English verbs can be both active and passive. Verbs that can't be passive are labeled **intransitive verbs** in the dictionary. The verbs *happen, occur, result from, disappear, vanish,* and *die* are a few that are sometimes mistakenly put in the passive voice.

◆   The tornado was happened yesterday.

◆   Much improvement was resulted from working with a tutor.

Even though they may take objects, certain verbs such as *have, weigh,* and *consist of* cannot be rephrased in the passive voice either.

ACTIVE   New York City has five boroughs.

INCORRECT   Five boroughs are had by New York City.

ACTIVE   The loaded truck *weighed* 70,000 pounds.

INCORRECT   The loaded truck *was weighed* 70,000 pounds.

BUT   The truck *was weighed* by the scale operator.

When a verb is in the **passive voice,** the recipient of the action becomes the subject, and there is no object.

subject of action	passive-voice verb	agent of action in prepositional phrase
The tickets	are taken	by Juana.

Using the active voice

By focusing on the actor, the active voice helps readers visualize what happens and who does it. Active-voice sentences usually use fewer words and have a more direct effect than passive-voice sentences.

◆   Andrew Karpinski is the most widely read business writer of our day.
     Millions have devoured his books,
     His books have been devoured by millions of executives seeking to
                              ^   ^
                              His   grow
enhance their management skills. The books are written directly from his
                                           ^   ^
years of experience as a consultant.

Using the passive voice

The passive voice de-emphasizes the actor and highlights the recipient of the verb's action. This may be what you want to do in certain cases.

TO STRESS RESULTS OVER ACTIONS	A $500 million reduction in the national debt *was approved* by Congress.
TO LEAVE THE AGENT UNSTATED	The city's first homeless shelter *was established* in a vacant warehouse.
TO ASSERT OBJECTIVITY IN RESEARCH WRITING	In the experiment, the samples *were* first *tested* for bacteria.

17 ◆ CONCISE WRITING

Most writing strives to convey information clearly and efficiently, to help the reader understand without undue effort. Strive to make your writing **direct**—expressing ideas plainly—and **concise**—using few unnecessary words. By doing so, you avoid being imprecise, wordy, or obscure.

Writing concisely takes careful editing. Some writers call this process "boiling down," the way a cook turns large quantities of thin broth into hearty soup. Here's a passage from a draft of this chapter.

> Public speakers are often advised, "Tell them what you're going to say; say it; then tell them what you said." In other words, say the message at least three times so that the audience will understand it clearly. This advice reflects the patterns of spoken language. When you write, though, try to make your point once, concisely.

The second sentence seemed merely to rephrase the first, so we combined it with the third sentence.

◆ In ~~other words, say~~ the message ~~at least three times so that~~ the audience
   spoken language, repeating   will help
~~will~~ understand it clearly. ~~This advice reflects the patterns of spoken language.~~

Then we started eliminating unnecessary words:

◆ In spoken language, ~~repeating the message will help the audience~~ under-
                       repetition helps listeners
stand ~~it clearly.~~

Vague generalities   17a

Generalizations are broad statements without specific detail that enable us to express the large concepts essential to abstract thinking. Sometimes, however, writers lapse into **generalities,** statements so broad as to be obvious: *It is our duty today to take responsibility for our actions.* (And when was it not?)

Some generalities indulge in circular reasoning: *During the harsh winters of the 1870s, the weather was very cold.* Others announce that a point is going to be made but don't make it: *Many factors played a part in the Republican landslide.* (What factors?)

Although generalities can occur anywhere, look particularly at your openings and conclusions, where you may be trying hard to impress. Here is how one student edited the opening paragraph of his paper for greater impact.

◆   Fetal alcohol syndrome affects one of every 750 newborn babies. ~~It is clearly not good for them,~~ causing coordination problems, malformed organs, small brains, short attention spans, and behavioral problems.

Idle words   17b

In speaking, we allow ourselves many extra words. This habit often carries over into writing. As you edit, test each word to see whether you can eliminate it. If the meaning of the sentence is unchanged, leave it out.

Automatic and other wordy phrases

Phrases like *in my opinion, it has come to my attention that, and due to the fact that* contribute nothing to a discussion. They are no more than a writer's "throat-clearing." These **automatic phrases** most often appear at the beginnings of sentences, but look for them anywhere. When you find an automatic phrase, remove it and reread the passage. If no meaning is lost, leave it out. If some meaning seems to be missing, write a condensed version of the phrase.

◆   ~~In this day and age~~ ^{Today} children ~~in many instances~~ ^{often} know more about black holes than they do about Black Beauty.

Wordy phrases can be condensed too. Vague, abstract nouns—*area, aspect, factor, kind, manner, nature, tendency, thing,* and *type*—may signal that wordiness is afoot. Often you can delete imprecise phrases, condense them, or find more concrete substitutes.

WORDY PHRASES

WORDY	MORE CONCISE
most of the people	most people
all of the work	all the work
due to the fact that	because, since
despite the fact that	although
at that (or this) point in time	then, now
communicate to (or with)	tell
impact on	affect
in this day and age	today, now
in any case	anyway
in the case of	regarding, concerning
in most instances	usually
in some instances	sometimes
subsequent to	after
in case	if
in the final analysis	finally, at last

◆ One of the ~~factors that gave them~~ problems in the lab was ~~the tendency toward~~ contamination.

Useless modifiers

Writers often use modifiers such as *clearly, obviously, interestingly, undoubtedly, absolutely, fortunately, hopefully, really,* and *totally* to make a sentence sound forceful or authoritative. These **intensifiers** usually add little, and they can be deleted. Be careful, though, to test for altered meaning.

◆ The strike against General Motors ~~clearly~~ disrupted production of light trucks. It was undoubtedly intended to do so.

The writer decided to leave undoubtedly *because it tells the reader that the assessment is her own conclusion.*

17c Redundancy

Public speakers are often advised, "Tell them what you're going to say; say it; then tell them what you said." In speaking, repetition helps listeners under-

---

TIGHTENING GRAMMATICAL CONSTRUCTIONS

To fight wordiness, consider simplifying grammatical constructions.

◆ Change a verb from the **passive voice** to the **active voice**. (See 16c.)

◆ Substitute **strong verbs** for **expletive constructions** such as *there were, there are, it is, it was*. (See 16b.)

◆ Shorten **dependent modifier clauses** to phrases and reduce **modifier phrases** to single words. (See also 14c and 29b.)

CLAUSE	The research project *that we were assigned* involves a complex experiment.
PHRASE	The research project *assigned to us* involves a complex experiment.
WORD	*Our assigned* research project involves a complex experiment.

---

stand. When you write, though, try to make your point once, concisely. (Deliberate repetition does have special uses; see 13c and 14g.)

Needless repetition is called **redundancy.** As you edit, evaluate each instance of repetition. Take out the repeated word or phrase and compare both versions. Ask yourself whether the repetition links ideas, sustains an established rhythm, or prevents confusion. If it doesn't, take it out.

◆ The ~~general~~ consensus ~~of opinion~~ among students was that the chancellor had exceeded her authority.

Consensus *means a generally held opinion.*

REDUNDANT PHRASES

first ever	refer back
first and foremost	basic fundamentals
full and complete	initial preparation
past history	terrible tragedy
round in shape	final result
red in color	free gift
general consensus of opinion	true facts
a faulty miscalculation	completely destroyed
old and outdated	

If you find yourself repeating the same word or using a similar one, look for ways to eliminate one of them.

◆ A very high percentage *About 90 percent* of the prison's inmates take advantage of the special education program, about ninety percent.

You can often eliminate ineffective repetition by coming two sentences. (See Chapter 14.)

◆ As you edit your writing, be alert to possible redundancy. One kind of redundancy is , such as an unnecessary repetition.

17d Elliptical constructions

By omitting words that readers can be expected to supply for themselves, an **elliptical construction** helps avoid unneeded repetition. Such constructions are usually used in the second part of a parallel construction.

◆ Her words suggested one thing, her actions suggested another.

However, elliptical constructions work only when the words dropped are exactly the same as the words that remain.

◆ Of Shakespeare's female characters, Lady Macbeth is the most ruthless, Desdemona and Juliet *are* the most loving, and Portia *is* the most resourceful.

The plural subject Desdemona and Juliet requires the verb are, so the omitted verbs are and is have to be reinstated.

17e Pretentious language

It is tempting, when you want to sound authoritative, to use technical, obscure, or ornate language. When such language is needlessly complicated or overinflated, it is called **pretentious.**

Not only does pretentious language use two or three words where one would do, it also relies on the third-person point of view and the passive voice. When editing such constructions, try to find concrete subjects for your verbs and address your readers more directly.

PRETENTIOUS LANGUAGE

PRETENTIOUS	MORE CONCISE
incarcerated offenders	prisoners
client populations	people served
voiced concern that	said, worried
range of selections	choice
minimizes expenditures	saves money
of crucial importance	important, crucial
provide an occasion for investigation	be worth investigating
institution of higher learning	college, university

ORIGINAL The range of audiovisual services provided includes examinations to determine optical or auditory impairment and the specification, provision, and instruction in the use of prosthetic devices, including corrective lenses and auditory amplification devices.

EDITED We can examine your eyes and ears, prescribe and sell glasses and hearing aids, and teach you how to use them.

Euphemisms   17f

A **euphemism** is an inoffensive word or phrase deliberately substituted for one considered harsh or indelicate. Our conversations are full of euphemisms, especially those that deal with money, death, sex, and body functions. Job cuts and massive firings are called *corporate downsizing*. People say *I lost my grandmother last week* instead of *My grandmother died last week.*

In academic writing, you strive to inform, not to obscure, but you must balance directness with your audience's comfort. If in doubt, ask a peer or an instructor to check your choices.

◆ As a result of ~~the reordering of~~ budget ~~priorities~~ _{cuts, the} library ~~acquisitions will be deferred and maintenance activities reduced~~ will stop buying books and staff will clean the building less often.

18 ◆WORD CHOICE

The English language has a particularly rich vocabulary. The place you live, for instance, might be your *house, home, residence, abode, dwelling, domicile, habitation, quarters, lodging, apartment, pad, place, shack, spot,* or *digs.* The choice is yours. Your task as a writer is finding the word that conveys the shade of meaning you have in mind.

The more words you know how to use, the more clearly you will be able to communicate. Enlarge your vocabulary by reading widely and listening actively to the words others use. Make word lists to study; paraphrase new words right away and use them in sentences, and try to learn the meaning of an unfamiliar word from its context.

18a The dictionary and the thesaurus

All writers rely on dictionaries and thesauruses to guide them in their use of language. If you consult these books regularly, your word skills and your writing will improve.

The dictionary

An **unabridged dictionary** offers the most comprehensive listing of words in American English plus information on word origins, definitions, and usage. Examples include *Webster's Third New International Dictionary,* with 470,000 entries, and the 615,000-word *Oxford English Dictionary.* A searchable edition of the *OED* is now available on CD-ROM.

An **abridged dictionary** omits less frequently used words and some obsolete or archaic definitions. The *American Heritage Dictionary* (2nd college ed.), *Merriam-Webster's Collegiate Dictionary* (10th ed.), and the *Random House Webster's College Dictionary* are good for everyday use.

The thesaurus

A **thesaurus** (the word comes from the Greek for "treasure") lists synonyms for each entry. Many thesauruses list antonyms as well. A thesaurus can help you find the right word for a particular context or level of formality. *Roget's Thesaurus of English Words and Phrases* lists words by concept. *Roget's 21st Century Thesaurus* lists words alphabetically, with a concept index.

To find the word that best expresses the meaning you wish to convey, place each word in the context of your sentence and assess it. When the thesaurus suggests a word you are unfamiliar with, be sure to look it up in the dictionary as well.

WHAT'S IN A DICTIONARY ENTRY?

Most dictionaries follow the format found in the tenth edition of *Merriam-Webster's Collegiate Dictionary.*

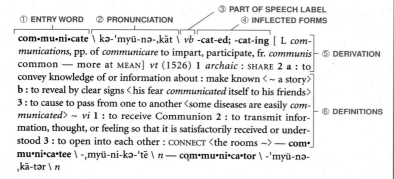

① ENTRY WORD   ② PRONUNCIATION   ③ PART OF SPEECH LABEL
④ INFLECTED FORMS
⑤ DERIVATION
⑥ DEFINITIONS

com•mu•ni•cate \ kə-'myü-nə-,kāt \ *vb* -**cat-ed; -cat-ing** [L *com-munications,* pp. of *communicare* to impart, participate, fr. *communis* common — more at MEAN] *vt* (1526) **1** *archaic* : SHARE **2 a :** to convey knowledge of or information about : make known ⟨~ a story⟩ **b :** to reveal by clear signs ⟨ his fear *communicated* itself to his friends⟩ **3 :** to cause to pass from one to another ⟨some diseases are easily *com-municated*⟩ ~ *vi* **1 :** to receive Communion **2 :** to transmit infor-mation, thought, or feeling so that it is satisfactorily received or under-stood **3 :** to open into each other : CONNECT ⟨the rooms ~⟩ — **com•mu•ni•ca•tee** \ -,myü-ni-kə-'tē \ *n* — **com•mu•ni•ca•tor** \ -'myü-nə-,kā-tər \ *n*

1   The **entry word** appears in bold type. Bars, spaces, or dots be-tween syllables show where the word can be hyphenated. If two spellings are shown, the first is more common, although both are ac-ceptable. If two spellings are dissimilar, entries are cross-referenced: **gaol** (jal) *n Brit. sp.* of JAIL. A superscript numeral before an entry in-dicates that two or more words have identical spellings.

2   **Pronunciation** is spelled phonetically, set in parentheses or be-tween slashes. (The phonetic key is at the bottom of the page.) If two pronunciations are given, the first is more common, although both are acceptable.

3   **Parts-of-speech labels** are set in italic type. The abbreviations are *n* for noun, *vb* for verb, *vt* for transitive verb, and so forth.

4   **Inflected forms** are shown, including plurals for nouns and pro-nouns, comparatives and superlatives, and principal parts for verbs. Ir-regular spellings also appear here.

5   The **derivation** of a word that has roots in other languages is set between brackets or slashes (*OE* and *ME* = Old English and Middle Eng-lish, *L* = Latin, *Gr* = Greek, *OFr* = Old French, *Fr* = French, *G* = German, and so on).

6   **Definitions** appear with major meanings numbered and arranged from the oldest to the most recent or from the most common to the least common. An example using the word may be enclosed in brackets.

◆   **Synonyms** or **antonyms** may be listed, often with comments on how the words are similar or different.

◆   **Usage labels** are used for nonstandard words or meanings.
        archaic: from a historic period; now used rarely if at all
        colloquial (coll.): used informally in speech or writing

> *dialect (dial.):* used only in some geographical areas
> *obsolete (obs.):* no longer used, but may appear in old writings
> *slang:* highly informal, or an unusual usage
> *substandard (substand.):* widely used but not accepted in formal usage
> *British (Brit.), Irish, Scottish (Scot.)* and so on: a word used primarily in an area other than the United States. Some dictionaries use an asterisk to mark Americanisms.

◆   **Usage notes** may follow definitions. They may also comment on acceptability or unacceptability.

18b   Words and their meanings

Roots, prefixes, and suffixes

Roots, prefixes, and suffixes provide substantial clues to a word's meaning. A **root** is a base word, or part of a word, from which other words are formed: *mile* in the word *mileage*.

A **prefix** is a group of letters attached to the beginning of a root that changes its meaning: *un-* in *unfinished*. The word *prefix* itself consists of a root, *-fix*, which means "attach," and a prefix, *pre-*, meaning "before." A **suffix** is a group of letters attached to the end of a root: *-age* in *mileage*.

Both prefixes and suffixes change the meaning of the root to which they are attached. For example, the words *antebellum, bellicose,* and *belligerent* share the root *bellum*, Latin for "war." If you already know that *belligerent* means "warlike or at war," you might guess that *antebellum* means "before war."

Denotations and connotations

The **denotation** of a word is its direct, literal meaning. *Fragrance, odor,* and *smell* denote the same thing: a perception detected by your olfactory sense. But the associations the words bring to mind differ. "You have a distinct fragrance" is quite different from "You have a distinct odor." *Fragrance* suggests a pleasant smell; *odor* suggests an unpleasant one. The associated or indirect meaning of a word is its **connotation.**

The connotations of your words affect the meaning you convey, so consider them when you edit. You might say that the filmmaker Ingmar Bergman is *concerned* or *fascinated with childhood,* but you might not want to say that he is *obsessed* with it. Edit carefully to eliminate unintended connotations.

Idiomatic expressions

Why do we ride *in* a car but *on* a train? Why do we *take* a picture but *make* a recording? Such conventional—that is, widely accepted—speech patterns are called **idioms.** Sometimes idiomatic patterns do not follow rules of logic or grammar, so it's easy to misuse one you are not familiar with.

A **preposition**—such as *at, by, for, out,* or *to*—shows a relationship between a noun or a pronoun and other words in the sentence. The only guide to the correct use of prepositions with nouns and verbs and in standard expressions about time and space is to learn the conventional idioms.

> This novel shows a great similarity *to* that one. The similarity *of* [or *between*] the stories is remarkable.

> I will meet *with* you *in* the evening, *at* sunset.

VERB-PREPOSITION IDIOMS

AMUSE	My cousin was amused *by* the clown. I was amused *at* my cousin's delight. The clown amused us *with* her tricks.
ARRIVE	They arrived *at* the airport. They arrived *in* Los Angeles. They arrived *on* the scene.
DIFFER	Margot differs *with* Harriet on this subject. One's opinion differs *from* the other's. They differ *over* whether to go skiing.
IDENTIFY	You can identify her *by* her red hair. You must identify her *to* the authorities. I have always identified *with* my father.
OCCUPY	This room is occupied *by* Mario. He is occupied *with* his book.
PREJUDICE	The coach was prejudiced *against* nonathletes. The jury was prejudiced *by* pretrial publicity.
REWARD	The dog was rewarded *for* her behavior. She was rewarded *with* liver treats.
TRUST	He trusts *in* you. He trusts you *with* his investments.
VARY	The colors vary *in* intensity. They vary *from* one another. People's tastes vary *over* time. Mood varies *with* the weather.

WORD ORDER WITH PHRASAL VERBS

A **phrasal verb** consists of a verb plus a **particle**—a word such as *on, up, by,* or *through.* Both the verb and the particle are needed to convey the full meaning of the phrasal verb: *put on, give up, get by, muddle through.* (See 18c.)

Determining where in a sentence to place the particle of a phrasal verb is sometimes difficult. Here are some guidelines.

Some phrasal verbs are **intransitive**—that is, they do not take a direct object. The most common phrasal verbs in this category include *break down, come back, come out, come over, pass out* ("faint"), and *play around.* The particle for such a phrasal verb should always come directly after the verb.

The stray dog *came back* the next day.

Some phrasal verbs are **transitive**—that is, they can take a direct object. The phrasal verbs in this category can be further divided into three types according to whether the direct object can come between the verb and the particle.

1   For some transitive phrasal verbs, the particle cannot be separated from the verb by the object. Common verbs of this type include *come across, get on, get off, get over, get through* ("finish"), *look into, run into, see through* ("not be deceived by").

INCORRECT   Please *go* this report *over* carefully.

CORRECT   Please *go over* this report carefully.

2   For some transitive phrasal verbs, the particle may be separated from the verb by the object. Common verbs of this type include *call off, cut up, do over, fill out, fill up, find out, give up, look over, leave out, make up, put on, throw away, turn off,* and *turn on.*

CORRECT   The president *called* the meeting *off.*

CORRECT   The president *called off* the meeting.

If the object of such a verb is a pronoun, however, the particle must be separated from the verb.

INCORRECT   Why did she *call off* it?

CORRECT   Why did she *call* it *off?*

3   For a few transitive phrasal verbs, the particle must be separated from the verb by the object. The most common verbs of this type include *get through* ("communicate") and *see through* ("preserve").

INCORRECT   I tried to *get through* the idea to him.

CORRECT   I tried to *get* the idea *through* to him.

Particles—such as *up, down, out, in, off,* and *on*—look like prepositions, but they combine with verbs to form **phrasal verbs,** or two-word verbs. Both the verb and the particle are needed to convey the meaning of a phrasal verb, which may be quite different from the meaning of the verb alone. The meanings of these phrasal verbs, for instance, have little in common with the verb *to come.*

How did this *come about?* (happen)

When did the question *come up?* (when was it raised)

Of course, I expected things to *come out* all right. (end)

I was unconscious for a moment, but I soon *came to.* (revived)

When editing, check your use of idiomatic expressions, and whenever you are in doubt, consult a dictionary.

Slang, regionalisms, and colloquialisms   18d

Everyone uses **slang,** informal language that originates in and is unique to small groups such as students, musicians, athletes, or politicians. Some slang words eventually enter the mainstream and become part of standard English. A *jeep* was originally slang for a general-purpose (g.p.) military vehicle used in World War II. Now it is the brand name of a four-wheel-drive vehicle driven by many Americans.

Regionalisms are expressions used in one part of the country but not common elsewhere. The name for a *carbonated beverage,* for example, varies by region from *pop* to *soda* to *soft drink* to *seltzer.* Some bits of regional dialect are regarded as **nonstandard,** that is, not widely used in academic writing.

A **colloquialism** is an expression common to spoken language but seldom used in formal writing. For example, the noun *pot* can mean "a cooking vessel," "marijuana," "the amount of money bet on a hand of cards," and "ruination," (as in *go to pot*).

Use slang words, regionalisms, and colloquialisms sparingly, if at all, in your writing. They may not be understood, and they are usually too informal for academic writing. They can, however, convey immediacy and authenticity in descriptions and dialogue.

18e   Jargon

Every profession or field develops terms to express its special ideas. Such specialized or technical language is called **jargon.**

As you edit, you must decide whether the special terms you have used are appropriate for your audience. Using fewer technical terms helps you communicate better with a general audience, but a specialized audience expects you to use technical language appropriately. For example, for what kind of audience would you substitute *femur* for *thigh bone* or vice versa? Avoid jargon that is added merely to make your writing sound important.

JARGON   It is incumbent on us to challenge the prevailing proposition that critical-theoretical approaches are the most enlightened ways of introducing students to literary experience.

EDITED   We should question the widely held idea that using theories of criticism is the best way to introduce students to literature.

Sometimes you need a technical term to communicate a complex concept. In such a case, introduce it in a context that helps the reader grasp its meaning, perhaps with an explicit definition. This passage was written for car enthusiasts, not mechanical engineers, so the writer had to explain the terms *lean* and *stoichiometric*.

Running an engine *lean* means that there is less fuel in the cylinders than is needed to completely burn all the available air. With gasoline, 14.7 pounds of air are required to burn 1 pound of fuel. This air-fuel ratio is referred to as *stoichiometric*.

Frank Markus, *"Lean-Burn Engines"*

18f   Figurative language

Figurative language, which likens one thing to another in imaginative ways, brings freshness and resonance to writing. When well done, figurative language, often in the form of comparisons and analogies, can help readers gain insight better than any other language.

One of the most common problems writers have is inadvertently juxtaposing incongruous images. A **mixed metaphor** combines two or more unrelated images, often with unintended effects. When you find a mixed metaphor in your writing, eliminate the weaker one and extend the more appropriate one.

SOME COMMON FIGURES OF SPEECH

Examine these examples of figurative language, and consider using some of these strategies in your own writing.

◆   A **simile** is a comparison that explicitly expresses a resemblance between two essentially unlike things, using *like, than,* or *as.*

> German submarines swam the seas like sharks, suddenly seizing their prey without warning.

◆   A **metaphor** implicitly equates one thing with another.

> Her life became a whirlwind of design meetings, client conferences, production huddles, and last-minute decisions.

◆   An **analogy** uses an extended comparison to show similarities in structure or process.

> The course catalog at a large university resembles a smorgasbord. Courses range from differential calculus to American film, from Confucianism to liberation theology. Students receive little advice as to which classes are the salads, which the desserts, and which the entrees of a college education. Even amid this feast, a student risks malnutrition.

◆   **Personification** is the technique of attributing human qualities or behavior to a nonhuman event or phenomenon.

> The ship sailed into the teeth of the hurricane.

◆   Deliberate exaggeration is called **hyperbole.**

> No book in the world is more difficult than this economics text. Reading it is absolute torture.

◆   The opposite of hyperbole is deliberate **understatement.**

> With temperatures remaining below zero all day, it will seem just a bit chilly outside tomorrow.

◆   **Irony** is the use of words to mean the opposite of what they seem to mean on the surface.

> "Houseguests for three weeks? Terrific."

◆   A **paradox** contains a deliberately created contradiction.

> For a moment after she spoke, the silence was deafening. Then the audience erupted in cheers.

◆   We must swim against the tide of cynicism that threatens to ~~cloud our vision~~ *drown our hope*

of a world without hunger.

The author decided swim/tide/drown/hope *made a more consistent image than* swim/tide/cloud/vision.

18g   Clichés

Our language is full of overused, worn-out expressions called **clichés**. The word itself, interestingly, is a metaphor. *Cliché* is a French word for the sound a stamping press makes in a process of making multiple, identical images. In other words, something has become a cliché if it is ordinary, run-of-the-mill:

the last straw	needle in a haystack
as strong as an ox	handwriting on the wall
better late than never	tried and true
lay your cards on the table	hit the nail on the head
a drop in the bucket	best thing since sliced bread

To edit a cliché, try improving on it. Go back to the original image and describe it in new words or add fresh details.

◆   Outside, the wind ~~howled~~ *keened as though it had lost a child.*

If you can't revive it, replace the cliché with a direct statement of what you are trying to say.

◆   It was ~~dark as night~~ *, so dark* inside the cave. *that we waited in vain for our eyes to adjust.*

19 ◆ UNBIASED LANGUAGE

Using a generalization about a group of people to predict, describe or interpret the behavior or characteristics of an individual in that group is both insensitive and illogical. Careless generalizations based on race, ethnicity, gender, cultural background, age, physical characteristics, or lifestyles are called **stereotypes**.

Whether they refer to gender, race, ethnicity, or sexual preference, stereotypes are oversimplified generalizations. Positive or negative, they substitute a simplistic formula for an appreciation of individual differences and the richness of human variation.

At best, stereotypes represent laziness on the part of a writer who uses a stereotype — a phrase like *small-town sheriff* — and assumes that readers know what is intended rather than taking the time to provide individual detail. At worst, stereotypes represent appeals to unexamined prejudice rather than to reason.

Recognizing stereotypes   19a

Many stereotypes stem from ignorance and from fear of people who are perceived as "different." These stereotypes often penetrate our language both in descriptions of people — *liberal politician* — and in descriptive images — *sleepy Southern town.* Calling a doctor or a lawyer *he* reinforces the stereotype that all doctors and lawyers are men. **Biased language** that contributes to stereotypes may offend your readers so much that they disregard your other judgments.

If you find you have used stereotypes, edit your writing to eliminate them. Qualify broad generalizations, and replace sweeping statements with specific factual evidence. In some cases, you may want to drop the stereotypical observation altogether.

◆ Like most ~~teenage~~ _{inexperienced} drivers, he didn't know what to do when the car started

to skid.

The problem is inexperience, not age.

◆ ~~Like so many of his race,~~ Michael Jordan is a superbly gifted athlete. His

tremendous achievements have provided an inspiration to ~~many black~~

children everywhere.

Jordan's race is irrelevant to his athletic gifts, and not all the children who admire him are black.

◆ Frank Peters, stooped from years in the woods ~~but still alert~~, remembers

the dry, hot summer of the Tillamook Burn.

The original implies that people of Peters' age are not expected to be still alert.

ELIMINATING STEREOTYPES

As you edit, ask yourself four questions.

1 Have I relied more on stereotypes than on evidence to make my point? A stereotype is shorthand that nudges your readers with "You know what I mean." But they may not know what you mean, or they may disagree.

2 Do my generalizations follow logically from factual evidence? Make sure your facts are accurate and sufficient. Then check your logic. That someone is Canadian and likes to dance the tango does not mean that being Canadian causes people to do the tango or that all Canadians enjoy it.

3 Am I using generalizations properly? Generalizations about a group cannot be used to predict the knowledge, attitudes, abilities, beliefs, or behaviors of an individual who belongs to the group. For example, anthropologists may observe that traditional Japanese culture emphasizes group values over individual ones, but that alone does not enable you to characterize any one Japanese person.

4 Have I used euphemism to mask a stereotype? Even a positive stereotype can be a slur in disguise, as it is when someone praises a wife for being "a wonderful asset to her husband" as if that were the wife's identifying role in life.

19b Choosing group labels

People often label themselves in terms of the groups to which they belong. However, labels inevitably emphasize a single feature of a person's identity, ignoring other characteristics. They also may offend people who do not want to be so characterized. Furthermore, many labels go beyond simple identification and become explicitly or implicitly derogatory. As you edit, examine any labels you have used; try to use only those acceptable to the members of the group themselves, and avoid labels with negative connotations.

Using a group's own labels

Even though members of a particular group may not agree on what they should be called, whenever possible, refer to such a group by the label most of its members prefer. Labels sometimes move quickly into or out of favor as they acquire unintended connotations, so be sure to check current practice.

Designations of race, ethnicity, and nationality

The terms *black, African American,* and *people of color* all refer to those people who used to be called *Negroes* or *colored.* Some spokespeople and many of the media have adopted the term *African American* as both an adjective and a noun.

The terms *Asian* and *Asian American* have begun to replace *Oriental* for people of Asian ancestry, although some individuals and groups prefer to use a specific country of origin: *Japanese, Korean, Malaysian, Chinese.* To refer to national origin or ancestry, using a specific country is always correct.

Today some Americans of Spanish-speaking heritage refer to themselves as *Hispanics* while others prefer *Latino* and *Latina* and some Mexican Americans *Chicano* and *Chicana.* Many *Native Americans* prefer that term to *Indian,* but using the name of the tribe or nation is often a better choice: *Navajo, Lakota Sioux, Seneca.* Some *Inuit* prefer that term to *Eskimo.*

If the religion of a particular group has relevance in your writing, use the preferred terms; for example, a follower of Islam is a *Muslim.*

Designations of gender and sexual orientation

Most adult women prefer to be called *women* rather than *girls* or *ladies.* *Girl* is particularly inappropriate in reference to salespeople, administrative staff, or those in service jobs.

USING LABELS DERIVED FROM ADJECTIVES   ESL

Many labels that describe groups are derived from adjectives: *the wealthy, the poor, the homeless.* If you have decided to use one of the many collective nouns, check to make sure you have used it correctly.

1 Always use the definite article *the* before the noun.

♦ The legislature passed a new law to help ^the^ hearing impaired.

2 Use a plural verb when the collective noun is the subject.

♦ The wealthy in this country is ^are^ going to be taxed more.

3 Use the collective noun only in reference to a group. A collective noun usually cannot refer to a single person. If you refer to one person in the group, use an adjective-plus-noun construction.

♦ We interviewed a homeless ^person^ about her search for a job.

When writing about sexual orientation, keep in mind that people have widely different views about the role of sexuality in our personal and public lives. Be aware that not everyone may share your perspective, and consider using a group's own chosen term.

Designations of ability
People with physical limitations often prefer *disabled* to *handicapped;* others prefer *differently abled.*

Designations of age
Modern American culture does not extol old age, and even accepted terms can describe it bluntly or condescendingly. Think about using *senior citizens* rather than the *elderly.* If a person's age is critical to what you want to say, cite the person's actual age or decade of life: *68-year-old, septuagenarian.*

Checking labels for negative connotations

Some labels that on the surface seem neutral hide negative connotations. For example, the terms *AIDS victims* implies that such people are blameless, which you may intend, but also that they are helpless, which you may not.

As you edit, watch for such unnecessary or unintended negative connotations, and substitute more neutral alternatives. Because neutral phrases can be cumbersome, they are easily mocked as too "politically correct." Your editing job therefore often involves finding a balance between directness, which you may lose, and sensitivity, which you may gain.

Here are two general rules to follow.

1 Focus on people's strengths: people *live with* cancer, or they are *cancer survivors* rather than *suffering from* the disease.
2 Focus on the person first and the characteristic or condition second: *a woman who is quadriplegic,* not a *quadriplegic.*

19c Using nonsexist language

When you use words that embody sexual stereotypes, you run the risk of alienating half—or more—of your potential audience. Gender bias can arise from unexamined habits of thought and language.

Pronoun choice
English does not have a singular personal pronoun of indefinite gender. In speaking, people often use plural pronouns to avoid the masculine forms:

Everybody had fun on their vacations. But in a sentence with a singular subject (*everybody*), any pronoun you use later in the sentence should be singular, so you have to choose between *his* and *her*.

Until recently, *he, him,* and *his* were used generically to refer to singular nouns or pronouns whose gender was unknown, unstated, or irrelevant: *Anyone who believes those promises should have <u>his</u> head examined.* (See also 25b.) Such usage is disappearing because many people believe that the generic *he* excludes women.

If you know the gender of the antecedent, use the pronoun of the same gender: *Each nun makes <u>her</u> own bed.* If you don't know the gender, choose one of these strategies.

1   Make the antecedent plural and adjust other agreement problems: *All the <u>residents</u> make <u>their</u> own beds.*
2   Use *his or her: Each resident makes <u>his or her</u> own bed.*
3   Eliminate the pronoun by restructuring the surrounding sentence or sentences: not *Everyone has done <u>his</u> part* but *Everyone has <u>helped</u>.*

The last of these strategies is often the most effective approach.

Universal terms

The use of *man* and *mankind* to refer to the whole of humanity seems to ignore the female half of the species. As you edit, substitute more inclusive terms such as *humanity, the human race, humankind,* or *people.*

Occupational terms

In choosing terms for an occupation, focus on the occupation, not the gender of the person who holds it. There are almost no jobs that are "naturally" held by either men or women. Avoid language that implicitly identifies an occupation with gender, that assumes all fight attendants, nurses, secretaries, or teachers to be female or all airline pilots, business executives, streetcar conductors, or bronco busters to be male.

◆   **A ~~male~~ nurse assisted the surgeon in the operating room.**

Avoid using occupational terms with feminine suffixes: *actor/actress, author/authoress, poet/poetess, executor/executrix.* Such feminine forms have become obsolete, and the formerly male form has become neutral: *author, poet, actor,* and *executor.* Others, such as *waitress,* are changing to more inclusive terms: *server.*

AVOIDING THE GENERIC _HE_

A singular indefinite pronoun—_someone, anyone_—does not specify gender, yet a singular personal pronoun that refers to the indefinite pronoun must specify gender _(he, she)_. There are four ways to avoid the generic _he_ in referring back to an antecedent.

1 If there is no doubt about the gender of the antecedent, use a pronoun of the same gender.

◆ Anyone who wants to be an operatic soprano must train ~~their~~ her voice carefully.

2 Make the antecedent plural. (But watch for other words in the sentence that need to be made plural as well.)

◆ ~~Everyone knows~~ All the singers know their ~~part.~~ parts

3 Use _his or her._ Do this sparingly because repeating the phrase becomes monotonous.

◆ Everyone knows ~~their~~ his or her part.

4 Rewrite to eliminate the pronoun.

◆ Everyone has ~~done their best~~ worked hard to make the recital succeed.

◆ ~~Everyone~~ Every writer wrestles with this problem ~~in his or her own writing.~~

Occupational terms that end in -_man_ imply that everyone who does that job is male. Sex-neutral substitutes for many occupations are readily available.

GENDER-SPECIFIC (MALE)	NEUTRAL
statesman	diplomat
congressman	representative in Congress, congressional representative, representative
mailman	letter carrier, mail carrier
policeman	police officer
fireman	firefighter
businessman	executive, businessperson
salesman	sales representative

20 ◆ GLOSSARY OF USAGE

Like every other aspect of editing, good usage—selecting the most appropriate word for your purpose and context—seldom involves clear-cut distinctions and unvarying rules. Even language authorities do not agree on the acceptability of all usages. Where disagreement does exist, writers have greater liberty to make their own choices. For example, although some writers prefer to use *farther* only for physical distances and *further* for differences of degree, the two words have in fact been used interchangeably for hundreds of years.

You should strive to use words carefully and correctly, since your use of language shows how well you understand your material and reflects on the overall quality of your education.

This glossary provides information about many of the most frequently confused or misused words. Some usages listed here are acceptable or common in contexts other than formal academic writing. For example, **nonstandard** usages (such as *anyways* for *anyway*) reflect the speech patterns of particular communities but do not follow the conventions of the dominant American dialect. **Colloquial** usages (such as *flunk* for *fail* or *totally* meaning *very*) are often heard in speech but are usually inappropriate for academic writing. **Informal** usages (such as using *can* and *may* interchangeably) may not be acceptable in formal research essays or argument papers. Except as noted, this glossary recommends usage as found in formal academic writing.

a, an Use *a* before words that begin with a consonant sound (*a boy, a history, a shining star*), even if the first letter of the word is a vowel (*a useful lesson*). Use *an* before words that begin with a vowel sound (*an antelope, an hour, an umbrella*).

accept, except *Accept* is a verb meaning "to receive" or "to approve" (*I accept your offer*). *Except* is a verb meaning "to leave out" or "to exclude" (*He excepted all vegetables from his list of favorite foods*) or a preposition meaning "excluding" (*He liked to eat everything except vegetables*).

adapt, adopt *Adapt* means "to adjust" or "to accommodate"; it is usually followed by *to* (*It is sometimes hard to adapt to college life*). *Adopt* means "to take into a relationship" (*My parents are adopting another child*) or "to take and use as one's own" (*I have adopted my roommate's habit*).

adverse, averse *Adverse* is an adjective meaning "unfavorable" or "unpleasant," generally used to describe a thing or situation (*Adverse weather forced us to cancel the game*). *Averse*, also an adjective, means "opposed to" or "feeling a distaste for" and usually describes feelings about a thing or situation; it is usually followed by *to* (*We are averse to playing on a muddy field*).

advice, advise *Advice* is a noun meaning meaning "recommendation" or "information given." *Advise* is a verb meaning "to give advice to" (*I advise you to take my advice and study hard*).

affect, effect   *Affect* as a verb means "to influence" or "to produce an effect" (*That movie affected me deeply*). *Affect* as a noun means "feeling" or "emotion," especially in psychology. *Effect* is commonly used as a noun meaning "result," "consequence," or "outcome" (*That movie had a profound effect on me*); it is also used as a verb meaning "to bring about" (*Dr. Jones effected important changes as president*).

aggravate   *Aggravate* is a verb meaning "to make worse." *Aggravate* is sometimes used colloquially to mean "to irritate" or "to annoy," but in formal writing use *irritate* or *annoy* (*I was irritated by my neighbors' loud stereo; my irritation was aggravated when they refused to turn it down.*)

all ready, already   *All ready* means "fully prepared" (*The children were all ready for bed*). *Already* means "previously" (*The children were already in bed when the guests arrived*).

all right, alright   The two-word spelling is preferred; the one-word spelling is considered incorrect by many.

all together, altogether   *All together* means "all gathered in one place" (*The animals were all together in the ark*). *Altogether* means "thoroughly" or "completely" (*The ark was altogether too full of animals*).

allude, elude   *Allude* is a verb meaning "to refer to something indirectly"; it is usually followed by *to* (*Derek alluded to the rodent infestation by mentioning that he'd bought mousetraps*). *Elude* is a verb meaning "to escape" or "to avoid" (*The mouse eluded Derek at every turn*).

allusion, illusion   *Allusion* means "an indirect reference" or "the act of alluding to, or hinting at, something" (*Derek's allusion to lunchtime was not lost on his companions*). *Illusion* is a noun meaning "misapprehension" or "misleading image" (*Mr. Hodges created an optical illusion with two lines*).

a lot   *A lot* should be written as two words. Although *a lot* is used informally to mean "a large number" or "many," avoid using *a lot* in formal writing (*The prisoners had many* [not *a lot of*] *opportunities to escape*).

although, while   *Although* means "despite the fact that." The primary meaning of *while* is "at the same time that". In formal writing, do not substitute *while* for *although* (*Although* [not *while*] *John did the grocery shopping, he wished Mary would sometimes help.*) See *since.*

a.m., p.m., or A.M., P.M.   Use only with numbers to indicate time (6:30 P.M.), not as a substitute for *morning, afternoon, evening,* or *night.*

among, between   *Among* should be used when discussing three or more individuals (*It was difficult to choose among all the exotic plants*). *Between* is used when discussing only two individuals (*There were significant differences between the two candidates*).

amount, number   *Amount* should be used to refer to quantities that cannot be counted or cannot be expressed as a single number (*Fixing up the abandoned farmhouse took a great amount of work*). *Number* is used for quantities that can be counted (*A large number of volunteers showed up to clean out the abandoned farmhouse*).

an   See *a, an*.

and/or   *and/or* is used in technical and legal writing to connect two terms when either one or both apply (*Purchasers must select type and/or size*). Avoid this awkward phrasing by using the construction "*a* or *b* or both" (*Students may select chemistry or physics or both*).

anxious, eager   *Anxious* is an adjective meaning "worried" or "uneasy" (*Lynn is anxious about her mother's surgery*). Do not confuse it with *eager*, which means "enthusiastic," "impatient," or "marked by strong desire" (*I am eager* [not *anxious*] *to leave*).

anybody, anyone, any body, any one   *Anybody* and *anyone* are singular indefinite pronouns that refer to an unspecified person (*Anybody may apply for the new scholarship. Anyone on the hill could have seen our campfire*). *Any body* and *any one* are noun phrases consisting of the adjective *any* and the noun *body* or the pronoun *one*; they refer to a specific body or to a single member of a group (*Each child may select any one toy from the toy box*).

anyplace, anywhere   In formal writing, do not use *anyplace*; use *anywhere* instead (*We could not find the game piece anywhere* [not *anyplace*]).

anyways, anywheres   Use the standard terms *anyway* and *anywhere*.

as   *As* may be used to mean "because" (*We did not go ice skating as the lake was no longer frozen*), but only if no confusion will result. For example, *We canceled the meeting as only two people showed up* could mean that the meeting was canceled at the moment when the two people showed up or because only two showed up.

as, as if, like   To indicate comparisons, *like* should be used only as a preposition followed by a noun phrase to compare items that are similar but not equivalent (*Ken, like his brother, prefers to sleep late*). In formal writing, *like* should not be used as a conjunction linking two clauses. Use *as* or *as if* instead (*Anne talks as if* [not *like*] *she has read every book by Ernest Hemingway*).

assure, ensure, insure   *Assure* is a verb meaning "to reassure" or "to convince" (*The lawyer assured her client that the case was solid*). *Ensure* and *insure* both mean "to make sure, certain, or safe," but *insure* generally refers to financial certainty (*John hoped his college degree would ensure him a job, preferably one that would insure him in case of injury or illness*).

as to   Do not use *as to* as a substitute for *about* (*We had questions about* [not *as to*] *the company's affirmative action policies*).

averse   See *adverse, averse*.

awful, awfully   *Awful* is an adjective meaning "inspiring awe." In formal writing, do not use it to mean "disagreeable" or "objectionable." Similarly, the adverb *awfully* means "in an awe-inspiring way"; in writing, do not use it in the colloquial sense of "very."

awhile, a while   The one-word form *awhile* is an adverb that can be used to modify a verb (*We rested awhile*). Only the two-word form *a while*, that is, the article *a* and the noun *while*, can be the object of a preposition (*We rested for a while*).

bad, badly   *Bad* is an adjective, so it must modify a noun or follow a linking verb, such as *be, feel,* or *become* (*John felt bad about holding the picnic in bad weather*). *Badly* is an adverb, so it must modify a verb (*Pam played badly today*).

being as, being that   *Being as* and *being that* are nonstandard expressions for *because* (*Anna withdrew from the tournament because* [not *being as*] *her shoulder was injured*).

beside, besides   *Beside* is a preposition meaning "by the side of" or "next to" (*The book is beside the bed*). *Besides* can be used as a preposition meaning "other than" or "in addition to" (*No one besides Linda can build a good campfire*). *Besides* can also be used as an adverb meaning "furthermore" or "in addition" (*The weather is bad for hiking; besides, I have a cold*).

between   See *among, between.*

breath, breathe   *Breath* is a noun (*I had to stop to catch my breath*); *breathe* is a verb (*It became difficult to breathe at higher elevations*).

bring, take   The verb *bring* describes movement from a distant place to a nearer place; the verb *take* describes movement away from a place (*Dr. Gavin asked us to bring our rough sketches to class; she said we may take them home after class*).

burst, bust   *Burst* is an irregular verb meaning "to break open, apart, or into pieces." Its past tense and past participle are both *burst; bursted* is nonstandard and should not be used (*Lee burst the balloon with the point of a pen*). *Bust* is an informal verb meaning "to burst," "to break," and "to arrest"; avoid it in formal writing.

but, however, yet   Each of these words should be used alone, not in combination (*We finished painting the house, but* [not *but however*] *there was still much work to do*).

can, may   In informal usage, *can* and *may* are often used interchangeably to indicate permission. But in formal writing, only *may* should be so used (*May I borrow your dictionary?*). *May* is also used to indicate possibility (*It may snow tomorrow*); *can* is used only to indicate ability (*I can see much better with my new glasses*).

capital, capitol   *Capital* is an adjective meaning "punishable by death" (*capital punishment*) or is used to refer to uppercase letters (*A, B*). As a noun it means "accumulated wealth" (*We will calculate our capital at the end of the fiscal year*) or "a city serving as a seat of government" (*Albany is the capital of New York*). *Capitol* is a noun indicating a building in which lawmakers meet (*The civics class toured the state capitol last week*).

censor, censure   *Censor* is a noun or verb referring to the removal of material that is considered objectionable. *Censure* is a verb meaning "to blame or condemn sternly" (*Plans to censor song lyrics have been censured by groups that support free speech*).

cite, site   *Cite* is a verb meaning "to quote for purposes of example, authority, or proof" (*Tracy cites several legal experts in her paper on capital punishment*). *Site* as a noun means "place or scene" (*Today we poured the foundation on the site of our future home*). As a verb it means "to place or locate" (*The house was carefully sited to take advantage of the view*).

climactic, climatic *Climactic* is an adjective derived from *climax;* it refers to a moment of greatest intensity (*In the climactic scene of the play, the murderer's identity is revealed*). *Climatic* is an adjective derived from the noun *climate;* it refers to weather conditions (*Some people fear that climatic changes are caused by environmental pollution*).

compare to, compare with *Compare to* means "to liken" or "to represent as similar" (*Jim compared our new puppy to an unruly child*). *Compare with* means "to examine to discover similarities or differences" (*We compared this month's ads with last month's*).

complement, compliment *Complement* is a verb meaning "to fill out or complete"; it is also a noun meaning "something that completes or fits with" (*The bouquet of spring flowers complemented the table setting*). *Compliment* is a verb meaning "to express esteem or admiration" or a noun meaning "an expression of esteem or admiration" (*Russ complimented Nancy on her choice of flowers*). As a noun, *complement* means a set (*The ship's complement of sails included two mains, a spinnaker, a genoa, and a storm jib*). The noun *compliment* means a flattering remark or action (*The team voted her captain, which she took as a compliment*).

compose, comprise *Compose* means "to constitute or make up"; *comprise* means " to include or contain" (*Only eight members compose this year's club; last year's comprised fifteen*).

conscience, conscious *Conscience* is a noun referring to a sense of right and wrong (*His conscience would not allow him to lie*). *Conscious* is an adjective meaning "marked by thought or will" or "acting with critical awareness" (*He made a conscious decision to be more honest*).

contact *Contact* is often used informally as a verb meaning "to get in touch with," but it should not be used this way in formal writing. Use a verb such as *write* or *telephone* instead.

continual, continuous *Continual* means "recurring" or "occurring repeatedly" (*Liz saw a doctor about her continual headaches*). *Continuous* means "uninterrupted in space, time, or sequence" (*Eventually we grew used to the continuous noise*).

council, counsel *Council* is a noun meaning " a group meeting for advice, discussion, or government" (*The tribal council voted in favor of the new land-rights law*). As a noun, *counsel* means "advice" or "a plan of action or behavior" (*The priest gave counsel to the young men considering the priesthood*). It can also refer to a legal representative (*The company's legal counsel denied comment on the lawsuit*). *Counsel* may also be used as a verb meaning "to advise or consult" (*The priest counseled the young man*).

criteria *Criteria* is the plural of *criterion,* which means "a standard on which a judgment is based" (*Many criteria are used in selecting a president, but a candidate's hair color is not an appropriate criterion*).

data *Data* is the plural of *datum,* which means "an observed fact" or "a result in research." Some writers now use *data* as both a singular and a plural noun; in formal usage it is still better to treat it as plural (*The data indicate that a low-fat diet may increase life expectancy*).

different from, different than *Different from* is preferred to *different than* (*Hal's taste in music is different from his wife's*). But *different than* may be used to avoid awkward constructions (*Hal's taste in music is different than* [instead of *different from what*] *it was five years ago*).

differ from, differ with *Differ from* means "to be unlike" (*This year's parade differed from last year's in many ways*). *Differ with* means "to disagree with" (*Stephanie differed with Tom over which parade was better*).

discreet, discrete *Discreet* is an adjective meaning "prudent" or "modest" (*Most private donors were discreet about their contributions*). *Discrete* is an adjective meaning "separate" or "distinct" (*Professor Roberts divided the course into four discrete units*).

disinterested, uninterested *Disinterested* is an adjective meaning "unbiased" or "impartial" (*It will be difficult to find twelve disinterested jurors for such a highly publicized case*). *Uninterested* is an adjective meaning "indifferent" or "unconcerned" (*Most people were uninterested in the case until the police discovered surprising new evidence*).

don't *Don't* is a contraction for *do not,* not for *does not.* The contraction for *does not* is *doesn't* (*He doesn't* [not *don't*] *know where she's living now*).

due to *Due to* is an adjective phrase that is generally used after forms of the verb *be* (*The smaller classes were due to a decline in enrollment*). In formal writing, *due to* should not be used as a prepositional phrase meaning "because of" (*Class size decreased because of* [not *due to*] *a decline in enrollment*).

each *Each* is singular (*Each goes in its own place*).

effect See *affect, effect.*

e.g. *E.g.* is the Latin abbreviation for *exempli gratia,* which means "for example." In formal writing, use *for example* or *for instance.*

elicit, illicit *Elicit* is a verb meaning "to draw forth" or "to bring out" (*The investigators could not elicit any new information*). *Illicit* is an adjective meaning "unlawful" or "not permitted" (*The investigators were looking for evidence of illicit drug sales*).

elude See *allude, elude.*

emigrate, immigrate *Emigrate* means "to leave one's country to live or reside elsewhere" (*His grandparents emigrated to Israel*). *Immigrate* means "to come into a new country to take up residence" (*His grandparents immigrated to the United States*).

eminent, imminent *Eminent* means "lofty" or "prominent" (*Her operation was performed by an eminent surgeon*). *Imminent* means "impending" or "about to take place" (*The hurricane's arrival is imminent*).

ensure See *assure, ensure, insure.*

enthused, enthusiastic In formal writing, *enthused,* a past-tense form of the verb *enthuse,* should not be used as an adjective; use *enthusiastic* (*Barbara is enthusiastic* [not *enthused*] *about her music lessons*).

especially, specially   *Especially* is an adverb meaning "particularly" or "unusually" (*The weather was especially cold this winter*). *Specially* is an adverb meaning "for a special reason" or "in a unique way" (*The cake was specially prepared for Sandy's birthday*).

etc.   An abbreviation for the Latin expression *et cetera, etc.* means "and so forth." In formal writing, avoid ending a list with *etc.*; indicate that you are leaving items out of a list with *and so on* or *and so forth*. Use *etc.* alone, not with *and,* which is redundant.

eventually, ultimately   Although these words are often used interchangeably, *eventually* means "at an unspecified later time," while *ultimately* means "finally" or "in the end" (*He knew that he would stop running eventually, but he hoped that he would ultimately win a marathon*).

everybody, everyone, every body, every one   *Everybody* and *everyone* are singular indefinite pronouns that refer to an unspecified person (*Everybody wins in this game*). *Every body* and *every one* are noun phrases consisting of the adjective *every* and the noun *body* or the pronoun *one;* they refer to each individual body or each single member of a group (*Every one of these toys must be picked up*).

except   See *accept, except.*

expect   *Expect* means "to anticipate or look forward to." Avoid using it colloquially to mean "to think or suppose" (*I suppose* [not *expect*] *I should go study now*).

explicit, implicit   *Explicit* means "perfectly clear, direct, and unambiguous" (*Darrell gave me explicit directions to his house*). *Implicit* means "implied" or "revealed or expressed indirectly" (*His eagerness was implicit in his cheerful tone of voice*).

farther, further   Although these words are often used interchangeably, some writers prefer to use *farther* to refer to physical distances (*Boston is farther than I thought*) and *further* to refer to quantity, time, or degree (*We made further progress on our research project*).

fewer, less   *Fewer* is an adjective used to refer to people or items that can be counted (*Because fewer people came to the conference this year, we needed fewer programs*). *Less* is used to refer to amounts that cannot be counted (*We also required less space and less food*).

finalize   Many writers avoid using *finalize* to mean "to make final." Use alternative phrasing (*We needed to complete* [not *finalize*] *plans*).

firstly, secondly, thirdly   These expressions are awkward; use *first, second,* and *third.*

former, latter   *Former* is used to refer to the first of two people, items, or ideas being discussed, *latter* to refer to the second (*Monet and Picasso were both important painters; the former is associated with the Impressionist school, the latter with Cubism*). *Former* and *latter* should not be used when referring to more than two items; use *first* and *last* instead.

further   See *farther, further.*

get   The verb *get* has many colloquial uses that should be avoided in formal writing. *Get* can mean "to provoke or annoy" (*He gets to me*), "to start" (*We should get going on* *this project*), or "to become" (*She got worried when he didn't call*). *Have got to* should not be used in place of *must* (*I must* [not *have got to*] *finish by five o'clock*).

goes, says The verb *goes* is sometimes used colloquially for *says*, but avoid this usage in formal writing (*When the coach says* [not *goes*] *"Now," everybody runs*).

good and *Good and* should not be used for *very* in formal writing (*My shoes were very* [not *good and*] *wet after our walk*).

good, well *Good* is an adjective; it should not be used in place of the adverb *well* in formal writing (*Mario is a good tennis player; he played well* [not *good*] *today*).

hanged, hung *Hanged* is the past-tense and past-participle form of the verb *hang* meaning "to suspend by the neck until dead" (*Condemned prisoners were hanged at this spot*). *Hung* is the past-tense and past-participle form of the verb *hang* meaning "to suspend" or "to dangle" (*All her clothes were hung neatly in the closet*).

hardly, scarcely *Hardly* and *scarcely* are adverbs meaning "barely," "only just." Do not use phrases like *can't scarcely* and *not hardly* in formal writing; these are double negatives (*I can scarcely* [not *can't scarcely*] *keep my eyes open*).

has got, have got These are colloquial expressions; in formal writing use simply *has* or *have* (*He has* [not *has got*] *his books packed*).

have, of The auxiliary verb *have* (not *of*) should be used in verb phrases beginning with modal auxiliaries such as *could, would,* and *might* (*We could have* [not *could of*] *gone to the concert*).

he/she, his/her When you require both female and male personal pronouns in formal writing, use *he or she* (or *she or he*) and *his or her* (or *her or his*). For more on avoiding sexist language, see 19c.

herself, himself, itself, myself, ourselves, themselves, yourself, yourselves These are reflexive or intensive pronouns and should be used only to reflect the action of a sentence back toward the subject (*He locked himself out of the apartment*) or to emphasize the subject (*I myself have no regrets*). Do not use these pronouns in place of personal pronouns such as *I, me, you, her,* or *him* (*He left an extra key with Bev and me* [not *myself*]).

hisself *Hisself* is nonstandard; use *himself*.

hopefully *Hopefully* is an adverb meaning "in a hopeful manner" (*The child looked hopefully out the window for her mother*). In formal writing, do not use *hopefully* to mean "I or we hope that" or "It is hoped that" (*I hope that* [not *Hopefully*] *Bob will remember his camera*).

hung See *hanged, hung*.

i.e. *I.e.* is an abbreviation for the Latin phrase *id est,* which means "that is." In formal writing, use *that is* instead of the abbreviation (*Hal is a Renaissance man; that is* [not *i.e.*], *he has many interests*).

if, whether Use *if* in a clause that refers to a conditional situation (*I will wear my new* *boots if it snows tomorrow*). Use *whether* (or *whether or not*) in a clause that expresses or implies an alternative (*I will decide whether to wear my boots when I see what the weather is like*).

illusion   see *allusion, illusion.*

immigrate   see *emigrate, immigrate.*

imminent   See *eminent, imminent.*

implicit   See *explicit, implicit.*

imply, infer   *Imply* is a verb meaning "to express indirectly" or "to suggest" ; *infer* is a verb meaning "to conclude" or "to surmise" (*Helen implied that she had time to visit with us, but we inferred from all the work on her desk that she was really too busy*). A speaker implies; a listener infers.

incredible, incredulous   *Incredible* is an adjective meaning "hard to believe"; *incredulous* is an adjective meaning "skeptical" or "unbelieving" (*My parents were incredulous when I told them the incredible story*).

infer   See *imply, infer.*

ingenious, ingenuous   *Ingenious* means "resourceful" or "clever" (*Elaine came up with an ingenious plan*). *Ingenuous* means "innocent" or "simple" (*It was a surprisingly deceptive plan for such an ingenuous person*).

in regards to   *In regards to* is an incorrect combination of two phrases, *as regards* and *in regard to* (*In regard to* [or *As regards;* not *In regards to*] *the first question, refer to the guidelines you received*).

inside, inside of; outside, outside of   The prepositions *inside* and *outside* should not be followed by *of* (*The suspect is inside* [not *inside of*] *that building*).

insure   See *assure, ensure, insure.*

invitation, invite   *Invitation* is a noun; *invite* is a verb (*I will invite her to the party and hope she will accept the invitation*). Do not use *invite* as a noun (*Thanks for the invitation* [not *invite*]).

irregardless, regardless   Do not use the nonstandard *irregardless* in place of *regardless* (*We will have the party regardless* [not *irregardless*] *of the weather*).

is when, is where   Avoid these awkward expressions in formal writing to define terms (*Sexual harassment refers to* [not *is when someone makes*] *inappropriate sexual advances or suggestions*).

its, it's   *Its* is the possessive form of the pronoun *it; it's* is a contraction for *it is* (*It's hard to tear a baby animal away from its mother*).

kind, sort, type   *Kind, sort,* and *type* are singular nouns; each should be used with *this* (not *these*) and a singular verb (*This kind of mushroom is* [not *these kind of mushrooms are*] *expensive*). The plural forms—*kinds, sorts,* and *types*—should be used with *these* and with a plural verb (*These three types of envelopes are the only ones we need*).

kind of, sort of   In formal writing, avoid using the colloquial expressions *kind of* and *sort of* to mean "somewhat" or "rather" (*My paper is rather* [not *kind of*] *short; my research for it was somewhat* [not *sort of*] *rushed*).

later, latter   *Later* means "after some time"; *latter* refers to the second of two people, items, or ideas (*Later in the evening Jim announced that the latter of the two guest speakers was running late*). See *former, latter*.

lay   See *lie, lay*.

lead, led   As a verb, *lead* means "to go first" or "to direct"; as a noun, it means "front position" (*Hollis took the lead in organizing the files*). *Led* is the past-tense and past-participle form of the verb *lead* (*He led me to the cave*).

learn, teach   *Learn* means "to gain knowledge or understanding"; *teach* means "to cause to know" or "to instruct" (*Tonight James will teach* [not *learn*] *us a new dance step; I hope we can learn it quickly*).

leave, let   *Leave* means "to depart"; it should not be used in place of let, which means "to allow" (*When you are ready to leave, let* [not *leave*] *me give you a ride*). The expressions *leave alone* and *let alone*, however, may be used interchangeably (*I asked Ben to leave* [or *let*] *me alone while I worked on my paper*).

led   See *lead, led*.

less   See *fewer, less*.

liable, likely   *Liable* means "inclined" or "tending," generally toward the negative (*If you do not shovel the sidewalk, you are liable to fall on the ice*). *Liable* is also a legal term meaning "responsible for" or "obligated under the law" (*The landlord is liable for the damage caused by the leak*). *Likely* is an adjective meaning "probable" or "promising" (*The school board is likely to cancel classes if the strike continues*).

lie, lay   The verb *lie* meaning "to recline" or "to rest in a horizontal position" has the principal forms *lie, lay, lain*. *Lie* should not be confused with the transitive verb *lay*, which means "to put or set down" and is followed by an object; the principal forms of *lay* are *lay, laid, laid* (*Lay the blanket on this spot and lie* [not *lay*] *down; She laid the book next to the spot where he lay on the bed*).

like   See *as, as if, like*.

likely   See *liable, likely*.

loose, lose   *Loose* is an adjective meaning "not securely attached"; it should not be confused with the verb *lose*, which means "to misplace," "to fail to keep," or "to undergo defeat" (*Be careful not to lose that loose button on your jacket*).

lots, lots of   *Lots* and *lots* of are colloquial expressions meaning "many" or "much"; avoid them in formal writing (*The senator has much* [not *lots of*] *support; she is expected to win many* [not *lots of*] *votes*).

man, mankind   These terms were once used to refer to all human beings. Now such usage is considered sexist; use terms such as *people, humanity,* and *humankind* instead (*What has been the greatest invention in the history of humanity* [not *mankind*]?).

may See *can, may.*

may be, maybe *May be* is a verb phrase (*Charles may be interested in a new job*); *maybe* is an adverb meaning "possibly" or "perhaps" (*Maybe I will speak to him about it*).

media the term *media,* frequently used to refer to various forms of communication such as newspapers, magazines, television, radio, is the plural form of the noun *medium;* it takes a plural verb (*Some people feel that the media were responsible for the candidate's loss*).

moral, morale *Moral* is the message or lesson of a story or experience (*The moral is to treat others as you wish to be treated*). *Morale* is the mental condition or mood of a person or group (*The improvement in the weather lifted the crew's morale*).

most In formal writing, do not use *most* to mean "almost" (*Prizes were given to almost* [not *most*] *all the participants*).

myself See *herself, himself.* . . . .

neither The pronoun *neither* is singular (*Neither of my parents is able to come this weekend*).

nor, or *Nor* should be used with *neither* (*Neither Paul nor Sara guessed the right answer*); *or* should be used with *either* (*Either Paul or Sara will drive me home*).

number See *amount, number.*

of See *have, of.*

off of Use *off* alone; *of* is not necessary (*The child fell off* [not *off of*] *the playground slide*).

OK, O.K., okay All three spellings are acceptable, but this colloquial term should be avoided in formal writing (*John's performance was all right* [or *adequate* or *tolerable,* not *okay*], *but it wasn't his best*).

on account of In formal writing, avoid *on account of* to mean "because of" (*The course was canceled because of* [not *on account of*] *lack of interest*). Also see *due to.*

outside, outside of See *inside, inside of; outside, outside of.*

passed, past *Passed* is the past-tense form of the verb *pass* (*She passed here several hours ago*). *Past* may be an adjective or a noun referring to a time before the present (*She has forgotten many details about her past life*).

penultimate See *ultimate, penultimate.*

per The Latin term *per* should be reserved for commercial or technical use (*miles per gallon, price per pound*) and avoided in other formal writing (*Kyle is exercising three times each* [not *per*] *week*).

percent, percentage The term *percent* (or *per cent*) refers to a specific fraction of one hundred; it is always used with a number (*We raised nearly 80 percent of our budget in one night*). Do not use the symbol % in formal writing. The term *percentage* is more general and is not used with a specific number (*We raised a large percentage of our budget in one night*).

perspective, prospective   *Perspective* is a noun meaning "a view"; it should not be confused with the adjective *prospective* meaning "potential" or "likely" (*Mr. Harris's perspective on the new school changed when he met his son's prospective teacher*).

phenomena   *Phenomena* is the plural of the noun *phenomenon,* which means "an observed fact, occurrence, or circumstance" (*Last month's blizzard was an unusual phenomenon; there have been several such phenomena this year*).

plenty   *Plenty* means "full" or "abundant"; in formal writing, do not use it to mean "very" or "quite" (*The sun was quite* [not *plenty*] *hot*).

plus   *Plus* is a preposition meaning "increased by" or "with the addition of" (*With wool socks plus your heavy boots, your feet should be warm enough*). Do not use *plus* to link two independent clauses; use *besides* or *moreover* instead (*Brad is not prepared for the advanced class; moreover* [not *plus*], *he can't fit it in his schedule*).

precede, proceed   *Precede* is a verb meaning "to go or come before"; *proceed* is a verb meaning "to move forward or go on" or "to continue" (*The bridal attendants preceded the bride into the church; when the music started, they proceeded down the aisle*).

pretty   In formal writing, avoid *pretty* to mean "quite" or "somewhat" (*Dave is quite* [not *pretty*] *tired this morning*).

principal, principle   *Principal* is an adjective meaning "first" or "most important"; it is also a noun meaning "head" or "director" or "an amount of money" (*My principal reason for visiting Gettysburg was my interest in the Civil War. My high school principal suggested the trip*). *Principle* is a noun meaning "a rule of action or conduct" or "a basic law" (*I also want to learn more about the principles underlying the U.S. Constitution*).

proceed   See *precede, proceed.*

quotation, quote   *Quotation* is a noun, and *quote* is a verb. Avoid using *quote* as a noun (*Sue quoted Jefferson in her speech, hoping the quotation* [not *quote*] *would have a powerful effect on her audience*).

raise, rise   *Raise* is a transitive verb meaning "to lift" or "to increase"; it takes a direct object (*The store owner was forced to raise prices*). *Rise* is an intransitive verb meaning "to go up"; it does not take a direct object (*Prices will rise during periods of inflation*).

rarely ever   Do not use *rarely ever* to mean "hardly ever"; use *rarely* alone (*We rarely* [not *rarely ever*] *travel during the winter*).

real, really   *Real* is an adjective meaning "true" or "actual" (*The diamonds in that necklace are real*). *Really* is an adverb, used informally to mean "very" or "quite"; do not use *real* as an adverb (*Tim was really* [not *real*] *interested in buying Lana's old car*). In formal writing, it is generally best to avoid using *really* altogether.

reason is because   *Reason is because* is redundant; use *reason is that* or *because* instead (*The reason I am late is that* [not *because*] *I got stuck in traffic. Yesterday I was late because* [not *The reason I was late yesterday was because*] *I overslept*).

reason why   *Reason why* is redundant; use *reason* alone (*The reason* [not *The reason why*] *we canceled the dance is that no one volunteered to chaperone*).

regardless   See *irregardless, regardless.*

relation, relationship   *Relation* is a connection or association between things; *relationship* is a connection or involvement between people (*The analyst explained the relation between investment and interest. The relationship between a mother and child is complex*).

respectfully, respectively   The adverb *respectfully* means "in a respectful manner" (*The children listened to their teacher respectfully*). The adverb *respectively* means "in the order given" (*The sessions on Italian, French, and Spanish culture are scheduled for Tuesday, Wednesday, and Thursday, respectively*).

rise   See *raise, rise.*

says   See *goes, says.*

scarcely   See *hardly, scarcely.*

sensual, sensuous   *Sensual* means "arousing or exciting the senses or appetites"; it is often used in reference to sexual pleasure (*His scripts often featured titillating situations and sensual encounters*). *Sensuous* means "experienced through or affecting the senses," although it generally refers to aesthetic enjoyment or pleasure (*Her sculpture was characterized by muted colors and sensuous curves*).

set, sit   *Set* is a transitive verb meaning "to put" or "to place"; it takes a direct object, and its principal forms are *set, set, set* (*Mary set her packages on the kitchen table*). *Sit* is an intransitive verb meaning "to be seated"; it does not take a direct object, and its principal forms are *sit, sat, sat* (*I sat in the only chair in the waiting room*).

shall, will   In the past, *shall* (instead of *will*) was used as a helping verb with the first-person subjects *I* and *we*. Now *will* is acceptable with all subjects (*We will invite several guests for dinner*). *Shall* is generally used in polite questions (*Shall we go inside now?*) or in legal writing (*Jurors shall refrain from all contact with the press*).

since   *Since* should be used to mean "continuing from a past time until the present" (*Carl has not gone skiing since he injured his knee*). Do not use *since* to mean "because" if there is any possibility that readers will be confused about your meaning. For example, in the sentence *Since she sold her bicycle, Lonnie has not been getting much exercise,* the word *since* could mean either "because" or "from the time that." Use *because* to avoid confusion.

sit   See *set, sit.*

site   See *cite, site.*

so, so that   The use of *so* to mean "very" can be vague; use *so* with a *that* clause of explanation (not *Gayle was so depressed,* but *Gayle was so depressed that she could not get out of bed*).

somebody, someone, something   These singular indefinite pronouns take singular verbs (*Somebody calls every night at midnight and hangs up; I hope someone does something about this problem soon*).

someplace, somewhere   Do not use *someplace* in formal writing; use *somewhere* instead (*The answer must lie somewhere* [not *someplace*] *in the text*).

some time, sometime, sometimes   The phrase *some time* (an adjective and a noun) means "a length of time" (*We have not visited our grandparents in some time*). *Sometime* is an adverb meaning "at an indefinite time in the future" (*Let's get together sometime*); *sometimes* is an adverb meaning "on occasion" or "now and then" (*Sometimes we get together to talk about our assignments*).

sort   See *kind, sort, type*.

stationary, stationery   *Stationary* is an adjective meaning "not moving" (*All stationary vehicles will be towed*). *Stationery* is a noun meaning "writing materials" (*Karen is always running out of stationery*).

supposed to, used to   Both of these expressions consist of a past participle (*supposed, used*) followed by *to*. Do not use the base forms *suppose* and *use* (*Ben is supposed* [not *suppose*] *to take the garbage out; he is used* [not *use*] *to his mother's reminders by now*).

sure, surely   In formal writing, do not use the adjective *sure* to mean "certainly" or "undoubtedly"; use *surely* or *certainly* or *undoubtedly* instead (*It is certainly* [or *surely*; not *sure*] *cold today*).

sure and, try and   *Sure and* and *try and* are colloquial expressions for *sure to* and *try to*, respectively; avoid them in formal writing (*Be sure to* [not *and*] *come to the party. Try to* [not *and*] *be on time*).

take   See *bring, take*.

teach   See *learn, teach*.

than, then   *Than* is a conjunction used in comparisons (*Dan is older than Eve*). *Then* is an adverb indicating time (*First pick up the files and then deliver them to the company office*).

that   See *that, which* and *which, who, that*.

that, which   A clause introduced by *that* is always a restrictive clause; it should not be set off by commas (*The historical event that interested him the most was the Civil War*). Many writers use *which* only to introduce nonrestrictive clauses, which are set off by commas (*His textbook, which was written by an expert on the war, provided useful information*); however, *which* may also be used to introduce restrictive clauses (*The book which offered the most important information was an old reference book in the library*). See 24h.

their, there, they're   *Their* is the possessive form of the pronoun *they* (*Did they leave their books here?*). *There* is an adverb meaning "in or at that place" (*No, they left their books there*); it may also be used as an expletive with a form of the verb *be* (*There is no time to look for their books*). *They're* is a contraction of *they are* (*They're looking all over for their books*).

theirselves   *Theirselves* is nonstandard; always use *themselves.*

then   See *than, then.*

'til, till, until   *Till* and *until* are both acceptable spellings; *'til,* however, is a contraction and should be avoided in formal writing (*We will work until we are finished; you should not plan to leave till then*).

to, too, two   *To* is a preposition often used to indicate movement or direction toward something (*Nancy is walking to the grocery store*). *Too* is an adverb meaning "also" (*Sam is walking too*). *Two* is a number (*The two of them are walking together*).

toward, towards   *Toward* is preferred, but both forms are acceptable.

try and   See *sure and, try and.*

type   In colloquial speech, *type* is sometimes used alone to mean "type of," but avoid this usage in formal writing (*What type of* [not *type*] *medicine did the doctor prescribe?*). Also see *kind, sort, type.*

ultimate, penultimate   *Ultimate* literally means "the last." In formal writing, do not use it in the colloquial sense of "the best" (*the toughest challenge,* not *the ultimate challenge*). *Penultimate* is also sometimes used to mean "the best", but it means "next to last."

ultimately   See *eventually, ultimately.*

uninterested   See *disinterested, uninterested.*

unique   *Unique* is an adjective meaning "being the only one" or "having no equal." Because it refers to an absolute, unvarying state, it should not be preceded by a word that indicates degree or amount (such as *most, less,* or *very*) (*Her pale blue eyes gave her a unique* [not *very unique*] *look*). The same is true of other adjectives that indicate an absolute state: *perfect, complete, round, straight,* and so on.

until   See *'til, till, until.*

usage, use   The noun *usage* means "an established and accepted practice or procedure" (*He consulted the glossary whenever he was unsure of the correct word or usage*). Do not substitute it for the noun *use* when the intended meaning is "the act of putting into service" (*Park guidelines forbid the use* [not *usage*] *of gas grills*).

used to   See *supposed to, used to.*

utilize   The verb *utilize,* meaning "to put to use," is often considered inappropriately technical for formal writing. It is generally better to use *use* instead (*We were able to use* [not *utilize*] *the hotel kitchen to prepare our meals*).

wait for, wait on   *Wait for* means "to await" or "to be ready for." *Wait on* means "to serve"; in formal writing they are not interchangeable (*You are too old to wait for* [not *on*] *your mother to wait on you*).

way, ways   Do not use *ways* in place of *way* when referring to long distances (*Los Angeles is a long way* [not *ways*] *from San Francisco*).

well See *good, well.*

where *Where* is nonstandard when used in place of *that* (*I read that* [not *where*] *several of the company's plants will be closed in June*).

where . . . at, where . . . to *Where* should be used alone, not in combination with *at* or *to* (*Where did you leave your coat?* [not *Where did you leave your coat at?*] *Where are you going next?* [not *Where are you going to next?*]).

whether See *if, whether.*

which See *that, which.*

which, who, that Use the relative pronoun *which* to refer to places, things, or events; use *who* to refer to people or to animals with individual qualities or given names; use *that* to refer to places, things, or events or to groups of people (*The parade, which was rescheduled for Saturday, was a great success. The man who* [not *which*] *was grand marshall said it was the best parade that he could remember*). *That* is also occasionally used to refer to a single person (*Beth is like the sister that I never had*). See 24h.

while See *although, while.*

who See *which, who, that.*

who, whom, whoever, whomever Use *who* and *whoever* for subjects and subject complements; use *whom* and *whomever* for objects and object complements (*Who revealed the murderer's identity? You may invite whomever you wish*). See 25c.

who's, whose *Who's* is a contraction of *who is* (*Who's coming for dinner tonight?*). *Whose* is the possessive form of *who* (*Whose hat is lying on the table?*).

will See *shall, will.*

-wise The suffix *-wise* indicates position or direction in words such as *clockwise* and *lengthwise*. In formal writing, do not add it to words to mean "with regard to" (*My personal life is rather confused, but with regard to my job* [not *jobwise*], *things are fine*).

yet See *but, however, yet.*

your, you're *Your* is the possessive form of the pronoun *you* (*Your table is ready*); *you're* is a contraction of *you are* (*You're leaving before the end of the show?*).

EDITING GRAMMAR

EDITING GRAMMAR

The **sentence,** a group of words expressing a complete thought, is the basic unit of speech and writing. Sentence grammar describes how sentences are organized and structured. It also describes the function of each word in a sentence. An understanding of grammar helps you identify and improve places where your writing may be confusing. It also helps you find nonstandard structures or usages that may distract the reader from your meaning.

21 ◆ ELIMINATING SENTENCE FRAGMENTS

A sentence expresses a complete idea. A group of words punctuated as a sentence that is not grammatically complete is called a **fragment.** One kind of fragment neglects to tell what it is about (the subject) or what happened (the verb).

> None of us understood the result. *Or even how it had happened.*

> *Seven graduate students in microbiology. Without any idea.*

Other fragments cannot stand alone because they contain a subordinating element: they are dependent clauses punctuated as sentences.

> This was devastating. *Because the unusual results had not been predicted by our hypothesis.*

Fragments occur often in everyday speech and in informal writing. In academic writing, however, most instructors regard sentence fragments as errors.

As you edit, check to make sure that each sentence is complete. When you discover fragments in your writing, decide which element is missing, and then turn each fragment into a complete sentence by doing one of three things.

◆ Add the missing subject or verb (or both) to make the fragment a complete sentence.

◆ Find a sentence nearby and incorporate the fragment into that sentence.

◆ If the fragment is a dependent clause standing alone, remove the subordinating element to create an independent clause.

Often you can eliminate sentence fragments simply by repunctuating or by changing a few words.

RECOGNIZING FRAGMENTS

If you're unsure whether a group of words is a sentence fragment, ask yourself the following questions.

1 Does it contain a verb? If not, it is a fragment. (See 21a.)

◆ A controlled experiment *was conducted* comparing the effect of light on plants.

A gerund, an infinitive, or a participle without an auxiliary or helping verb cannot serve as the main verb of a sentence. (See 23d.)

2 Does it contain a subject? If not, it is a fragment. (See 21a.)

◆ During the night, the protesters talked quietly and slept,/ ~~And~~ *and* prayed.

Certain sentences in the imperative mood (commands, orders, and requests) do not require explicit subjects: *Come at noon.* The subject is understood to be *you,* so an imperative sentence is not considered a fragment. (See 23f.)

3 Does it contain a subordinating word or phrase? If a group of words contains both a subject and a verb but is introduced by a subordinating conjunction (*until, because, after,* and so on) or a relative pronoun (*who, that, which*), it is a **dependent clause** and cannot stand alone as a complete sentence. (See 14c and 21b.)

◆ None of the test plants bloomed during the experiment,/ ~~Because~~ *because* of the limited time period.

21a Fragments lacking verbs or subjects

Providing missing elements

If a fragment lacks a verb or subject, you can simply add one.

◆ A fleet of colorful fishing boats *rocked* at anchor in the bay.

◆ The snowboarder cleared the rock ledge and flew out into space. ~~Spun~~ *She spun* twice in midair and sliced into the clean powder below.

Joining the fragment

Another solution is to make the fragment part of a nearby sentence. There may be several ways to do that.

◆ Few employees interviewed held the company president in high regard./ ~~Or~~ *or*
    believed he could bring the business back to profitability.
    Repunctuating the sentence provides a subject for believed.

◆ Symbolism is an important technique in Alice Walker's "Everyday ~~Use". A~~ *Use," which*
    ~~story that~~ portrays cultural differences between generations.

Use a colon or a dash to join a list or set of examples to the sentence that introduces it.

◆ Taking the boat out alone for the first time, I struggled to remember every-
    thing my father had shown me over the ~~summer. Centerboard,~~ *summer: centerboard,* halyards,
    jib sheets, main sheet, tiller, and telltales.
    The list punctuated as a sentence actually renames everything my father had
    shown me *and therefore fits well in the same sentence.*

    Katharine Hepburn influenced a generation of current screen actresses./ —
    Meryl Streep, Glenn Close, Sigourney Weaver, and Kathleen Turner.

Sometimes a fragment lacks both a subject and a complete verb. The best move then is usually to find it a home in a nearby sentence.

◆ Last month I visited Detroit's Institute of Arts./ ~~With~~ *with* my mother. We saw a
    wonderful collection of futurist paintings.

◆ Returning to the lab, he found that the bacterial specimens were dying./, *suffering,*
    ~~Suffering,~~ apparently, from the effects of some sort of wild mold.

Dependent clause fragments   **21b**

A **dependent clause** is a clause introduced by a **subordinating conjunction** (such as *after, although, since, because, when, where,* or *whether*) or a **rela-**

◇ **ESL** **PREPOSITIONS OF TWO OR MORE WORDS**

Fragments introduced by multiple-word prepositions are difficult to spot. Whenever you use one of these prepositions, make sure the phrase it introduces is attached to an independent clause.

according to	contrary to	instead of
along with	due to	on account of
as a result of	except for	regardless of
as compared with	for the sake of	relative to
as for	in contrast with	up until
aside from	in favor of	with respect to
as well as	in spite of	with the exception of
because of		

in
♦ Our basketball team was not picked for the invitational tournament./ ~~In~~
  spite of our winning record, which we worked hard to attain.

tive pronoun (such as *who, which,* or *that*). Even though it contains both a subject and a predicate, a dependent clause cannot stand alone as a sentence.

To fix a dependent clause fragment, you can either create a new independent clause by removing the subordinating word or attach the dependent clause to the nearby independent clause it modifies.

He
♦ This is my cousin Jacob. ~~Who~~ has never missed a day of school.

after
♦ The trees stood bare./ ~~After~~ the leaves had all fallen.

Sometimes the emphasis you want dictates which adjoining sentence you choose to absorb the dependent clause.

, although
♦ It sounds like an excellent opportunity./ ~~Although~~ the starting pay is barely minimum wage. The position provides more training than many entry-level jobs.

♦ It sounds like an excellent opportunity. Although the starting pay is barely minimum wage. *,the* ~~The~~ position provides more training than many

entry-level jobs.

The first version uses the clause starting with although *to qualify the value of the opportunity. The second uses the clause to stress the value of the training provided.*

(See 31b and 31c for punctuation of dependent clauses.)

Creating special effects 21c

Writers occasionally use fragments to create special effects—to reproduce the sound of spoken language, for example, or create dramatic emphasis. Intentional fragments appear in fiction, personal essays, and narratives and wherever dialogue is reproduced.

> I knew that I was no legitimate resident in any world of ideas. I knew I couldn't think. All I knew then was what I couldn't do. All I knew then was what I wasn't, and it took me some years to discover what I was.
> Which was a writer.
> By which I mean not a "good" writer or a "bad" writer, but simply a writer, a person whose most absorbed and passionate hours are spent arranging words on pieces of paper.
>
> Joan Didion, *"Why I Write"*

Fragments are almost never used in academic writing. If you want to use a fragment, think carefully about its effect. Will your readers be swept along, or will they think you have made a grammatical error? If you decide to use a fragment, make sure that it seems intentional. Use it to create emphasis. When your point warrants disrupting readers' expectations, consider using a fragment. If it works.

22 ◆ CORRECTING COMMA SPLICES AND FUSED SENTENCES

An **independent clause** includes a **subject** and **predicate.** It can stand alone as a complete sentence because it expresses a complete idea. (See Chapter 29, "Grammar Review.")

subject   predicate

Professional athletes can earn huge salaries.

Two independent clauses may be joined in one sentence if they are linked in a clear, conventional way: with a comma and a coordinating conjunction; with a semicolon alone; with a semicolon and a conjunctive adverb or transitional phrase; or with a colon. These markers tell readers that a new idea is beginning and clarify the relationship between the ideas.

Two independent clauses that are joined (or "spliced") only by a comma make a **comma splice.**

independent clause   independent clause

COMMA SPLICE   **Professional athletes can earn huge salaries, some are paid millions of dollars a year.**

Seeing the comma without a coordinating conjunction, readers expect what follows to be part of the first clause rather than a new clause.

A **fused sentence** occurs when two independent clauses are joined without any marker.

independent clause   independent clause

FUSED SENTENCE   **Professional athletes can earn huge salaries some are paid millions of dollars a year.**

There are several ways to eliminate comma splices and fused sentences from your writing.

1 Use a comma and a coordinating conjunction to create a complete sentence.
2 Use a semicolon, alone or with a conjunctive adverb or a transitional phrase, to create a complete sentence.
3 Use a colon when the second clause explains or illustrates the first.
4 Divide the sentence into two sentences.
5 Subordinate one clause to the other.
6 Rewrite the sentence as one independent clause.

Which remedy you choose depends on the meaning you wish to convey, the length of the sentence, and the rhythm and wording of surrounding sentences.

RECOGNIZING COMMA SPLICES AND FUSED SENTENCES

Comma splices and fused sentences often occur when two clauses express ideas closely linked in the writer's mind. Here are some common writing situations in which such sentence errors occur.

1   The second clause offers an example, explanation, or elaboration of the first.

◆   The tribes gathered every summer along the banks of the river ~~they~~ $\overset{\text{. They}}{\wedge}$

fished and hunted and picked berries.

2   The second clause contains a meaning that contrasts with the first.

◆   Everyone was asked to express an opinion on the plans, $\overset{\text{but}}{\wedge}$ Mr. Johnson

was out of town.

3   The subject of the second clause is a pronoun that renames the subject of the first clause.

◆   The instructor asked us to write our thoughts down $\overset{\text{. She}}{\wedge}$ ~~he~~ said just to write

whatever came to mind as fast as we could.

4   A conjunctive adverb or transitional phrase is incorrectly used to join two sentences.

◆   I remember playing with Ernest and Mike $\overset{;}{\wedge}$ in fact $\overset{,}{\wedge}$ I can barely remember

playing with anyone else.

Using a comma and a coordinating conjunction   22a

Coordinating conjunctions specify a relationship between equal grammatical elements: *and* (addition); *but* and *yet* (contrast); *so* and *for* (cause); *or* and *nor* (choice). (See 14a.) To join independent clauses, use an appropriate coordinating conjunction preceded by a comma. (See 31a).

◆   Maya Angelou has worked as an actress and director, $\overset{\text{but}}{\wedge}$ her greatest success

came as an autobiographer and poet.

22b   Adding a semicolon

A semicolon after an independent clause signals that the following independent clause is just as important as the first one.

Semicolon alone

Two independent clauses may be joined with a semicolon alone (see 32a) only if the ideas in the clauses are closely and clearly related. If they are not, make them separate sentences or use a conjunction to clarify the relationship for the reader. (See 14a.)

◆   **For years the Federal Communications Commission has advocated legislation to allow competitive auctions for broadcast licenses; so far Congress has refused.**

Semicolons are especially useful in sentences that contain more than two independent clauses.

◆   **The sculpture was monstrous; its surface was rough and pitted, and its colors were garish.**

Here the semicolon clarifies the relationship among the three clauses. The second and third clauses together illustrate the point of the first clause.

Semicolon with a conjunctive adverb or transitional expression

Conjunctive adverbs (*finally, however,* and others listed in the box [opposite]) and **transitional expressions** (*in fact, for example,* among others; see box) can be used to join two independent clauses. To do so, you need a stronger mark of punctuation than a comma; use a semicolon.

◆   **The rebel forces were never completely defeated; moreover, they still controlled several strategic highland passes.**

Conjunctive adverbs, like other adverbs, can be moved around in a sentence. Coordinating conjunctions cannot.

CONJUNCTIVE ADVERB

YES   The mayor presented her budget plans; *however,* the council had its
own ideas.

YES   The mayor presented her budget plans; the council, *however,* had its
own ideas.

COORDINATING CONJUNCTION
YES   The mayor presented her budget plans, *but* the council had its own
ideas.

NO   The mayor presented her budget plans, the council, *but,* had its own
ideas.

Adding a colon   22c

Use a colon to join two independent clauses when the second clause explains,
elaborates, or illustrates the first.

◆   My mother gave me one important piece of advice: never wear stripes
with plaids.

Writing separate sentences   22d

The two independent clauses in a comma splice or fused sentence may read
better as two separate sentences, especially when one clause is much longer

---

CONJUNCTIVE ADVERBS

accordingly	incidentally	now
also	indeed	otherwise
anyway	instead	similarly
besides	likewise	still
certainly	meanwhile	subsequently
consequently	moreover	then
conversely	namely	therefore
finally	nevertheless	thus
furthermore	next	undoubtedly
hence	nonetheless	whereas
however		

than the other or when the two clauses are dissimilar in structure or meaning. Making two sentences out of one can emphasize the second.

◆ My last year of high school was an eventful one ~~and everything~~ $_\wedge^{. Everything}$

seemed to be happening all at once.

22e Using subordination

To show how one idea depends on another, use **subordination** to revise comma splices or fused sentences. Subordinating a clause makes it **dependent;** that is, it can no longer stand on its own.

Dependent clauses are introduced by a **subordinating conjunction** such as *after, although, as, because, if, than, whenever,* or *while* or by a **relative pronoun** such as *who, which,* or *that.* (Lists of subordinating conjunctions and relative pronouns appear on pp. 223-224 and 91.)

To use subordination, place the less important idea in a dependent clause, and choose the subordinating conjunction that best describes the relationship you want to establish between the two.

◆ $_\wedge^{Because\ the}$ ~~The~~ rain had frozen as it hit the ground $_\wedge^{,}$ the streets were slick with glare ice.

◆ The panel studied the issue $_\wedge^{that}$ ~~it~~ decided to recommend allowing the group to participate.

22f Creating one independent clause

When two independent clauses in a fused sentence or comma splice are very closely related in meaning, they can often be collapsed into one clause. If the two clauses have the same subject, try dropping the second subject and forming a compound predicate in a single independent clause. Note that no comma appears between elements of a compound predicate.

◆ This book held my attention $_\wedge^{and}$ ~~it~~ gave a lot of information about the colonial period.

Since book *and* it *are the same,* it *can be dropped. This leaves one independent clause with the compound predicate* held . . . *and gave.*

You can also turn one clause into a modifier clause.

◆   The huge chestnut oak cast a heavy blanket of shade on the ground
       dwarfing
      beneath it, ~~it dwarfed~~ the saplings nearby.
                     ^

              , my favorite author,
◆   Mary Stewart steeps her stories in historic detail. ~~She is my favorite author.~~
              ^

23 ◆ SELECTING CORRECT VERBS

Effective writing employs strong verbs that show action. Verbs can express a great deal of other information as well. They show who performed the action (**person**), indicate how many people performed the action (**number**), tell when the action occurred (**tense**), suggest the speaker's attitude toward the action (**mood**), and show whether the subject of the sentence acts or is acted upon (**voice**). When drafting, revising, and editing, select correct verb forms that best convey the meaning you intend.

Standard verb forms   23a

Except for the verb *be,* all English verbs have five forms.

The five verb forms

Two verb forms express action occurring now, in the present: (1) the **base form,** which is used with *I, we, you,* and *they;* and (2) the **-s form,** which is used for *he, she,* and *it.*

Two verb forms express action that occurred in the past: (3) the **past tense** and (4) the **past participle.** For regular verbs, the past tense and the past participle are formed by adding *-d* or *-ed* to the base form. Verbs that form the past tense and past participle in other ways are called **irregular verbs.** Past participles must be used with some form of *be* or *have.* (See auxiliary verbs, 23d.)

For all verbs, both regular and irregular, the (5) **present participle** is formed by adding *-ing* to the base form. It is used to express continuing action in both the past and the present. Like the past participle, it does not change form according to person and number. To serve as the main verb of a sentence, it must be used with a form of *be.* (See *be,* 23b.)

TERMS USED TO DESCRIBE VERBS

◆ **Person** indicates who or what performs an action. (See 23a.)

first person	the one speaking	*I read.*
second person	the one spoken to	*You read.*
third person	the one spoken about	*He reads.*

◆ **Number** indicates how many people or things perform the action. (See 23a.)

singular	one	*I think.*
plural	more than one	*We think.*

◆ **Tense** indicates the time of the action (See 23e.)

present	at this time	*I learn.*
past	before this time	*I learned.*
future	after this time	*I will learn.*

◆ **Mood** expresses the speaker's attitude toward or relation to the action (See 23f.)

indicative	states a fact or asks a question	*You are quiet.*
imperative	gives a command or a direction	*Be quiet!*
subjunctive	expresses a desire, wish, or requirement or states a condition contrary to fact	*I would be happier if you were quiet.*

◆ **Voice** indicates whether the grammatical subject of the sentence performs the action or is acted upon. (See 16c.)

active	the subject acts	*She read the book.*
passive	the subject is acted on	*The book was read by her.*

Using -*s* and -*ed* forms

Speakers of some English dialects, some nonnative speakers, and people speaking informally sometimes do not use the -*s* and -*ed* endings. In academic writing, such usage is considered nonstandard. As you edit your work, keep the following points in mind.

SUMMARY OF VERB FORMS

ESL

BASE FORM	-s FORM	PAST TENSE	PAST PARTICIPLE	PRESENT PARTICIPLE
REGULAR				
act	acts	acted	acted	acted
seem	seems	seemed	seemed	seeming
IRREGULAR				
know	knows	knew	known	knowing
eat	eats	ate	eaten	eating
hit	hits	hit	hit	hitting

The *-s* form, or third-person singular form, adds *-s* or *-es* to all verbs in the present tense except *be* and *have*.

◆   He ~~don't~~ need to study.
doesn't

The past tense of all regular verbs is created by adding *-d* or *-ed* to the base form.

◆   She walk her dog even though it was raining.
walked

Irregular verb forms   23b

Irregular verbs, those that do not form the past tense and past participle by adding *-d* or *-ed,* form their past tense and participles in many different ways. Some, including *bet, bid, burst, cost, cut, hit,* and *quit,* do not change in any form. Others have a pattern of vowel changes — for example, *ring, rang, rung; sing, sang, sung; drink, drank, drunk.*

Such patterns are not reliable enough to predict, however. When you edit, look for all the irregular verbs and consult the following chart or a dictionary.

FORMS OF IRREGULAR VERBS

BASE FORM	PAST TENSE	PAST PARTICIPLE
arise	arose	arisen
awake	awoke, awakened	awakened, awoken
be	was, were	been
bear	bore	borne
beat	beat	beaten, beat
become	became	become
begin	began	begun
bend	bent	bent
bet	bet	bet
bind	bound	bound
bite	bit	bitten
blow	blew	blown
break	broke	broken
bring	brought	brought
build	built	built
burst	burst	burst
buy	bought	bought
catch	caught	caught
choose	chose	chosen
cling	clung	clung
come	came	come
cost	cost	cost
creep	crept	crept
deal	dealt	dealt
dig	dug	dug
dive	dived, dove	dived
do	did	done
draw	drew	drawn
dream	dreamed, dreamt	dreamed, dreamt
drink	drank	drunk
drive	drove	driven
eat	ate	eaten
fall	fell	fallen
feed	fed	fed
feel	felt	felt
fight	fought	fought
find	found	found
flee	fled	fled
fly	flew	flown
forbid	forbade	forbidden

continued

BASE FORM	PAST TENSE	PAST PARTICIPLE
forget	forgot	forgotten, forgot
forgive	forgave	forgiven
freeze	froze	frozen
get	got	gotten, got
give	gave	given
go	went	gone
grow	grew	grown
hang (suspend)	hung	hung
hang (execute)	hanged	hanged
have	had	had
hear	heard	heard
hide	hid	hidden
hold	held	held
hurt	hurt	hurt
keep	kept	kept
know	knew	known
lay (put)	laid	laid
lead	led	led
leap	leapt, leaped	leapt, leaped
leave	left	left
lend	lent	lent
let (allow)	let	let
lie (recline)	lay	lain
light	lit, lighted	lit, lighted
lose	lost	lost
make	made	made
mean	meant	meant
meet	met	met
mistake	mistook	mistaken
pay	paid	paid
prove	proved	proved, proven
read	read	read
rid	rid	rid
ride	rode	ridden
ring	rang	rung
rise	rose	risen
run	ran	run
say	said	said
see	saw	seen
seek	sought	sought
send	sent	sent
set	set	set

continued

23c SEL VERB

BASE FORM	PAST TENSE	PAST PARTICIPLE
shake	shook	shaken
shoot	shot	shot
show	showed	shown, showed
shrink	shrank	shrunk
sing	sang	sung
sink	sank	sunk
sit	sat	sat
slay	slew	slain
sleep	slept	slept
speak	spoke	spoken
spin	spun	spun
spit	spit, spat	spit, spat
spring	sprang	sprung
stand	stood	stood
steal	stole	stolen
stick	stuck	stuck
sting	stung	stung
stink	stank, stunk	stunk
strike	struck	struck, stricken
swear	swore	sworn
swim	swam	swum
swing	swung	swung
take	took	taken
teach	taught	taught
tear	tore	torn
tell	told	told
think	thought	thought
throw	threw	thrown
wake	woke, waked	woken, waked, woke
wear	wore	worn
win	won	won
write	wrote	written

23c Sit and set, lie and lay

The various forms of *sit* and *set* and of *lie* and *lay* are confusing because the verb forms in each pair sound alike and are related in meaning. To distinguish between them, remember that *sit* ("to be seated") and *lie* ("to recline") are **intransitive;** that is, they never take direct objects. *Set* ("to place") and *lay* ("to put or place") are **transitive;** that is, they always take direct objects.

	no direct object
INTRANSITIVE	People *sit* outside when it's warm.
	no direct object
	I often *lie* down after lunch.
	direct object
TRANSITIVE	We *set* the plants on the porch.
	direct object
	Each morning I *lay* the mail on her desk.

BASE FORM	PAST TENSE	PAST PARTICIPLE	PRESENT PARTICIPLE
sit	sat	sat	sitting
set	set	set	setting
lie	lay	lain	lying
lay	laid	laid	laying

Be sure to use the correct form of each of these troublesome verbs.

◆   The books were just ~~laying~~ lying on the table.

◆   She asked me to come in and ~~set~~ sit with her a while.

Auxiliary verbs   23d

On some occasions, the main verb of a sentence requires the presence of one or more **auxiliary verbs,** or **helping verbs.** The auxiliary and the main verb together form a **verb phrase.**

verb phrase

auxiliary main verb

Tyler has been working.

The most common auxiliary verbs are forms of *be, have,* and *do.* These verbs help to form certain tenses (see 23e), add emphasis, ask questions, make negative statements, and form the passive voice.

PRESENT PROGRESSIVE	The student council *is considering* what to do about it.
EMPHASIS	They *do want* to go to the conference.
QUESTION	*Has* he received the blueprints?
NEGATIVE STATEMENT	He *does* not *intend* to leave without them.
PASSIVE VOICE	The blueprints *were delivered* on Friday.

Modal auxiliaries

The **modal auxiliary** verbs *can, could, may, might, must, shall, should, will,* and *would* are used with a main verb to express condition, intent, permission, possibility, obligation, or desire. These auxiliary verbs do not change form to show person, tense, number, or mood.

A modal auxiliary cannot stand alone as a main verb. It always appears with the base form of the main verb, unless the meaning of the main verb can be understood from context.

Staying in touch with friends *can become* difficult as we grow old.
Can she *dance?* Yes, she *can.*

Modal auxiliaries are also used to form certain tenses. (See 23e.)

Using auxiliary verbs correctly

In some dialects, participles serve alone as main verbs, that is, without any auxiliary verb. In standard English, however, present participles and irregular past participles need a form of the auxiliary verbs *be* or *have* to function as main verbs in a sentence.

◆   Gina is running for student council.

◆   She has spoken to everyone about it.

A form of *be*—*is, are, was, were*—along with the main verb is needed to create the passive voice.

◆   She has been a good leader in her classes.

PHRASAL MODALS

In addition to one-word modal auxiliary verbs [*can, should*], English also has **phrasal modals.**

PHRASAL MODAL	MEANING
be able to	possibility, ability
be allowed to	permission, possibility
be going to	future action, obligation, intent
be supposed to	obligation
had better	obligation
have to	obligation
have got to	obligation
ought to	obligation
used to	habitual past action

Most phrasal modals change form to show number, person, and tense. The main verbs following them do not change form.

> She *has to* take the bus today.

> They *have to* take the bus today.

The phrasal modals *had better* and *used to* do not change form.

> We *used to* spend time in the library every day.

> You *used to* spend time in the library every day.

Verb tense   23e

A verb's **tense** places its action in time and shows how that action relates in time to other actions.

The three **simple tenses** place action in the present, past, or future.

PRESENT   He *looks* happy today.

PAST   He *looked* a little depressed yesterday.

FUTURE   He *will look* different tomorrow.

The three **perfect tenses** indicate action completed by a specific time. They also place that action in the present, past, or future.

◆ **Present perfect** (action completed in the past or a completed action still occurring)

She *has looked* for the file already.

She *has looked* for it every day this week.

◆ **Past perfect** (one action completed before another past action took place)

She *had looked* for the file ten times before she found it.

◆ **Future perfect** (an action will be completed at some specific time in the future)

Once she goes through the last drawer, she *will have looked* everywhere.

The three **progressive tenses** describe continuing action in the present, past, or future.

◆ **Present progressive** (continuous or ongoing action in the present)

She *is anticipating* the holidays.

◆ **Past progressive** (continuous or ongoing action in the past with no specified end)

Before her father's illness, she *was anticipating* the holidays.

◆ **Future progressive** (continuous or ongoing action in the future which often depends on some other action or circumstance)

Once her father is better, she *will be anticipating* the holidays again.

The three **perfect progressive tenses** describe action that continues up to a specific time of completion in the present, past, or future.

◆ **Present perfect progressive** (ongoing action that began in the past and still continues)

He *has been looking* for a job since August.

◆ **Past perfect progressive** (ongoing action that was completed before some other action)

Before he found work, he *had been looking* for a job since August.

◆ **Future perfect progressive** (continuous action that will be completed at some future time)

By August, he *will have been looking* for a job for six months.

VERBS THAT DO NOT HAVE A PROGRESSIVE FORM

ESL

Verbs that express action, processes, or events are called **dynamic verbs.** Such verbs can usually be used in a progressive *-ing* form to express an action in progress.

> I *am walking* through the park.

Other verbs express attitudes, conditions, or relationships. These are called **stative verbs,** and they cannot usually be used in a progressive *-ing* form.

believe
◆ I ~~am believing~~ your story.

COMMON STATIVE VERBS

admire	dislike	like	see
agree	doubt	look	seem
appear	hate	love	smell
believe	have	need	sound
belong	hear	own	taste
contain	imagine	possess	think
cost	include	prefer	understand
disagree	know	remember	want

Sometimes these verbs are used as dynamic verbs to describe an activity or a process. In these cases, the progressive form may be used.

> Don't bother me while I *am thinking*.

> I was agreeing with you until you started the argument.

Sequence of tenses

Verb tenses throughout a piece of writing must relate logically to one another. The dominant, or prevailing, tense of a piece is its **governing tense,** which affects the choice of tense for every other verb.

In sentences, many combinations of verb tenses are possible, but the **sequence of tenses**—the way in which one verb's tense relates to the tense of others nearby—needs to describe events accurately and to make sense.

present   future

I think that you will enjoy this movie.

present   present

I know that you like foreign films.

present   past

I believe that you misunderstood me.

Changing the tense of any verb can change the meaning of a sentence, so edit carefully for verb tense.

Sequence with infinitives and participles

The tense of an infinitive or a participle must be in proper sequence with the tense of a main verb. The **present infinitive,** the base form of the verb preceded by *to* (*to know*), shows action occurring at the same time as, or later than, the action of the main verb.

Some children *like to play* with educational toys.
Liking and playing take place at the same time.

The committee *plans to vote* on the proposal next week.
Voting takes place later than planning.

The **perfect infinitive,** in which the past participle is preceded by *to have* (*to have known*), generally indicates action that occurred before the action of the main verb.

I *seem to have misplaced* my bank machine card.

The **present participle,** using the *-ing* form of the verb (*knowing*), shows action taking place at the same time as the action of the main verb.

Working feverishly, he *wrote* late into the night.

The **present perfect participle,** which includes the past participle plus *having* (*having known*), shows action completed before that of the main verb.

Having worked feverishly all night, at dawn he *saw* the sunrise.

The **past participle** (*known*) shows action taking place at the same time as or completed before the action of the main verb.

Guided by instinct, the birds *returned* as usual on March 19.
Guiding and returning take place at the same time.

Born in 1917, John F. Kennedy *became* the country's youngest president in 1961.
He was born before he became president.

SPECIAL USES OF THE PRESENT TENSE

Beyond its literal sense of action happening now, the present tense has some specialized uses.

◆ **Habitual or regular actions.** Use the present tense to describe actions that are characteristic of someone or something or that are regularly repeated.

I *run* three miles every weekday morning.

◆ **Future action.** The present tense can also indicate future action when used with other words that locate the action in the future.

He *is speaking* tomorrow night.

◆ **Universal truths.** The present tense is used to state scientific fact, a definition, or a piece of accepted wisdom.

Newton showed that the moon's orbit *is* a result of the earth's gravity.

Jarosite *is* a hydrous sulfate of iron and potassium.

◆ **Literary present.** Use the present tense when writing about literary or artistic works. When you use the literary present, make sure you use it consistently.

◆ In *The Tempest*, the wizard Prospero seems to control the very heavens.
describes   has
As Shakespeare ~~described~~ him, he ~~had~~ extraordinary powers.

23f   SEL VERB

Sequence for habitual actions and universal truths
When a dependent clause expresses a habitual action or a universal truth, the verb in the dependent clause stays in the present tense regardless of the tense in the independent clause. (See also 23f.)

He *told* me he *works* for Teledyne.

Copernicus *demonstrated* that the earth *revolves* around the sun.

Notice that shifting to the past tense in a dependent clause can suggest that something is not true or habitual.

He *told* me that he *worked* for Teledyne, but the company had no record of him.

Ptolemy *believed* the earth *was* the center of the universe.

23f   Verb mood

The **mood** of a verb expresses the speaker's attitude toward or relation to the action described.

♦   The **indicative mood,** used for facts, opinions, and questions, states things that have happened, are happening, or will happen.

He *believes* that the theory is valid.

When *did* she *graduate?*

♦   The **imperative mood,** consisting of the base form of the verb, expresses commands, orders, or directions. The subject, which is understood to be *you,* is omitted.

Sit down and *fill* out these forms.

Knead the dough until it forms a ball.

♦   The **subjunctive mood,** expresses wishes, desires, requirements, and conditions that the speaker knows not to be factual.

The subjunctive mood

Verbs in the subjunctive mood have three forms.

◆ The **present subjunctive** is the base form of the verb for all persons and numbers.

I asked that she *leave* early to avoid traffic.

◆ The **past subjunctive** uses the simple past tense for all verbs except *be*, which always uses *were*.

If you *donated* a million dollars, your college would name a hall after you.

If he *were* willing to help, what would we ask him to do?

◆ The **perfect subjunctive** uses the past perfect tense of a verb — that is, the past participle, along with *had*.

If he *had caught* the ball, the run would not have scored.

Using the subjunctive

In standard idiomatic expressions
The subjunctive appears in some idiomatic expressions.

Long live the queen!   as it were
if I were you   far be it from me

Word these and other idiomatic phrases as is customary.

After as if, as though, *or* if
Dependent clauses beginning with *if, as if,* and *as though* specify conditions that are contrary to fact. Use the past or perfect subjunctive in these cases.

He screamed as though the house *were* on fire.

If it *were* sunny, he could go out.

When the *if* clause expresses an actual condition, use the indicative mood.

If the baseball game *has begun*, we will know where to find him.

Do not use conditional auxiliaries in both the dependent clause and the main clause.

◆ If I ~~could have~~ ^had^ left earlier, I would have been on time.

To express a wish, a requirement, or a request
Use the past or perfect subjunctive in dependent clauses expressing wishes. (Sometimes the relative pronoun *that* is omitted.)

◆ I wished there ~~was~~ ^had been^ some way to help them.

When a dependent clause follows a verb that states a requirement, such as *demand, insist, require, recommend, request, suggest, specify,* or *ask,* put the verb in that clause in the present subjunctive.

◆ Courtesy requires that he comes in formal attire.

◆ Barbara insisted she ~~goes~~ ^go^ alone.

24 ◆ MAINTAINING SUBJECT-VERB AGREEMENT

Verbs and their subjects must **agree**; that is, they must correspond in **person** (first, second, or third) and **number** (singular or plural). Such agreement helps the reader interpret relations between parts of the sentence. When editing, identify the subjects of your sentences and determine verb agreement according to the following guidelines.

24a Ignoring words between subject and verb

When a word or words separate a verb from its subject, confusion can arise as to whether the subject is singular or plural. In such cases, it may help to restate the sentence in your mind in its simplest form—just subject and verb.

People interested in helping campaign for an incumbent who wants to run for reelection typically (*volunteer/volunteers?*) time as well as money.

Reduced to its simple subject and main verb, the sentence reads People volunteer; *both subject and verb are clearly plural.*

PRINCIPLES OF SUBJECT-VERB AGREEMENT

Matters of agreement often come down to a single letter: *s*. Most English nouns form plurals by adding *-s* or *-es*.

SINGULAR	PLURAL
house	houses
rock	rocks
box	boxes

Most present-tense, third-person singular verbs end in *-s* or *-es*.

I
you
we   think
they

she
he   thinks
it

The verbs *have* and *be* also end in *-s* in the third-person singular: *he is, she has.*

Here is a simple rule of thumb. If the subject ends in *-s* or *-es* (is plural), the verb probably shouldn't; if the verb ends in *-s* or *-es* (is singular), the subject probably shouldn't.

The mansions seem elegant and sophisticated.

The mansion seems elegant and sophisticated.

Nouns with irregular plurals—*children, men*—don't follow this rule, of course. These plurals still require a verb without an *-s* or *-es*: *The children walk home.* Another exception is nouns that end in *-s* but are singular: *Politics is a dirty business.* (See 24f and 24i.)

Often the words intervening between subject and verb are prepositional phrases.

The bowl of apples (*is/are?*) very tempting.

Is the subject of the verb bowl *(singular) or* apples *(plural)? Here,* apples *is the object of the preposition* of, *not the subject.* Bowl *is the subject and needs the singular verb* is.

Intervening phrases that begin with words such as *including, as well as, along with, together with,* and *in addition to* do not affect the number of a subject. Think of such phrases as parenthetical asides, and ignore them when making decisions about agreement.

◆   Mr. Johnson, along with his children, ~~were~~ waiting outside.
(was)

24b   Finding the subject when it follows the verb

When the subject follows the verb, mentally restoring normal word order to the sentence can help you find the subject.

> Underneath the freeway overpass (*huddle/huddles?*) a ramshackle collection of cardboard shelters.

Restoring normal word order yields this sentence.

> A ramshackle *collection* of cardboard shelters *huddles* underneath the freeway overpass.

Questions   In questions, part of the verb almost always precedes the subject. Find the subject and check for proper agreement.

◆   *Are* those *seats* next to you empty?

◆   Without help from his friends, *is Juan* able to finish on time?

Expletives   Sentences introduced by the expletives *here* and *there* also have inverted word order. *Here* and *there* are never subjects, so look for the subject elsewhere in the sentence.

◆   There *are* a million *stories* in the Naked City.

When *it* is used in an expletive construction, it is considered the grammatical subject of the sentence. *It* is singular, so it is always followed by a singular verb.

◆   *It is* management, not the workers, who want this change.

24c   Creating agreement with linking verbs

Linking verbs, such as *be, become, seem,* and *appear,* connect the subject of the sentence to a **subject complement** that renames, identifies, or describes the subject. As you edit sentences containing a subject complement, make sure the verb agrees with the subject, not the complement.

subject   complement

One pleasure in life is flowers.

subject   complement

Pets are another source of delight.

◆   *are*
    Her hobbies is the one thing that makes her happy.

◆   **His promises to change appears to be a waste of breath.**

Making verbs agree with subjects joined by *and*   24d

When the conjunction *and* links two or more parts of a subject, it creates a **compound subject.** Such a subject is almost always considered plural, and it thus requires a plural verb.

◆   **Peter and Patrick *play* on the lacrosse team.**

There are several important exceptions.

1 When the two elements joined by *and* comprise a single entity, the subject is considered singular and takes a singular verb.

◆   *is*
    Red beans and rice are my favorite dish.

2 If all the parts of a compound subject refer to the same person or thing, the verb is singular.

◆   *has*
    My friend, partner, and mentor have brought expertise to the firm.

3 *Each* has different effects on a verb. When *each* precedes singular subjects joined by *and*, the resulting structure is singular.

◆   *has*
    Each river, brook, and stream in the country have suffered from pollution.

4 When *each* follows a compound subject, the subject and verb are plural.

◆ The pianist and the singer each deserves special praise.

24e Making verbs agree with subjects joined by *or* and *nor*

Two or more parts of a subject joined by *or, nor, either . . . or, neither . . . not,* or *not only . . . but also* form a compound subject. When one element of a compound subject joined by *or* or *nor* is singular and another is plural, by convention the verb agrees with the part of the subject that is closer to the verb.

◆ Neither the researchers nor the *professor accepts* the results.

◆ Neither the professor nor the *researchers accept* the results.

If a singular verb sounds awkward, try rearranging the subject to put the plural part closer to the verb.

◆ ~~Two crabs or one~~ lobster ~~makes~~ an excellent dinner.
   One   *or two crabs make*

24f Creating agreement with collective nouns

Collective nouns—for example, *couple, flock, crowd, herd,* and *committee*—designate groups of people, animals, or things. Whether collective nouns take singular or plural verbs depends on whether the members of the group are seen as acting as individuals or as one unit.

1 When members of a group act as one unit, use a singular verb.

The *jury has* reached a verdict.

2 When the members of a group act individually, use a plural verb.

The *jury have* returned to their homes.

To emphasize the individual members of the group, try replacing the subject with one that is clearly plural.

◆ The *members* of the jury *have* returned to their homes.

The collective noun *number* when used in the expression *the number* refers to a group as a single unit, and it takes a singular verb. The phrase *a number* implies "more than one" or "several," and it takes a plural verb.

The number of visitors *has* been small.

A number of visitors *have* been enthusiastic about exhibits, however.

Certain collective nouns, such as *media, data, curricula, criteria,* and *phenomena,* look like singular words in English, but in fact they are plural forms of the singular *medium, datum,* and *curriculum* from Latin and *crite-rion* and *phenomenon* from Greek. Such words take plural verbs.

◆ The media ~~has~~ ^{have} continued to focus on crime even as data ~~shows~~ ^{show} cities are

becoming safer.

Check your dictionary to see whether a noun that ends in -*a* is singular or plural.

VERB AGREEMENT WITH NONCOUNT NOUNS   ◆ ESL

Count nouns name persons, places, or things that can be counted: *one apple, two oranges.* **Noncount nouns** (also called *mass nouns*) refer to things that can't be counted–*oil*–or refer to things in a sense that does not imply counting—*money, sand* (see 29a).

NONCOUNT NOUNS	ABSTRACTIONS	EMOTIONS	QUALITIES
equipment	behavior	anger	confidence
water	education	happiness	honesty
homework	health	love	integrity
money	knowledge	surprise	sincerity

Noncount nouns are usually used in the singular—most have no plural forms—and take singular verbs.

◆ Public transportations in Atlanta ~~make~~ ^{makes} getting around easy.

◆ ^{This information is} ~~These informations are~~ intended to help you when you edit.

24g SUB VERB AGR

24g Creating agreement with indefinite pronouns

Indefinite pronouns do not refer to a specific person or thing. Most of them are either always singular or always plural.

SINGULAR   Someone *has* been sleeping in my bed.

PLURAL   Luckily, few of the passengers *were* injured.

ESL **VERB AGREEMENT WITH QUANTIFIERS**

FEW **AND** *A FEW*

> *Few:* "not many" or "not enough"
>
> *A few:* "some," "several," or "a small number"

Both take plural verbs.

> Many students are taking exams today. *A few are* out sick.
>
> *Few have* failed in past years.

LITTLE **AND** *A LITTLE*

> *Little:* "not much," "not enough"
>
> *A little:* "some," "a small amount"

Both take singular verbs.

> *Little has* been done to address the problem of poverty.
>
> When it comes to jalapeños, *a little goes* a long way.

MOST **AND** *MOST OF THE*

> *Most:* "the majority"
>
> *Most of, most of the:* "the majority of"

For *most*, use a singular or plural verb, depending on the noun or pronoun it modifies or refers to. For *most of*, use a plural verb when followed by a plural noun or pronoun; use a singular verb when followed by a noncount noun or a singular pronoun.

SINGULAR   *Most* violence on TV *is* unnecessary.

SINGULAR   *Most is* encouraged by producers who want higher ratings.

PLURAL   *Most of* the neighborhood dogs *bark* in the morning.

PLURAL   *Most* dogs *are* tied up when their owners are away.

The pronouns *everyone, everybody,* and *someone* are singular, even though people often treat them as plural (see 25b).

◆   Everybody wears $\overset{a}{\underset{\wedge}{}}$ heavy coats in this weather.

To determine *whether some, any, all, more, most, what,* and *which* are singular or plural, look at their meaning and the nouns to which they refer.

◆   Some of the team $\overset{are}{\underset{\wedge}{\text{is}}}$ planning to evaluate our information using a computer.

All is plural when it means "the entire group." It is singular when it means "everything" or "the only thing."

All are required to take the foreign language exams.

All I have *is* a rough idea of how to proceed.

When an indefinite pronoun renames a specific antecedent, the number of the antecedent determines the number of the pronoun.

◆   Of the *time* that remained, more *was* spent arguing than making decisions. *Antecedent is* time.

COMMON INDEFINITE PRONOUNS

ALWAYS SINGULAR

someone	another	nobody	everybody	either
somebody	anybody	no one	everyone	neither
something	anyone	nothing	everything	each
	anything			much
				one

EITHER SINGULAR OR PLURAL

some	any	none	all	more
				most
				what

ALWAYS PLURAL

few	both	several	many	others

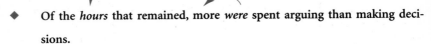

◆ Of the *hours* that remained, more *were* spent arguing than making decisions.
Antecedent is hours.

Used alone, *none* is always singular. Followed by a prepositional phrase, however, *none* may be singular or plural depending on the object of the phrase. However, some experts argue that because *none* means "not one" or "no one," it should be treated as singular. When in doubt, use a singular verb.

The birds all escaped, and *none was* recaptured.

24h Making verbs agree with *who, which,* and *that*

To decide whether a verb following the **relative pronoun** *who, which,* or *that* should be singular or plural, find the word to which the pronoun refers—the **antecedent**—and use a singular or plural verb.

plural antecedent

◆ Barbara and Robin, who wants to join the project, have applied in writing.

singular antecedent

slips

◆ A bale of shingles that slip off the roof could hurt someone.

Relative pronouns can be troublesome when they follow *one of the* or *the only one of the.* If the pronoun refers to *one,* it is singular, and so is the verb. If it refers to whatever comes after *one of the* or *the only one of the,* it is plural, and so is the verb.

◆ The only *one* of the women who *disagrees* is Maria.

◆ One of the *areas* that *have* suffered is voter participation.

24i Creating agreement with nouns ending in *-s,* with nouns that specify amounts, with titles, and with words used as words

Using verbs with nouns ending in *-s*

Many nouns ending in *-s,* such as *statistics, politics, economics, athletics, measles, news, acoustics,* and *aesthetics,* appear to be plural but take singular verbs when used to mean a field of study, a body of ideas, a disease, or a profession. They are plural, however, when they refer to specific instances, activities, or characteristics.

Economics *is* sometimes called "the dismal science."

The economics of the project *make* no sense.

Nouns such as *pants, sunglasses, binoculars,* and *scissors* refer to single objects but take plural verbs.

◆ The binoculars ~~was~~ *were* useful for spotting birds.

When you use *pair of,* as in *pair of pants,* however, the verb is singular because the subject is now *pair,* not *pants.*

◆ The pair of pants you wanted ~~are~~ *is* ready.

Using verbs with nouns that specify amounts

Words that describe amounts of time, money, distances, measurements, or percentages can take singular or plural verbs depending on whether the subject is considered as a group of individuals (plural) or as a single unit or a sum (singular).

Four hours *have* passed since we saw each other.
Hours pass one at a time, individually.

Fifteen minutes *is* too long to keep the boss waiting.
Minutes here are considered as a block of time.

Using singular verbs with titles, with words used as words, and with terms

Use singular verbs with the titles of books, plays, and movies, even when they are plural in form. The name of a company or firm also takes a singular verb.

"Shake, Rattle and Roll" *was* recorded by Bill Haley and the Comets.

General Motors *is* an important employer in Michigan.

In discussing a word used as word or as a term, use a singular verb even if the word is plural.

Hyenas was what my father lovingly called us children.

SOME NOUNS THAT TAKE PLURAL VERBS

◆   Some collective nouns derived from adjectives refer to groups of people: *the wealthy, the homeless.* These nouns are considered plural and take plural verbs.

   The young often *ignore* the advice of their elders.

◆   The noun *people* is always plural and takes a plural verb. To indicate the singular, use *person.*

   People are wondering who will be the next governor.

   That *person is* asking where to register to vote.

◆   The noun *police* is always plural. It never refers to only one person. T*he police* is also always plural. The article *a* is never used before *police.* To indicate one member of the police force, use *police officer.*

   Police have been stationed in front of the courthouse all day.

   A *police officer is* always on duty inside the courthouse.

25 ◆ CHOOSING PRONOUNS

A **pronoun** is a word that substitutes for a noun or another pronoun. Choosing correct pronoun forms helps convey your meaning clearly.

25a   Pronoun reference to antecedents

The word or words to which a pronoun refers is called its **antecedent.** The word to which a pronoun refers must be clear. Pronouns that have more than one possible antecedent can be confusing. In the sentence *Marco met Roger as he arrived at the gym,* the pronoun *he* might refer to either *Marco* or *Roger.* Edit such a sentence so that the pronoun has only one possible antecedent, or eliminate the pronoun.

◆   *Roger*
   Marco met Roger as ~~he~~ arrived at the gym.

◆   *As*   *, he met Roger.*
   Marco ~~met Roger as he~~ arrived at the gym.

   In sentences that involve more than one person and verbs such as *said* and *told,* you can often use a direct quotation to clarify the pronoun reference.

◆ Barbara told Stephanie that she passed the test."

(handwritten annotation above "that she": , "you)

Providing explicit antecedents

In general, a pronoun's antecedent should be explicitly stated. (Indefinite pronouns such as *somebody* and *everybody* are exceptions. See 24g.)

◆ Interviews with several television news people made it seem like a fascinating career.

(handwritten annotation above "made it": reporting)

The implied antecedent television news reporting *does not appear in the sentence, so a noun must be substituted for the pronoun.*

A pronoun must refer to an antecedent that is a noun, a noun phrase, or another pronoun. It cannot refer to the possessive form of a noun or to an adjective. Make sure that any pronoun you use refers to a grammatically acceptable antecedent that is explicitly stated.

◆ The ~~committee's~~ bitter argument reflected badly on all of them.

(handwritten annotation above: among the committee members)

A possessive form of a noun or pronoun can be an antecedent, however, if the pronoun that refers to it is also possessive.

◆ The bitter argument ~~among the committee members~~ reflected badly on all its members.

(handwritten annotation: committee's)

UNNECESSARY PRONOUNS   ◈ ESL

Speakers of some dialects use a pronoun immediately following its antecedent. In academic writing or when paraphrasing such a speaker, don't use the extra pronoun unless you are deliberately trying to achieve a colloquial effect.

◆ After Ann used it, the wagon/ ~~it~~ just seemed to fall to pieces.

Do not use a personal pronoun (*he, her*) and a relative pronoun (*who, whom, which, that*) in the same clause to refer to the same antecedent.

◆ I know the teacher whom my sister had ~~him~~ for history.

◆ I corrected the errors that you pointed ~~them~~ out to me today.

Pronoun reference for *this, that,* **and** *which*

This, that, and *which* can be used as adjectives—*I don't like this one*—
or as pronouns—*That is my favorite.* Confusion can arise when *this* or *that,*
used alone, has no clear antecedent. You can usually clarify a pronoun reference by explicitly restating its antecedent.

◆   No one has suggested taxing health care. This is unlikely.
      tax
      What is unlikely? The tax, not the suggestion.

When *which* and *that* introduce clauses, they are called **relative pronouns.** A relative pronoun usually introduces a clause that immediately follows the pronoun's antecedent.

◆   This book, *which* I heartily recommend, is out of print.

Confusion can arise if other sentence elements intervene or if the relative pronoun has more than one possible antecedent. To clarify the pronoun
reference, add an unambiguous antecedent or replace *which* or *that* with another construction.

◆   She took the situation seriously, which I found laughable.
      a response

◆   She took the situation seriously, which I found laughable.
      , although   it

◆ **WP TIP** Use the search function to find *this, that,* and *which* in your
papers. Make sure these pronouns always have explicit antecedents.

ESL   **USING *THIS* AND *THAT***

The **demonstrative adjectives** *this* and *that* mean "near" and "far," respectively. This concept of distance applies to space, to time, and to
relative importance.

SPACE   *This* vase right here is a better choice than *that one* in the back.

TIME   *That* article I showed you last week was too technical. *This* book I
just found is better.

IMPORTANCE   *This* testimony is central to our case, but we may not use *that*
testimony.

Vague reference with *it, they,* or *you*

In casual speech, people often use *it, they,* or *you* without a clear antecedent. In academic writing, use specific constructions.

◆ ~~It said on~~ the news this morning *According to* that the game was canceled.

◆ *The club doesn't* ~~They don't~~ let anyone in without a shirt or shoes.

You presents another special case. When your tone need not be entirely formal, you may use *you* to refer to the reader—as we just did. In academic writing, however, avoid using *you* to mean "people in general." One alternative is to use an indefinite pronoun such as *one* or *someone.*

◆ If this rain keeps up, ~~you~~ *one* could see flooding in low-lying areas.

Who, which, or *that?*

The relative pronouns *who, which,* and *that* are used in similar ways, but in different contexts.

1 Use *who* for people or for animals with names.

Black Beauty is a horse *who* lives in a world that no longer exists.

2 Use *which* and *that* for objects, ideas, unnamed animals, and anonymous people or groups of people.

This is the policy *that* the administration wants to enforce.

He tried to rope the last steer, *which* twisted to avoid him.

The tribes *that* built these cities have long since vanished.

Avoid using *which* to refer to a person.

◆ He met scores of interesting people in the logging camps, of ~~which~~ *whom* Jake was the most memorable.

In talking about an inanimate object, if *of which* sounds awkward, use *whose.*

◆ This is an idea ~~the~~ time ~~of which~~ *whose* has come.

CHOOSING BETWEEN *THAT* AND *WHICH*

◆ *That* always introduces a **restrictive** modifier, one that is necessary to identify what it modifies. A *that* clause is never set off by commas.

Ann's money *that was in a trust fund* has been embezzled.

The modifier that was in a trust fund *restricts, or limits, the phrase it modifies,* Ann's money. *It implies that she has more money elsewhere.*

◆ A **nonrestrictive** modifier, one that merely adds more information but is not necessary to identify or limit, must be set off by commas and must be introduced by *which.*

Ann's money, *which was in a trust fund,* has been embezzled.

The modifier which was in a trust fund *does not restrict the subject,* Ann's money, *all of which has been embezzled. The modifier merely adds information about the subject.*

◆ *That* can only be used for restrictive modifiers, but *which* can be used for nonrestrictive or restrictive modifiers.

When in the course of human events it becomes necessary for one people to dissolve the political bonds *which* have connected them with another . . . a decent respect for the opinions of mankind requires that they should declare the reasons *which* impel them to the separation. [Italics added.]
Declaration of Independence

Just to avoid confusion, some writers choose to use *which* only for nonrestrictive modifiers.

◆ *Who* may introduce both restrictive and nonrestrictive modifiers.

NONRESTRICTIVE Americans, *who* eat a richer diet than Europeans, have higher rates of heart disease.

RESTRICTIVE Americans *who* cut down on fatty foods may live longer than those *who* don't.

25b Agreement with antecedents

Personal pronouns (see 25c) should **agree** with, or match, their antecedents in number, person, and gender.

◆ Personal pronouns should agree with their antecedents in number—singular or plural.

◆ A *pronoun* is singular if *it* has a singular antecedent.

◆ *Pronouns* are plural if *they* have plural antecedents.

- Personal pronouns should match their antecedents in person—first person (*I, we, my, our*) second person (*you, your*), or third person (*he, she, it, they, his, her, its, their*).

    - Call *me Ishmael.*

    - When the *tree* fell, *it* shook the forest.

- Singular personal pronouns should match their antecedents in gender—feminine, masculine, or neuter. No distinction is made in the plural.

    - *Mrs. Shah* held the door for *her* daughter.

    - *The Shahs* were on *their* way to the antique show.

Agreement with antecedents joined by *and*

A **compound antecedent** has two or more parts joined by a conjunction such as *and, or,* or *nor*. Elements linked by *and* are considered plural. Any pronoun that refers to a compound antecedent, then, is plural.

- The book and the folder *are* in their places on the shelf.

There are a few exceptions. Use a singular pronoun to refer to a compound antecedent joined by *and* when (1) a compound antecedent is preceded by *each* or *every*, (2) the parts of a compound antecedent refer to the same person or thing, or (3) the elements linked by *and* constitute a single entity.

- *Each* book and folder is in *its* place on the shelf.

- As my *sociology professor and thesis advisor, she* helped me select this semester's courses.

- *Beans and rice* is my favorite dish; *it* always tastes good on cold days.

Agreement with antecedents joined by *or* and *nor*

The conjunctions *or* and *nor* can also join two or more parts of an antecedent to form a compound antecedent. When all parts of the antecedent are singular, the pronoun is singular.

- Either the assessor's *office* or the *court* will have to cut *its* budget.

When one element of a compound antecedent is singular and one is plural, convention has the pronoun agree with the antecedent closer to it.

◆   Either the equipment failures or the bad *weather* will take *its* toll.

If the resulting sentence sounds awkward, try placing the plural antecedent last to receive a plural pronoun.

◆   Either the bad weather or the equipment *failures* will take *their* toll.

Agreement with collective nouns

Collective nouns, such as *couple, flock, crowd, herd,* and *committee,* are singular in form yet refer to groups that can be regarded as plural. In these cases, the meaning of the sentence determines which pronoun to use.

Use a plural pronoun if members of the group are acting separately.

◆   The *crew* gathered ~~its~~ their belongings and prepared to leave the ship.

Use a singular pronoun if the group acts as a unit.

◆   The *flock* rose suddenly from the pond and took up ~~their~~ its usual formation.

◆   **WP TIP** Search for collective nouns you use frequently and examine each instance for correct pronoun-antecedent agreement.

Agreement with indefinite pronouns

An indefinite pronoun—*anyone, all, both, most, either*—does not require an explicit antecedent because it does not refer to any specific person or thing. Problems arise when an indefinite pronoun serves as the antecedent for yet another pronoun. Should that second pronoun be singular or plural?

◆   We sampled the grapes and the blackberries. *Both* were at the height of *their* seasons.

◆   *None* of the fruit was disappointing in *its* taste or *its* appearance.

(For use of indefinite pronouns and nonsexist language, see 19c.)

Some indefinite pronouns are always singular: *anyone, everyone, someone, anybody, everybody, somebody, anything, everything, something, either, neither, each, nothing, much, one,* and *no one.* Pronouns that refer to them should also be singular.

Someone has lost *his* necktie.

These pronouns remain singular even when followed by a prepositional phrase with a plural object.

> *Neither* of these books has *its* original cover.

Be careful when *each* is used with compounds joined by *and*. When it precedes such a compound, *each* is an indefinite pronoun and the subject of the clause. The pronoun that follows should agree with the subject of the clause.

INDEFINITE PRONOUN *Each* Boy Scout leader and guide carried *his* own pack.

When it follows such a compound, however, *each* is an adjective, and the compound itself is the subject of the clause.

ADJECTIVE The Boy Scout leader and the guide *each* carried *their* own packs.

The indefinite pronouns *few, many, both,* and *several* are always plural. Pronouns that refer to them should be plural as well.

> *Few* of the students have completed *their* work.

The indefinite pronouns *some, any, all, more, most,* and *none* can be singular or plural depending on their context.

> In a survey of young voters, *some* said *they* were conservative.

> The money is still in the safe. *Some* is still in *its* bags.

> *None* of the money could be traced to *its* owners.

> *None* of the coins could be identified from *their* markings.

◆ **WP TIP** If you have trouble with a particular indefinite pronoun, search for and highlight each appearance so that you can locate its antecedent and check on its agreement.

Pronoun case 25c

In speaking, we say *I saw him* rather than *me saw him,* and *my car* rather than *I car,* without ever thinking about it. These changes of form, called **case**, help indicate a pronoun's role in a sentence.

25c   CHOS PRO

PRONOUN CASE

PERSONAL PRONOUNS

SINGULAR	SUBJECTIVE	OBJECTIVE	POSSESSIVE
1st person	I	me	my/mine
2nd person	you	you	your/yours
3rd person			
Masculine	he	him	his
Feminine	she	her	her/hers
Neuter	it	it	its

PLURAL			
1st person	we	us	our/ours
2nd person	you	you	you/yours
3rd person	they	them	their/theirs

INTERROGATIVE OR RELATIVE PRONOUNS*

	SUBJECTIVE	OBJECTIVE	POSSESSIVE
	who	whom	whose
	whoever	whomever	—

*These pronouns are called **interrogative pronouns** when used to ask questions: *Whose book is that?* They are called **relative pronouns** when used to introduce dependent clauses: *The writer whose book we read visited the university.*

◆ The **subjective case** (*I, he,* or *she,* for example) indicates a subject—a person or thing that performs the action of the sentence.

◆ The **objective case** (*me, him, her*) indicates an object—a person or thing that receives the action.

◆ The **possessive case** (*mine, ours, his, hers, theirs*) shows possession or ownership.

Compound elements

Joining two or more words by *and, or,* or *nor*—creating a compound element—does not affect their case. Many of us use the wrong case after *and* when we speak. It is not uncommon to hear errors such as *Joe and <u>me</u> were talking* or *He talked to Joe and <u>I</u>.* As you edit, determine whether the pronouns you have used are subjects or objects, and then make sure you have them in the right case.

Sometimes it helps to simplify a compound structure by mentally dropping all but the pronoun in question. It is easy to see that _Me was talking_ or _He talked to I_ is not right.

Subjective case for compound subjects and subject complements

A subject with two or more parts joined by *and, or,* or *nor* is a **compound subject.** Both parts of a compound subject should use the subjective case. When the first-person pronoun (*I*) is one part of a compound subject, put it last.

◆   Todd and ~~me~~ pruned the tall white pine.
                 I

◆   Ralph, Otto, and ~~him~~ planned to go bowling tonight.
                       he

A **subject complement** follows a **linking verb** (see 24c) and renames the subject or completes its meaning in the sentence. As with subjects, both parts of a compound structure use the subjective case.

◆   The real winners were my father and ~~me~~.
                                         I

If you have trouble choosing between the subjective and objective case following a linking verb, turn the sentence around and simplify the compound complement to a single pronoun: *I was the real winner.*

Objective case for compound objects

An object with two or more parts joined by *and, or,* or *nor* is a **compound object.** Use the objective case for each part of a compound object, whether it is the object of a verb or the object of a preposition.

◆   The judges chose neither ~~he~~ nor ~~I~~.
                              him   me

◆   I spoke to Nancy and ~~they~~ about the competition.
                          them

> *To clarify the correct choice quickly in your mind, mentally drop all but one pronoun from the compound object:* The judges chose him. The judges chose me. I spoke to them.

Even though it sometimes sounds awkward, the prepositions *between* and *among,* like all others, take objects in the objective case.

◆   Among the chairman, the other committee members and ~~I~~, there was little
                                                        me

enthusiasm for that battle.

USING THE PRONOUN CASES

SUBJECTIVE CASE

Use the **subjective case** (*I, you, he, she, it, we, they, who, whoever*) for the subject of a sentence or the subject of a dependent clause.

> *We* planted a winter garden.

> James knew *who* would answer.

Also use the subjective case for a subject complement—a term that follows a linking verb (*be, seem, become, appear*) and renames the subject.

> It is *they* who will benefit most.

OBJECTIVE CASE

Use the **objective case** (*me, you, him, her, it, us, them, whom, whomever*) for the object of a verb or a preposition.

> The judges chose *her* first.

> They awarded the prize to *us*.

POSSESSIVE CASE

Use the **possessive case** to show ownership, possession, or connection. The adjective form (*my, your, his, her, its, their, whose*) is used before a noun.

> This is *my* coat.

> We heard the singer *whose* songs we liked.

The noun form (*mine, yours, his, hers, theirs*) can stand alone, without a noun.

> *Hers* is the black one.

> I traded *mine* for *his*.

Pronoun case for appositives

An **appositive** is a noun or pronoun that renames a preceding noun. Pronouns used as appositives must be in the same case as the nouns they rename.

> The *losers*—Jimmy and *I*—wanted a rematch.
>
> *The appositive renames the subject, losers, so the pronoun is in the subjective case.*

It was the victors, Paul and *he,* who wanted to leave well enough alone.

The appositive Paul and he *renames the subject complement,* victors, *so he is in the subjective case.*

They asked the medalists, Barbara and *me,* to pose for a picture.

The appositive Barbara and me *renames* medalists, *the object of the verb* asked, *so* me *is in the objective case.*

To decide whether to use the subjective or objective case in such sentences, simplify the construction and substitute the appositive pronoun for the noun: *They asked me to pose for a picture.*

Us or *we* before a noun?

The case of a pronoun immediately followed by a noun depends on whether the noun serves as a subject or an object.

subjective case

We

SUBJECT   Us hikers were worried about the weather.

objective case

us

OBJECT   They told we hikers not to worry.

If you drop the noun following *us* or *we,* you can make the right choice: *We were worried about the weather. They told us not to worry.*

Pronoun case with verb forms

Participles, gerunds, and infinitives are called **verbals** because they are derived from verbs. (See 29a.) Verbals can have objects, and when a pronoun serves as the object of a verbal, it is in the objective case.

I saw Robert greeting *him.*

Seeing *her* made the holiday complete.

To know *him* is to love *him.*

Before -ing *words*

The case of a pronoun that appears before an -*ing* verbal depends on whether the verbal is used as a noun or a modifier. Both of the following sentences are correct, depending on the meaning intended.

199

He heard *their* shouting.

The gerund shouting *is used as a noun, in this case the object of the verb. There-fore, the possessive adjective* their *modifies* shouting.

He heard *them* shouting.

Them is the object of the verb, so them *is in the objective case.*

Use the possessive case for pronouns preceding verbals used as nouns, and use the objective case for pronouns preceding verbals used as modifiers.

◆   My
      M̧e leaving made them all sad.

◆   me
      He heard my leaving just before midnight.

Before infinitives

A pronoun just before an infinitive uses the objective case.

They want *her* to help.

It was hard for *him* to agree.

Case after *than* or *as*

The subordinating conjunctions *than* and *as* often mark **elliptical con-structions,** clauses with one or more words intentionally omitted. (See 17d.) Understanding exactly what is omitted is the key to choosing the correct case for a pronoun following *than* or *as*. Here the choice of case can really affect meaning.

She likes her dog better than (she likes) *me*.

Me is the object of the omitted verb likes.

She likes her dog better than *I*. (do)

I is the subject of the omitted verb.

The preposition *like* is sometimes used as a conjunction in place of *as* in casual speech and in advertising: *Winston tastes good like a cigarette should.* In academic writing avoid using *like* as a conjunction.

◆   the way
      I tried to do it like he does.

◆   as
      I tried to do it like he does.

Who or *whom?*

The distinction between *who* and *whom* and between *whoever* and *whomever* has all but disappeared from everyday speech. In writing, remember to use *who* and *whoever* for subjects, *whom* and *whomever* for objects.

To introduce questions

Who, *whom*, *whoever*, and *whomever* act as interrogative pronouns when they introduce questions. When the pronoun is the subject of the question, use *who* or *whoever*. Sometimes it helps to turn the question into a statement by substituting *he* or *him*. If *he* fits, use *who*. If *him* fits, use *whom*.

Who had the authority to enter the building at night?
He *had the authority, so use* who.

When a pronoun is the object of the verb or the object of a preposition, use *whom* or *whomever*.

To *whom* are you speaking?
You *are speaking to* him, *so use* whom.

Be careful when the preposition is left at the end of a question but its object comes first.

Whom did you give it to?

Placing the preposition with its object makes the choice clear.

To *whom* did you give it?

In independent clauses

Who, *whom*, *whoever*, and *whomever* are relative pronouns when they introduce dependent clauses. Choose the case according to the pronoun's role in the clause, not according to the role of the clause in the rest of the sentence. Use *who* and *whoever* when the pronoun is the subject of its clause.

I know *who* found your books.
Who *is the subject of the clause* who found your books.

Use whom and whomever when the pronoun is the object of its clause.

That woman, *whom* I met last week, won the Nobel prize for chemistry.
Whom *is the object of the verb* met, *even though it renames the subject of the main clause*, woman.

To check the case of a relative pronoun, turn the dependent clause into a question introduced by the pronoun, then answer that question with a personal pronoun. Again, if *he* or *she* fits, use *who*; if *him* or *her* fits, use *whom*.

◆   I want a list of everyone ~~whom~~ visited the plant today.
> who

> Who *or* whom *visited the plant today?* He, she, *or* they *did. Use the subjective case* who.

◆   The police will talk to ~~whoever~~ they want to interview.
> whomever

> Who *or* whom *do the police want?* They want to interview *him, her, or* them. *Use the objective case* whomever.

◆ **WP TIP** Search for *who, whom, whoever,* and *whomever,* and evaluate each instance. If you tell the computer to search for [space]*who* with no space after the *o,* it will find all four pronouns (along with some other *who-* words) with one extended search.

Using reflexive pronouns

A **reflexive pronoun** reflects the action of the verb back toward the subject, making it clear that the object and the subject of the verb are one and the same. The reflexive pronouns are *myself, yourself, himself, herself, itself, ourselves, yourselves,* and *themselves.*

Never use a reflexive pronoun as a subject.

◆   My partner and ~~myself~~ were invited to the reception.
> I

Use a reflexive pronoun as the object of a verb only when it names the same person as the subject.

◆   John cut ~~him~~ with the scissors.
> himself

> Himself *makes it clear that the person who has been cut is the same as the person who did the cutting.*

◆   John cut ~~myself~~ with the scissors when he handed them to me.
> me

> *The subject of the verb* cut *is John. The words* myself *and* John *do not name the same person, so* myself *is incorrect.*

Use a reflexive pronoun as the object of a preposition only when it names the same person as an earlier noun or pronoun in the sentence.

◆   I speak only for ~~me~~, not for my research partner.
> myself

> Myself *is correct because* I *precedes it in the sentence.*

◆   As for Toya and ~~myself~~, we want to work in Chicago after we graduate.

me

Myself *is incorrect because* I *or* me *does not precede it.*

◆ **WP TIP** Search for *myself* or any other reflexive pronouns. Check to make sure you have used these pronouns correctly.

26 ◆ USING ADJECTIVES AND ADVERBS

Adjectives and adverbs *modify*—that is, they describe, identify, or limit the meaning of—other words. **Modifiers** can enrich description, transforming a simple sentence like *The hikers were lost* into a more engaging one like *The exhausted hikers were hopelessly lost.*

Choosing adjectives or adverbs   26a

Adjectives modify nouns and pronouns.

noun   noun   noun

◆   Hector is a fine father who has gentle hands and abundant patience with

noun

crying babies.

pronoun

◆   He is loving, careful, and dependable.

Adverbs modify verbs, adjectives, other adverbs, and sometimes whole clauses.

verb   adjective   adverb   verb

◆   He often takes care of the baby at truly late hours and nearly always quiets

her quickly.

clause

◆   Amazingly, he loves doing it.

ESL **ORDER OF ADJECTIVES**

The order of adjectives preceding nouns is somewhat flexible, but some types of adjectives typically occur before others. For example, an adjective describing size occurs before one describing color: *the large white house* rather than *the white large house.*

The following list shows the typical order of adjectives before nouns. Of course, you generally should avoid long strings of adjectives.

1 **Determiner:** *a, the, her, Bob's, that, these, a few*
2 **Order:** *first, next, third*
3 **Evaluation:** *good, pretty, happy, interesting*
4 **Appearance—size:** *big, small, minuscule*
5 **Appearance—shape:** *oblong, squarish, round*
6 **Appearance—condition:** *broken, shiny*
7 **Appearance—age:** *old, young, new*
8 **Appearance—color:** *blue, green, magenta*
9 **Material:** *wooden, cotton*
10 **Noun used as adjective:** *flower* garden

1   2   6   7   10
One never forgets that first shiny new sports car.

1   4   5   9
A few large square wooden boxes were stacked on the floor.

Suffixes

Many adjectives and adverbs are formed by adding **suffixes,** or endings, to other words.

◆ Adjectives are often formed by adding endings such as *-able, -ful,* and *-ish* to nouns and verbs: *acceptable, beautiful, foolish.*

◆ Adverbs are often formed by adding *-ly* to an adjective: *nearly, amazingly, brilliantly.* However, an *-ly* suffix does not always mean that a word is an adverb. A number of adjectives end in *-ly: brotherly, friendly, lovely.* And many adverbs do not end in *-ly.*

Commonly confused modifiers

In casual speech, adjectives are sometimes used instead of adverbs to modify verbs: *It fit real well* instead of *It fit really well.* As you edit, take care to use the correct forms of the following pairs.

Bad *and* badly

In academic writing, use *bad* only as an adjective with a linking verb and *badly* as an adverb with any other verb.

◆ She looked as though she felt ~~badly~~. *bad*

◆ They were playing so ~~bad~~ that I left at halftime. *badly*

Good *and* well

Good is always an adjective; *well* can be an adjective meaning "healthy" or an adverb meaning "skillfully."

Good and *well* are often confused in speaking, partly because they share the same comparative and superlative forms: *good, better, best; well, better, best.* Check these two words carefully when you edit.

◆ She sings ~~good~~ enough to get the lead. *well*

◆ The hat looked ~~well~~ on my mother. *good*

Real *and* really

Real is properly used as an adjective meaning "genuine, true, not illusory." *Really* is an adverb meaning "truly" or "very." These meanings are so closely related that you may sometimes use *real* as an adverb in casual speech. In writing, however, use *really* to modify adjectives and adverbs.

◆ He believed the interview was ~~real~~ important to his job prospects. *really*

Less *and* fewer

Less and *fewer* are both adjectives, but they function in different ways. *Less* describes something considered as a whole unit: *less hope, less money. Fewer* describes quantities that can be counted: *fewer hopes, fewer dollars.*

◆ The house would lose *less* heat if ~~less~~ windows were open. *fewer*

◆ **WP TIP** Search for any of the above words and check the way you have used them in each instance.

Using adjectives after linking verbs 26b

A modifier that follows a linking verb (see 24c) modifies the subject of the sentence, not the verb, to create what is known as a **subject complement.** Because a subject complement modifies a subject—a noun or a pronoun—it must be an adjective.

◆   I   linking verb *felt*   adjective *bad*   about not helping her.

◆   The samples   linking verb *seemed*   adjective *cool.*

Some linking verbs, such as *appear, look, smell, taste,* and *sound,* can also function as action verbs. In such cases, the words that modify them are adverbs.

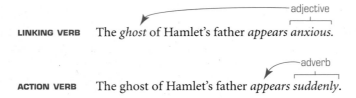

LINKING VERB   The *ghost* of Hamlet's father *appears anxious.* — adjective

ACTION VERB   The ghost of Hamlet's father *appears suddenly.* — adverb

26c Avoiding double negatives

In English, one negative modifier (*no, not, never*) is sufficient to change the meaning of a sentence. When a negative modifier is paired with another negative word or phrase (*no, neither, none, nobody,* or *nothing*), the two negatives cancel each other out: *I didn't have no money* literally means that I must have had *some* money.

Double negatives are common in some dialects, but in standard English, use only one negative modifier to make a statement negative.

◆   I ~~didn't have~~ no money.   *had*

◆   I didn't have ~~no~~ money.

Adverbs such as *hardly, barely,* and *scarcely* have negative meanings and do not need an additional negative word such as *no* or *not.*

◆   He has ~~not~~ barely gotten started.

◆   I ~~don't~~ have hardly any money.

However, to emphasize the negative aspects of a statement, you may deliberately use two negatives.

He said it was *not* true that he had *no* money.

USING NEGATIVES: *NOT* VERSUS *NO*

Use *not* to express negation in these situations.

◆   To make a verb phrase negative.

I do *not* agree with the author's opinion.

◆   With forms of *any* or with number modifiers.

There are *not any* places to sit in the theater.

There is *not one* place to sit in the theater.

◆   To negate the indefinite pronouns *everybody* and *everyone*.

Not everyone would have dealt with that problem so easily.

◆   To emphasize negation, you can use *no* in front of a noun instead of *not* in a verb phrase.

NEGATIVE	I do *not* see *any* reason to assume he is lying.
EMPHATIC NEGATIVE	I see *no* reason to assume he is lying.

Using comparatives and superlatives   **26d**

Both adjectives and adverbs describe qualities or properties that can be stated on their own or compared.

The **positive form,** the basic form of an adjective or adverb, describes a quality or property: *large, delicious, dirty, late, eagerly.*

The **comparative form** makes a comparison between two people or two things. Most one-syllable adjectives and adverbs add -*er* (*ier*): *smarter, funnier.* Adjectives of three or more syllables, adjectives ending in -*ful,* adverbs of two or more syllables, and most adverbs ending in -*ly,* however, generally use *more* to form comparatives: *more impressive, more sharply.*

She arrived *later* than I did but was greeted *more warmly.*

My schedule is *tighter* than it had been, so I am *more eager* to start.

The **superlative form** makes a comparison among three or more people or things. Adjectives that use -*er* in the comparative use -*est* in the superlative. Adjectives and adverbs that use *more* in the comparative use *most* in the superlative.

Of all their guests, she arrived *latest* and was greeted *most warmly.*

My schedule is the *tightest* it has ever been, so I am *most eager* to start.

ARTICLES WITH COMPARATIVES AND SUPERLATIVES

◆ Do not use an article (*a, an,* or *the*) when a comparative adjective is used by itself.

> This house is *larger* than the other one.

> But

> A *larger* house almost always requires more work.

DEFINITE ARTICLE *THE*

◆ Use *the* when a comparative or superlative adjective is followed by a specific noun or pronoun renaming a specific noun.

> This house is *the larger one.*

> This house is *the largest one.*

◆ The use of *the* is optional when the comparative or superlative adjective is used without a noun but the noun is implied.

> Of the two houses, which one is *the larger?*

> The larger house *is what is implied.*

> Of the two houses, which one is *larger?*

INDEFINITE ARTICLES *A/AN*

◆ Use *a* or *an* with comparative adjectives that modify a nonspecific noun.

> A *larger* house usually requires more work.

> The meaning is "any larger house."

◆ Use *a* or *an* with superlative adjectives only if the superlative means "very."

> That was *a most refreshing* glass of grapefruit juice.

> The meaning is "very refreshing."

When you choose a comparative or a superlative modifier, you also tell your reader something important about the number of units you are comparing.

Of the brothers, Joe was the *stronger* athlete. (*There are two brothers.*)

Of the brothers, Joe was the *strongest* athlete. (*There are at least three brothers.*)

Negative comparisons are formed using *less* for comparatives and *least* for superlatives: *less often, least hopeful.*

Don't use double comparatives or superlatives. When forming comparatives, use either *-er* or *more,* not both. When forming superlatives, use either *-est* or *most,* not both.

◆ After eating, he felt ~~more~~ better.

Irregular comparatives and superlatives

A few adjectives and adverbs form their comparatives and superlatives in different ways.

◆ Paul did ~~gooder~~ better work today.

Adjectives: good, better, best

◆ She said she felt ~~weller~~ better.

Adverbs: well, better, best

Absolute modifiers do not have comparative or superlative forms. The positive forms of *perfect, unique, equal, essential, final, total,* and *absolute,* for example, imply the superlative.

◆ The turbo engine makes this car ~~even more~~ unique.

IRREGULAR ADJECTIVES AND ADVERBS

POSITIVE	COMPARATIVE	SUPERLATIVE
good	better	best
well	better	best
bad	worse	worst
badly	worse	worst
ill	worse	worst
many	more	most
much	more	most
some	more	most
little*	less	least

*Little meaning "not much" is irregular. *Little* meaning "small" is regular: *little, littler, littlest.*

27 ◆ POSITIONING MODIFIERS

In English, word order is critical to meaning. It makes a difference, for example, whether you say *The man ate the fish* or *The fish ate the man*.

Most of us put subjects and verbs in a conventional order. Most word order problems in writing involve **modifiers:** adjectives, adverbs, and phrases or clauses used as adjectives or adverbs. There may be more than one place within a sentence to put a modifier, but if the modifier is not positioned so that what it modifies is clear, readers may misinterpret the sentence.

27a Repositioning misplaced modifiers

A modifier usually modifies the nearest grammatically acceptable element in a sentence, so if there is uncertainty about what is modified, readers will look first for such an element. A **misplaced modifier** is one that because of its placement seems to modify some element other than the one the writer intended.

> We wanted our ordeal to end *desperately.*

Unless the writer wanted things to turn out badly, the modifier is misplaced. Putting the adverb next to the verb it modifies, *wanted,* clarifies what the writer intended.

> We *desperately* wanted our ordeal to end.

A **limiting modifier,** such as *almost, even, hardly, just, merely, nearly, only, scarcely,* or *simply,* restricts the words it modifies by limiting the possibilities. If *only A* is true, then *B* and *C* are not. Readers usually understand a modifier to modify the sentence element that directly follows it. Consider the differences in meaning created by moving the limiting modifier *just* in the following sentences.

> They *just* want her to sing this song.

> They want *just* her to sing this song.

> They want her *just* to sing this song.

> They want her to sing *just* this song.

◆ **WP TIP** Evaluate your use of limiting modifiers by searching for ones you regularly use and checking how you have placed each of them.

Clarifying squinting modifiers   27b

A **squinting modifier** seems to modify two things at once and thus can produce conflicting meanings.

◆ Students who follow directions *consistently* score well on tests.

To edit a squinting modifier, decide which sentence element the modifier should go with and rearrange the sentence so that your meaning is unambiguous.

◆ Students who follow directions ~~consistently~~ score well on tests.
consistently

Students who follow directions ~~consistently~~ score well on tests.
consistently

Attaching dangling modifiers   27c

A **dangling modifier** is one that cannot be attached to any element in the sentence. Either the element it is supposed to modify does not appear in the sentence, or that element appears in the wrong grammatical form. Thus it leaves the reader dangling as well.

Often a dangling modifier consists of a prepositional phrase or a verb phrase at the beginning of a sentence.

Running through the rain, our clothes got soaked.

Our clothes were running through the rain? Not likely. But we does not appear anywhere in the sentence, only our, a form that cannot be modified by the dangling phrase.

To correct a dangling modifier, add an element that can be modified, or change the form of the existing element. Place the new subject directly after the modifier, and supply a new verb if necessary.

◆ *we got*
Running through the rain, our clothes ~~got~~ soaked.

◆ *she earned an A on*
Having completed her research, the paper. ~~earned her an A.~~

◆ *residents prepared for*
Still digging out from Thursday's snowfall, another big storm ~~is~~ due on Sunday.

When the main clause is in the passive voice, an introductory phrase is often left floating, with no subject to modify. One solution is to change the main verb into the active voice. That sometimes means finding a subject for it. (See 16c for more on active and passive voice.)

◆ *researchers have forced*
In studying the effects of cigarette smoking, monkeys ~~have been forced~~ to inhale the equivalent of a hundred cigarettes a day.

27d Moving disruptive modifiers

A **disruptive modifier** distracts readers by interrupting the flow of a sentence. Check carefully for any disruptive modifier that splits an infinitive, divides a verb phrase, or needlessly separates major sentence elements.

Split infinitives

An **infinitive** consists of the word *to* plus the base form of a verb: *to fly, to grow, to achieve*. Whenever possible, avoid putting anything between the word *to* and the verb. Such **split infinitives** occur often in speech, but they are considered careless and awkward in writing.

◆ *whenever possible.*
He promised to ~~whenever possible~~ avoid splitting infinitives /

If you have trouble finding a suitable place for the word or words, change the construction of the sentence in another way.

◆ *vividly*
The director wanted to ~~vividly~~ re-create a bullfight for the second act.

◆ *planned a vivid re-creation of*
The director ~~wanted to vividly re-create~~ a bullfight for the second act.

Split verb phrases

A **verb phrase** consists of one or more auxiliary verbs—often a form of *be, do,* or *have*—and a participle or the base form of a verb: *have been formed, does mention.*

Most instructors accept a single adverb, or *not* plus an adverb, between the elements of a verb phrase. Intervening phrases or clauses, however, are disruptive, and you should rewrite the sentence to remove them.

◆ ~~The Roanoke colony had, by~~ the the time a supply ship arrived four years later,
   By
   the Roanoke colony had ^
   mysteriously disappeared without a trace.
  ^

Separated sentence elements

Major sentence elements—subjects, verbs, objects, and complements—need to be near each other to make their relationships clear. At the same time, modifiers need to be near the sentence elements they modify. When these needs conflict, you have to make some choices.

PLACEMENT OF ADVERBS WITHIN VERB PHRASES

◆   When an adverb is used between elements of a verb phrase, it usually appears after the first auxiliary verb.

   Our baseball stadium has *rarely* been filled to capacity.

◆   In questions, the adverb appears after the first auxiliary verb and the subject, but before the other parts of the verb.

   In the past, have you *usually* found yourself writing a paper the day before it's due?

◆   When *not* negates another adverb, it should appear directly after the first auxiliary verb and before the other adverb.

   This newspaper does *not usually* put sports on the front page.

   Not *negates* usually; *the phrase* not usually *means "seldom."*

◆   *Not* should appear after the adverb when it negates the action expressed by the main verb.

   The senators have *often not* paid much attention to the voters who elected them.

   Not *negates* paid.

◆ ~~Mary Pickford, because~~ of her great popularity with audiences, became the
        Because   *Mary Pickford*

first silent film actor to be publicized by name.

◆ ~~African American spirituals influenced, through~~ their distinctive rhythms
                         Through

African American spirituals influenced
and harmonies, the development of most twentieth-century popular music.

Your desired emphasis can help guide your choice.

◆ ~~Kentucky was, even~~ though many of its residents fought on the side of the
       Even   *Kentucky was*
Confederacy during the Civil War, never a stronghold of slavery.

◆ Kentucky was / even though many of its residents fought on the side of the
         never a stronghold of slavery,

Confederacy during the Civil War, ~~never a stronghold of slavery.~~

Unfortunately, no sweeping rule can be made about where to place
modifier phrases and clauses. When editing, let the goals of clarity and precision guide your decisions about modifier placement.

28 ◆ ELIMINATING UNNECESSARY SHIFTS AND MIXED CONSTRUCTIONS

Readers are like bus riders: they like to know where they are being taken.
Good writers keep their passengers comfortable. They drive smoothly to the
expected destination, usually by a direct route.

Throughout a piece of writing, readers expect continuity in point of
view and references to time. Within sentences, they expect consistency, with
no puzzling shifts in the person and number of subjects (see Chapter 24), the
forms of verbs (see Chapter 23), or the way quotations are reproduced. There
should also be no twists and turns in grammar, logic, or sense.

28a Editing unnecessary shifts in person and number

Unnecessary shifts in person often occur when pronouns are used in sentences about groups or about unidentified people.

◆ When the researchers mixed the two chemicals, ~~you~~ saw a surprising
                                                      they

reaction.

Some writers shift needlessly from third person (*he, she, it, one, they*) to second person (*you*) when trying to make a comprehensive statement.

◆   **With the cost of prescription drugs spiraling upward every day,** ~~you~~ ^one^ **can see**

   that some regulation of the pharmaceutical industry is inevitable.

Unnecessary shifts in number, from singular to plural or plural to singular, generally occur when a plural pronoun is used to refer to a singular noun or pronoun of indeterminate gender in the same sentence. Make the antecedent plural or substitute a singular pronoun.

◆   **Every employee sets** ~~their~~ ^his or her^ **own work pace.**

Editing unnecessary shifts in tense   28b

Tense places the action of the verb in time.

We *will play* tennis before we *eat* breakfast but after we *have had* coffee.

ESL

SHIFTING TENSE

Sometimes you have to shift from one verb tense to another within a sentence or paragraph in order to support or comment on an idea. Here are some acceptable reasons for shifting tense.

FROM PRESENT TENSE TO PAST TENSE
◆   To provide background information
◆   To support a claim with an example from the past
◆   To compare a present situation with a past one

Here is an example of supporting a claim with an example from the past.

   Truly dedicated writers *find* time to write regardless of the circumstances. Jane Austen *wrote* most of her novels in short bursts of activity between receiving visitors and taking care of household duties.

FROM PAST TENSE TO PRESENT TENSE
◆   To express a comment, opinion, or evaluation

   On May 6, the town council *voted* against the school bond issue. The decision *is* unfortunate.

28c SHIFT

The dominant, or prevailing, tense throughout a piece of writing is called the **governing tense.** A writer may use different tenses to show actions occurring at different times (see 23e), but any departures from the governing tense without good reason can be confusing.

CONFUSING   When the letter *arrived,* it *says* nothing about the contract.

The **literary present tense** is used to discuss literature or art. (See 23e.) Once the literary present tense is established as your governing tense, be sure to maintain it.

◆   In *The Glass Menagerie,* Tom realizes how trapped he is after the Gentle-
man Caller ~~departed.~~
        departs.

28c   Editing unnecessary shifts in mood

English verbs have three moods: the **indicative mood,** used for statements and questions; the **imperative mood,** used for commands, orders, and directions; and the **subjunctive mood,** used for wishes and for statements that are known to be not factual. (See 23f.)
        Watch for unnecessary shifts from the imperative to the indicative, particularly in instructions.

◆   First cover your work surface with newspapers, and then ~~you~~ make sure

your materials are within easy reach.

The indicative mood and the subjunctive mood often appear in the same sentence.

My instructor *wishes* that I *were* more attentive.

But watch out for unnecessary shifts from the subjunctive to the indicative or the imperative.

◆   The contract requires that you be in Denver on July 1 and that you ~~will~~ be

in Houston on August 1.

Editing unnecessary shifts in voice and subject   28d

The subject of an active-voice verb performs the verb's action: <u>He</u> hit the ball. The subject of a passive voice verb is acted upon: The <u>ball</u> was hit by <u>him</u>. (See 16c.)

If a sentence has two verbs with the same subject, a shift of voice can be acceptable.

> The students *completed* the project first and *were awarded* the prize.
>
> *The verbs shift from active* (completed) *to passive* (were given) *but have the same subject* (students).

Avoid shifting from the active to the passive voice, or passive to active, when doing so requires a change of subject as well.

◆   As we peered out of the tent, the waning moon ~~was seen~~ through the trees.
      we saw

Editing unnecessary shifts between direct and indirect quotation   28e

Direct quotation, or *direct discourse,* reproduces someone's exact words, which are enclosed in quotation marks: *"I love my wife," he said.*

Indirect quotation, or *indirect discourse,* paraphrases someone else's words and does not appear in quotation marks: *He insisted that he loved his wife.* (See Chapter 35.)

Be careful when shifting from indirect to direct quotation. Either use indirect quotation consistently, or rewrite the sentence so that the direct quotation is introduced by a new verb and enclosed in quotation marks.

◆   He said that he loved his wife and ~~"Why did~~ she ~~have~~ to leave ~~me?"~~
      wondered why   had   him.

◆   He insisted that he loved his wife and ~~why~~ did she have to leave him?
      cried, "Why   me?"

Avoid using one verb to introduce both an indirect quotation and a complete sentence of direct quotation. Either use indirect quotation in both instances, quote less than the full sentence directly, or start a new sentence.

◆   Dr. Ryan claims that the play was composed before 1600 and ~~"It shows the~~
      ~~clear hand of~~ Shakespeare.ᵖ
      *that it was
      written by*

◆ Dr. Ryan claims that the play was composed before 1600 and "~~It shows~~ the *that it "shows*

clear hand of Shakespeare."

◆ Dr. Ryan claims that the play was composed before 1600. ~~and~~ "It shows the *He says,*

clear hand of Shakespeare."

28f Eliminating mixed constructions

The term **mixed construction** applies to sentences that begin in one way, then take a sudden turn in another.

One kind of mixed construction uses a grammatically unacceptable element as a subject or predicate. For example, in English a prepositional phrase cannot be the subject of a sentence. To edit such a sentence, either convert the phrase into something that can be a subject or supply a new subject for the sentence.

◆ ~~By listening~~ closely and paying attention to nonverbal signals helps a *Listening*

doctor make a fuller diagnosis.

◆ ~~By~~ listening closely and paying attention to nonverbal signals. ~~helps a~~ *A doctor can make a fuller diagnosis by*

~~doctor make a fuller diagnosis.~~

A modifier clause beginning with a subordinating conjunction (such as *after, before, when, where, while, because, if, although,* or *unless*) cannot be the subject of a sentence. To edit such a construction, provide the sentence with a new subject.

◆ ~~Because the doctor is~~ an expert does not mean a patient should never *The doctor's status as*

question a diagnosis.

The subject is now status *rather than the modifier clause beginning with* Because.

Watch for inappropriate elements used as predicates as well. A dependent clause, for example, cannot contain the main verb of a sentence. To edit such a sentence, either supply a new verb or change a verb already present so that it functions as the main verb.

◆ The fact that most patients are afraid to ask questions,/~~which~~ gives doctors

complete control.

Removing which *turns* gives *into the main verb.*

Revising illogical constructions   28g

Even though the intended meaning of a sentence may be clear, the literal meaning sometimes gets muddled. If you find some elements don't make sense, reduce your sentence to its most basic elements—subject and verb—to see where the problem lies.

◆   Most
    ~~The opinion of most~~ people believe that dogs make better pets than cats.

    Reduce the sentence to subject and verb; the opinion *cannot believe; people* can. People *is the subject.*

◆   Repeat offenders whose licenses have already been suspended for drunk
    have their licenses
    driving will ~~be~~ revoked.

    It is not offenders *who will be* revoked *but rather their* licenses.

A **subject complement,** which renames the subject following a linking verb (*is, seems,* or *appears*), must rename or comment on the subject. If it does not, you must edit the resulting mixed construction.

◆   My father's favorite kitchen appliance is ~~using~~ the microwave oven.

    The subject, linking verb, and complement are appliance is using, *which doesn't make sense. In the edited version, the sequence* appliance is the microwave oven *makes more sense.*

Eliminating faulty predication   28h

Faulty predication describes a mixed construction that is both ungrammatical and illogical. It often consists of a modifier clause, especially one introduced by *when, where,* or *because,* following a linking verb such as *is.* This construction requires the modifier to serve as a subject complement, which it can't do. A person or thing (the subject) cannot be renamed as *when, where,* or *because.* Use *where* and *when* clauses only to refer to location or time, not to introduce concepts or conditions.

◆   based on
    Pop art is ~~where an artist reproduces~~ images from commercial products

    and the popular media.

◆   In sudden-death
    ~~Sudden-death~~ overtime, ~~is when~~ the game is extended until one team

    scores.

219

Faulty predication occurs often in sentences that have *reason . . . is because* constructions. You must change one part of the sentence to match the other.

◆ ~~The reason little~~ has been done to solve the problem ~~is~~ because Congress is deadlocked.

     Little ^

◆ The reason little has been done to solve the problem is ~~because~~ Congress is deadlocked.

     that ^

29 ◆ GRAMMAR REVIEW

One approach to English grammar looks at individual words and asks, "What kind of word is this?" This question leads to a consideration of words as parts of speech: nouns, pronouns, verbs, adjectives, prepositions, conjunctions, and interjections. A second approach examines sentence organization and asks, "What function does each word or group of words serve in the sentence?" This question leads to an analysis of sentence elements: subject, predicate, object, complement, and so forth. A third question, "What kind of sentence is this?" leads to a discussion of sentence patterns.

29a Parts of speech

What part of speech a word is depends on its meaning and position in a sentence. Some words change parts depending on the context in which they appear. The word *ride,* for example, can be either a verb or a noun.

    NOUN   They went for a *ride.*

    VERB   They *ride* their horses.

To know what part of speech a word is, you must look not only at the word itself but also at its relation to other words in the sentence.

Nouns

Nouns are words that name persons, animals, places, things, or ideas: *woman, Flipper, Grand Canyon, velociraptor,* and *virtue* are all nouns.

Proper nouns name particular people, animals, places, or things: *Marie Curie, Black Beauty, Kentucky, Catholicism.* They are almost always capitalized. (See 38c.) Generic nouns, or common nouns, can apply to any member of a class or group: *scientist, horse, state, ship, religion.* They are generally not capitalized.

Concrete nouns refer to things that can be seen, heard, touched, smelled, or tasted: *butterfly, telephone, ice, fudge.* **Abstract nouns** refer to ideas or concepts that cannot be directly sensed: *nature, communication, temperature, temptation.* (For the uses of concrete and abstract nouns, see 16a.)

Count nouns refer to one or more individual items that can readily be counted: *one book, two books.* Count nouns usually name something concrete, though some are abstract: *one idea, several ideas.* **Noncount nouns** refer to entities that either cannot be counted individually — *water, oil* — or are used in a sense that does not imply counting — *sand, money.* These are seldom made plural. The things denoted by **mass nouns** are counted only as part of a phrase that specifies some measurement: *grains of sand, pails of water, gallons of oil.* Most abstract nouns are mass nouns.

Collective nouns, such as *crowd, couple,* and *flock,* refer to groups of similar things.

Singular and plural nouns

Nouns that refer to an individual thing or person are **singular:** *boy, town, box.* Those that refer to two or more are **plural:** *boys, towns, boxes.*

Most nouns add *-s* or *-es* to the singular to create the plural. A few nouns change spelling in other ways to form the plural: *goose, geese; child, children; man, men; medium, media.* And a few stay the same regardless of number: *sheep, sheep.* (For more on forming plurals, see 34c and 37b.)

Possessive forms of nouns

Nouns change form to show possession, ownership, or connections, usually by adding an apostrophe and an *-s: the king's son, the town's mayor.* This form is called the **possessive case.** (For guidelines on forming possessives of plural nouns and nouns that end in *-s,* see 34a.)

Pronouns

A **pronoun** is a word that substitutes for a noun or for another pronoun. The word which the pronoun replaces is called its **antecedent.**

antecedent   pronoun

Sean helped Alicia paint her room.

Usually an antecedent appears before the pronoun, but it may also follow shortly after the pronoun. (For a description of pronoun reference to clear antecedents, see 25a.)

pronoun   antecedent

Because of its construction, the boat was unsinkable.

A pronoun must **agree** with (or correspond to) its antecedent in terms of person, number, and gender. (See 25b.)

Personal pronouns

Personal pronouns, such as *me, you, their,* and *it,* refer to specific people, animals, places, things, or ideas.

I asked *you* to buy *it.*

Personal pronouns change their form to show **person.** First-person pronouns refer to the speaker or writer directly: *I, we.* Second-person pronouns refer to those being addressed: *you.* Third-person pronouns refer to someone other than the speaker or writer or those being addressed: *he, she, it, they.*

Personal pronouns change form to show **number.** They are either singular (*I, he, she, it*) or plural (*we, they*). The pronoun *you* is the same whether it is plural or singular.

Singular personal pronouns change form to show **gender.** They are masculine (*he*), feminine (*she*), or neuter (*it*).

Personal pronouns change form to show **case.** (See 25c.)

Indefinite pronouns

Indefinite pronouns, such as *anyone, everybody, something, many, few,* and *none,* do not require an antecedent because they do not refer to any specific person, animal, place, thing, or idea. Often they are used to denote a quantity.

Many are called, but *few* are chosen.

Indefinite pronouns change form to indicate the possessive case by adding an apostrophe and an -*s: anyone's idea, everyone's preference.* They do not change form to show person, number, or gender. Most are either always singular (*someone*) or always plural (*many*). A few can be either singular or plural, depending on the context. (See 25b.)

Demonstrative pronouns

Demonstrative pronouns, such as *this, that, these,* and *those,* are used to identify or point out a specific person, place, or thing.

This is the largest one we have.

Demonstrative pronouns change form to show number: *this* and *that* are singular; *these* and *those* are plural.

These words are demonstrative pronouns only when they are not immediately followed by a noun, in which case they are adjectives: *I enjoyed reading <u>this</u> book.*

Relative pronouns

A **relative pronoun,** such as *who, whom, which,* or *that,* introduces a dependent clause and "relates" that clause to an antecedent elsewhere in the sentence.

◆   She chose the knife *that* cut best.

Some relative pronouns are also indefinite: *whoever, what, whatever, whichever.* Relative pronouns change form to show case. (See 25c.)

Interrogative pronouns

Interrogative pronouns, such as *who, what,* and *whose,* are used to ask questions. They change form only to show case.

Who is there?

Whose footsteps did I hear?

Reflexive and intensive pronouns

Pronouns ending in *-self* or *-selves,* such as *myself, yourself,* and *themselves,* are **reflexive pronouns** when they refer back to, or "reflect," the subject of the sentence.

◆   Dave cut *himself* while shaving.

The same pronouns are called **intensive pronouns** when they are used to emphasize, or "intensify," an antecedent.

I talked to the president *herself.*

Unlike reflexive pronouns, intensive pronouns can be omitted without changing the sense of the sentence: *I talked to the president.*

Reflexive and intensive pronouns change form to show person, number, and gender, just as personal pronouns do.

Reciprocal pronouns

The **reciprocal pronouns** *each other* and *one another* are used to describe an action or state that is shared between two people, animals, places, things, or ideas.

The investigators helped *one another* with the research.

PRONOUNS

PERSONAL
I, me, my, mine   it, its
you, your, yours   we, us, our, ours
he, him, his   they, them, their, theirs
she, her, hers

INDEFINITE

all	each	many	none	somebody
any	either	more	no one	someone
anybody	everybody	most	nothing	something
anyone	everyone	much	one	what
anything	everything	neither	several	
both	few	nobody	some	

DEMONSTRATIVE

this	that	these	those

RELATIVE

that	whatever	whichever	whoever	whomever
what	which	who	whom	whose

INTERROGATIVE

what	which	who	whom	whose
whatever	whichever	whoever	whomever	

REFLEXIVE AND INTENSIVE

myself	yourself	himself	herself	itself
ourselves	yourselves	themselves	oneself	

RECIPROCAL

each other	one another

Reciprocal pronouns have possessive forms; *each other's, one another's.* Otherwise, they do not change form.

Pronoun case

Case indicates the role a word plays in a sentence, whether it is a subject, an object, or a possessive. Nouns change form to show the possessive case, usually by adding an apostrophe and *-s* to the end of the word. In the subjective and objective cases, nouns have the same form. Personal pronouns, indefinite pronouns, and the relative or interrogative pronouns *who* and *whoever* change form to show all three cases. Indefinite pronouns change form to show the possessive case by adding an apostrophe and *-s,* as nouns do.

subject		possessive	object	object
Julia	**carried**	**Juan's**	**coat**	**for him.**
She	carried	*his*	coat	for him.

SUBJECTIVE		OBJECTIVE		POSSESSIVE	
SINGULAR	PLURAL	SINGULAR	PLURAL	SINGULAR	PLURAL
I	we	me	us	my, mine	our, ours
you	you	you	you	your, yours	your, yours
he	they	him	them	his	their, theirs
she	they	her	them	her, hers	their, theirs
it	they	it	them	its	their, theirs
who		whom		whose	
whoever		whomever			

The **subjective case** indicates that a pronoun is the subject of a clause or is a subject complement.

We should leave now.

It was *she who* wanted to leave.

The **objective case** indicates that a pronoun is the object of a verb, a preposition, or a verbal.

Whom did they choose?

The judging seemed unfair to *us.*

Seeing *her* made the holiday complete.

The **possessive case** indicates possession, ownership, or connection. Possessive personal pronouns have two forms: adjective forms (*my, your*) modify a noun or gerund; noun forms (*mine, yours*) stand alone as a subject or complement.

That is *my* hat.

The hat is *mine.*

For more on pronoun case, see 25c.

Verbs

A **verb** describes an action or state of being.

The logger *fells* the tree.

The air *is* fragrant with the scent of pine.

The verb of a sentence changes form to show person, number, tense, voice, and mood.

◆ **Person** indicates who performed the action: *I write; she writes.*

◆ **Number** indicates how many people performed the action: *He sings, they sing.*

◆ **Tense** indicates when the action was performed: *She argue̲s, she argue̲d.*

◆ **Voice** indicates whether the verb's grammatical subject acts or is acted upon: *She paid the bill; the bill was paid.*

◆ **Mood** indicates the speaker's attitude toward or reaction to the action: *I am a millionaire; if I were a millionaire.*

A verb with a specific person and number is called a **finite verb.** A verb form without these properties is called a **verbal.** (See 25c. For more on verb person, number, tense, and mood, see Chapter 23. For more on verb voice, see 16c.)

In addition to one-word verbs, English has many **phrasal verbs,** or multiple-word verbs. These consist of a verb plus a **particle,** a word that may be a preposition in other contexts but has become an integral part of the phrasal verb. Both the verb and the particle are necessary to convey the meaning of the phrasal verb.

The rocket *went off* with a bang.

Went off is a phrasal verb. Its meaning ("detonated, fired") is not easy to determine by considering only the separate meanings of the words went *and* off.

Auxiliary verbs

One sentence may have several verbs in it. The verb that expresses the action or state of the subject of the sentence is the **main verb.**

main verb

◆   After swimming for an hour, he decided to go home.

When the main verb of a sentence is preceded by one or more **auxiliary verbs,** or **helping verbs,** the result is a **verb phrase.**

verb phrase

auxiliary verb   main verb

◆   My eldest sister was doing a crossword puzzle.

The most common auxiliary verbs—forms of *be, do,* and *have*—are used to form certain tenses, to add emphasis, to ask questions, to make negative statements, and to form the passive voice. They can also stand alone as main verbs. When used as auxiliaries, these verbs change to show person, number, and tense.

Other auxiliary verbs add to the verb the meanings of desire, intent, permission, possibility, or obligation. These **modal auxiliaries,** or **modals,** are not generally used alone as main verbs. English has both one-word modals and phrasal modals (or multiple-word modals).

ONE-WORD MODALS

can	may	must	should	would
could	might	shall	will	

PHRASAL MODALS

be able to	be supposed to	have got to
be allowed to	had better	ought to
be going to	have to	used to

One-word modals do not change form to show person, number, or tense: *I can sing, and you can dance.*

Most phrasal modals do change form to show person, number, and tense: *I am able to sing, and you are able to dance.* The phrasal modals *had better, ought to,* and *used to* do not change form.

Transitive and intransitive verbs

Some verbs require a **direct object,** a word or words that indicate who or what received the action of the verb. (See 29b.)

direct object

◆   They documented their results.

A verb that has a direct object is a **transitive verb.** A verb that does not have a direct object is an **intransitive verb.** Many verbs may be either transitive or intransitive, depending on the context.

TRANSITIVE   Joey *grew* tomatoes last summer.

INTRANSITIVE   The tomatoes *grew* rapidly.

Linking verbs

Linking verbs include *be, become, seem,* and verbs describing sensations — *appear, look, feel, taste, smell, sound,* and so on. They link the subject of a sentence to a subject complement, an element that renames or identifies the subject. Subject complements can be nouns or adjectives. (See 24c.)

A linking verb, like an equal sign, links two equivalent terms.

Sue is nice.   Sue = nice
They felt tired.   They = tired
Jake was a recent graduate.   Jake = graduate

Voice

Most transitive verbs may be either active or passive. In the **active voice,** the subject of the sentence is the person or thing performing the action expressed by the verb. In the passive voice, the subject of the sentence is the person or thing acted upon. The **passive voice** uses the past participle of the verb with a form of the verb *be* as an auxiliary. (See 15c and 23d.)

ACTIVE   The woman *pushes* the baby carriage.

PASSIVE   The baby carriage *is pushed* by the woman.

The object of the sentence in the active voice becomes the subject of the passive-voice sentence. The subject of the active-voice sentence, if it appears at all in the passive-voice sentence, is usually an **agent** following the preposition *by: Movies are often seen by teenagers.* Some passive-voice sentences do not have agents: *Movies are often shown at night.*

Verbals

A **verbal** is a verb form that does not change form to show person or number. There are three types of verbals.

1   **Infinitive:** the base form of the verb, usually preceded by the word *to*
2   **Gerund:** the *-ing* form of the verb functioning as a noun
3   **Participle:** either the past participle (usually ending in *-ed* or *-d*) or the present participle (ending in *-ing*)

The infinitive changes form to show tense.

PRESENT INFINITIVE	*To sing* at Carnegie Hall is her ambition.
PAST INFINITIVE	*To have sung* so well last night is something you should be proud of.

After prepositions and certain verbs, the *to* of an infinitive does not appear: *He did everything except* wash *the floor. She let them* visit *their cousins.*

A verbal can function as a noun, an adjective, or an adverb, but it cannot be the main verb of a sentence or a clause.

NOUN	*Jogging* is a great form of exercise.
ADJECTIVE	We had *boiled* eggs for breakfast.
ADVERB	This machine was designed *to last.*

Verbals can form verbal phrases by taking objects, complements, and modifiers. (For more on verbal phrases, see the chart in 23d on phrasal modals.) For more on verb selection, see 23. For subject-verb agreement, see 24.

Adjectives and adverbs

Adjectives and adverbs *modify*—that is, they alter and specify—the meaning of other words. They have many similar properties, so they are sometimes grouped together as **modifiers.** The difference between them lies in what they modify. **Adjectives** modify nouns, pronouns, or phrases and clauses used as nouns.

The bird-watchers spotted *scarlet* tanagers. (*Modifies noun* tanagers.)

They were *beautiful.* (*Modifies pronoun* they.)

To see them would be *delightful.* (*Modifies phrase* to see them.)

Adverbs modify verbs, adjectives, verbals, or other adverbs; they can also modify clauses or entire sentences.

His judgment was made *hastily*. (*Modifies verb* was made.)

The feathers are *quite* beautiful. (*Modifies adjective* beautiful.)

Writing *well* takes practice. (*Modifies verbal* writing.)

She sings *very* nicely. (*Modifies adverb* nicely.)

Surprisingly, the band played for hours. (*Modifies entire sentence.*)

Adjectives and adverbs have three **degrees:** positive, comparative, and superlative. A **positive modifier** is one that makes no comparison. A **comparative modifier** makes a comparison between two things. A **superlative** adjective or adverb distinguishes among three or more things.

POSITIVE   He lives in an *old* house.

COMPARATIVE   It is *older* than mine.

SUPERLATIVE   It is the *oldest* house in the country.

For more on forming comparatives and superlatives, see 26d.

Kinds of adjectives

Adjectives that describe qualities or attributes are called **descriptive adjectives:** <u>gray</u> sky, <u>beautiful</u> garden. Adjectives that identify or specify the words they modify are called **limiting adjectives:** <u>this</u> sky, <u>my</u> garden.

Limiting adjectives include articles, the words *a, an,* and *the. The* is a **definite article** because it identifies, or "defines," precisely which person or thing is being referred to. *A* and *an* are **indefinite articles.** The choice between *a* and *an* depends on the initial sound of the following word: *a* precedes a consonant sound or a long *u* sound (*a monster, a university*) and *an* precedes any other vowel sound (*an apron*).

Several types of pronouns can also serve as limiting adjectives when they are directly followed by a noun. (See 25a.)

PERSONAL   She is going to buy *her* dog today.

RELATIVE   She hasn't decided *which* dog she will pick.

DEMONSTRATIVE   She likes *that* dog very much.

INDEFINITE   But *all* look cute to her.

Numbers can also be limiting adjectives when they are directly followed by a noun: <u>two</u> *dogs*.

Adjectives derived from proper nouns are called **proper adjectives:** *Alaskan, Shakespearean, British*. Like proper nouns, proper adjectives are almost always capitalized. (See 38c.)

Sometimes a noun is used as an adjective without any change of form. Such a noun is called a **noun modifier.**

He works as a *masonry* contractor.

The police dispersed the rioters with a *water* cannon.

Kinds of adverbs

In addition to the usual kind of descriptive adverb (*quickly, often*), several special groups of words are also classified as adverbs. The **negators** *no* and *not* are adverbs. **Conjunctive adverbs,** such as *however* and *therefore,* are words that modify an entire clause and express its relationship to another clause. (For a list of common conjunctive adverbs, see 14a.) **Relative adverbs,** such as *where, why,* and *when,* introduce adjective or adverb clauses. (See 29b.)

NEGATOR   We were *not* ready.

CONJUNCTIVE ADVERB   *However,* the train was leaving.

RELATIVE ADVERB   We were visiting the house *where* I grew up.

For editing tips on using adjectives and adverbs, see 26. For tips on positioning modifiers, see 27.

Prepositions

Words such as *to, with, by,* and *of* are **prepositions.** English has both one-word prepositions and phrasal prepositions, or multiple-word prepositions, which are made up of two or more words: *because of, except for, instead of.*

A preposition shows the relationship between a noun or pronoun—the *object* of the preposition—and other words in the sentence. The preposition, its object, and any associated modifiers are together called a *prepositional phrase.*

```
              prepositional phrase
          ┌──────────┴──────────┐
        preposition       object
          ┌──┴──┐        ┌──┴──┐
 ◆   I   sat   on    the   bed.
```

COMMON PREPOSITIONS

aboard	beneath	including	regarding
about	beside	in front of	since
above	besides	inside	through
according to	between	in spite of	throughout
across	beyond	into	till
after	but	like	to
against	by	near	together with
ahead of	concerning	next to	toward
along with	despite	notwithstanding	under
among	down	of	underneath
apart from	due to	off	unlike
around	during	on	until
as	except	onto	up
as for	except for	on top of	upon
at	for	other than	up to
away from	from	out	via
because of	in	out of	with
before	in addition to	outside	within
behind	in back of	over	without
below	in case of	past	

Words usually used as prepositions may also function as adverbs or as particles when they are parts of phrasal verbs.

PREPOSITION   I looked *up* the street.

ADVERB   The woman looked *up*.

PARTICLE   He looked *up* the word in the dictionary.

For more on adverbs, see 26a. For more on phrasal verbs, see 23d.

Conjunctions

The word *conjunction* comes from Latin words meaning "join" and "with." **Conjunctions** join two or more words, phrases, or clauses with one another. The **coordinating conjunctions**—*and, or, nor, for, but, yet,* and *so*—imply that the elements linked are equal or similar in importance.

Bill *and* I went shopping.

The bus will take you to the market *or* to the theater.

Correlative conjunctions always appear in pairs: *either . . . or, neither . . . nor, both . . . and, not only . . . but also, whether . . . or.* Correlative conjunctions join pairs of similar words, phrases, or clauses.

Neither Jack *nor* his brother was in school this morning.

She *not only* sings *but also* dances.

Subordinating conjunctions, such as *after, although, because, before, if, unless, when, where,* and *while,* introduce ideas in dependent clauses that are less important to the point of the passage than the ideas in main or independent clauses. (For a list of subordinating conjunctions, see 14c.)

While you finish sewing, I will start dinner.

I left *because* I was angry.

Conjunctive adverbs, such as *however, therefore,* and *furthermore,* link independent clauses. The clauses they link must be separated by a semicolon. (See 32a.)

I am finished; *therefore,* I am going home.

Interjections

Interjections are words inserted, or "interjected," into a sentence. They may show surprise, dismay, or strong emotion. They most often appear in speech or dialogue, and their presence often calls for an exclamation point.

Ouch! That pipe is hot!

Yes, it is.

Elements of a sentence   29b

The principal **elements of a sentence** are the subject and the predicate. Usually, the **subject** names who or what performs the action of the sentence or, if there is no action, tells who or what the sentence is about. It consists of a noun, a pronoun, or another word or group of words that can serve as a noun, along with any modifiers. The **predicate** contains the verb of the sentence, along with its objects, its modifiers, and any complements or modifiers that refer to the subject.

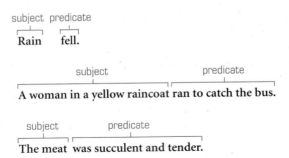

subject predicate

Rain fell.

subject   predicate

A woman in a yellow raincoat ran to catch the bus.

subject   predicate

The meat was succulent and tender.

The subject usually comes at the beginning of a sentence and the predicate at the end. Sometimes, as in questions, the subject may follow part of the predicate.

subject   predicate

Do *you know a good roofing contractor?*

Subjects

Simple subject The simple subject of a sentence is the person or thing that performs the action of the predicate. Usually this is a noun or pronoun, but it can also be a verbal, a phrase, or a clause that is used as a noun.

NOUN   Long *shadows* crept along the lawn.

PRONOUN   *He* looked exactly like a cowboy.

VERBAL   *Singing* pleases Alan.

PHRASE   *To work hard* is our lot in life.

CLAUSE   *That LeeAnn could dance* amazed us all.

Complete subject The complete subject consists of the simple subject and all words that modify or directly relate to it, such as adjectives, adverbs, phrases, or clauses.

> *Winning the last game of a dreadful season that included injuries, losing streaks, and a strike* was small consolation to the team.

The simple subject here is the gerund *Winning. The last game* is the object of *Winning;* the prepositional phrase *of a dreadful season* modifies *game;* and the clause *that included injuries, losing streaks, and a strike* modifies *season.*

Compound subject A compound subject includes two or more subjects linked by a coordinating conjunction such as *and* or *or*.

Books, records, and videotapes filled the room.

Implied subject An implied subject is one that is not stated directly but may be understood.

Come to the meeting to learn about the preschool program.

Here the subject is understood to be *you*. Commands with verbs in the imperative mood often have the implied subject *you*.

Predicates

Simple predicate The simple predicate consists of the main verb of the sentence and any auxiliaries.

The candidate who wins the debate *will win* the election.

Complete predicate The complete predicate consists of the simple predicate and all words that modify or directly relate to it. Objects and complements are part of the predicate, along with any modifiers, including phrases, clauses, and single words.

The farmer *gave the pigs enough food to last the weekend.*

The verb *gave* is the simple predicate; *food* is the direct object of the verb, and *pigs* is the indirect object of the verb. The words *the* and *enough* modify *pigs* and *food,* respectively. The phrase *to last the weekend* also modifies *food.*

Compound predicate A predicate in which two or more verbs have the same subject is a compound predicate.

At the beach we *ate* our picnic, *swam* in the surf, *read* to each other, and *walked* on the sand.

The sentence has four verbs with the same subject: *ate, swam, read,* and *walked* all have the subject *we.*

Objects of verbs

A **direct object** receives the action of a transitive verb.

The company paid its *workers* a day early.

The direct object *workers* and its modifiers receive the action of *The company paid.* Asking a *whom* or *what* question about the subject and verb of a sentence is a good way to find its direct object: *Whom did the company pay?* (For more on transitive verbs, see pp. 227–228.)

An **indirect object** is a person or thing to whom (or for whom) the action of the verb is directed. It must be a noun or a pronoun that precedes the direct object. If it is accompanied by a preposition, it becomes the object of the preposition and cannot be the object of the verb.

indirect   direct
object   object

Kordell Stewart threw *Thigpen* the *ball.*

To find an indirect object, identify the verb and the direct object and ask *To or for whom?* or *To or for what?* The answer is the indirect object. *He threw the ball to whom?* He threw it to *Thigpen.*

Complements

A **complement** renames or describes a subject or an object. A complement can be a noun, a pronoun, or an adjective.

A **subject complement** renames or describes the subject of a sentence. It follows a *linking verb*—a verb such as *be, become, seem,* or *appear.* (See 24c.) A linking verb, acting like an equal sign, links two equivalent terms. Whatever appears before the linking verb is the subject; whatever appears after is the subject complement.

subject   subject complement

My mother's *uncle* is the factory *foreman.*

subject   subject complement

The factory *foreman* is my mother's *uncle.*

An **object complement** follows a direct object and modifies or renames it.

Tonight we will paint the town *red.*

The adjective red *describes the direct object* town.

A noun or pronoun used as a complement is sometimes called a **predicate noun.** An adjective used as a complement is sometimes called a **predicate adjective.**

Phrases

A group of related words lacking a subject, a predicate, or both is a **phrase.**

Verb phrase   A verb phrase consists of the main verb of a clause and its auxiliaries. It functions as the verb of a sentence.

verb phrase

The college *has been having* a difficult year.

Noun phrase   A noun phrase consists of a noun, a pronoun, or an infinitive or gerund serving as a noun, and all its modifiers.

noun phrase

The famous and venerable institution is bankrupt.

Noun phrases may function as subjects, objects, or complements.

SUBJECT   *The college's president* is distraught.

OBJECT   He addressed *the board of trustees.*

COMPLEMENT   They became *a terrified mob.*

Modifier phrase   Modifier phrases function as adjectives or adverbs; they may be prepositional phrases, infinitive phrases, participial phrases, or absolute phrases. Appositive phrases are sometimes considered modifier phrases.

Prepositional phrases   A prepositional phrase consists of a preposition, its object, and any related modifiers.

prepositional phrase

The new book was hailed *with great fanfare.*

A prepositional phrase may function as an adjective or an adverb.

ADJECTIVE   He knows the difficulty *of the task.*

ADVERB   She arrived *at work* a little early.

Verbal phrase   A verbal phrase contains a verbal plus any objects, complements, or modifiers. There are three kinds of verbals: infinitives, gerunds, and participles.

An **infinitive phrase** is built around an infinitive, the base form of the verb usually preceded by *to*. Infinitive phrases can function as nouns, adjectives, or adverbs. When they function as nouns, they are usually subjects, complements, or direct objects.

NOUN   *To raise a family* is a lofty goal.

ADJECTIVE   He has the duty *to protect his children.*

ADVERB   My father worked *to provide for his family.*

A **gerund phrase** is built around a gerund, the *-ing* form of a verb functioning as a noun. Gerund phrases always function as nouns, subjects, subject complements, direct objects, or as the objects of prepositions.

SUBJECT   *Studying these essays* takes a lot of time.

SUBJECT COMPLEMENT   The key to success is *reading all the assignments.*

DIRECT OBJECT   My roommate likes *reading novels.*

OBJECT OF PREPOSITION   She can forgive me for *preferring short stories.*

A **participial phrase** is built around a participle, either the past participle (usually ending in *-ed* or *-d*) or the present participle (ending in *-ing*). A participial phrase always functions as an adjective.

ADJECTIVE   *Striking a blow for freedom,* the Minutemen fired the "shot heard around the world."

Appositive phrase   An appositive phrase appears directly after a noun or pronoun and renames or further identifies it. (See 31c.)

appositive phrase

Ralph Nader, *a longtime consumer advocate,* supports the new auto emissions proposal.

Absolute phrase   An absolute phrase modifies an entire sentence or clause. It consists of a noun or pronoun and a participle, together with any accompanying modifiers, objects, or complements.

absolute phrase

The opposition notwithstanding, the committee approved the resolution.

Clauses

Any group of related words with a subject and a predicate is a **clause.** A clause that can stand alone as a complete sentence is called an **independent clause** or the **main clause** of the sentence.

The moon rose.

main clause

The winner will be the candidate who best communicates with voters.

A clause that cannot stand by itself as a complete sentence is called a **dependent clause** or **subordinate clause.** It is dependent because it is introduced by a subordinating word, usually either a subordinating conjunction (such as *because, when,* or *unless*) or a relative pronoun (such as *who, which,* or *that*). (For lists of subordinating conjunctions and relative pronouns, see 14c and 25a.)

The little girl laughed *when the moon rose.*

I know *that the best candidate will win the election.*

Dependent clauses must be joined to independent clauses. They can be classified as noun, adjective, or adverb clauses by the role they play in the sentence.

Noun clause A **noun clause** is one used in the same way as a noun — as a subject, an object, or a subject complement. It is usually introduced by a relative pronoun (such as *who, what,* or *which*) or by a subordinating conjunction (*how, when, where, whether,* or *why*).

SUBJECT	*What I want* is a good job.
DIRECT OBJECT	In class we learned *how we can improve our writing.*
OBJECT OF PREPOSITION	We wondered *to whom we should send them.*
SUBJECT COMPLEMENT	English history is *what I know best.*

Adjective clause   An adjective clause modifies a noun or pronoun elsewhere in the sentence. Most adjective clauses begin with relative pronouns such as *who, whose,* or *that.* They can also begin with the relative adverbs *when, where,* or *why.* Adjective clauses are sometimes called **relative clauses.**

Adjective clauses and noun clauses are often confused. Remember that a noun clause functions as a noun, while an adjective clause modifies a noun or pronoun. To determine whether a dependent clause is an adjective clause, look for the noun or pronoun it modifies. Usually, an adjective clause directly follows the word it modifies.

> The book *that you reserved* is now available. (*Modifies* book.)

> The graduating seniors, *who had just completed their exams,* were full of high spirits.

Adjective clauses, along with adverb clauses, are also known as **modifier clauses.**

Adverb clauses   An adverb clause modifies a verb, an adjective, an adverb, or an entire clause. Adverb clauses tell when, where, why, or how, or they specify a condition. They are introduced by subordinating conjunctions such as *although, than, as,* or *since.*

> The fish ride the tide *as far as it will carry them.*

> Now they can be caught more easily *than at any other time.*

29c   Sentence classification and sentence patterns

Sentences can be classified by function and by grammatical structure. They can also be described in terms of their sentence patterns.

Classifying sentences by function

Declarative sentences make statements. The normal word order for a declarative sentence is subject followed by predicate.

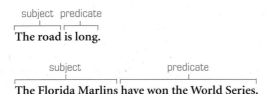

Word order is occasionally inverted, however. (See 15d.)

predicate   subject

At the top of the hill stood a tree.

Interrogative sentences ask questions. They can be introduced by an interrogative pronoun, or the subject can follow part of the verb.

Who goes there?

Can pigs really fly?

Imperative sentences make commands or requests. The subject, *you*, usually is not stated but implied. The verb form used for the imperative is always the base form.

Drive slowly.

Signal before changing lanes.

Exclamatory sentences exclaim (and usually end with an exclamation point).

Oh, how I hate to get up in the morning!

(See 15c for more on the uses of these different types of sentences.)

Classifying sentences by grammatical structure

Sentences are classified by grammatical structure according to how many dependent and independent clauses they contain.

A **simple sentence** consists of a single independent clause and no dependent clause. Some simple sentences are brief. Others, if they contain modifier phrases or compound subjects, verbs, or objects, can be quite long.

Marmosets eat bananas.

Benny and Griselda, marmosets at our local zoo, eat at least fifteen bananas a day, in addition to lettuce, nuts, oranges, and apples.

A **compound sentence** has two or more independent clauses and no dependent clause.

      independent   independent

They grew tired of waiting, so they finally hailed a taxi.

A **complex sentence** contains one independent clause and at least one dependent clause.

     independent   dependent

The students assemble outside when the bell rings.

A **compound-complex sentence** contains at least two independent clauses and at least one dependent clause.

               independent

The first motorcyclists to arrive never ordered anything to eat;

   independent   dependent

they just sat quietly until their hands stopped shaking.

Understanding sentence patterns

Most independent clauses are built on one of five basic patterns. (For more on these sentence elements, see Chapter 14.)

1 The simplest pattern has only two elements, a subject and a verb (s−v).

   s   v

Nobody noticed.

Even when expanded by modifying phrases, the basic pattern of an independent clause may still be only subject-verb.

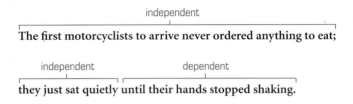

        s   v

Heavy tropical rain fell Tuesday and Wednesday in the Philippines, causing mud slides and driving hundreds from their homes.

2 The next simplest pattern includes a subject, a verb, and a direct object (s−v−do).

   s   v   do

Gloria read the book.

    s   v   do

Robins eat worms.

3 A third pattern is subject−verb−indirect object−direct object (s−v−io−do).

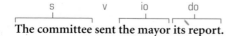

The committee sent the mayor its report.

    s   v   io   do

The waiter brought her an appetizer.

4 A fourth pattern is subject−verb−subject complement (s−v−sc).

    s   v   sc

The commissioner seems worried.

  s v   sc

She is a Republican.

5 The fifth basic pattern is subject−verb−direct object−object comple-ment (s−v−do−oc).

    s   v do   oc

His friends call him an achiever.

  s   v   do oc

That makes him proud.

IV

EDITING PUNCTUATION

EDITING PUNCTUATION

Certain forms for punctuation are conventional in written English. Using the conventions for periods, commas, semicolons, colons, dashes, quotation marks, brackets, and so on—and using them correctly—shows that you know what you're doing when you write. It also shows that you have your readers' needs in mind.

30 ◆ END PUNCTUATION

The full stop at the end of every written sentence requires one of three marks of punctuation: a **period,** a **question mark,** or an **exclamation point.** Which mark you use at the end of a sentence depends largely on the meaning you wish to express: *They won. They won? They won!*

Periods

Periods at the ends of sentences

Use a period at the end of a statement, a mild command, or a polite request.

The administration has canceled classes.

Do not attempt to drive to school this morning.

Please sit down.

Use a period, not a question mark, after an **indirect question** (a question that is reported but not asked directly).

I wonder who made the decision.

Use a single period to end the sentence when an abbreviation containing a period falls at the end of a sentence.

Her flight leaves at 6:15 a.m.

Periods with abbreviations

Use a period in most abbreviations.

Mr., Mrs., Ms.	in., ft., yd., mi.	etc., e.g., i.e., vs., ca.
Dr., Rev., Msgr.	Mon., Tues., Wed.	p., para., fig., vol.
Atty., Gov., Sen.	Jan., Feb., Mar.	St., Ave., Rd.

Do not use a space after the periods in abbreviations that stand for more than one word.

U.S., U.K.	B.C., A.D.	B.A., Ph.D., M.D.

Do not use periods with **acronyms** (words formed from initials and pronounced as words) or with abbreviated names of government agencies, corporations, and other entities. (See 42e.)

NASA, NATO, HUD, AIDS	CNN, IBM, SAT
FBI, CIA, EPA, IRS	IRA, LAPD, NCAA

30b   Question marks

Use question marks at the end of **direct questions.** (Direct questions are usually signaled either by an interrogative pronoun such as *what, where,* or *why,* or by inverted word order, with the verb before the subject.)

Where is Times Square?   How can I get there?

Use a question mark or a period at the end of a polite request. A question mark emphasizes politeness.

Would you please sit down?

Use a question mark for a sentence with a dependent clause containing a question when the independent clause is a question. When the independent clause contains an **indirect question,** however, don't use a question mark.

independent clause   dependent clause

Are you asking me which subway to take?

independent clause   dependent clause

He wants to know how he can get to Times Square.

Use a question mark when a sentence ends with a **tag question**—one that is added at the end—even though the independent clause is declarative.

◆   **This train goes to Times Square, doesn't it?**

Use a question mark for a direct question in quotation marks, even when it is part of a declarative sentence. Put the question mark before the closing quotation mark, and use no other end punctuation.

◆   **"Have we missed the train?" she wailed.**

Use question marks after each question in a series of questions, even if they are not all complete sentences. Capitalization is optional, but be consistent.

◆   **Where did Mario go? Did he go to the library? To the cafeteria? To class?**

Use a question mark after a direct question enclosed within dashes.

◆   **When the phone rang—was it 7 a.m. already?—I jumped out of bed.**

Use a question mark in parentheses to indicate uncertainty about a specific fact.

◆   **The plays of Francis Beaumont, 1584–1616(?) were as popular in their day as Shakespeare's.**

Do *not* use a question mark to convey irony or sarcasm.

◆   **Some people think it is funny (?) to humiliate other people.**

Exclamation points   30c

Use an exclamation point to convey emphasis and strong emotion in sentences that are exclamations, strong commands, or interjections.

Wow! It's late!   Stop the train!

In a direct quotation, place the exclamation point inside the quotation marks and do not use any other end punctuation.

◆ "Ouch"!/my brother cried. "That hurts!"/

Use an exclamation point after an exclamation enclosed between dashes.

They told me — I couldn't believe it! — that I'd won the lottery.

In most college writing, however, use exclamation points sparingly, if at all.

31 ◆ COMMAS

The **comma** is the most frequently used mark of punctuation in English. Commas show how a sentence is divided into parts and how those parts are related.

◆ **WP TIP** If you have trouble with commas, use the search function to locate all the commas in your paper. Evaluate each one and edit wherever necessary.

31a Commas before coordinating conjunctions that join independent clauses

Use a comma before two or more independent clauses when they are joined by a coordinating conjunction (*and, or, for, but, nor, yet,* or *so*) in a compound sentence.

We must act quickly, *or* the problem will only get worse.

The farmers ate lunch at 10:00, *and* they rested in the shade whenever they got too hot.

The comma before the conjunction may be omitted when the two independent clauses are very short and closely related: *The sun rose and the fog lifted.*

Do not use a comma without a coordinating conjunction to join independent clauses. This error is called a **comma splice.** (See 22a.)

GUIDELINES FOR USING COMMAS

As you edit, make sure you have used commas in the following places.

- ◆ Before coordinating conjunctions that join independent clauses
- ◆ To set off introductory elements
- ◆ To set off nonrestrictive modifiers and appositives
- ◆ Between items in a series
- ◆ Between coordinate adjectives
- ◆ To set off parenthetical elements
- ◆ To set off elements of contrast, tag sentences, and words of direct address
- ◆ With quotations
- ◆ With numbers, dates, names, and addresses

(For a list of common comma errors, see pp. 259–260.)

---

                                                and

◆   His hobby is raising geese, he proudly displays the blue ribbons his gander

    won at the state fair.

Commas after introductory elements   **31b**

An introductory element is a clause, phrase, expression, or word that precedes and introduces an independent clause.

Use a comma after an introductory **adverb clause** (a dependent clause beginning with *when, because, if,* and so on).

> *When Elizabeth I assumed the throne of England in 1558,* the country was in turmoil.

In most cases, use a comma following an introductory phrase to separate it from the independent clause.

PREPOSITIONAL PHRASE   *In every taste test,* the subjects chose the new flavor over the old.

INFINITIVE PHRASE   *To do the job properly,* they need more time.

PARTICIPIAL PHRASE   *Taking a cue from her instructor,* the nervous student eased the car into the parking spot.

ABSOLUTE PHRASE   *His dream of glory destroyed,* the boxer died an embittered man.

The comma is optional when a phrase has no more than two or three words and when its absence will not cause confusion.

In 1963 an assassin's bullet shocked the world.

Use a comma after introductory interjections, transitional expressions, and adjectives and adverbs that need to be separated from the independent clause.

INTERJECTION   *Yes,* we need to improve our parks.

TRANSITIONAL EXPRESSION   *In fact,* most students prefer to study in the library.

ADJECTIVE   *Angered,* the bull charged once more.

ADVERB   *Surprisingly,* the chef was not disheartened.

CONJUNCTIVE ADVERB   *Nevertheless,* taxes must be raised.

31c   Commas to set off nonrestrictive elements

Words or groups of words that are considered essential to the meaning of the sentence are called **restrictive** elements. **Nonrestrictive** elements provide additional information that is not essential to the meaning of the word or words they modify.

Do not use commas around a restrictive modifier or appositive.

Students *who are late* will be prohibited from taking the exam.
The modifier limits those who will be prohibited to a specific group.

Use commas before and after nonrestrictive modifiers and appositives.

Bus drivers, *who are generally underpaid,* work long hours at straight pay.
The modifier tells you something extra about bus drivers, but it does not identify a specific group.

Often the only clue to whether or not a modifier is essential to meaning is the way a sentence is punctuated. Rewrite the sentence, leaving out the modifier. If the meaning does not change, the modifier is probably nonrestrictive. If it does change, the modifier is restrictive.

◆ **Athletes,/who want a risky short cut to muscle bulk,/take steroids.**

Omitting the modifier who want a risky short cut to muscle bulk *alters the meaning of the sentence, so the element is restrictive. The commas are unnecessary.*

◆ **Olympic athletes ,who are in excellent physical condition ,usually perform well in this lung-capacity test.**

Without the modifier who are in excellent physical condition, *the meaning of the sentence remains the same, so the element is nonrestrictive. Commas are needed.*

Adjective clauses

Adjective clauses, those that begin with *that, where, which, who, whom,* or *whose,* can be either restrictive or nonrestrictive. *That* is used only in restrictive clauses. *Which* is always used for nonrestrictive clauses and may be used for restrictive clauses. (See 24h.)

RESTRICTIVE

The team *that scores the most points* will receive a bronze trophy.

NONRESTRICTIVE

The dinner party, *which had been carefully planned,* went smoothly.

An adjective clause that modifies an indefinite pronoun is usually restrictive because it describes or limits the indefinite pronoun. Thus it is not set off with commas. A clause that modifies a proper noun, however, is almost always nonrestrictive; thus, it needs commas.

RESTRICTIVE CLAUSE

◆ **Anyone,/who visits the National Air and Space Museum,/can touch a piece of the moon.**

NONRESTRICTIVE CLAUSE

◆ **Col. John Glenn ,who was one of the first astronauts ,later was elected to the Senate from Ohio.**

Phrases

Phrases can be either restrictive or nonrestrictive. Use commas to set off nonrestrictive phrases.

> **RESTRICTIVE PHRASE**
> ◆ A house⁄ *destroyed by fire*⁄ can smolder for days.

> **NONRESTRICTIVE PHRASE**
> ◆ This book, *written by an authority on camping*, contains valuable infor-
> mation on tents.

Appositives

An **appositive,** a noun or phrase that immediately follows a noun and renames it, can be either restrictive or nonrestrictive. Use commas to set off nonrestrictive appositives.

> **RESTRICTIVE APPOSITIVE**
> ◆ Former president *Theodore Roosevelt* was an avid big-game hunter.
> *There are many former presidents; the appositive* Theodore Roosevelt *restricts the statement to one.*

> **NONRESTRICTIVE APPOSITIVE**
> ◆ My sister, *Margaret,* often listens to music in the evening.
> *In this sentence, the speaker has only one sister, the appositive* Margaret. *Omitting the commas around the name would imply that the speaker had more than one sister.*

31d Commas between items in a series and between coordinate adjectives

A **series** consists of three or more words, phrases, or clauses that are equal in grammatical form and in importance. A coordinating conjunction—*and, or nor, for, but, yet, so*—usually precedes the final element.

Use a comma after each element in a series, including the one that precedes the conjunction.

WORDS He studied all the notes, memos, letters, and reports.

PHRASES To accelerate smoothly, to stop without jerking, and to make correct turns can require many hours of driving practice.

CLAUSES He reported that some economists believe the recession is over, that some believe it continues, but that most agree a slow recovery is under way.

Although some writers omit the comma between the last two items in a series, it is used in academic writing to avoid confusion.

Coordinate adjectives are two or more adjectives modifying the same noun—*a warm, sunny day*—that each relate independently to the noun they modify. To see whether adjectives are coordinate, try inserting *and* between them or reversing their order. If the resulting sentence still makes sense, the adjectives are coordinate and require a comma to separate them.

ADJECTIVES COORDINATE: COMMAS REQUIRED

YES   He put on a clean, pressed shirt.

YES   He put on a clean and pressed shirt.

YES   He put on a pressed, clean shirt.

ADJECTIVES NOT COORDINATE: USE NO COMMAS

YES   I found five copper coins.

NO   I found five and copper coins.

NO   I found copper five coins.

Commas to set off parenthetical elements   31e

A **parenthetical element** is a word, phrase, or clause that interrupts a sentence but does not affect its meaning. It may appear anywhere in the sentence and can be moved from one place to another without changing the meaning.

Use commas to set off parenthetical elements, no matter where they appear.

Surprisingly enough, none of the bicycles was stolen.

None of the bicycles, *surprisingly enough,* was stolen.

None of the bicycles was stolen, *surprisingly enough.*

Common sentence elements that are treated parenthetically include **transitional expressions** (*indeed, for example, in addition*), **conjunc-**

tive adverbs (*however, furthermore, therefore*), and **interjections** (*alas, oh, hey*).

TRANSITIONAL EXPRESSION

One Saturday, *for example,* we had marshmallows for breakfast.

CONJUNCTIVE ADVERB

The commissioner was unable to influence the striking players, *however.*

INTERJECTION

The replacement players were, *alas,* doomed from the start.

Parentheses and dashes are also used to set off parenthetical elements. (See 36a, 36b.)

31f Commas to set off elements of contrast, tag sentences, and direct address

Use commas around **elements of contrast,** which are words, phrases, or clauses that describe something by emphasizing what it is not or by citing some opposite condition.

The experience was illuminating, *but unnerving,* for everyone.

Jeremiah was a bullfrog, *not a toad.*

Use a comma before **tag sentences,** which are short statements or questions at the ends of sentences that express or elicit an opinion.

You received my application in time, *I hope.*

They meet every Monday, *don't they?*

Use commas to set off words of **direct address** that name the person or group to whom a sentence is directed. Such words can appear at the beginning, middle, or end of a sentence.

Lilith, I hope you are well.

That, *my friends,* is not the end of the story.

Commas with quotations   31g

A direct quotation may be accompanied by **attributory words** that identify the source of the quotation.

Use commas to set off attributory words, whether they appear before, after, or in the middle of the quotation. The comma before attributory words appears *inside* the quotation marks, not outside.

◆   **"When I went to kindergarten and had to speak English for the first time,"/**

   writes Maxine Hong Kingston, "I became silent."

Use a question mark or an exclamation point alone, without any comma, at the end of a quoted question or exclamation and before the attributory words.

◆   **"What does the latest survey show,?" Marion asked.**

Do not use commas when a quotation is preceded by *that* or when the quotation is worked into the sentence structure in some other way.

◆   **He closed by saying that/time "will prove us right."**

◆   **According to the brochure, coffee lovers have/"reason to lift their cups in celebration."**

Do not use commas with indirect discourse that uses no quotation marks.

◆   **Emerson wrote that/we should trust ourselves.**

(For more on punctuating quotations, see 35a, 35b.)

Commas with numbers, dates, names, and addresses   31h

Many different rules and conventions govern the use of commas in the following situations.

Numbers

Counting from the right, use a comma after every three digits in numbers with five or more digits. The comma is optional in four-digit numbers.

2700 (or 2,700)   79,087   467,391

Do not use a comma in page numbers, street numbers, zip codes, or years. (For numbers as figures, see 41a, 41b.)

see page 1269   21001 Southern Boulevard

Dates

Use a comma before and after the year when a date giving month, day, and year is part of a sentence.

◆   Louis Armstrong was born on July 4ˬ1900ˬin New Orleans.

When only the month and year are given or when the day precedes the month, do not use a comma.

◆   The war broke out in August,/1914,/and ended on 11 November,/1918.

Names

Use a comma to set off a title or abbreviation following a name.

◆   Joyce B. Wongˬ M.D.ˬsupervised the CPR training.

Do not use commas to enclose roman numerals following a name.

◆   Frank T. Winters,/III,/opened the meeting.

(For more on abbreviations used with names, see 42a.)

Places and addresses

Use a comma before and after the state when naming a city and state in a sentence.

◆   She was born in Lexingtonˬ Kentuckyˬand brought up in ~~New York.~~ Los Angeles.

Use a comma to separate each element of a full address given in a sentence. The zip code does not have a comma before or after it.

◆   Please note that my address will be 169 Elm Streetˬ Apartment 4ˬ Bostonˬ

MA 02116 as of July 6.

EDITING MISUSED COMMAS

Commas are the most frequently used mark of punctuation and therefore the most frequently misused. As you edit, keep the following points in mind.

Eliminate single commas between subjects and verbs, between verbs and their objects, between linking verbs and their complements, or between objects and their complements.

◆ A season of drought / worried the farmers.

  subject   *verb*

◆ The agreement entails / training the part-time staff.

  verb   *object*

◆ The laid-off workers seem / surprisingly calm.

  linking verb   *complement*

◆ The extra pay made him / quite happy.

  object   *complement*

Eliminate commas between the parts of compound elements. (See comma splices, Chapter 22.)

COMPOUND SUBJECT

◆ The members of the senior class / and their parents were invited.

COMPOUND VERB

◆ Maria quickly turned off the lights / and locked the door.

COMPOUND OBJECT

◆ Shawan put the books on the shelf / and the pens in the drawer.

COMPOUND COMPLEMENT

◆ The weather was unbearably hot / and much too humid.

COMPOUND OBJECT

◆ Gina tried to save more / and spend less.

COMPOUND COMPLEMENT

◆ The rule applies to students who have maintained their grades / and
    who have paid all their fees.

continued

Eliminate commas after an introductory phrase when the word order of the sentence is inverted.

◆ With the changing colors of fall / comes the time for cider.

Eliminate commas after an introductory phrase that functions as the subject of the sentence.

◆ Hearing that song / evokes warm memories.

Eliminate commas before and after restrictive modifiers or apposi-tives. (See 31c.)

◆ The information / that we requested / has arrived.

Make sure to use two commas where necessary to set off nonre-strictive modifiers; parenthetical elements; words of direct address; at-tributory words; elements of contrast; and dates, states, titles, and ab-breviations in the middle of a sentence. (See 31c–31h.)

◆ This book ˌ which he has read three times, is slightly tattered.

◆ Carla, on the other hand ˌ is always on time.

◆ Do you think ˌ Alex, that you could hurry a bit?

Eliminate commas that separate relative pronouns or subordinat-ing conjunctions from the dependent clauses they introduce. (See 14c.)

◆ He wrote that / home accidents are the cause of most childhood injuries.

◆ Our legislators have no idea how to proceed because / we have not come to a consensus.

Eliminate commas before the first element or after the last ele-ment in a series unless another rule requires one. (See 31d.)

◆ The primary colors are / red, yellow, and blue.

◆ They went to London, Paris, and Rome / on their last trip.

Eliminate commas between a final coordinate adjective and the noun it modifies and between adjectives that are not coordinate. (See 31d.)

◆ His old / blue / boat was finally ready for the water.

◆ Andy bought a new / black / leather motorcycle jacket.

(For guidelines on where to use commas, see p. 251.)

Commas to prevent misreading   31i

Even when no specific rule requires one, a comma is sometimes added to prevent misreading.

> We will all pitch in, in the event of a problem.

> Those who can, do what they can.

32 ◆ SEMICOLONS

A semicolon marks a stop within a sentence. It tells readers that what precedes it is complete, that what follows it is complete, and that both elements are equal in weight and closely related.

◆ **WP TIP** Use the search function to highlight semicolons in your papers and check them for correct and effective usage.

Semicolons between independent clauses   32a

You may use a semicolon instead of a comma and a coordinating conjunction to join two or more independent clauses when the clauses are closely related, especially when the relationship is one of contrast or contradiction. (See coordination, 14a – 14b.)

◆ Most dogs aim to please their owners/; ~~but~~ cats are more independent.

Use a semicolon between independent clauses joined by a **conjunctive adverb** (*however, furthermore, therefore*) or a **transitional expression** (*indeed, for example, on the other hand*). (See 22b.)

◆ Many in the community were angry/; however, they lacked a strong leader.

◆ The contract was approved/; indeed, no one questioned the restrictions.

A semicolon may also be used with a **coordinating conjunction** to join complex or long independent clauses, particularly when the clauses contain commas.

32b   SEMI

◆   If the weather clears, we'll leave at dawn,/; and if it doesn't, given the dangerous trail conditions, we'll pack up and go home.

32b   Semicolons between items in a series containing commas

Use semicolons between elements in a series when at least one element of the series includes a comma.

◆   The candidates for the award are Darnell, who won the essay competition,/; Elaine, the top debater,/; and Kiesha, who directed the senior play.

EDITING MISUSED SEMICOLONS

A few semicolons go a long way, so save them for places where they are most effective.

Eliminate semicolons that come between an independent clause and a dependent clause.

◆   Even though my head continued to hurt;/, we sat in the emergency room for an hour.

◆   He ran down the block to the old mailbox;/, where he dropped his letter into the slot.

Eliminate semicolons that come between an independent clause and a phrase.

◆   Having failed in my exasperating search of the old files and dusty records;/, I longed for a simpler research assignment.

Do not use a semicolon to introduce a list. Use a colon instead.

◆   It was a fine old house, but it needed work;/: plaster repairs, wallpaper, rewiring, paint, and a thorough cleaning.

---

33 ◆ COLONS

The **colon** indicates a more forceful stop within a sentence than does a semi-colon. As a mark of introduction, a colon alerts the reader that the information following it will provide further explanation. The colon is also used by convention in certain other situations.

◆ **WP TIP** Use the search function to locate all the colons you have used in a paper. This makes it easier to see how you have used them and simplifies the task of editing them.

Colons as marks of introduction   33a

Use a colon to introduce an explanation, example, list, or quotation. What precedes the colon must be an independent clause. The explanation or example can be a single word, a phrase, or a clause.

He has but one objective: success.

The budget agreement erected a wall between the mayor and the school board: the mayor controlled the money, and the board controlled policy.

Capitalization after a colon may vary. Some writers capitalize the first word after the colon when the first independent clause introduces a second clause that conveys the main point. A lowercase letter after a colon is always correct, however.

◆ This year's team is suprisingly inexperienced/: seven of the players are juniors and six are sophomores.

Use a colon to emphasize a list that follows an independent clause. Such a clause often contains an expression such as *the following* or *as follows*.

◆ To serve, proceed as follows/: ~~Transfer~~ *transfer* the meat to a warm platter, arrange the cooked vegetables, ladle on some of the sauce, and sprinkle with chopped parsley.

Use a colon to introduce a quotation when an independent clause precedes the quotation.

◆ As he left, he quoted Puck's final lines from *A Midsummer Night's Dream,/*: "Give me your hands, if we be friends, / And Robin shall restore amends."

Use a comma before a quotation, however, if the words preceding it do not constitute an independent clause.

◆ As the song from *South Pacific* puts it:/, "You've got to be carefully taught."

Use a colon to introduce a long quotation set off from the main text in block format. (See 35a.)

33b Colons between divisions of time, biblical chapters and verses, titles and subtitles, and in business communication

Use a colon to separate the numerals expressing hours, minutes, and seconds; to separate the numerals indicating chapter and verse in biblical citations; to separate main titles from subtitles; and after salutations and memo headings in business communications.

HOURS, MINUTES, AND SECONDS
Court convened promptly at 9:00 a.m.

The official elapsed time for the race was 2:45:56.

BIBLICAL CITATIONS
Isaiah 14:10

Note that the Modern Language Association suggests a period instead of a colon in biblical citations.

Isaiah 14.10

MAIN TITLES AND SUBTITLES
Blue Highways: A Journey into America

"A Deep Darkness: A Review of *Out of Africa*"

SALUTATIONS AND MEMO HEADINGS
Dear Mr. Nader:

To: Alex DiGiovanni
From: Paul Nkwami
Subject: 1996 budget

34 ◆ APOSTROPHES

The **apostrophe** is used primarily to show the possessive form of a noun or pronoun, to mark certain plural forms, and to indicate where a letter has been dropped in contractions. (For its use as a single quotation mark, see Chapter 35.)

Apostrophes to form the possessive case of nouns   34a

The possessive case of a noun or pronoun indicates ownership or association between the noun or pronoun and the word it modifies. To form the **possessive case,** add either an apostrophe and *-s* or just an apostrophe to nouns and some indefinite pronouns.

Singular nouns

Use an apostrophe and *-s* to form the possessive of any noun that does not end in *-s.*

Brad Pitt's new movie is his best yet.

She has long been an advocate for *children's* rights.

Use an apostrophe and -s to form the possessive of a singular noun ending in -s. If pronouncing the additional syllable is awkward, you may use the apostrophe alone.

Don't waste the *class's* time.

The company produced *Yeats'* cycle of plays about the Irish hero Cuchulain.

Plural nouns

Use an apostrophe alone to form the possessive case of a plural noun ending in -s.

They owe her several *months'* pay.

Compound nouns

To form the possessive of a hyphenated or unhyphenated compound noun, use an apostrophe and -s on only the last word.

◆ He borrowed his mother's-in-law's car.

◆ The secretary's of ~~state~~ state's office certified the election results.

Joint possession

When nouns joined by *and* form a unit that has joint possession, use an apostrophe and -s on only the last noun.

◆ My aunt's and uncle's anniversary party was a disaster.

When nouns joined by *and* are individuals with separate possession, add an apostrophe and -s to each noun.

◆ The documentary compared *Aretha ~~Franklin~~ Franklin's and Diana Ross's* early careers.

34b Apostrophes to form the possessive case of indefinite pronouns

An **indefinite pronoun** is a pronoun that does not refer to any specific person or thing.

Use an apostrophe and -s to form the possessive case of some indefinite pronouns, including *someone, anybody, no one, one,* and *another.*

POSSESSIVE FORMS

SINGULAR	SINGULAR POSSESSIVE	PLURAL	PLURAL POSSESSIVE
school	school's	schools	schools'
box	box's	boxes	boxes'
class	class's	classes	classes'
Duvalier	Duvalier's	Duvaliers	Duvaliers'
Jones	Jones's	Joneses	Joneses'

When spoken, the singular possessive, the plural, and the plural possessive sound the same for most words. In writing, the spelling and the placement of the apostrophe help readers distinguish among the three forms.

Someone's umbrella was left at the bank.

It's *no one's* business but my own.

Do not use an apostrophe and -*s* with the indefinite pronouns *all, any, both, each, few, many, most, much, none, several, some,* and *such.* Use the preposition *of* to show possession with these pronouns, or use a pronoun that has a possessive form.

◆   The syllabus for the Dickinson and Crane seminar requires that we read
     the   of both.
     ~~both's~~ complete works.

◆   With so many applicants, we find it difficult to provide a personal response
     everyone's
     to ~~each's~~ questions.

Apostrophes to form plurals of words used as words and letters, numbers, and symbols

Use an apostrophe and -*s* to form the plural of a word discussed as a word or term and to form the plural of letters, numbers, and symbols.

There are two *perhaps*'s in that sentence.

The word *occurrence* is spelled with two *r*'s.

34c APOS

EDITING MISUSED APOSTROPHES

Possessives and contractions often sound alike—*whose* and *who's, its* and *it's, your* and *you're*. So do plurals and plural possessives. As you edit, be especially careful to check the placement and appropriateness of the apostrophes you use.

Eliminate apostrophes you may have used to make the possessive forms of plurals.

◆   Theirs'\ is the glory, theirs'\ the fame.

Eliminate apostrophes you may have used in forming the plural of a noun. (See the box on p. 267.)

◆   Although they seemed like a happy family, the ~~Simpson's~~ *Simpsons* did not always

behave that way.

Make sure you have not confused a possessive with a contraction, or a contraction with a possessive.

◆   ~~Your~~ *You're* late.

When you see a word with an apostrophe, spell out the contraction. If it is a true contraction, the sentence will still make sense: *You are late.*

◆   ~~You're~~ *Your* hat looks like a biscuit box.

Spell out the contraction. You are hat *is nonsense.*

◆   The accused are innocent until proven guilty, ~~its~~ *it's* said.

When you see a pronoun such as its, your, *or* their, *substitute the prepositional phrase* of it, of you, *or* of them. *If the possessive is correct, the sentence will make sense.* Of it said *doesn't make sense.*

◆   Can you hear ~~it's~~ *its* heartbeat?

The heartbeat of it *does make sense.*

Some children have difficulty learning to write *8*'s.

A row of ***'s marks the spot where I'm having trouble.

Note that words, numbers, and letters referred to as themselves are italicized—that is, underlined in typescript. The apostrophe and the final *s*, however, are not italicized.

You may use an apostrophe and -s for the plural of centuries and decades expressed in figures. (The Modern Language Association recommends the letter -s with no apostrophe.) Do not use an apostrophe when the century or decade is expressed in words.

the 60s (or the 60's)   the 1800s (or the 1800's)   the sixties

Use an apostrophe and -s for plurals of abbreviations ending with periods. Use -s alone for abbreviations without periods.

My science professor has earned two *Ph.D.'s.*

Like all politicians, she has some *IOUs* to call in.

Apostrophes to form contractions   34d

A **contraction** is a word in which one or more letters are intentionally omitted and replaced by an apostrophe.

Use an apostrophe to replace one or more letters intentionally omitted in a contraction: *they're, 'bye.* An apostrophe can also be used to show that digits have been dropped from a number, especially a year: *the class of '99.*

COMMON CONTRACTIONS

cannot	can't	does not	doesn't
do not	don't	would not	wouldn't
has not	hasn't	have not	haven't
will not	won't	was not	wasn't
she would	she'd	it is	it's
who is	who's	you are	you're
I am	I'm	they are	they're
let us	let's	we have	we've
there is	there's	she has	she's

35 ◆ QUOTATION MARKS

Quotation marks indicate that certain words you have used in your writing are not your own. They also distinguish certain titles, foreign expressions, and special terms from the main body of the text. American English uses **double quotation marks** (" ") for quotations, titles, and so on and **single quotation marks** (' ')—apostrophes on the typewriter and on many computers—for quotations within quotations (or titles within titles).

In **direct quotation**—quoting another person's exact words, either written or spoken—you must enclose those words in quotation marks and indicate your source of information when appropriate. In **paraphrase** or **indirect quotation,** you do not use quotation marks, although you should acknowledge the source. (For more on identifying sources, see 46b.)

Quotation style varies somewhat from discipline to discipline. This chapter follows the conventions of the Modern Language Association, the authority for papers written in the languages and literature. (For more information on quoting and documenting sources using the MLA style, see Chapter 47. For more information on quoting and documenting sources in other disciplines, see Chapters 48–49.)

◆ **WP TIP** To check that you have used quotation marks correctly and in pairs, have your computer search for all beginning quotation marks. Then examine the passages that follow them and verify that you have ended with closing quotation marks every time.

35a Quotation marks for direct quotations

When quoting another person's exact words directly, keep in mind the following two conventions for quoting short or long passages.

Short passages

Use quotation marks to enclose brief direct quotations of up to four typed lines of prose or up to three lines of poetry. Any parenthetical citation of a source goes after the closing quotation marks but before the period.

> In *Lives under Siege,* Ratzenburger argues that "most adolescents are far too worried about the next six months and far too unconcerned about the next sixty years" (84).

Use single quotation marks for a quotation within a quotation.

After the election, the incumbent said, "My opponent will soon learn, as someone once said, 'You can't fool all of the people all of the time.' "

When quoting poetry within the body of your essay, use a slash preceded and followed by a single space to indicate line breaks. (See 36e.)

Shakespeare concludes Sonnet 18 with this couplet: "So long as men can breathe or eyes can see, / So long lives this, and this gives life to thee."

Long passages

Set off longer quotations from the main text in **block format.** Start a new line for the quotation, indent all lines of the quotation ten spaces, and do not use quotation marks. If the words that introduce a block quotation are a complete sentence, use a colon or a period after them. If they are not a complete sentence, use either a comma or no punctuation, depending on the structure. (See 31g.) Place a source in parentheses one space after the end punctuation of the quotation. Here is an example of a block quotation.

```
A recent editorial describes the problem:

        In countries like the United States, breast-
        feeding, though always desirable, doesn't mean
        the difference between good and poor nutrition--
        or life and death. But it does in developing
        countries, where for decades infant food manu-
        facturers have been distributing free samples of
        infant formulas to hospitals and birthing cen-
        ters. (Daily Times 17)

The editorial goes on to argue that the samples last only
long enough for the mothers' own milk to dry up; then the
mothers find they cannot afford to buy the formula.
```

Use double quotation marks for a quotation within a block quotation, since the outer quotation has none.

Note that paragraph indents are not used for quoting single paragraphs or parts of paragraphs. For two or more paragraphs, indent the first line of each new paragraph after the first (use three additional spaces).

For poetry, copy as precisely as possible the line breaks, indents, spacing, and capitalization of the original.

In *Patience,* W. S. Gilbert has the character Reginald Bunthorne proclaim,

> This air severe
> Is but a mere
> Veneer!
>
> This cynic smile
> Is but a wile
> Of guile! (5–10)

35b Quotation marks for dialogue

Use quotation marks to set off dialogue. Start a new paragraph every time the speaker changes. This pattern tells readers who is speaking even without attributory words.

> "Early parole is not the solution to overcrowding," the prosecutor said. "We need a new jail."
> The chairman of the county commission asked, "How do you propose we pay for it?"
> "Increase taxes if you must, but whatever you do, act quickly."

If one speaker's words continue for more than a single paragraph, use quotation marks at the beginning of each new paragraph but at the end of only the last paragraph. (For commas to set off attributions, see 31g.)

35c Quotation marks for certain titles

Use quotation marks for the titles of brief poems, book chapters and parts, magazine and journal articles, episodes of television series, and songs. (Use italics or underlining for titles of longer works, such as books, magazines and journals, recordings, films, plays, and television series.)

"Araby" is the third story in James Joyce's book *Dubliners*.

This chart appeared with the article "Will Your Telephone Last?" in November's *Consumer Reports*.

In my favorite episode of *I Love Lucy,* "Job Switching," Lucy and Ethel work in a chocolate factory.

The Beatles' *Sgt. Pepper's Lonely Hearts Club Band* includes the song "A Day in the Life."

(For more on italics and quotation marks, see 40a.)

Do not use quotation marks or italics for

1 Titles of parts of a work or series that are generic rather than specific

Chapter 6   Part II   Episode 43

2 Titles of sacred works, part of sacred works, and ancient manuscripts

the Talmud   the Koran   the Book of Kells

3 Documents

the Constitution   the Gettysburg Address

Use single quotation marks for quoted material that is part of a title enclosed in double quotation marks.

We read "'This Is the End of the World': The Black Death" by historian Barbara Tuchman.

TITLES WITHIN TITLES

Use the following models when presenting titles within titles. These guidelines also apply to other words normally indicated by quotation marks or by italics (or underscoring on the typewriter), such as quotations and foreign words, when they appear in titles.

1   A title enclosed in quotation marks within an italicized (or underscored) title

  "A Curtain of Green" and Other Stories

2   An italicized title within a title enclosed in quotation marks

  "Morality in *Death of a Salesman*"

3   A title enclosed in quotation marks within another title enclosed in quotation marks

  "Symbolism in 'Everyday Use'"

4   An italicized title within another italicized title

  Modern Critics on Hamlet *and Other Plays*

Do not use quotation marks of any sort for titles at the top of your own essays, poems, or stories. Do, however, use them for any part of a title or quotation that you use in your title.

An Analysis of the "My Turn" Column in *Newsweek*

35d Quotation marks for special purposes

Translations

Use quotation marks around the translation of a foreign word or phrase into English. (You can also use parentheses for this purpose: see 36a.) The foreign word or phrase itself is italicized.

I've always called Antonio *fratellino,* or "little brother," because he is six years younger than I.

Special terms

Use quotation marks around specialized terms when they are first introduced and defined.

The ecology of this "cryocore" — a region of perpetual ice and snow — has been studied very little.

He called the new vegetable a "broccoflower," a yellow-green cross between broccoli and cauliflower.

Irony

Quotation marks may be used around a word or phrase used ironically—that is, with a meaning opposed to its literal one.

Jonathan Swift's essay "A Modest Proposal" offers a quick "solution" to Ireland's poverty and overpopulation: eat the children.

Unusual nicknames

Use quotation marks around unusual nicknames at first mention.

When I joined the firm, the president was a man named Garnett E. "Ding" Cannon.

Quotation marks with other punctuation   **35e**

Which punctuation mark comes first when a word is followed by a quotation mark and another mark of punctuation? Both logic and convention govern the order.

Periods and commas

Put periods and commas inside quotation marks. (For more on the uses of periods and commas with quotations, see Chapter 30 and 31g.)

> After Gina finished singing "Memories," Joe began to hum "The Way We Were."

> "Denver is usually warm in the spring," he said, "but this year it's positively hot."

Colons and semicolons

Put colons and semicolons outside quotation marks. (For colons to introduce quotations, see 33a.)

> The sign read "Closed": there would be no cold soda for us today.

> In 1982, Bobbie Ann Mason wrote "Shiloh"; it is considered one of her finest works.

Question marks, exclamation points, and dashes

Put question marks, exclamation points, and dashes inside the quotation marks if they are part of the quotation, outside the quotation marks if they are not. (For the uses of these punctuation marks with quotations, see 30b, 30c, and 36b.)

> She asked, "Have you read 'The Tiger'?"
>
> Was it you who said "Who's there"?
>
> He began singing "Oklahoma!" and doing a square dance.
>
> I can't believe you've never read "The Lottery"!
>
> "Hold on a minute. I can't hear—"
>
> Emma's first word—"dada"—caused her father to beam.

(For the uses of brackets and ellipses with quotation marks, see 36c–36d.)

EDITING MISUSED QUOTATION MARKS

Quotation marks are used frequently in academic writing, and they can be tricky. Examining some of their common misuses can help you as you edit your own papers.

Quotation marks are like shoes: use them in pairs. (The only exception is in extended dialogue; see 35b.)

◆ "There are always a few students who boycott the assembly," he said, "but

that's no reason for us to call it off."

When quoting passages, make sure the material enclosed within the quotation marks is only quoted words. (For modifying quoted material, see uses of brackets, 36d.)

If the logic of a sentence dictates that a quotation end with a question mark or an exclamation point but sentence grammar calls for a period or comma as well, use the stronger mark (the question mark or exclamation point) and delete the weaker one (the period or comma).

◆ As soon as we heard someone shout "Fire!," we began to run for the exit.

Do not use quotation marks to indicate emphasis. Emphasis is achieved through rhythm and sentence structure, although you may use italics for emphasis when necessary.

◆ He was guilty of a "felony," not a misdemeanor.

Do not use quotation marks for slang or for terms you think are overused. Instead, consider substituting another word or phrase.

◆ Several of these companies should go into a "hall of shame" for their em-

ployment practices.

---

36 ◆ OTHER PUNCTUATION

Parentheses, dashes, ellipsis points, brackets, and slashes each have specific uses. Using them correctly gives extra polish to your writing.

Parentheses   36a

Parentheses enclose elements that would otherwise interrupt a sentence: explanations, examples, asides, and supplementary information. Parentheses are also used to set off cross-references, citations, and numbers in a list. Because they de-emphasize the material they enclose, use them carefully.

Explanations, examples, and asides

Use parentheses to enclose explanations, examples, and asides within a sentence.

Relatives of famous people now famous themselves include Angelica Huston (daughter of John) and Michael Douglas (son of Kirk).

Parentheses may also be used to enclose the translation of a specialized term or foreign word that appears in italics. (For quotation marks and dashes around translations, see 35d and 36b.)

English also borrowed the Dutch word *koekje* (cookie).

Dates, cross-references, and citations

Use parentheses to set off the date of an event or the dates of a person's birth and death.

The Oxford English Dictionary was first published under the editorship of James A. H. Murray (1888 – 1933).

Use parentheses to enclose cross-references to other parts of your paper or to enclose documentation. (For more on documentation styles, see Chapters 47 – 49.)

The map (p. 4) shows the areas of heaviest rainfall.

Nick Carraway felt unsettled to see Gatsby at the end of his dock beckoning in the direction of a "single green light" (21).

Numbers or letters in a list

Use parentheses to enclose numbers or letters that introduce items in a list within a sentence.

The dictionary provides (1) pronunciation, (2) etymology, (3) past meanings, and (4) usage citations for almost 300,000 words.

Using other punctuation with parentheses

Do not place a comma directly before a set of parentheses.

◆ His favorite American authors include Mark Twain, Emily Dickinson,/ (he always refers to her as "my favorite recluse"), and Zora Neale Hurston.

When a parenthetical sentence is not enclosed within another sentence, capitalize the first word and use end punctuation inside the final parenthesis.

◆ The countess of Dia is almost forgotten today. (she was quite well known *She* in her own time.)

When a parenthetical sentence falls within another sentence, use no period, and do not capitalize the first word.

◆ Uncle Henry (He is my mother's brother./) has won many awards for his *he* poetry.

(For help determining whether to use parentheses, dashes, or commas, see the box on p. 280.)

36b · Dashes

Dashes set off explanations, definitions, examples, appositives, and other supplementary information, as well as interruptions and pauses in speech. They call attention to the material they set off and thus may be used to emphasize contrasts.

To create a dash on the typewriter, use two hyphens with no space on either side (--).

Explanations, examples, and asides

Use dashes to set off explanations, definitions, examples, or appositives within sentences.

The *frijoles refritos* — refried beans — were home made.

At first we did not notice the rain—it began so softly—but soon we were soaked through.

◆ Of all the oddities in Richard's apartment, the contents in the bathtub—transistors, resistors, circuit boards, and odd bits of wire—were the strangest of all.

Contrasts, interruptions, or shifts in thought

Use dashes to emphasize contrasts.

We have all read the novels of British and American writers, but few of us know even the titles of novels by German or Spanish writers—not to mention those by Asian or African writers.

Use dashes to indicate a pause, interruption, or abrupt shift in thought.

"Well, I guess I was a little late—OK, an hour late."

"Hold on," she shouted, "while I grab this—"

◆ "Nothing is so exciting as seeing an eagle—there's one now!"

Using dashes with other punctuation

Do not capitalize the first word enclosed by dashes within another sentence. If the enclosed sentence is a question or an exclamation, use a question mark or an exclamation point at the end, but do not capitalize the first word.

◆ Ward and June Cleaver—who can forget their orderly world?—never once question their roles in life.

Do not use commas or periods immediately before or after a dash.

◆ My cousin Eileen—she was from Ireland—brought a strange flute with her when she came to visit.

◆ With so many things happening at once—graduation, a new job—Joan hardly knew who she was any more.

COMMAS, PARENTHESES, OR DASHES?

Commas, parentheses, and dashes can all be used to set off nonessential material within a sentence. Use **commas** when the material being set off is closely related in meaning to the rest of the sentence.

> A dusty plow, the kind the early Amish settlers used, hung on the wall of the old barn.

Use **parentheses** when the material being set off is not closely related and when you want to de-emphasize it.

> Two young boys found an old plow (perhaps as old as the first Amish settlement) hidden in an unused corner of the barn.

Use **dashes** when the material being set off is not closely related to the main sentence and you want to emphasize it.

> The old plow—the one his great-grandfather had used—was still in good working order.

Do not overuse dashes.

◆   He never told his father about his dreams—he couldn't bear to—but he

began to make plans—plans that would lead him away from this small

town.

36c   Ellipsis points

Ellipsis points are three periods, each preceded and followed by a space. They are used to mark an **ellipsis,** the deliberate omission of words or entire sentences from a direct quotation.

Use an ellipsis to indicate an omission within a sentence.

> In *Drawing on the Right Side of the Brain,* Betty Edwards tells the reader, "You may feel that . . . it's the drawing that is hard."

If the omission comes before the end of a sentence in the original, use a period or other end punctuation before an ellipsis.

Edwards addresses the reader directly with a provocative assertion: "Drawing is not really very hard. . . . You may not believe me at this moment."

Use a whole line of spaced ellipsis points when you omit a line or more of poetry.

> She walks in beauty, like the night
> . . . .
> And all that's best of dark and bright
> Meet in her aspect and her eyes.

Use ellipsis points to indicate a pause or interruption in dialogue.

"The panther tracks come from that direction, . . . but where do they go after that?" he wondered.

Brackets   36d

Brackets are used to enclose words that are added to or changed within direct quotations.

Use brackets to enclose small changes that clarify the meaning of a reference or of a word or to make quoted words read correctly within the context of a sentence.

E. B. White describes just such a spring day. "Any noon in Madison Square, you may see [a sparrow] pick up a straw in his beak, [and] put on an air of great business, twisting his head and glancing at the sky."

E. B. White describes a sparrow on a spring day. "Any noon in Madison Square [in New York City], you may see one pick up a straw in his beak, [and] put on an air of great business, twisting his head and glancing at the sky."

White concludes by noting that the bird "[hopped] three or four times and [dropped] both the straw and the incident."

Use the Latin word *sic* ("such") within brackets to indicate that an error in quoted material was present in the original.

In its statement, the commission said that its new health insurance program "will not effect [*sic*] the quality of medical care for county employees."

Within parentheses, use brackets to avoid double parentheses.

> Theodore Bernstein explains that a person who feels sick is *nauseated:* "A person who feels sick is not *nauseous* any more than a person who has been *poisoned* is *poisonous.*" (*Do's, Don'ts and Maybes of English Usage* [New York: *Times,* 1977]).

36e   Slashes

The **slash** (/) is a slanted line, also called a **solidus** or **virgule,** that is used to separate lines of poetry quoted in text, to indicate alternative choices, and to separate figures in certain situations.

Use a slash, preceded and followed by a space, to mark the end of a line of poetry incorporated in text.

> Shakespeare opens *The Passionate Pilgrim* with a seeming paradox: "When my love swears that she is made of truth, / I do believe her, though I know she lies."

Use a slash with no space before or after to separate alternatives.

> an either/or situation

> a pass/fail grading system

> the President and/or Congress

Use a slash to separate month, day, and year in a date given entirely in figures and to separate the numerator and the denominator in a typed fraction written entirely in figures. Use a hyphen to separate a whole number from its fraction.

> 7/16/99   2-1/16

V

EDITING MECHANICS

43 ◆ DOCUMENT PREPARATION 313

EDITING MECHANICS

The conventions that govern spelling and the use of capital letters, hyphens, italics, numbers, and abbreviations help readers to understand your meaning. The conventions that govern the preparation of documents, whether a two-page essay or a business letter, are equally important since a reader's first impression is often based on what a document looks like.

37 ◆ SPELLING

English spelling seems sometimes to defy reason. As the English language has borrowed and then absorbed words from other languages, it has assumed or adapted the spellings of the originals. Thus, pronunciation is often not a good key to spelling. The same sound may be represented in different letter combinations—such as with the long *e* sound in *meet, seat, concrete, petite, conceit,* and *piece.* Conversely, the same letter or letter combination can represent different sounds—such as the *a* in *amaze,* the *g* in *gorgeous,* and the *ough* in *tough, though,* and *through.*

Commonly confused words   37a

Homonyms

Homonyms are words with the same sound but different meanings: *great, grate; fair, fare.* Be especially careful when spelling similar-sounding words; see the chart of homonyms on pages 287–289. It is particularly easy to confuse contractions with their homonyms—*it's* for *its* and *their* for *there* or *they're.* (For more on contractions and apostrophe problems, see 34d.)

One word or two?

Some words can be written as one word or two, and the form that is used can make a difference in meaning. Some common examples are

all ready (completely prepared)	already (previously)
all together (all in one place)	altogether (thoroughly)
all ways (all methods)	always (at all times)
a lot (a large amount)	allot (distribute, assign)

every day (each day)	everyday (ordinary)
may be (could be)	maybe (perhaps)
some time (an amount of time)	sometime (at some unspecified time)

Consult a dictionary when in doubt as to whether a word should be one word or two. If it isn't in the dictionary, it isn't one word.

◆ **WP TIP** If you frequently confuse homonyms or other words, ask your computer to find your problem words, and then make sure you have used the right spelling for each one.

Words with similar spellings

Words spelled and pronounced very much alike—and perhaps closely related in meaning—are easy to misspell. Such pairs include these:

advice (noun)	human (of people)
advise (verb)	humane (merciful)
breath (noun)	personal (pertaining to a person)
breathe (verb)	personnel (employees; staff)
chose (past tense)	perspective (angle of view)
choose (present tense)	prospective (in the future)
device (noun)	prophecy (noun)
devise (verb)	prophesy (verb)
envelope (noun)	
envelop (verb)	

The only sure way to know how to spell troublesome words correctly is to memorize their spellings and meanings. However, differences in pronunciation can sometimes signal which spelling is the right one.

American versus British spellings

Use American spellings rather than British ones: *center,* not *centre; labor,* not *labour.* If you forget which is which, check your dictionary.

HOMONYMS AND OTHER SIMILAR-SOUNDING WORDS

accept (receive)
except (leave out)

access (approach)
excess (too much)

adapt (change)
adopt (choose)

affect (influence)
effect (result)

allot (assign, distribute)
a lot (a large amount)

allude (suggest)
elude (escape)

allusion (suggestion)
illusion (deception)

already (previously)
all ready (completely prepared)

altar (church table)
alter (change)

altogether (entirely)
all together (all in one place)

ascent (climb)
assent (agree)

always (at all times)
all ways (all methods)

bare (uncovered)
bear (carry; the animal)

bazaar (market)
bizarre (weird)

birth (childbearing)
berth (place of rest)

board (plank; food)
bored (drilled; uninterested)

born (given birth to)
borne (carried)

break (smash, split)
brake (stopping device)

canvas (fabric)
canvass (examine)

capital (city; wealth)
capitol (building)

censor (prohibit)
sensor (measuring device)

cite (mention)
site (place); sight (vision)

coarse (rough)
course (way, path)

complement (make complete)
compliment (praise)

conscience (moral sense)
conscious (aware)

council (committee)
counsel (advice; adviser)

cursor (computer marker)
curser (swearer)

dairy (milk-producing farm)
diary (daily book)

dessert (sweet food)
desert (dry land)

dissent (disagreement)
descent (movement downward)

continued

HOMONYMS AND OTHER SIMILAR-SOUNDING WORDS

dual (having two parts)
duel (fight between two people)

dye (color)
die (perish)

elicit (draw forth)
illicit (improper)

eminent (noteworthy)
imminent (impending)

ensure (make certain)
insure (indemnify)

everyday (ordinary)
every day (each day)

exercise (activity)
exorcise (drive out)

fair (just)
fare (food; fee)

faze (disturb)
phase (stage)

formerly (at an earlier time)
formally (according to a pattern)

forth (forward)
fourth (follows *third*)

forward (to the front)
foreword (preface)

gorilla (ape)
guerrilla (fighter)

hear (perceive)
here (in this place)

heard (perceived)
herd (group of animals)

heroin (drug)
heroine (principal female character)

hole (opening)
whole (entire)

holy (sacred)
wholly (entirely)

immigrate (come in)
emigrate (leave)

its (possessive of *it*)
it's (contraction of *it is*)

know (be aware)
no (negative, not yes)

lead (metal)
led (guided)

lesson (instruction)
lessen (reduce)

lightning (electric flash)
lightening (making less heavy)

maybe (perhaps)
may be (could be)

meat (food)
meet (encounter)

miner (excavator)
minor (person under a given age)

pair (two)
pear (fruit); pare (peel; reduce)

passed (went by)
past (an earlier time)

peace (absence of war)
piece (part, portion)

peer (look; equal)
pier (pillar)

plain (simple; flat land)
plane (flat surface; smooth off)

continued

pray (ask, implore)
prey (hunt down; what is hunted)

principle (rule)
principal (chief, chief person; sum of money)

quiet (silent)
quite (really, positively, very much)

rain (precipitation)
reign (rule)

right (proper; entitlement)
rite (ritual)

road (path)
rode (past of *ride)*

scene (setting, stage setting)
seen (perceived)

sense (perception)
since (from that time)

shone (past of *shine)*
shown (displayed)

sometime (at some time)
some time (an amount of time)

stationary (not moving)
stationery (writing paper)

straight (not curved)
strait (narrow place)

tack (angle of approach)
tact (sensitivity, diplomacy)

taut (tight)
taught (past of *teach)*

than (word of comparison)
then (at that time)

their (possessive of *them)*
there (in that place); they're (contraction of *they are)*

threw (past of *throw)*
through (by way of)

to (in the direction of)
too (also); two (the number)

waist (middle of the torso)
waste (squander)

weak (feeble)
week (seven days)

wear (carry on the body)
where (in what place)

weather (atmospheric conditions)
whether (if, in case)

which (what one)
witch (sorceress)

whose (possessive of *who)*
who's (contraction of *who is)*

write (inscribe, record)
wright (builder)
right (correct)

your (possessive of *you)*
you're (contraction of *you are)*

Basic spelling rules   37b

The *ie/ei* rule and its exceptions

The familiar rule that "*i* comes before *e* except after *c,* or when sounded like *ay* as in *neighbor* and *weigh*" holds true in most cases.

SPELLING TIPS

Misspellings can undermine your credibility as a writer. In some cases, your reader will even misunderstand what you mean.

◆ Always consult a dictionary when you are in doubt about how to spell a word.

◆ When checking the spelling of an unfamiliar word, note its *etymology,* or its origin and the history of its usage. This information will help you understand why a word is spelled in a particular way and thus fix the correct spelling in your mind.

◆ Keep a personal spelling list of difficult words you encounter in your notebook or journal. Check to see if the word shares a root, prefix, or suffix with a word you already know; the connection helps you learn the meaning, as well as the spelling, of the new word.

◆ Use the spelling checker on your word processor to proofread your papers. It locates transposed or dropped letters as well as misspellings.

◆ Proofread your work carefully, even when you use a spelling checker. If your spelling is right but the word is wrong, however, the computer can't help. For example, if you confuse *to, too,* and *two* or *its* and *it's,* the spelling checker won't catch it because it can't recognize the context in which the word is used.

◆ **WP TIP** Keep a list of words you frequently misspell in a special file on your computer disk. Use the search-and-replace function to locate and correct the words on your list.

---

i before *e:* belief, field, friend, mischief, niece, patience, piece, priest, review, shield, view

ei after *c:* ceiling, conceit, conceive, deceit, deceive, receipt

ei sounding like "ay": eight, feign, freight, sleigh

The common exceptions to this rule can be memorized.

ie after *c:* ancient, conscience, financier, science, species

ei not after *c* and not sounding like "ay": caffeine, codeine, counterfeit, either, feisty, foreign, forfeit, height, leisure, neither, seize, weird

---

PRONUNCIATION AND SPELLING

If you spell some words exactly as you pronounce them, you will probably misspell them. As you edit, try to pronounce each word in your mind the way it is spelled, not the way you normally say it.
The following words can be troublesome.

accidentally	literature	recognize
arctic	mathematics	relevant
arithmetic	memento	roommate
athlete	mischievous	sandwich
candidate	nuclear	similar
congratulations	possibly	surprise
environment	prejudice (noun)	temperature
extraordinary	prejudiced (adjective)	tentative
February	probably	usually
interference	pronunciation	veteran
laboratory	quantity	Wednesday
library	realtor	wintry

Spelling rules for suffixes

A **suffix** is a letter or a group of letters added to the end of a word that changes its meaning and sometimes its spelling.

> *The suffixes* -cede, -ceed, *and* -sede
> The syllables -cede, -ceed, and -sede sound alike and are often confused.
>
> **-cede** (most common): concede, intercede, precede, recede, secede, and so on
>
> **-ceed:** exceed, proceed, succeed
>
> **-sede** (appears in only one word): supersede

Suffixes after words ending in y
If the letter before the final *y* is a consonant, change the *y* to *i* before adding the suffix unless the suffix begins with *i*.

    friendly, friendlier   happy, happily   apply, applying

Keep the *y* if the letter before the *y* is a vowel.

    convey, conveyed   annoy, annoyed   pay, payment

Exception: Some very short words ending in *y* do not change the *y* to *i*: *dryly, shyly, wryly.* However, other short words do change the *y* to *i*: *daily, gaily.*

Suffixes after words ending in e
When the suffix begins with a consonant, keep the final *e* before the suffix.

    sure, surely   polite, politeness   hate, hateful

Exception: *acknowledgment, argument, judgment, truly, wholly, awful,* and *ninth.*

When the suffix begins with a vowel, drop the final *e* before the suffix except when the *e* is necessary to prevent misreading. (*Dyeing* is not the same thing as *dying,* for example.)

    admire, admirable   insure, insuring   close, closest

Exception: Keep the *e* after a soft *c* (which sounds like *s,* not *k*) or a soft *g* (which sounds like *j* or *jh*) when the suffix starts with an *a* or *o*.

    enforce, enforceable   outrage, outrageous

Suffixes after words ending in a consonant
When adding a suffix to a base word ending in a consonant, do not change the spelling, even if a double consonant results.

    benefit, benefited   girl, girllike   fuel, fueling

An exception to this rule is *format, formatting, formatted.*

When a suffix begins with a vowel, double the final consonant of a base

word if (1) it is preceded by a single vowel *and* (2) the base word is one syllable or the stress is on the last syllable.

    occur, occurrence   admit, admitting   slap, slapped

Final -y *or* -ally
The suffixes -*ly* and -*ally* turn nouns into adjectives or adjectives into
adverbs.

Add -*ally* to words that end in -*ic.* The one exception is *publicly.*

    basically   automatically   characteristically

Add -*ly* to words that do not end in -*ic.*

    absolutely   nationally   really

Spelling rules for plurals

Most English nouns are made plural by adding -*s.* The following are exceptions to this rule.

Nouns ending in ch, s, sh, *or* x
Add -*es* to form the plural of most nouns ending in *ch, s, sh,* or *x.*

    church, churches   glass, glasses   wish, wishes   box, boxes

Nouns ending in y
Add -*s* to form the plural of nouns ending in *y* if the letter before the *y* is a
vowel. Change the *y* to *i* and add -*es* if the letter before the *y* is a consonant.

    day, days   alloy, alloys   melody, melodies   dairy, dairies

Nouns ending in o
Add -*s* to form the plural of most nouns ending in *o.*

    video, videos   trio, trios   inferno, infernos   burro, burros

For a few nouns that end in an *o* preceded by a consonant, form the plural by
adding -*es.*

    embargo, embargoes   hero, heroes   potato, potatoes

For other nouns that end in *o,* the plural can be formed either way.

    zero, zeros, zeroes   cargo, cargos, cargoes   tornado, tornados, tornadoes

Nouns ending in f and fe
Change the *f* to *v* and add *-es* to form the plural of some nouns ending in *f.*

leaf, leaves	self, selves	half, halves	thief, thieves

Add *-s* to form the plural of other nouns ending in *f.*

brief, briefs	belief, beliefs	reef, reefs	proof, proofs

For still other nouns ending in *f,* the plural can be formed either way: *hoof, hoofs, hooves.*

For some but not all nouns ending in *-fe,* change the *f* to *v* before adding *-s.*

wife, wives	knife, knives	safe, safes	strife, strifes

Irregular and unusual plural forms
Learn the few nouns that form plurals without adding *-s* or *-es.*

woman, women	man, men	goose, geese
child, children	foot, feet	mouse, mice

A handful of words that do not add *-s* have the same form for singular and plural.

moose, moose	sheep, sheep	series, series

Plurals of proper nouns
Add *-s* to form the plural of most proper nouns.

the Chungs	the Kennedys	several Jennifers

Add *-es* when the plural ending is pronounced as a separate syllable, as happens when proper nouns end in *ch, s, sh, x,* or *z.*

the Ameses	the Bushes	the Lopezes

Do not use an apostrophe to indicate the plural of a proper noun. (See 34c).

Plurals of compound nouns
When a compound noun is written as one word, make only the last part of the compound plural. An exception to this rule is *passersby.*

newspapers	henhouses	notebooks

When a compound noun is written as separate words or when it is hyphenated, pluralize the word that expresses the main idea, usually a noun.

    attorneys general   brothers-in-law
    bath towels   ladies-in-waiting

(See also 34c.)

38 ◆ CAPITALIZATION

Capital letters mark the beginning of sentences and the first letters of names, titles, and certain other words. The first-person singular pronoun *I* (*I'm, I'll, I'd*) and the interjection *O* (*O best beloved* and *forgive us, O Lord*) are also capitalized. (For capitalization of abbreviations, see 42e.)

Capitalization of the first word of sentences   38a

Use a capital letter at the beginning of a sentence or an intentional sentence fragment.

    Alfred enjoyed working in the garden. And in the conservatory.

Capitalization is optional in a series of fragmentary questions, but be consistent.

    What, we wondered, was the occasion? A holiday? Someone's birthday?

Capitalization in quotations and lines of poetry   38b

Quotations

    Capitalize the first word of quoted sentences.

    "We'd like to talk to you about the women's sports budget," Carmen told the athletic director. "Ryan has the first question."

Do not capitalize the first word of the continuation of a quotation interrupted by attributory words.

> "Indeed," Mr. Kott responded, "we field men's and women's teams in track, swimming, and golf."

If the first word of a quotation does not begin a sentence, do not capitalize it.

> Recognizing details familiar from his childhood, E. B. White feels "the same damp moss covering the worms in the fishing can."

Feel free to change the capitalization from that in an original prose source to fit the needs of your own sentences. Be sure to enclose such changes in square brackets, however. (See 36d.)

Lines of poetry

Poets make deliberate decisions about when and how they use capital letters. When quoting poetry, always follow the capitalization of the original.

> The poem opens with Frost's usual directness and rhythmic formality: "Whose woods these are, I think I know. / His house is in the village, though." Compare this to Lucille Clifton's offhanded "boys / i don't promise you nothing. . . ."

For more on punctuating quotations, see 35a.

38c   Capitalization of proper nouns and their derivatives

Capitalize **proper nouns,** the names of particular persons, places, or things.

> Yukio Mishima   Persian Gulf   Mercedes Benz

Do not capitalize the articles, coordinating conjunctions, or prepositions that appear within such names.

Individual people and animals
Capitalize the names and nicknames of individual people and animals. Always look up foreign names in the dictionary.

> Hillary Rodham Clinton   Snoopy   Vincent van Gogh
> Catherine the Great   Buffalo Bill   Michael Jordan

Capitalize (and also italicize) the genus name but not the species of people, animals, and plants.

> *Homo erectus*   *Pan paniscus*   *Rosa rugosa*

Capitalize words describing family members when they are used as names.

Mother   my mother
Aunt Carol   his aunt

Religions and their members, deities, and sacred texts
Capitalize the names of religions, members of a religion, religious sects, deities, and sacred texts.

Judaism, Jews   Christianity, Christians
Roman Catholic   Protestant
God   Allah
the Koran   the Bible

Nationalities, ethnic groups, and languages
Capitalize the names of nationalities, ethnic groups, and languages.

French   Chinese   Hindustani
Chicano   African American   Slavic

Titles
Capitalize formal and courtesy titles and their abbreviations when they are used before a name and not set off by commas.

Gen. Colin Powell   Senator Dianne Feinstein   Professor Cox
Pope John Paul II   Baron De la Warr   Ms. Wu

Don't capitalize formal and courtesy titles when they are used alone or are separated from the name by commas.

my doctor, Robert Glickman
the chairwoman of the NAACP, Myrlie Evers-Williams

Capitalize titles not followed by a name when they indicate high station or office.

the Queen   the Pope   the President of
                                         the United States

Months, days of the week, and holidays
Capitalize the names of months, the days of the week, and holidays.

August 12, 1914   Tuesday   Arbor Day

Do not capitalize numbers written out or the names of seasons.

> the twentieth of April   spring

Geographic names, place names, and directions
Capitalize the formal and informal names of cities, states, countries, provinces, regions, bodies of water, and other geographic features.

> Little Rock, Arkansas   the Western Hemisphere   the Sahara
> the Grand Canyon   the Midwest   the Windy City

Capitalize common nouns like *river, street,* and *square* when they are part of a place name. Do not capitalize them when two or more proper nouns precede them.

> Rodeo Drive   Bleecker and MacDougal streets
> Hyde Park Boulevard   the Tigris and Euphrates rivers

Capitalize direction words when they indicate regions but not when they indicate compass directions.

> the West   we headed west on I-80

Institutions, organizations, and businesses
Capitalize the names of institutions, organizations, and businesses.

> Oberlin College   Federal Reserve Bank of New York
> Habitat for Humanity   the Internal Revenue Service
> the English Department   the United Nations

Historical documents, events, periods, and movements
Capitalize the names of historical documents and well-known events or periods.

> the Constitution   the Stone Age   the Gulf War
> Public Law 100-13   the Norman Conquest   the Great
> Depression

Capitalize the names of major movements in art, music, literature, and philosophy.

> the Romantic poets   the Renaissance
> an Impressionist painter   Logical Positivism

Ships, aircraft, spacecraft, and trains
Capitalize the names of individual vehicles. (For the uses of italics, see 40b.)

the U.S.S. *Constitution*   Air Force One   the *Spirit of St. Louis*

Derivatives of proper nouns
Capitalize most adjectives and other words derived from proper nouns.

Newtonian   Marxist   Texan

Prefixes before such derivatives are not capitalized unless the prefix has become part of the name.

neo-Marxist   anti-American   Postmodern

Words derived from proper nouns that have taken on independent meanings no longer require capitalization: *french fries, herculean, quixotic.* (For more on hyphenating prefixes, see 39b.)

Capitalization of titles   38d

Capitalize the first word, the last word, and all other words except articles, coordinating conjunctions, and prepositions in the titles and subtitles of books, plays, essays, stories, poems, movies, television programs, pieces of music, and works of art.

Pride and Prejudice   "What I Did for Love"
The Taming of the Shrew   *Beauty and the Beast*
"Why I Live at the P.O."   *La Traviata*
"The Idea of Order at   *Nude Descending a Staircase*
  Key West"

Words joined by a hyphen are usually both capitalized, except for articles, conjunctions, and prepositions.

The One-Minute   *The Social History of the Jack-in-the-Box*
Grammarian

(For more on the use of quotation marks and italics in titles, see 35c and 40a.)

38e Capitalization with other punctuation

Colons
Capitalization is optional after a colon when the colon joins two independent clauses and the second clause contains the main point of the sentence.

> The senators' courage failed them: The health-care bill was dead for another decade.

Use capitals after a colon that introduces a numbered list of complete sentences (but not a list of phrases).

> His philosophy can be reduced to three basic rules: (1) Think for yourself. (2) Take care of your body. (3) Never hurt anyone.

Parentheses and dashes
Capitalize the first word of a complete sentence set off by parentheses or dashes when it stands alone.

> In 1972 Congress attacked sex discrimination in sports by passing Title IX. (The changes made in 1974 are called the Bayh amendments.)

Do not capitalize the first word of a complete sentence set off by parentheses or dashes when it falls within another sentence.

> On many campuses Title IX has increased the number of competitive sports offered to women—even opponents of the law agree—but its effect on men's sports is more difficult to assess.

39 ◆ HYPHENS

Hyphens link words or parts of words to create new concepts and thus new meanings. They can also separate words into parts to clarify meaning. In addition, hyphens have many conventional uses in numbers, fractions, and units of measure.

Hyphens at the ends of lines 39a

Use a hyphen to break words that are too long to fit at the end of a line. If you don't know where to divide a word, look it up in the dictionary. The following guidelines will also help you determine how to hyphenate words.

- **Divide words only between pronounced syllables.** Words of only one pronounced syllable—eighth, through, dreamed, urged—cannot be divided without suggesting an incorrect pronunciation.

- **Don't leave just one letter at the end of a line or carry over only one or two letters to the next line.** A reader seeing only an *i-* (as in *idiot* or *idea,* for example) has no clue to what the complete word is or how to pronounce it. An *-ed* or an *-ing* alone on a new line is also confusing.

- **Divide at prefixes or suffixes rather than dividing base words.** Try to leave both parts of a word recognizable: not *an-tibody* but *anti-body,* not *ea-gerness* but *eager-ness.*

- **Divide between the words in closed compound words (two or more words run together).** The most natural place to divide a compound word is where its parts join: *mother-land, sword-fish.* Hyphenated compounds should be divided at one of the existing hyphens: *self-esteem, son-in-law.* (See also 39c.)

- **Watch out for double letters.** A word with an internal double letter is usually divided between those letters: *syl-la-ble, wil-low.* Keep double letters together if they fall at the end of a base word, and divide the word before a suffix: *access-ible, assess-ment.* But if the final consonant is doubled only when the suffix is added, put the second consonant with the suffix: *cut, cut-ting; abet, abet-ting.*

♦ **WP TIP** Many computer word-processing programs automatically hyphenate a document, but the computer's decisions about hyphenation may not be perfect. If you use your computer's program, be sure to double-check its choices.

Hyphens after some prefixes 39b

Most words with prefixes do not need hyphens. Some words do, however. When in doubt, consult your dictionary. These guidelines cover most of the common uses of hyphens following prefixes.

Use a hyphen when a prefix precedes a capitalized word or a date. The prefix itself is usually not capitalized.

pre-Columbian   pre-1994

Use a hyphen after a prefix attached to a term of two or more words.

post-World War II   anti-labor union

Use a hyphen in almost all cases after the prefixes *all-*, *ex-*, *self-*, and *quasi-*.

all-inclusive   ex-convict   self-hypnosis

To prevent misreading, hyphens are often used when a prefix ends with the same letter that begins the base word.

anti-intellectual   co-ownership

However, the hyphen has been dropped from many words, such as *cooperate, preexisting,* and *unnatural,* so check a dictionary if you are in doubt.

Use a hyphen to distinguish between words that are spelled with the same letters but have different meanings, especially when a misreading is likely.

We asked them to *refund* [give back] our money.

Congress will *re-fund* [fund again] the program for another year.

Use a hyphen when two prefixes apply to the same base word and are separated by a conjunction. Add a space after the first hyphenated prefix.

We compared the *pre-* and *post-election* analyses.

39c   Hyphens in compound words

Many **compound words**—two or more words used as a single unit—are written as one word: *workhorse, schoolteacher*. These are called **closed compounds.** Other compounds are written as two separate words, or **open compounds:** *hope chest, lunch break, curtain rod*. Still other compounds are hyphenated: *great-grandson, mother-in-law, stick-in-the-mud.*

Check the dictionary to see which compound words are written as one word and which are hyphenated. If you don't find a compound there, then it is written as an open compound—that is, as two words.

Hyphenate most compound nouns of three or more words: *jack-of-all-trades.*

Use a hyphen for most **compound adjectives,** which consist of two or more modifiers that act as a single adjective before a noun: *long-blooming peony, late-night party.* Such hyphens clarify which words go together.

Mr. Donovan is an old car collector.
The collector is old.

Mr. Donovan is an old-car collector.
The cars he collects are old.

Do not use a hyphen when compound adjectives come after the noun they modify and their meaning is unambiguous. (For more on using and positioning modifiers, see Chapter 27.)

The *well-liked* teacher has become a civic leader.

The teacher, who is *well liked,* has become a civic leader.

Do not use a hyphen in certain compound adjectives that are well established as nouns.

post office box   high school student

Do not use a hyphen between an adverb ending in *-ly* and the adjective it modifies.

a highly motivated employee   a strongly worded statement

Hyphens in numbers, fractions, and units of measure   **39d**

Use a hyphen in two-word numbers from twenty-one to ninety-nine. Never use a hyphen before or after the words *hundred, thousand,* or *million.*

fifty-seven   twenty-two thousand
two hundred fifty-seven   six hundred twenty thousand

Remember that long numbers are often easier to read as figures rather than as words. (For numbers as words or figures, see 41a.)

Use a hyphen between the numerator and denominator of a spelled-out fraction unless one of them is already hyphenated.

one-half   two-thirds   twenty-one fiftieths

Use a hyphen when a number that includes a unit of measure—feet, inches, miles, pounds—is used as a modifier. Do not use a hyphen when the unit of measure is used as a noun.

An ordinary dump truck has a *nine-cubic-yard* bed.

Only a gardener would delight in *nine cubic yards* of elephant manure.

Hyphenate ages when they are used as a noun or a modifier.

That *six-year-old* flour on the shelf is full of bugs.

Hyphens may be used to indicate ranges of page numbers, of other numbers, and of years, especially in technical writing and statistical passages.

pages 454-58   1992-1995   120-140 times a year

40 ◆ ITALICS

To distinguish certain words from the main body of your text, use *italics*. In typewritten or handwritten papers, <u>underline</u> words to indicate italics.

40a   Italics for titles

Use italics for the titles of books, plays, operas and other long musical works, movies, recordings, newspapers, magazines, television and radio series, long poems considered to be independent works, and works of art. (Use quotation marks for the titles of short stories, short poems, songs, and articles; see 35c.)

ITALICS	QUOTATION MARKS
Holy the Firm (book)	"*Newborn and Salted*" (chapter)
Here Lies (book of short stories)	"*Big Blonde*" (short story)
Leaves of Grass (book of poems)	"Song of Myself" (poem)
Song of Roland (long poem, an independent work)	
West Side Story (musical)	"Tonight" (song)
Carmen (opera)	
Throwing Copper (compact disc)	"I Alone" (song)
The Simpsons (television series)	"Homer Meets Godzilla" (episode)
Oprah (television show)	
All about Eve (movie)	
A Streetcar Named Desire (play)	
Wired (magazine)	"Free Speech in Cyberspace" (article)
Los Angeles Times (newspaper)	"High Tech, High Crime" (article)
The Boating Party (painting)	
Standing Woman (sculpture)	

Do not use italics (or quotation marks) for titles of sacred works, parts of sacred works, ancient manuscripts, and public documents.

the Bible	the Book of Kells
the Koran	the Bill of Rights
Genesis	the Civil Rights Act of 1964

Italics for the names of individual trains, ships, airplanes, and spacecraft 40b

Use italics for the official names of individual trains, ships, airplanes, and spacecraft, but not for the names of classes of such vehicles.

the *Phoebe Snow* (train)	*Spirit of St. Louis* (airplane)
the U.S.S. *Midway* (ship)	*Voyager* (spacecraft)
a Polaris rocket	a Trident submarine

Italics for foreign words 40c

Many words in English—for example, *moccasin, rococo, hors d'oeuvres,* and *burro*—have been absorbed by the language and do not require italics. Do use italics for recently borrowed foreign words, however. (A good dictionary indicates whether a word is considered foreign.)

The menu offered spaghetti, lasagne, and *pasticcio di faglioni.*

Use italics for foreign words and phrases that you are introducing for the first time. For the Latin names used to classify plants and animals, always use italics.

> The Hawaiian word for that smooth ropelike lava is *pahoehoe.*

> An early modern human ancestor, *Homo erectus,* migrated out of Africa about a million years ago.

40d Italics for words, letters, numbers used as words, and letters used as symbols

Use italics for words or numbers that stand only for themselves and for letters used as symbols in mathematics and other disciplines.

> By the term *liberal,* he meant anyone who disagreed with him.

> Every time I type quickly, I begin to substitute *y* for *u.*

> He read the *1* as a *7,* so his calculation was incorrect.

> Look up the *y* axis to point *A* on the *D* curve.

40e Italics for emphasis

Use italics to indicate that a certain word or words should receive special attention or emphasis.

> We all hear music in our heads, but how is music processed by the *brain?*

Be careful not to overuse italics. Too much emphasis of this sort can become monotonous.

41 ◆ NUMBERS

When you use numbers to describe data and research findings that support your positions, you should follow the conventions of the discipline in which you are writing. For general purposes, the following guidelines will help you decide when to spell out numbers and when to use figures.

Figures or spelled-out numbers? 41a

Spell out numbers of one hundred or less and numbers that can be expressed in one or two words.

thirty universities	three-fourths of the class
five hundred students	517 students
more than fifty thousand trees	52,331 trees

In technical writing, use figures for numbers over nine and in all measurements.

The pressure increased by 3 kilograms per square centimeter.

Fewer than 1/10 of the eggs failed to hatch.

Use a combination of words and figures for round numbers over one million.

The Census Bureau says that the U.S. population exceeds 250 million.

◆ **ESL** ▷ **SINGULAR AND PLURAL FORMS OF NUMBERS**

- ◆ When the word for a number is used as a plural noun without another number before it, use the plural form of the word. You may also need to use the word *of* after it.

  The news report said there were only a few protesters at the nuclear power plant, but we saw *hundreds*.

  Dozens of geese headed south today.

- ◆ When the word for a number is preceded by another number, use the singular form of the word, and do not use *of* with it.

  There were approximately *two hundred* protesters.

  At least *three dozen* geese flew over the lake today.

- ◆ When a word expressing a unit of weight, money, time, or distance is used with the word for a number as a hyphenated adjective, always use the singular forms for both words.

  That movie lasted *three hours*.

  It was a *three-hour* movie.

Spell out any number that begins a sentence. If this is awkward, rewrite the sentence.

◆ *Five hundred forty-seven*
~~547~~ students attended the concert.

◆ *Attending the concert were*
547 students. ~~attended the concert.~~

Consistency is important. Treat numbers that readers must compare with each other in the same manner. If convention dictates using a figure for one number, do the same for the other numbers.

◆ In Midville last year, ~~eighty-seven~~ *87* cats and 114 dogs were destroyed by the Humane Society.

41b   Conventional uses of numbers

In all types of writing, convention requires the use of figures in certain situations.

DATES

11 April 1999   the year 1616
July 16, 1999   A.D. 412

ADDRESSES

2551 Polk Street, Apt. 3
San Francisco, CA 94109

ABBREVIATIONS AND SYMBOLS

3500 rpm   37° C
65 mph $62.23
74%   53¢

You may use words to express percentages and amounts of money in passages that use numbers infrequently if you can do so in two or three words. If you spell out numbers, also spell out "percent," "dollars," and "cents."

seventy-four percent   fifty cents
five dollars

TIME

12:15   2330 hours

Numbers used with *o'clock, past, to, till,* and *until* are generally written out as words.

at seven o'clock   twenty past one

DECIMALS AND FRACTIONS
2.7 seconds   35.4 miles

CROSS-REFERENCES AND CITATIONS
Chapter 12   line 25
volume 3, pages 13–17   act 3, scene 2

(For more on other documentation formats, see Chapters 47–49.)

42 ◆ ABBREVIATIONS

Abbreviations are frequently used in tables, footnotes, endnotes, and bibliographies to help readers proceed through material quickly. The following abbreviations are acceptable in nontechnical writing.

Abbreviated titles and degrees   42a

Abbreviate titles of address when they precede a full name, except for *president* and *mayor,* which are never abbreviated.

Mr. Samuel Taylor   Dr. Ellen Hunter
St. Francis of Assisi   Prof. Ahmed Greenberg
Gen. Colin Powell   Sen. Trent Lott
Rep. Ben Nighthorse Campbell   Rev. Martin Luther King, Jr.

Except for *Mr., Ms., Mrs.,* and *Dr.,* do not abbreviate titles that appear before a surname alone: *Professor Greenberg, Senator Braun.* Do not abbreviate or capitalize titles that are *not* used with a proper name.

◆   Raissa Goldblum has been named assistant ~~prof/~~ professor of chemistry.

Always abbreviate titles and degrees that follow a name, such as *esq., M.D., LL.D., J.D.,* and *Ph.D.* Use either a title (such as *Dr.*) or a degree (such as *M.D.*), but not both.

Dr. Randall Marshall   Randall Marshall, M.D.

42b ABB

Always abbreviate generational titles such as *Jr.* and *Sr.* When used in a sentence, they are set off by commas.

> He talked to Thomas Burke, Jr., and to Karen Burke.

42b   Abbreviations with numbers

TIME

Use *A.M.* and *P.M.* (or *a.m.* and *p.m.*) for specific times of day.

3:45 P.M. (or p.m.)   12 noon

YEAR

Use *B.C.* (*before Christ*) and *A.D.* (*anno Domini*) for calendar years. Only *A.D.* precedes the year. To avoid religious reference, many writers substitute *B.C.E.* (*before the Common Era*) and *C.E.* (*Common Era*).

425 B.C. (or 425 B.C.E.)   A.D. 1215 (or 1215 C.E.)

DEGREES, NUMBERS, AND UNITS OF MEASURE

In nontechnical writing, use *F* for degrees Fahrenheit and *C* for degrees Celsius when writing out temperatures. Use *no.* or *No.* for *number.* Use *mph* for *miles per hour.*

> The prime minister's address is No. 10 Downing Street.

> The speed limit is 65 mph on the interstate and 55 mph on other roads.

In scientific and technical writing, abbreviate units of measure, usually without periods.

> To 750 ml of this solution he added 200 mg of sodium cyanate.

SYMBOLS

Use symbols in nontechnical writing for degrees (°), percents (%), and dollars ($) when they are used with figures. Spell out symbols in words when they are used without figures.

◆   He dreamed about what he would do with the $$. *money.*

◆   The temperature was 30°C.

Abbreviated geographic names 42c

Abbreviate geographic names when addressing mail. Use the U.S. Postal Service state abbreviations (see box below).

Lila Branch
100 W. Glengarry Ave.
Birmingham, MI 48009

STATE ABBREVIATIONS

Use the U.S. Postal Service abbreviations (capitalized, with no periods), for the names of the fifty states and the District of Columbia only on mail, in full addresses in text, or in documentation.

STATE	ABBREVIATION	STATE	ABBREVIATION
Alabama	AL	Missouri	MO
Alaska	AK	Montana	MT
Arizona	AZ	Nebraska	NE
Arkansas	AR	Nevada	NV
California	CA	New Hampshire	NH
Colorado	CO	New Jersey	NJ
Connecticut	CT	New Mexico	NM
Delaware	DE	New York	NY
District of Columbia	DC	North Carolina	NC
Florida	FL	Ohio	OH
Georgia	GA	Oklahoma	OK
Hawaii	HI	Oregon	OR
Idaho	ID	Pennsylvania	PA
Illinois	IL	Rhode Island	RI
Indiana	IN	South Carolina	SC
Iowa	IA	South Dakota	SD
Kansas	KS	Tennessee	TN
Kentucky	KY	Texas	TX
Louisiana	LA	Utah	UT
Maine	ME	Vermont	VT
Maryland	MD	Virginia	VA
Massachusetts	MA	Washington	WA
Michigan	MI	West Virginia	WV
Minnesota	MN	Wisconsin	WI
Mississippi	MS	Wyoming	WY

Do not abbreviate anything but the state name when presenting a full address in text. Do not abbreviate anything when giving place names with less than a full address.

His address was 1109 West Green Street, Harrisburg, PA 17102.

She was born in Harrisburg, Pennsylvania.

42d Common Latin abbreviations

Use certain common Latin abbreviations in documentation and notes, but write out their English equivalents in the text of your papers.

ABBREVIATION	LATIN	MEANING
c. or ca.	*circa*	about
cf.	*confer*	compare
e.g.	*exempli gratia*	for example
et al.	*et alii*	and others
etc.	*et cetera*	and so forth
ibid.	*ibidem*	in the same place
i.e.	*id est*	that is
N.B.	*nota bene*	note well
vs. or v.	*versus*	against (used in legal case names)

42e Acronyms and initials

An **acronym** is a word made up of initials and pronounced as a word—NATO for North Atlantic Treaty Organization, for example. Acronyms are written with no periods and no spaces between the letters.

Most initial abbreviations, such as *CD* for compact disc or *JFK* for John F. Kennedy, are written with neither periods nor spaces between the letters. Some abbreviations for countries do use periods but no spaces: *U.S., U.K.*

Make sure that acronyms and initial abbreviations are familiar to your readers. If you have any doubts, give the full name the first time, followed by the abbreviation or acronym in parentheses.

World commerce is governed in large part by a set of treaties called the General Agreement on Tariffs and Trade (GATT).

43 ◆ DOCUMENT PREPARATION

Whether you are handing in a paper to an instructor, sending a letter to a prospective employer, or submitting a report to a supervisor, a clean document in the required format makes a positive impression. For college papers, learn and follow your instructor's guidelines and use the documentation style for your discipline. (For further discussion of styles, see Chapters 47–49.)

Proofreading, the process of finding and correcting errors, is an important part of document preparation. The key to proofreading is to see what is *actually* on the page, not what you *meant* to put there. Plan to proofread twice: once on the edited draft from which you will prepare your final copy and once on the final copy itself.

Proofreading   43a

When you proofread, look for typographical errors and errors in spelling, punctuation, and mechanics. If you often make the same kinds of errors, list them in your journal and check for them when you do subsequent papers.

- ◆ **Proofread on hard copy.** If you have been composing on a word processor, print out a hard copy to proofread. Errors and awkward passages are much easier to see in print. Make your corrections immediately on the computer or enter them all at once when you finish, whichever works best.

- ◆ **Read your paper aloud.** Reading aloud will give you a fresh perspective and the chance to hear anything that isn't clear and natural. It will also help you to find dropped words and incorrect punctuation.

- ◆ **Ask someone else to read your paper.** Ask someone else to proofread your final draft for errors, omissions, or awkward passages. If that person also reads your work aloud, you may hear problems you didn't know you had.

- ◆ **Read your paper backward.** Most readers become distracted by meaning when they read and thus miss their mistakes. One way around this problem is to start with the last word and work back, one word at a time, to the first. Use a ruler to help you focus on a single line, or point a pencil at each word.

- ◆ **Use your computer's spelling checker.** Spelling checkers tell you when you have misspelled a word, not when you have used the wrong word or

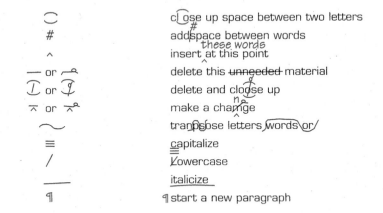

PROOFREADING MARKS

close up space between two letters

add space between words

insert *these words* at this point

delete this ~~unneeded~~ material

delete and close up

make a change

transpose letters words or

capitalize

lowercase

italicize

¶ start a new paragraph

Insert missing punctuation directly following the word where it should appear. All handwritten changes to a final manuscript should be made neatly.

left one out. Therefore, you should proofread after your computer has checked for spelling. Make sure that you have typed the words you intended, and use a dictionary to check questionable spellings.

When you find an error in your draft, use the standard proofreading symbols listed above. They provide a quick and efficient way to mark up your paper for correction later. If you have more than two corrections on a page, however, redo the page.

43b   Preparing the final manuscript

Typed or computer-printed papers are the most legible, although some papers may be written by hand. Your instructor will tell you what is acceptable.

◆   Use 8-1/2″ × 11″ white paper. Don't use onionskin, colored or "erasable" paper, or paper that is less than 16-pound weight, all of which are hard to handle.

Typed or computer-printed papers

◆ Double-space your manuscript, whether it is typed or printed.

◆ Use a standard roman typeface, not script or italics.

◆ If certain symbols are not available on your typewriter or word processor, add them to the final manuscript neatly by hand, using dark blue or black ink.

◆ If you use a typewriter, make sure the ribbon is fresh and the typewriter keys are clean.

◆ Make corrections before removing each page from the typewriter, or use lift-off film or correction fluid and write in corrections neatly by hand. If you have more than two corrections on a page, retype the page.

◆ If your printer uses continuous paper, remove the perforated edges, separate the pages, and put them in the proper order.

Handwritten papers

◆ For handwritten papers, write in blue or black ink on ruled white 8-1/2″ × 11″ paper. Don't use legal paper or pages torn from a spiral notebook.

◆ Write legibly and carefully, and use correction fluid if necessary.

Formatting the first page

◆ On the first page, start at the upper left-hand margin and, without indenting, write your name, your instructor's name, the course title, and the date the paper is due, each on a separate double-spaced line.

◆ On the next double-spaced line, center the title of the paper, using initial capital letters for all words except articles and prepositions. Do not underline your title or put it in quotation marks.

◆ Double-space again before beginning your text.

◆ Sometimes an instructor asks for a separate title page. In such cases, follow your instructor's guidelines.

Margins and indentions

◆ Use one-inch margins at the left, right, top, and bottom of each page.

◆ Indent the first word of each paragraph five spaces.

◆ To set off quotations of more than four lines, use the double-spaced block format with all text indented ten spaces. (For a detailed explanation, see 35a on quotations.)

Page numbers

◆   Number each page of your manuscript, including the first, in the upper right-hand corner about one-half inch from the top of the page unless otherwise instructed.

◆   You may also include your last name or an abbreviated title just before the page number, separated by a single space.

Models of this and other styles are shown on pages 372–379, 391–403, and 408–409.

Spacing

◆   Double-space the entire manuscript including block quotations of four lines or more and footnotes. (See 35a.)

◆   Space once after each word.

◆   Space once after any punctuation that ends a sentence.

◆   Space once after a comma, a semicolon, or a colon.

◆   Do not space after an opening quotation mark, parenthesis, or bracket or before a closing quotation mark, parenthesis, or bracket.

◆   Do not space between quotation marks and a period, a question mark, or an exclamation point.

◆   Do not space between single and double quotation marks.

◆   Do not space after a hyphen except in a suspended construction: *The rest of us are half- and quarter-time employees.*

◆   Do not space on either side of a dash, which on a typewriter or word processor consists of two hyphens with no spaces between them.

◆   Do not space before or after a slash except when you use it to separate lines of poetry quoted within your text.

43c   Formatting business correspondence

Businesses value efficiency and accuracy, and business communications mirror those objectives. Business writing should be simple, direct, and brief; it should convey correct information and conform to standard conventions, and it should be honest and courteous.

Audience is particularly important in business writing. Ask yourself to whom the communication is being written. What information do they already

---

GUIDELINES FOR BUSINESS WRITING

◆ Get to the main point quickly. Avoid unnecessary information and repetition. Your reader's time, as well as your own, is valuable.

◆ Write in simple, direct language. Keep your sentences straightforward and readable.

◆ Choose the active voice over the passive.

◆ Use technical terminology and jargon sparingly. Write out complete names of companies, products, and titles. Explain any unusual terms.

◆ Avoid emotional or offensive language and sexist constructions. Always be courteous, even when lodging a complaint.

◆ Use numbers or descriptive headings to help readers locate information quickly.

◆ Use graphs, charts, and other illustrations when they convey information more clearly than words.

---

have? What else do they need to know? Who else will read what you have written? In general, adopt an objective and fairly formal tone.

And, of course, think about presentation. To make a good impression, any piece of writing must be neat, clean, and correct.

Business letters

Business letters commonly request, inform, or complain, and they are often addressed to a reader unknown to the writer. State your purpose clearly and provide all the information needed to make it easy for the reader to respond.

Business letters are typed on 8-1/2″ × 11″ paper, one side only. Most use block format; that is, every element of the letter is typed flush with the left margin. All business letters include the following elements.

Heading Type the sender's address (but not name) and the date single-spaced, approximately one inch from the top of the first page. Spell out street and town names and months in full. Abbreviate state names using standard postal abbreviations. Include the zip code.

If you use letterhead stationery, type the date two line spaces below the letterhead address.

Inside address Type the recipient's address two line spaces below the heading. (If the letter is very short, add space here so that the letter will be

COVER LETTER

405 Martin Street
Lexington, Kentucky 40508   **HEADING**
February 10, 19xx

Barbara McGarry, Director
Kentucky Council on the Arts   **INSIDE ADDRESS**
953 Versailles Road
Box 335
Frankfort, Kentucky 40602

Dear Ms. McGarry: **GREETING**

John Huff, one of my professors at the University   **BODY,**
of Kentucky, recommended that I write to you   **NO**
regarding openings in the Council's internship   **INDENTS**
program this summer. I would like to apply for
one of these positions and have enclosed my
résumé for your consideration.

As you will note, my academic background combines
a primary concentration in business administration with a minor in the fine arts. My interest in
the arts goes back to childhood when I first heard
a performance by the Lexington Symphony, and I
have continued to pursue that interest ever
since. My goal after graduation is a career in
arts administration, focusing on fund-raising and
outreach for a major public institution.

I hope you'll agree that my experience, particularly my work with the local Community Concerts
association, is strong preparation for an internship with the Council. I would appreciate the
opportunity to discuss my qualifications with you
in greater detail.

I will call your office within the next few weeks
to see about setting up an appointment to meet
with you. In the meantime, you can reach me at
the above address or by phone at 555-4033.
Thank you for your attention.

Sincerely,

Chris Aleandro   **CLOSING**
    SIGNATURE

Chris Aleandro   **ADDITIONAL INFORMATION**

centered on the page.) Include the person's full name (and title, if appropriate), followed by her or his position (if needed); the name of the department or division within the company; the company name; and the full street, city, and state address.

When writing to an unknown person, always try to find out the name and its spelling, perhaps by calling the company switchboard. If you can find no name, use an appropriate title (*Personnel Director* or *Claims Manager,* for example) in place of a name.

Greeting   Type the opening salutation two line spaces below the inside address (*Dear Dr. Schmertz, Dear Mei Ling Wong*) followed by a colon. If you and the recipient are on a first-name basis, you may use only the first name alone (*Dear Mei Ling*).

If you do not know the recipient's name, use *To Whom It May Concern* or some variation of *Dear Claims Manager,* or *Attention: Marketing Director* (the latter without a second colon). Avoid the old-fashioned *Dear Sir* or *Dear Sir or Madam.*

Body   Begin the body of the letter two line spaces below the greeting. Single-space within paragraphs; double-space between paragraphs.

If your reason for writing is clear and simple, state it directly in the first paragraph. If it is absolutely necessary to detail a situation, provide background, or supply context, do so in the first paragraph or two; then move on to state your purpose in writing.

If your letter is more than a page long, type the addressee's last name, the date, and the page number flush with the right margin of each subsequent page.

Closing   Type the complimentary closing two spaces after the last line of the body of the letter. The most common closings are *Sincerely, Cordially, Yours truly, Respectfully yours* (formal), and *Best regards* (informal). Capitalize only the first word of the closing, and follow it with a comma.

Signature   Type your full name, including any title, four line spaces below the closing. Sign the letter with your full name (or just your first name if you have addressed the recipient by first name) in blue or black ink in the space above your typed name.

Additional information   You may provide additional brief information below your signature, flush with the left margin. This may include recipients of copies of the letter (*cc Jennifer Rodriguez*); the word *Enclosures* (or the abbreviation *enc.*) to indicate that you are also enclosing additional material mentioned in the letter; and, if the letter was typed by someone other than the writer, the writer's initials and the typist's initials (*TF/jwl*).

Résumés

A résumé is a brief summary of an applicant's qualification for employment. It outlines education, work experience, and other activities and interests so that a prospective employer can decide quickly whether or not an applicant is a good prospect for a particular job. Try to tailor your résumé for the position you are seeking by emphasizing experience that is most relevant to the job. Preparing a résumé on a computer lets you revise it easily and quickly.

Generally, a résumé is sent out with a cover letter that introduces the applicant, indicates the position applied for, and offers additional information that cannot be accommodated on the résumé itself.

Résumés should be brief and to the point, preferably no more than one page long (if relevant experience is extensive, more than one page may be acceptable). Résumé formats vary in minor ways, but most include the following information.

Personal information　Résumés begin with the applicant's name, address, and phone number, usually centered at the top.

Objective　Many résumés include a line summarizing the applicant's objective, naming either the specific job sought or describing a larger career goal.

Education　Most first-time job applicants list their educational background first, because their employment history is likely to be fairly limited. Name the last two or three schools attended (including dates of attendance and degrees), starting with the most recent. Indicate major areas of study, and highlight any courses relevant to the job. Consider including your grade point average, awards, and anything else that shows you in a good light.

When employment history is more detailed, educational background is often put at the end of the résumé.

Work experience　Starting with the most recent, list all relevant jobs, including company name, dates of employment, and a brief job description or list of duties. Use your judgment about listing jobs where you had difficulties with your employer.

Special skills or interests　It is often useful to mention special skills, interests, or activities that provide additional clues about your abilities and personality.

References　Provide the names, addresses, and phone numbers of two or three people — teachers, supervisors, employers — whom you trust to give a good reference for you. (Make sure you get their permission first, however.) You may want to conclude with the line "References available on request."

RÉSUMÉ

Chris Aleandro
405 Martin Street
Lexington, Kentucky 40508
(606) 555-4033

Objective: Internship in arts administration

Education

University of Kentucky: 1995 to present.
    Currently a sophomore majoring in business
    administration with a minor in art history.
    Degree expected May 1999.

Henry Clay High School (Lexington, KY): 1991 to 1995.
    College preparatory curriculum, with emphasis in
    art and music.

Related Work Experience

Community Concerts, Inc.: 1996 to present.
    Part-time promotion assistant, reporting to the
    local director. Responsibilities include assisting
    with scheduling, publicity, subscription/ticketing
    procedures, and fund-raising. Position involves
    general office duties as well as heavy contact with
    subscribers and artists.

Habitat for Humanity: September to November 1995.
    Co-chaired campus fund-raising drive that included
    a benefit concert, raising $55,000.

Art in the Schools Program: 1993–1995.
    Volunteer, through the Education Division of the
    Lexington Center for the Arts. Trained to conduct
    hands-on art appreciation presentations in grade
    school classrooms, visiting one school a month.

Other Work Experience

Record City: 1996 to 1998 (part time and summers).
    Sales clerk and assistant manager in a music store.

Special skills: Word 7; desktop design of brochures,
    programs, and other materials.

References

Professor John Huff	Ms. Joan Thomas
School of Business	Community Concerts,
Administration	Inc.
The University of Kentucky	1200 Fayette Stree'
Lexington, KY 40506	Lexington, KY 40⁵
(606) 555-3110	(606). 555-290'

VI

THE RESEARCH PROCESS

THE RESEARCH PROCESS

A research paper is the end result of the process of finding, evaluating, and synthesizing information you have selected from a wide variety of sources. Often it is the most important project you will work on during a semester.

44 ◆ MANAGING THE RESEARCH PROCESS

Although doing a research paper is demanding, it also can be rewarding if the subject interests you. Start on it immediately so that you have enough time for all the activities involved.

STRATEGIES FOR MANAGING THE RESEARCH PROCESS

◆ **Ask questions.** Begin by asking questions about a subject, both of yourself and of others. Preliminary questions lead to more specific inquiries.

◆ **Read extensively.** Texts of all kinds—books, journal and magazine articles, and studies—are the raw material from which you will build your research paper.

◆ **Question knowledgeable people.** Start with people you know. If they can't help, ask who can. Then broaden that circle to include people with specialized knowledge.

◆ **Seek out firsthand information and experience.** No matter how many answers other people offer you, seek out information yourself.

◆ **Evaluate your sources and double-check the information you find.** Sources vary in their accuracy and objectivity. Try to confirm the information you gather by checking more than one reliable source.

◆ **Write at every stage.** The notes you take on your reading, the field notes you write, and the research log you keep all help you gain control of your subject.

44a   Keeping a research log

A research log is essentially a journal dedicated to thinking methodically about a research project. Your log helps you keep track of the whole research project from beginning to end—to write about your curiosity, to pose questions, to brainstorm where answers might be found, to keep track of sources found (and not found), and to explore modifications of research questions as new information leads your thinking in new directions. Use the log to answer questions such as these:

- What subject do I want to research?
- Am I starting with a working thesis or looking for one?
- What evidence best supports my working thesis?
- What evidence challenges my working thesis?
- What information do I still need to find?
- Where am I likely to find it?

Writing out answers to these questions in your log clarifies your tasks as you go along. It forces you to articulate ideas and examine supporting evidence critically. This, in turn, helps you focus your research activities.

When you keep notes in a research log, record them as if they were on separate note cards. (See 45d.) Here is a sample from a research log for an investigation of ozone holes in the atmosphere.

11/12 Checked the subject headings—found no books on ozone depletion. Ref. librarian suggests looking at magazines because books take much longer to get published. Found twenty articles in the General Science Index—got printouts on about half. Start obtaining the sources and reading them tomorrow.

11/17 Conference today with professor about the ozone-hole thesis—said I didn't really have much of a thesis yet, just a lot of notes on the same subject. I should look at what I've got, then step back and decide what question it answers—that will probably point to my thesis.

44b   Finding a topic

The first step in finding a topic is to understand the purpose of your paper by studying the assignment requirements: What are the course goals? What approach makes the most sense? Where are the best sources? What documentation system is required? When is the paper due, and how long should it be? If your instructor assigns you a topic, make sure you understand the scope before you begin.

Choosing a topic

Many instructors let students choose their own topics. Try using some invention techniques to brainstorm about topics (see Chapter 3). What class discussions, labs, or lectures have you enjoyed most in your courses? What current events interest you? Whether your topic is assigned or created, you will probably need to narrow a large subject down to a manageable size.

BROAD TOPIC	American fatherhood today
NARROW TOPIC	The economic implications of being a Mr. Mom in the year 2000.
NARROW TOPIC	America's newest vision of the engaged father: at home and involved

Owning the topic

When you conduct research, you enter into a conversation with a select community of people who are knowledgeable about a subject. As you collect information, you too become an author, an *authority* who can teach your classmates, and your instructor, something they didn't know before.

The best way to exercise your newfound authority is to put the facts and ideas you collect into your own words at every chance—in your research log, on your note cards, in your drafts. Finding your own language to express an idea guarantees that you understand the idea and, at the same time, increases your chances of saying something useful, interesting, or provocative.

Developing a research question   44c

Research projects are designed to answer questions, so spend some time formulating a good **research question** about your subject. By isolating a particular aspect of the subject, the research question helps you tighten and maintain the focus you want.

What makes a good research question?

1 It encourages you to focus on a topic in which you are interested.
2 It asks you to explore a topic that is reasonably complex, with plenty of gray areas for investigation and argument.
3 It can probably be answered by investigation using your school's resources.

> **RESEARCH QUESTION**   What factors do today's parents consider in deciding whether the father should remain at home to care for the children?

If source materials you need are not available, you may have to adapt your question to fit the materials at hand. Ask your instructor to check your research question before you invest a lot of time in it. She or he can help you hone the question and save you time on a project too large to manage.

44d   Formulating a working thesis

When an answer to your research question starts to take shape, it's time to construct a **working thesis.** Your working thesis is a preliminary answer that helps you investigate further. If more research leads you in a different direction, be ready to redirect your investigation and revise your working thesis.

If you don't yet know the answer to your research question, begin to do **informational research.** Start with an open mind and focus on your research question. This may lead to an opinion you can argue in greater detail with more research, or it may turn up explanatory material for later use. Either way, you need to answer your research question. Informational research, then, is *thesis finding.*

In **argument research,** you begin by knowing the answer to your question and which side of a debate you want to support. The research you do focuses on supporting and strengthening your position. Such research is *thesis driven.*

44e   Using the writing process

Research writing, like all important writing, goes through all the stages of the writing process: planning, researching, drafting, revising, and editing. In research writing, however, managing information and incorporating sources present special problems.

Planning

The technical requirements of research writing—length, format, the nature and number of the sources you need, and the special documentation system required—take extra time and attention.

When you have an idea of what information is available, plan schedules for trips to the library, dates for retrieving books, and time for conducting interviews. Most important, allow enough time for writing, revising, and editing your paper. Whenever you fall behind in your schedule, revise your plan.

Researching

To evaluate sources, you first need to understand how different kinds of sources work as evidence. **Primary sources** contain original material and/or raw information. **Secondary sources** report on, describe, interpret, or analyze someone else's work. If you explore the development of a novelist's style, for example, the novels themselves are primary sources. Other people's reviews and interpretations of the novels are secondary sources.

What constitutes a primary source differs, depending on the field of study and on your research question. The novel *Moby Dick* is a primary source if you are making claims about it as a piece of literature. It is a secondary source if you are investigating nineteenth-century whaling and referring to chapters that describe harpooning.

Many research essays use both primary and secondary sources. Primary sources ground a paper in firsthand observations and facts; secondary sources supply context and support for your own analysis and argument.

Drafting

Write your first draft early so you have time for further research in case you find yourself creating a new working thesis or discover gaps in your coverage. The tentative answer to your research question has been your working thesis. As you gather material and begin drafting, however, this answer crystallizes into a more definite **thesis statement.**

In an *informational* paper—one that defines, describes, or explains—your thesis makes a statement about the information presented in the paper but does not advance one position over another. For example, if you are asked to report on holes in the ozone layer, your paper will define, describe, or explain ozone holes but will not argue any point about them. Your research question *What are ozone holes?* becomes the thesis statement: *Huge gaps in the earth's stratospheric ozone layer are caused by chlorofluorocarbons and other chemicals that react with and destroy ozone.*

In an *argument* paper—one that interprets, argues, or assesses—your thesis states your position on an issue. You begin research by looking for information to substantiate your point, with a research question such as *Should Congress regulate handgun ownership?* After conducting research that supports a particular side, you refine the thesis statement to *The ownership of handguns in the United States should be strictly regulated by the federal government.*

Many research essays present the thesis statement at the beginning, in the first or second paragraph, where it establishes what will follow. Some research papers delay the thesis statement until the end, where it acts as a conclusion or a summary. If you take the delayed-thesis approach, be sure that the topic and scope of your paper are clear to your readers in the beginning paragraphs.

Revising

In a research paper, revising entails not only modifying the writing of the paper but also the research that underlies it. Once you begin conducting research, your questions and answers multiply and change. Be prepared to find new questions more interesting to you than your original question. The research process must remain flexible if it is to be vital and exciting. Keep an open mind, but also keep an eye on your topic.

Be ready to spend a good deal of time revising your draft, adding new research information, and incorporating sources smoothly into your prose. Such work takes a great deal of thought, and you'll want to revise your paper several times.

Editing

Editing and proofreading a research paper require extra time. Not only should you check your own writing; you should also pay special attention to where and how you document sources, making sure you use the correct documentation format. The editing stage is a good time to assess your use of quotation, paraphrase, and summary to make sure you have not misquoted or used a source without crediting it.

TESTING YOUR THESIS

A good thesis not only helps readers understand your paper; it also helps you organize your thoughts as you write. Once you have drafted as detailed and accurate a thesis statement as you can, ask yourself the following questions.

◆ **Is it interesting?** An informational thesis answers a question that is worth asking. An argument thesis takes a position on a debatable issue and probably includes a proposal for change.

◆ **Is it precise and specific?** Sharpen your understanding of the thesis and the language you use to express it. This helps you define more exactly what you want your paper to say.

◆ **Is it manageable?** You may have more information than you can write about. This is your chance to narrow your thesis and tighten the paper you are about to write.

◆ **Does it reflect your research and match the expected shape of your paper?** Determine whether all the major points you want to make in your paper are reflected in your thesis. Consider, too, whether you have enough support for each of your points.

---

45 ◆ CONDUCTING RESEARCH

Before agonizing too long over your next research project, remember that in your nonacademic life you conduct *practical* research of one kind or another every time you investigate a new stereo, read movie reviews, or plan a vacation. You probably do not make note cards or report the results in writing as you do with *academic* research, but whenever you ask questions and systematically look for answers, you are conducting research. Practical research usually results in an action—seeing a movie or buying a stereo. Academic research results in a different kind of action—writing a paper that presents information or argues a position.

PLANNING LIBRARY RESEARCH

◆   **Go to the library early.**   Find and use resources on your subject as soon as you can because they might not be readily available.
◆   **Prepare to take notes.**   Take careful notes the first time around so you won't have to retrieve the sources again to pick up bibliographic information.
◆   **Keep a research log.**   Write in your research log as you work to help you keep track of what you've already done and what you still have to do.
◆   **Consult general sources before specific ones.**   On your first visit, check general sources—dictionaries, encyclopedias, atlases, and yearbooks—for a quick overview of your topic and for guidance in locating additional sources.
◆   **Talk to library personnel.**   Describe your assignment to your reference librarian, and ask for help finding sources. Librarians often know about sources you don't—it's their job.

Conducting library research   45a

The modern college library is the complex, multifaceted heart of the academic community. While field and Internet research will be useful for researching many topics, there is no substitute for the quantity and quality of sources available in a college library. Explore your library early, before your deadlines come due.

45b Locating sources

Most library information is contained in reference books, in cataloged books, or in periodicals—journals, magazines, and newspapers. Consult the following reference centers when you do initial research on a subject.

- ◆ The **book and periodical catalogs** list all the books your library owns and identifies where they are located.

- ◆ The **book stacks** contain all the library's cataloged books as well as older periodicals and pamphlets.

- ◆ The **circulation desk** is the place to check out and reserve books as well as to get general information about the library.

- ◆ The **periodical room** houses current issues of magazines, journals, and newspapers.

- ◆ The **reference room** contains general reference works—dictionaries, encyclopedias, guides, bibliographies, and indexes to more specific sources.

- ◆ **Nonprint media reference rooms** contain computerized databases, sound and video recordings, CD-ROMs, microfiche, microfilm, and other nonprint sources.

Consulting reference works

General reference works—almanacs and yearbooks, atlases, general dictionaries and biographical dictionaries, encyclopedias, and many field- or discipline-specific references—provide background information and basic facts about a topic. They contain summaries, overviews, and definitions that can tell you whether to pursue a topic further and where to turn next for the information you need. Such works do not make strong sources to cite in research papers, however. For better information, you will want to consult specialized sources.

Bibliographies, indexes, and databases identify the location of books and periodicals that contain the more specific information.

Bibliographies

Bibliographies list books alphabetically by title, by author, or by subject. Many books include bibliographies of the works the author consulted while writing the book. When you find a useful book, follow up on the items in its bibliography. Many other bibliographies are published separately as reference tools.

Indexes

Indexes are guides to material published sometimes in books but more often in periodicals. Each index covers a particular group of periodicals, so be sure to look in the index that deals with your subject.

Indexes list works alphabetically by author or by subject. To do a subject search, use the keywords associated with your topic or the subject headings given in the *Library of Congress Subject Headings.*

Most indexes are available both in printed form and in computerized form. Many are also available on microfiche or microfilm that must be read on special machines. Indexes in book form are usually the most comprehensive; those on microfilm, microfiche, or computers usually cover only the past ten or twenty years.

General periodical indexes list articles in magazines, journals, and newspapers that are of interest to the general public. Specialized periodical indexes list articles of interest to people in specific academic disciplines or professional fields. Both kinds of indexes are useful, but you need to know what each does and which you need.

Using the catalogs

The library catalog lists every book a library owns. Many libraries also catalog their periodicals.

Books

Whether the lists are stored on cards in drawers, on microfiche or microfilm, or computerized in online catalogs (or circulation computers), all library catalogs provide the same basic information. They list books by author, title, and subject; they provide basic information about format and content; and they tell you where in the library a book can be found.

Even if your library doesn't own a source you want, it can obtain a work owned by another library through an interlibrary loan. Your librarian will help you arrange this.

All **online catalog systems** work in much the same way, and they offer the quickest way to search for research sources. While the format of these catalogs can vary, generally they allow you to look up works simply by entering author name, title, or subject. Most online catalog systems allow you to search with partial information, so if you know only the first two words of a title, for example, the catalog computer will present you with a list of all the works that begin with those words, including the title you are looking for if the library owns it.

Searching by subject is generally the most useful method of finding sources. By entering **subject headings** (names for subject areas—check the list in the *Library of Congress Subject Headings*) or keywords (words identifying or describing your topic that can be entered alone or in combination, sometimes with *and*), you can locate books you might never have found otherwise. Finding these books can help you to make connections that can move your research in new directions, or it can simply help you narrow your search for sources and so focus your research topic.

To do a **keyword search,** use the words you've identified as describing your topic, linked by *and* or *or*. The computer will present you with a list of works that fit that description. As with all computer searches, the more specific your request, the more useful your list will be.

Once you find the book you want, the online catalog provides complete information on it. This is much the same data you would find in the card catalog, but it may also tell you whether the book is in or checked out. To find the book, use the book's **call number** to locate it in the stacks. The first letters or numbers in a call number indicate its general subject area, and this tells you, in turn, where in the library to find the book.

Periodicals

Periodicals can be found in general indexes and specialized indexes. Some are in print, while others are available in computerized form; many exist in both forms. They include subject-specific CD-ROM or online indexes to journals (some also including books), newspapers, and magazines.

As with books, the quickest and most efficient way to find periodicals is by computer. You search for articles in these databases the same way that you look for books: by author, title, or subject headings and keywords.

Once you identify sources that interest you, consult your library's list of periodical holdings. This list may be in print or in a computer library catalog like the one for books; in either case, you will find out whether your library has the periodical, whether it has the specific issue or volume you want, and where you can find it.

Computerized sources

Computerized sources—CD-ROMs, diskettes, online databases, and networks—contain many types of information from previously published books and periodicals to online reports, journals, and conferences. Your librarian should have guides and lists of these materials as well.

Databases

Databases are large collections of electronically stored bibliographic information that function like indexes. Often they also provide summaries, and occasionally they contain copies of the sources themselves.

The database most commonly found in college libraries is DIALOG, which tracks more than a million sources of information. DIALOG is divided into nearly a thousand specialized databases listed in the DIALOG *Blue Sheets,* so you must find out which database you need before you begin your search.

DIALOG and similar databases are available online. Before you use an online database, a reference librarian will ask you to list the keywords you have identified for your project. The library pays a fee for each search, and some libraries limit your time or ask you to pay the fee.

If the databases you want are available on CD-ROM, you can usually search through them without the aid of a librarian.

Other sources

Many libraries own materials other than books and periodicals that often do not circulate. Ask a librarian about your library's holdings.

Government documents   The U.S. government publishes numerous reports, pamphlets, catalogs, and newsletters on most issues of national concern. Reference books that can lead you to these sources include the *Monthly Catalog of United States Government Publications* and the *United States Government Publication Index,* both available on CD-ROM and online.

Nonprint media   Records, audio CDs, audiocassettes, videotapes, slides, photographs, and other media are generally cataloged separately from book and periodical collections.

Pamphlets   Pamphlets and brochures published by government agencies and private organizations are generally stored in a library's **vertical file.** The *Vertical File Index: A Subject and Title Index to Selected Pamphlet Material* (1932/35 – present) lists many of the available titles.

Special collections   Rare books, manuscripts, and items of local interest are commonly found in a special room or section of the library.

Developing a working bibliography   45c

Taking accurate notes makes the whole research process easier. Sometimes an instructor requests a working bibliography in the form of an alphabetized listing of all works you have consulted or are planning to consult. One option for keeping track of this bibliographic information is on 3″ × 5″ index cards, easily arranged later in alphabetical order to prepare your reference list. Another option is to type such information directly into an alphabetized computer file; this latter option has the advantage of being easily transformed into your Works Cited or Reference list at the end of your paper (see Chapters 47 and 48). In either case, make notes of the following information.

BOOKS

1 Call number or other location information
2 Full name(s) of author(s)
3 Full title and subtitle
4 Edition or volume number

5 Editor or translator (if any)
6 Place of publication
7 Publisher and date of publication
8 Inclusive page numbers for sections you used

PERIODICALS

1 Full name(s) of author(s)
2 Full title and subtitle of article
3 Periodical title
4 Periodical volume and number

5 Periodical date
6 Inclusive page numbers of the article
7 Library call number or other location information

45d Taking notes

Make note cards, perhaps using the larger 4″ × 6″ index cards, so that you have room to record the relevant information found in your sources. Keep these separate from your bibliography cards. Put only one piece of information or one idea on a card; later you can arrange and rearrange your notes in different ways as you draft.

In addition to text notes, each card should carry the following information.

1 Author and title of the source
2 Page numbers
3 Brief statement of the topic or argument the note supports
4 The information quoted, paraphrased, or summarized
5 Notes to yourself—placed in brackets or parentheses—with ideas on how you might use the material or with cross-references to other material

When recording information on your cards, think ahead about how you might use the information. Make preliminary decisions about whether you will quote, paraphrase, or summarize the material. Will you want to quote the author directly because he or she is an expert? Will you want to summarize concisely the history of something? Quoting may seem easiest, but writing out every potential quotation takes time and prevents you from thinking about the meaning of what is being said in relation to your research question. On the other hand, it is useful to quote a particularly persuasive argument or an original wording of a point. (For more information on quoting, paraphrasing, and summarizing, see 46b–46d.)

DIRECT QUOTATION, PARAPHRASE, AND SUMMARY

Use this list to help you choose which note-taking technique to use.

◆   **Direct quotation** duplicates the exact words from a source. Keep direct quotations brief, and put prominent quotation marks around them on your note cards.
◆   **Paraphrase** restates the author's ideas in your own words simply, clearly, and accurately. This device captures content without exposing you to the risk of unacknowledged quotations, but your text may run as long as the original.
◆   **Summary** condenses the main point(s) of an original passage. Summarize in your own words, and use quotation marks around any of the author's language you include.

Evaluating library sources   45e

Not all the sources you uncover through your library research will be equally useful. You will have to evaluate them to see how they further your claims and thus benefit your paper.

Learn to assess library sources in the same way you do your own writing. Is each resource a well-written, balanced study? Are the author's claims supported by sound evidence? The following guidelines will help you evaluate library sources.

EVALUATING LIBRARY SOURCES

◆   **Subject.**   Does the subject directly relate to my research question? Does it provide plenty of details and helpful background information? Does it provide information that supports my view? Does it contain facts or quotable passages that I want to use?
◆   **Author.**   What is the reputation of the author or authors? (An author who is often cited by other authors is probably reliable.) Does he or she reveal any biases that might limit credibility? Is the work a careful study or slanted and opinionated?
◆   **Date.**   When was this source published? Does it discuss current thinking, or is it dated? (In social science and the sciences, material older than ten years will be questionable.)
◆   **Publisher.**   Is the book published by a reputable publisher? Is the publication funded or endorsed by any special-interest group that is known to have a particular bias?

45f Using field research

Depending on your research question, you may also need to conduct research outside the library, commonly called **field research.** Field researchers collect information about people, places, events, or objects that has never before been recorded or assessed. Take careful notes in your research log to record your observations or interviews and give the information you've gathered a critical look before you use it in a paper.

Field observation tips

◆ **Select good sites.** Choose a site either because it could be the primary focus of your paper or because it offers the supplementary details you need to support your major points.

◆ **Do your homework.** To observe well and use your time on-site efficiently, gather information in advance about the place you are visiting.

◆ **Plan your visit.** Call ahead for directions, an appointment, and a contact.

◆ **Take good notes.** Write down a vivid description of the scene, and include your impressions, both general and specific. Review and rewrite your notes as soon after your visit as possible.

Use a notebook with a stiff cover so that you can write while walking or standing. A double-entry notebook allows you to record facts in one column and your reactions in the other. Make sketches if you like, or use a camera or camcorder. Dictating on-site notes into a tape recorder also captures your immediate impressions.

Interview tips

◆ **Select the right people.** Make sure you choose people who can give you the information you need. Ask yourself what information you need, who is likely to have it, and how you might approach them to get it before you make appointments.

◆ **Make an appointment.** Call ahead for an appointment, or drop by in advance with your request. Let the person know ahead of time if you must cancel or reschedule.

◆ **Do homework.** Before you talk to an expert, make sure you are generally familiar with your topic and what this person has said about it.

Preparation will help you ask better questions and makes the interview more interesting and profitable for you both.

◆ **Plan appropriate questions.**   Plan in advance a series of questions, starting with more general questions to establish context, then moving to more specific questions to obtain particular facts. This approach will help establish a meaningful conversation.

◆ **Ask open and closed questions.**   Open questions usually elicit general information, while closed questions allow you to zero in on specifics. Use open questions when you do not want to limit the answers: *What are your plans for the future?* Use closed questions when you need facts or concrete details to support a point: *What day did you announce your national campaign against the increase in poverty plaguing single parents?*

◆ **Ask follow-up questions.**   Listen closely. If the answers are incomplete or confusing, don't be afraid to ask follow-up questions right away. You want to get all the information you need in one sitting.

◆ **Use silence.**   Give your subject time to think about and respond to your question or to ask you to rephrase it. Don't worry if you don't get an immediate response; in many cases your subject is formulating a thoughtful answer.

◆ **Read body language.**   Notice how your subject acts while he or she answers questions. Is the person meeting your eyes? Fidgeting? Looking bored? Smiling? Such clues tell whether someone is speaking honestly, avoiding your question, or tiring fast. Watch as well as listen for useful information.

◆ **Take good notes.**   A pad that is spiral-bound on top lets you flip pages quickly. Write down major ideas and critical statements in your subject's own words. Omit small words and use abbreviations (like *b/c* for *because* or *w/* for *with*) to simplify the process.

◆ **Use a tape recorder.**   If you use a tape recorder, ask permission in advance. Even when you are recording, however, continue to take notes of the conversation's highlights. Jot down questions that occur to you during the interview, and record your impressions of the subject's appearance and manner.

◆ **Confirm important assertions.**   Read back important or controversial statements to your subject to check for accuracy and allow for further explanation.

◆ **Review notes soon after the interview.**   Within twenty-four hours of your interview, go back over your notes and fill in any missing details while you still remember them. Put this information onto note cards or into a computer file.

EVALUATING FIELD SOURCES

◆   **What is the most important point this source makes?** How does it address my research question? How might this point fit into my paper?

◆   **Did the source provide evidence that supports my point?** Can I use it and build on it? Should I question or refute it?

◆   **Does the information support or challenge my working thesis?** If so, how? Do I need to change my thinking?

◆   **Does this information support or contradict information from other sources?** How do I resolve contradictions? Do I need to consult other sources?

◆   **Is the source reliable?** Does anything from this source seem incorrect or illogical? Has any of the information been contradicted by a more authoritative source? Does this cast doubt on everything from this source?

◆   **Is the source biased?** Does the interview subject have any special cause to push or a reputation to protect? Would a different person—or site—have yielded different information?

45g   Analyzing field sources

Once you've returned from your field research, take the time to see how the information relates to your research topic. The series of questions above will help you assess information gathered at site visits and from interviews.

46 ◆ USING SOURCES

As you prepare to draft, you need to assess all the information you've found and decide which sources you will use and how. Read your notes critically to see how useful each source is, and synthesize the material into a new, coherent whole.

Synthesizing material involves looking for connections among different pieces of information and formulating ideas about what these connections mean. The connections may be similar statements made by several sources or contradictions between two sources. Try to reach some conclusions on your own that extend beyond the information in front of you, and then use those conclusions to form the goals for your paper.

Next make decisions on how you will use your source information, based on your goals for the paper and not on the format of your research notes. Source-driven papers, written in an effort "to get everything in," read like patch jobs. You want to be the director of the research production, with *your* ideas at center stage and your sources the supporting cast. Whenever you do quote, paraphrase, or summarize, be sure to document your source.

Organizing sources   46a

Your research notes exist in three basic formats: direct quotation, paraphrase, and summary. (See 45d.) Field notes may be more rambling. The format of your notes, however, should not dictate how you present that material in your paper.

The logic of your ideas, not a large stack of research notes, should be your blueprint. *First* make an outline of the conclusions you reached when synthesizing the source material; *then* organize your note cards according to it. If you do it the other way around, organizing your notes in order and then writing an outline based on that sequence, you'll be tempted to find a place for every note and miss the areas where you haven't done research. The point is, don't just repeat what you've read. Present your own ideas.

Quoting accurately   46b

Direct quotations, which cite an author's or speaker's exact words, provide strong support for your assertions. Too many quotations, however, indicate that you haven't adequately thought through what others have said and made it your own. Reserve direct quotations for places where you cannot express the ideas better yourself, when the original words are especially clear, powerful, or vivid.

Too many brief quotations can be distracting, so limit them to two per page. Long quotations slow readers down and invite them to skip something you think is important. Use only as much of a quotation as you need to support your point. As a rule, limit long quotations to about one every three pages.

WHEN TO USE DIRECT QUOTATIONS

Use direct quotations when an idea is so well said in the original source that you cannot do it justice in your own words.

◆   **Precision.** Use direct quotations when the words are important in themselves or when the author makes fine but important distinctions.
◆   **Clarity.** Use direct quotations when the author's ideas are complex and difficult to paraphrase.
◆   **Power.** Use direct quotations when the words are especially powerful and authoritative.
◆   **Vitality.** Use direct quotations when the language is lively, vivid, or unique to the writer or speaker.

Shortening quotations

Although you can't change what a source says, you can control how much of it you use. When you shorten a quotation, be careful not to change or distort its meaning. If you omit words within quotations, indicate the missing words with ellipsis points. Any changes or additions must be indicated by including the new words in brackets. (See 36c for more on ellipses, 36d for more on brackets.)

ORIGINAL
    The human communication environment has acquired biological complexity and planetary scale, but there are no scientists or activists monitoring it, theorizing about its health, or mounting campaigns to protect its resilience. Perhaps it's too new, too large to view as a whole, or too containing—"we swim in a sea of information," in poet Gary Snyder's phrase. All the more reason to worry. New things have nastier surprises, big things are hard to change, and containing things is impossible.

—Stewart Brand, *The Media Lab*

INACCURATE QUOTATION
    In *The Media Lab,* Stewart Brand describes the control that is exerted by watchdog agencies over modern telecommunications: "The human communication environment has . . . activists monitoring it, theorizing about its health . . ." (258).

By omitting certain words, the writer has changed the meaning of the original source.

ACCURATE QUOTATION

In *The Media Lab,* Stewart Brand notes that we have done little to monitor the growth of telecommunications. Modern communication technology may seem overwhelmingly new, big, and encompassing, but these are reasons for more vigilance, not less: "New things have nastier surprises, big things are hard to change, and containing things is impossible" (258).

Integrating quotations into your paper

Integrate direct quotations smoothly into the flow of your paper by providing an explanatory "tag" or sentence of explanation. Readers should be able to follow your meaning easily and to see the relevance of the quotation immediately.

Using embedded or block format

Brief quotations should be embedded in the main body of your paper and enclosed in quotation marks. According to MLA style guidelines, a brief quotation consists of four or fewer typed lines. The short quotation in the following passage is from a personal interview.

```
Photo editor Tom Brennan took ten minutes to sort through
my images and then told me, "Most photography editors
wouldn't take more than two minutes to look at a portfolio."
```

Quotations of five lines or longer should be set off in block format. Begin a new line and indent ten spaces. Do not use quotation marks. The end punctuation precedes parenthetical documentation. (See also 47a.)

```
Katie Kelly focuses on Americans' peculiarly negative
chauvinism, in this case, the chauvinism of New York
residents:
        New Yorkers are a provincial lot. They wear their
        city's accomplishments like blue ribbons. To
        anyone who will listen they boast of leading the
        world in everything from Mafia murders to porno
        movie houses. (89)
```

(See Chapter 35 for more on punctuating quotations.)

Introducing quotations

Introduce all quoted material with a **signal phrase** that tells readers who is speaking, what the quotation refers to, and where it is from. If the author is well known, be sure to mention his or her name as part of the signal phrase.

COMMON VERBS IN SIGNAL PHRASES

The verb you choose for a signal phrase should accurately reflect the intention of the source. Unless the context requires a past-tense verb, use the present-tense form of the verb, as modeled in the passages quoted in Chapter 46.

acknowledges	concludes	illustrates	reports
admits	declares	implies	reveals
agrees	denies	insists	says
argues	disagrees	maintains	shows
asserts	disputes	notes	states
believes	emphasizes	observes	suggests
claims	endorses	points out	thinks
comments	finds	refutes	writes
concedes	grants		

Henry David Thoreau asserts in *Walden,* "The mass of men lead lives of quiet desperation" (5).

If the title of your written work is well known, you can introduce a quotation with the title rather than the author's name, as long as the reference is clear.

Walden sets forth one individual's antidote against the "lives of quiet desperation" led by the working class in mid-nineteenth-century America (Thoreau 5).

If neither the author nor the title is well known, introduce the quotation with a brief explanation to provide a context.

    Mary Catherine Bateson, daughter of anthropologist Margaret Mead, has become, in her own right, a student of modern civilization. In Composing a Life, she writes, "The twentieth century has been called the century of the refugee because of the vast numbers of people uprooted by war and politics from their homes" (8).

Explaining quotations
Sometimes you will need to explain a quotation in order to clarify why it's relevant and what it means in the context of your discussion.

In <u>A Sand County Almanac</u>, Aldo Leopold invites modern
urban readers to confront what they lose by living in the
city: "There are two spiritual dangers in not owning a farm.
One is the danger of supposing that breakfast comes from the
grocery, and the other that heat comes from the furnace"
(6). Leopold sees city dwellers as self-centered children,
blissfully but dangerously unaware of how their basic needs
are met.

You may also need to clarify what a word or reference means. Do this by using square brackets. (See 36d.)

UNCLEAR

Observing the remains of earwigs, sow bugs, moths, and spiders, Dillard reminds us that everything is changing, even in death: "Next week, if the other bodies are any indication, he will be shrunken and gray, webbed to the floor with dust."

CLEAR

Observing the remains of earwigs, sow bugs, moths, and spiders, Dillard reminds us that everything is changing, even in death: "Next week, if the other bodies are any indication, [the earwig] will be shrunken and gray, webbed to the floor with dust."

Adjusting grammar in quoted passages

A passage containing a quotation must follow all the rules of grammatical sentence structure—tenses should be consistent, verbs and subjects should agree, and so on. If the form of the passage doesn't fit the grammar of your own sentences, quote less of the original source, change your sentences, or slightly alter the quotation. Use this last option sparingly, and always indicate any changes with brackets. (See 36d.)

GRAMMATICALLY INCOMPATIBLE

If Thoreau thought that in his day, "The mass of men lead lives of quiet desperation" (Walden 5), what would he say of the masses today?

GRAMMATICALLY COMPATIBLE

If Thoreau thought that in his day the masses led "lives of quiet desperation" (Walden 5), what would he say of the masses today?

GRAMMATICALLY COMPATIBLE

In the nineteenth century, Thoreau stated, "The mass of men lead lives of quiet desperation" (Walden 5). What would he say of the masses today?

GRAMMATICALLY COMPATIBLE

If Thoreau thought that in his day the "mass of men [led] lives of quiet desperation" (Walden 5), what would he say of the masses today?

46c   Paraphrasing effectively

To paraphrase, you restate a source's ideas in your own words. The point of paraphrasing is to make the ideas clearer (both to your readers and to yourself) and to express the ideas in the way that best suits your purpose. In paraphrasing, attempt to preserve the intent of the original statement and to fit the paraphrased statement smoothly into the immediate context of your essay.

Paraphrases should generally re-create the original source's order, structure, and emphasis, and they should include most of its details. This means that a paraphrase is seldom briefer than the original. Use paraphrases only when the original is already quite brief or when you need to present an author's or speaker's ideas in detail; otherwise, use a summary.

A paraphrase should say neither more nor less than the original source, and it should never distort the meaning of the source. The best way to make an accurate paraphrase is to stay close to the order and structure of the original passage, to reproduce its emphases and details. However, don't use the same sentence patterns or vocabulary, or you risk inadvertently plagiarizing the source. (See 46e.)

You may be tempted to paraphrase by substituting synonyms for a few of an author's words while keeping others and by using much of the same sentence structure; however, doing so is considered plagiarism. (See 46e.)

WHEN TO PARAPHRASE IN YOUR PAPER

◆   **Clarity.** Use paraphrase in your draft to make complex ideas clear to your readers.

◆   **Details.** Use paraphrase when you need to present briefly certain details that an author or speaker has described at greater length.

◆   **Emphasis.** Use paraphrase when including an author's or speaker's point suits the goals of your own paper.

- Make sure you understand the meaning of a passage before you begin to paraphrase. Look up any words you don't know in the dictionary.

- When you write your paraphrase, look away from the original, and write down the ideas in your own words.

- Try to convey the meaning of an entire passage. Don't paraphrase one sentence at a time.

- Look at the context around the text you are paraphrasing, and include anything necessary to explain the passage.

- Use a thesaurus if you need to, but remember that not every synonym listed is equally appropriate in every sentence. Use only words you are familiar with.

ORIGINAL

The human communication environment has acquired biological complexity and planetary scale, but there are no scientists or activists monitoring it, theorizing about its health, or mounting campaigns to protect its resilience. Perhaps it's too new, too large to view as a whole, or too containing—"we swim in a sea of information," in poet Gary Snyder's phrase. All the more reason to worry. New things have nastier surprises, big things are hard to change, and containing things is impossible.

—Stewart Brand, *The Media Lab*

INACCURATE PARAPHRASE

In *The Media Lab,* Brand points out that the "communication environment" we live within is as complex and vast as any ecosystem on the planet. Yet no one monitors this environment, keeping track of its growth and warning us if something is about to go wrong. This is because the communication environment has become so large and all-encompassing in such a short time that we don't worry about it (258).

ACCURATE PARAPHRASE

In *The Media Lab,* Brand points out that the "communication environment" we live within is as complex and vast as any ecosystem on the planet. Yet no one monitors this environment, keeping track of its growth and warning us if something is about to go wrong. This may be understandable, since the communication environment has become so large and all-encompassing in such a short time that we often overlook it. But this is exactly why we should worry: it's the very qualities of being recent, large, and all-encompassing that make this environment potentially so dangerous (258).

46d   Summarizing effectively

When you summarize, you distill the main ideas of a passage and state them in your own words. Because a summary includes only the essentials of the original and not all the specific details, you should use a summary only when those details are not important to your research question.

The length of the original source has no bearing on the length of your summary. You may summarize several paragraphs or an entire chapter in just a few sentences. The more material you summarize in a short space, however, the more you have to generalize and abstract it. Be sure to keep all the information your readers need to understand what you are saying, and be careful not to distort the meaning of the original.

ORIGINAL

> The human communication environment has acquired biological complexity and planetary scale, but there are no scientists or activists monitoring it, theorizing about its health, or mounting campaigns to protect its resilience. Perhaps it's too new, too large to view as a whole, or too containing—"we swim in a sea of information," in poet Gary Snyder's phrase. All the more reason to worry. New things have nastier surprises, big things are hard to change, and containing things is impossible.
>
> —Stewart Brand, *The Media Lab*

INACCURATE SUMMARY

> The current telecommunications networks compose a nasty, unchangeable, and inescapable environment (Brand 258).

ACCURATE SUMMARY

> Stewart Brand warns that we may soon regret not keeping a closer watch on the burgeoning telecommunications networks (258).

WHEN TO SUMMARIZE IN YOUR PAPER

◆   **Main points.**   Use summary when your readers need to know the main points from an original source but not the supporting details.

◆   **Overviews.**   Use summary to provide an overview or an interesting aside without digressing too far from your paper's focus.

◆   **Condensation.**   Use summary to condense lengthy or rambling notes from your note cards into a few effective sentences.

Avoiding plagiarism   46e

In general, you do not need to document **common knowledge.** Common knowledge is information that an educated person can be expected to know and factual information that appears in multiple sources—for example, the dates of historical events, the names and locations of states and cities, the general laws of science, and statements of well-known theories. If an author offers opinions or interpretations of any type of common knowledge, these should be credited using the proper documentation style.

A **documentation style** is a systematic method for acknowledging sources. Correct documentation helps readers quickly and easily find the sources you have used. Each discipline has its own conventions for documentation. Languages and literature use Modern Language Association (MLA) style. (See 47a-47c.) Other humanities use a system like that in the *Chicago Manual of Style* (CMS). (See 49a.) The social sciences use the style of the American Psychological Association (APA). (See 48a–48c.) The natural and physical sciences use either the style recommended by the Council of Biology Editors (CBE) or something similar. (See 49b.)

Plagiarism is taking someone else's idea or information and passing it off as your own. Failure to cite a source is dishonest, and in the academic community, plagiarism has serious consequences. However, much plagiarism is unintentional and can be avoided. Many writers simply don't know how to identify borrowed words and ideas correctly. In fact, most plagiarism occurs when a writer paraphrases or summarizes a source but stays too close to the wording or sentence structure of the original.

ORIGINAL
> Notwithstanding the widely different opinions about Machiavelli's work and his personality, there is at least one point in which we find a complete unanimity. All authors emphasize that Machiavelli is a "child of his age," that he is a typical witness to the Renaissance.
> —Ernst Cassirer, *The Myth of the State*

PLAGIARIZED PARAPHRASE
> Despite the widely different opinions about Machiavelli's work and personality, everyone agrees that he was a representative witness to the Renaissance (Cassirer 43).

ACCEPTABLE PARAPHRASE
> Although views on the work and personality of Machiavelli vary, everyone agrees that he was "a typical witness to the Renaissance" (Cassirer 43).

MLA

47 ◆ MLA DOCUMENTATION

The most common form for documenting sources in English papers is the MLA (Modern Language Association) system described here in detail. It is a simple, economical, and thorough way for writers to acknowledge the sources they use in research-based papers. Pay careful attention to the practical mechanics of documentation so that readers can readily identify, understand, and locate your sources. The general rules of the MLA system are simple.

- ◆ All sources are briefly documented in the text by an identifying name and page number (generally in parentheses).
- ◆ A list of works cited at the end of the paper lists full publication data for each source cited.
- ◆ Additional explanatory information provided by the writer of the paper (but not from external sources) goes in footnotes either at the foot of the page or in a Notes section after the body of the paper.

The MLA system is explained in more detail in the *MLA Handbook for Writers of Research Papers,* 5th ed. (New York: MLA, 1998).

47a In-text citations

MLA parenthetical citations in text feature author names, text titles, and page numbers that refer readers to the list of works cited at the end of the paper, where they can find complete publication information about each source. MLA style is economical, providing only as much in-text information as readers need in order to locate more complete information on the Works Cited page. Following are some examples of how in-text citation works.

1. Single work by one or more authors

When you quote, paraphrase, or summarize a source, include in the text of your paper the last name of the source's author, if known, and, in parentheses, the page or pages on which the original information appeared. Do not include the word *page* or the abbreviations *p.* or *pp.* You may mention the author's name in the sentence or put it in parentheses preceding the page number(s).

```
Carol Lea Clark explains the basic necessities
for the creation of a page on the World Wide
Web (77).

Provided one has certain "basic ingredients,"
the Web offers potential worldwide publication
to individuals (Clark 77).
```

Note that a parenthetical reference at the end of a sentence comes before the period. No punctuation is used between the author's last name and the page number(s).

For a work by two or three authors, include all authors' names.

```
(Rombauer and Becker 715)

(Child, Bertholle, and Beck 215)
```

For works with more than three authors, list all the authors or, to avoid awkwardness, use the first author's name and add *et al.* without a comma. *Et al.* is an abbreviation for the Latin *et alii*, translated "and others."

```
(Britton et al. 395).
```

2. Two or more works by the same author

If your paper has references to two or more works by the same author, each citation should clearly identify the specific work. Either mention the title of the work in the text or include a shortened version of the title (usually the first one or two important words) in the parenthetical citation.

```
According to Lewis Thomas in Lives of a Cell,
many bacteria become dangerous only if they
manufacture exotoxins (76).

According to Lewis Thomas, many bacteria become
dangerous only if they manufacture exotoxins
(Lives 76).

Many bacteria become dangerous only if they
manufacture exotoxins (Thomas, Lives 76).
```

Put a comma between the author's last name and a title in a parenthetical citation. Do not put a comma between the title and the page number.

3. Unknown author

When the author of a work is unknown, either give the complete title in the text or a shortened version in the parenthetical citation, along with the page number. Be sure to identify the shortened title by quotation marks or underlining as appropriate.

```
According to Statistical Abstracts, the
literacy rate for Mexico stood at 75 percent in
1990, up 4 percent from census figures ten years
earlier (374).
```

DIRECTORY FOR MLA DOCUMENTATION GUIDELINES

IN-TEXT CITATIONS (47a)

1   Single work by one or more authors
2   Two or more works by the same author
3   Unknown author
4   Corporate or organizational author
5   Authors with the same last name
6   Works in more than one volume
7   One-page works
8   Quotation from an indirect source
9   Literary works
10   More than one work in a citation
11   Long quotation set off from text

ENDNOTES AND FOOTNOTES (47b)

THE WORKS CITED LIST (47c)

DOCUMENTING BOOKS

1   Book by one author
2   Book by two or three authors
3   Book by more than three authors
4   Book by a corporation, organization, association, or foundation
5   Revised edition of a book
6   Edited book
7   Book with an editor and author
8   Book in more than one volume
9   One volume of a multivolume book
10   Translated book
11   Book in a series
12   Reprinted book
13   Introduction, preface, foreword, or afterword in a book
14   Work in an anthology or chapter in an edited collection
15   Essay or periodical article reprinted in a collection
16   Article in a reference book
17   Anonymous book
18   Government document
19   Dissertation

continued

```
The literacy rate for Mexico stood at 75 percent
in 1990, up 4 percent from census figures ten
years earlier (Statistical 374).
```

4. Corporate or organizational author

When no author is listed for a work published by a corporation, foundation, organization, or association, indicate the group's full name in any parenthetical reference.

```
(Florida League of Women Voters 3)
```

If the name is long, cite it in the sentence and put only the page number in parentheses.

5. Authors with the same last name

When you cite works by two or more different authors with the same last name, include the first initial of each author's name in the parenthetical citation.

```
(C. Miller 63; S. Miller 101-04)
```

6. Works in more than one volume

Indicate the pertinent volume number for each citation. Place the volume number before the page number, and follow it with a colon and one space.

```
(Hill 2: 70)
```

If your source is in only one volume of a multivolume work, you need not specify the volume number in the in-text citation, but you should specify it in the Works Cited list.

7. One-page works

When you refer to a work that is only one page long, it is not necessary to include the page number since that will appear in the Works Cited list.

8. Quotation from an indirect source

When a quotation or any information in your source is originally from another source, use the abbreviation *qtd. in.*

```
Lester Brown of Worldwatch feels that
international agricultural production has
reached its limit and that "we're going to be
```

```
in trouble on the food front before this decade
is out" (qtd. in Mann 51).
```

9. Literary works

In citing literary prose works available in various editions, provide additional information (such as chapter number or scene number) for readers who may be consulting a different edition. Use a semicolon to separate the page number from this additional information and periods to indicate abbreviations.

```
(331; bk. 10, ch. 5)
```

In citing poems, provide only line numbers; include the word *line* or *lines* in the first such reference. This information will help your audience find the passages in any source where those works are reprinted, which page references alone cannot provide.

```
In "The Mother," Gwendolyn Brooks remembers
"the children you got that you did not get"
(line 1); children that "never giggled or
planned or cried" (30).
```

Cite verse plays using act, scene, and line numbers, separated by periods. For major works such as *Hamlet,* use identifiable abbreviations.

```
(Ham 4.4.31-39)
```

10. More than one work in a citation

To cite two or more works, separate them with semicolons.

```
(Aronson, Golden Shore 177; Didion 49-50)
```

11. Long quotation set off from text

To set off quoted passages of four or more lines, indent one inch or ten spaces from the left-hand margin of the text (not from the paper's edge); double-space, and omit quotation marks. The parenthetical citation follows end punctuation (unlike citations for shorter, integrated quotations) and is not followed by a period.

```
Fellow author W. Somerset Maugham had this to
say about Austen's dialogue:
          No one has ever looked upon Jane
          Austen as a great stylist. Her
```

> spelling was peculiar and her grammar
> often shaky, but she had a good ear.
> Her dialogue is probably as natural
> as dialogue can ever be. To set down
> on paper speech as it is spoken would
> be very tedious, and some arrangement
> of it is necessary. (434)

47b   Endnotes and footnotes

MLA style uses notes primarily to offer comments, explanations, or additional information (especially source-related information) that cannot be smoothly or easily accommodated in the text of the paper. In general, however, you should omit additional information, outside the "mainstream" of your paper, unless it is necessary for clarification or justification. If a note is necessary, insert a raised (superscript) numeral at the reference point in the text. Introduce the note itself with a corresponding raised numeral, and indent it.

TEXT WITH SUPERSCRIPT

The standard ingredients for guacamole include avocados, lemon juice, onion, tomatoes, coriander, salt, and pepper.[1] Hurtado's poem, however, gives this traditional dish a whole new twist (lines 10–17).

NOTE

[1] For variations see Beard 314, Egerton 197, Eckhardt 92, and Kafka 26. Beard's version, which includes olives and green peppers, is the most unusual.

The references listed in the notes should appear in the Works Cited list.

Notes may come at the bottom of the page on which the citation appears—as footnotes—or may be included as endnotes, double spaced on a separate page at the end of your paper. Endnote pages should be placed between the body of the paper and the Works Cited list, with the title "Note" or "Notes."

47c   The Works Cited list

Every source mentioned in your paper should be identified in a Works Cited list at the end of the paper using the following format.

♦   Center the title—"Works Cited," with no quotation marks, no underlining, and no boldface—one inch from the top of a separate page that follows the final page of the paper. (If asked to include works you read but did not actually cite in your paper, you may attach an additional page titled "Works Consulted.")

◆ Number this page, following in sequence from the last text page of your paper. If the list runs more than a page, continue the page numbering in sequence, but do not repeat the "Works Cited" title.

◆ Double-space between the title and first entry and within and between entries.

◆ Begin each entry at the left-hand margin, and indent subsequent lines the equivalent of a paragraph indention (five spaces or one-half inch).

Order of entries   Alphabetize entries according to authors' last names. If an author is unknown, alphabetize according to the first word of the title (but do not use an initial *A, An,* or *The*).

Entry formats   Here are the three most commonly used formats.

BOOKS

ONE SPACE   ONE SPACE

Author(s). Book Title. Place of publication:

INDENT 5
  SPACES ——Publisher, year of publication.   ONE SPACE
             ONE SPACE

JOURNAL ARTICLES

ONE SPACE   ONE SPACE   ONE SPACE, NO PUNCTUATION

Author(s). "Article Title." Journal Title volume

INDENT 5
  SPACES ——number, (year of publication): inclusive page
         numbers.   ONE SPACE   ONE SPACE

MAGAZINE AND NEWSPAPER ARTICLES

ONE SPACE   ONE SPACE   ONE SPACE, NO PUNCTUATION

Author(s). "Article Title." Publication Title date

INDENT 5
  SPACES ——of publication: inclusive page numbers.
              ONE SPACE

Authors   List the author's last name first, followed by a comma and then the rest of the name as it appears on the publication, followed by a period. Never alter an author's name by replacing full spellings with initials or by dropping middle initials.

◆ For more than one author, use a comma rather than a period after the first author and list the other authors first name first, separated by a comma. Do not use an ampersand (&). Put a period at the end.

◆ For more than one work by the same author, use three hyphens for the name after the first entry. (See page 379.)

Titles List full titles and subtitles as they appear on the title page, not on the book's cover. Separate titles and subtitles with colons (followed by one space). Capitalize according to 38d.

◆ Underline titles of entire books and periodicals. Use quotation marks around the titles of essays, poems, and other parts of a larger work.

◆ Put a period after a book or article title. Use no punctuation after a journal, magazine, or newspaper title.

Places of publication Places of publication are given for books and pamphlets, not for journals or magazines.

◆ Give the city of publication from the title page or copyright page. If several cities are given, use only the first.

◆ If the city could be unfamiliar or if there are several cities with the same name, abbreviate the state or country, preceded by a comma.

◆ Use a colon to separate the place of publication from the publisher.

Publishers The name of the publisher is given for books and pamphlets.

◆ Shorten the publisher's name as described below under "Abbreviations." If a title page indicates both an imprint and a publisher (for example, Arbor House, an imprint of William Morrow), list both shortened names, separated by a hyphen (*Arbor-Morrow*).

◆ Use a comma to separate the publisher from the publication date.

Date For books, give the year of publication followed by a period. For other publications, give the year of publication within parentheses followed by a colon. For newspapers, put the day before the month and year—*25 May 1954*—with no commas separating the elements. For magazines and newspapers, put a colon after the date.

Page numbers Page numbers are included for publications other than books.

◆ Use a hyphen, not a dash, between inclusive page numbers, with no extra space on either side.

◆ Use all digits for ending page numbers up to 99 and the last two digits only for numbers above 99 (*130–38*) unless the full number is needed for clarity (*198–210*).

◆ If subsequent pages do not follow consecutively, use a plus sign after the last consecutive page number (*39+; 52–55+*).

Abbreviations   Use standard postal abbreviations (see 42c) to identify the state after the city of publication.

◆ To shorten a publisher's name, drop the words *Press, Company,* and so forth in the publisher's name (*Blair* for *Blair Press*). Use the abbreviation *UP* for *University Press* (*Columbia UP; U of Chicago P*).

◆ Use only the first name if the publisher's name is a series of names (*Farrar* for *Farrar, Straus & Giroux*). Use only the last name if the publisher's name is a person's name (*Abrams* for *Harry N. Abrams*).

◆ If no publisher or date of publication is given for a book, use the abbreviations *n.p.* or *n.d.*

◆ For periodicals, abbreviate months using the first three letters followed by a period (*Apr.; Dec.*) except for May, June, and July. If an issue covers two months, use a hyphen to connect the months (*Apr.-May* and *June-Aug.*). (See model 20 below.)

Documenting books

1. Book by one author

```
Thomas, Lewis. Lives of a Cell: Notes of a Biology Watcher.
     New York: Viking, 1974.
```

2. Book by two or three authors

```
Fulwiler, Toby, and Alan R. Hayakawa. The Blair Handbook. Boston;
     Blair-Prentice, 1994.
```

Second and third authors are listed first name first. Do not alphabetize the author's names within an individual Works Cited entry. The final author's name is preceded by *and.* Do not use an ampersand (&). A comma always follows the inverted ordering of the author's first name.

3. Book by more than three authors

Britton, James, et al. <u>The Development of Writing Abilities</u>
   <u>(11-18)</u>. London: Macmillan Education, 1975.

With more than three authors, you have the option of using the abbreviation
et al. ("and others") or listing all the authors' names in full as they appear on
the title page of the book. Do not alphabetize the names within the Works
Cited entry.

4. Book by a corporation, organization, association, or foundation

U.S. Coast Guard Auxiliary. <u>Boating Skills and Seamanship</u>.
   Washington: Coast Guard Auxiliary National Board, 1988.

Alphabetize by the name of the organization.

5. Revised edition of a book

Hayakawa, S. I. <u>Language in Thought and Action</u>. 4th ed. New York:
   Harcourt, 1978.

6. Edited book

Hoy, Pat C., II, Esther H. Shor, and Robert DiYanni, eds.
   <u>Women's Voices: Visions and Perspectives</u>. New York: McGraw,
   1990.

7. Book with an editor and author

Britton, James. <u>Prospect and Retrospect</u>. Ed. Gordon Pradl. Upper
   Montclair: Boynton, 1982.

The abbreviation *Ed.* when followed by a name replaces the phrase "edited by"
and cannot be made plural. (See models 13 and 14.).

8. Book in more than one volume

Waldrep, Tom, ed. <u>Writers on Writing</u>. 2 vols. New York: Random,
   1985-88.

When separate volumes were published in different years, use inclusive dates.

9. One volume of a multivolume book

Waldrep, Tom, ed. <u>Writers on Writing</u>. Vol. 2. New York: Random,
   1988.

When each volume has its own title, list the full publication information for
the volume you have used first, followed by information on the series (number of volumes, dates).

Churchill, Winston S. <u>Triumph and Tragedy</u>. Boston: Houghton,
    1953. Vol. 6 of <u>The Second World War</u>. 6 vols. 1948–53.

10. Translated book

Camus, Albert. <u>The Stranger</u>. Trans. Stuart Gilbert. New York:
    Random, 1946.

11. Book in a series

Magistrate, Anthony. <u>Stephen King, The Second Decade</u>: Danse
    Macabre <u>to</u> The Dark Half. Twayne American Authors Series
    599. New York: Twayne, 1992.

A book title appearing in a book's title is not underlined (or italicized). Add
series information just before city of publication.

12. Reprinted book

Hurston, Zora Neale. <u>Their Eyes Were Watching God</u>. 1937. New
    York: Perennial-Harper, 1990.

Add the original publication date after the title, then cite current edition information.

13. Introduction, preface, foreword, or afterword in a book

Holroyd, Michael. Preface. <u>The Naked Civil Servant</u>. By Quentin
    Crisp. New York: Plume-NAL, 1983. ii–v.

Odell, Lee. Foreword. <u>Writing across the Disciplines: Research
    into Practice</u>. Ed. Art Young and Toby Fulwiler. Upper
    Montclair: Boynton, 1986. N.p.

14. Work in an anthology or chapter in an edited collection

Donne, John. "The Canonization." <u>The Metaphysical Poets</u>. Ed.
    Helen Gardner. Baltimore: Penguin, 1957. 61–62.

Gay, John. <u>The Beggar's Opera</u>. 1728. <u>British Dramatists from Dry-
    den to Sheridan</u>. Ed. George H. Nettleton and Arthur E. Case.
    Carbondale: Southern Illinois UP, 1975. 530–65.

Lispector, Clarice. "The Departure of the Train." Trans.
    Alexis Levitin. <u>Latin American Writers: Thirty Stories</u>.
    Ed. Gabriella Ibieta. New York: St. Martin's, 1993. 245–58.

MLA

Use quotation marks around the title of the work unless the work was originally published as a book. In that case, underline (or italicize) the title. Add inclusive page numbers for the selection at the end of the entry.

When citing two or more selections from one anthology, you may list the anthology separately under the editor's name. Selection entries will then need to include only a cross-reference to the anthology entry.

```
Donne, John. "The Canonization." Gardner 61-62.
```

15. Essay or periodical article reprinted in a collection

```
Emig, Janet. "Writing as Mode of Learning." College Composition
     and Communication 28 (1977): 122-28. Rpt. in The Web of
     Meaning. Ed. Janet Emig. Upper Montclair: Boynton, 1983.
     123-31.

Gannet, Lewis. Introduction. The Portable Steinbeck. New York:
     Viking, 1946. 1-12. Rpt. as "John Steinbeck's Way of
     Writing" in Steinbeck and His Critics: A Record of
     Twenty-five Years. Ed. E. W. Tedlock, Jr., and C. V. Wicker.
     Albuquerque: U of New Mexico P, 1957. 23-37.
```

Include the full citation for the original publication, followed by *Rpt. in* ("Reprinted in") and the publication information for the book. Include inclusive page numbers for the article or essay found in the collection; include inclusive page numbers for the original source when available.

16. Articles in a reference book

```
"Behn, Aphra." The Concise Columbia Encyclopedia. 1983 ed.

Miller, Peter L. "The Power of Flight." The Encyclopedia of
     Insects. Ed. Christopher O'Toole. New York: Facts on File,
     1986. 18-19.
```

For a signed article, begin with the author's name. For commonly known reference works, full publication information and editors' names are not necessary. For entries arranged alphabetically, page and volume numbers are not necessary.

17. Anonymous book

```
The World Almanac and Book of Facts. New York: World
     Almanac-Funk, 1995.
```

Alphabetize by title, excluding an initial *A, An,* or *The.*

18. Government document

```
United States. Central Intelligence Agency. National Basic
     Intelligence Fact Book. Washington: GPO, 1980.
```

If the author is identified, begin with that name. If not, begin with the government (country or state), followed by the agency or organization. The U.S. Government Printing Office is abbreviated *GPO*.

19. Dissertation

```
Kitzhaber, Albert R. "Rhetoric in American Colleges." Diss. U of
  .  Washington, 1953.
```

Use quotation marks for the title of an unpublished dissertation. Include the university name and the year. For a published dissertation, underline (or italicize) the title and give publication information as you would for a book, including the order number if the publisher is University Microfilms International (UMI).

Documenting periodicals

20. Article, story, or poem in a monthly or bimonthly magazine

```
Linn, Robert L., and Stephen B. Dunbar. "The Nation's Report Card
     Goes Home." Phi Delta Kappan Oct. 1990: 127-43.
```

Abbreviate all months except May, June, and July. Hyphenate months for bimonthlies.

```
(July-Aug. 1993)
```

Do not list volume or issue numbers.

21. Article, story, or poem in a weekly magazine

```
Updike, John. "His Mother Inside Him." New Yorker 20 Apr. 1992:
     34-36.
```

Note that the publication date is inverted.

22. Article in a daily newspaper

```
Brody, Jane E. "Doctors Get Poor Marks for Nutrition Knowledge."
     New York Times 10 Feb. 1992, natl. ed.: B7.
```

```
"Redistricting Reconsidered." Washington Post 12 May 1992: B2.
```

For an unsigned article, alphabetize by the article's title.

Give the full name of the newspaper as it appears on the masthead, but drop any introductory *A, An,* or *The.* If the city is not in the name, it should follow in brackets: *El Diario* [Los Angeles].

With the page number, include the letter that designates any separately numbered sections. If sections are numbered consecutively, list the section number (*sec. 2*) before the colon, preceded by a comma.

23. Article in a journal paginated by volume

```
Harris, Joseph. "The Other Reader." Journal of Advanced
     Composition 12 (1992): 34-36.
```

If the page numbers are continuous from one issue to the next throughout the year, include only the volume number (always in Arabic numerals) and year. Do not give the issue number or month or season. Note that there is no space between the end parenthesis and the colon.

24. Article in a journal paginated by issue

```
Tiffin, Helen. "Post-Colonialism, Post-Modernism, and the
     Rehabilitation of Post-Colonial History." Journal of
     Commonwealth Literature 23.1 (1988): 169-81.
```

If each issue begins with page 1, include the volume number followed by a period and then the issue number (both in Arabic numerals, even if the journal uses Roman). Do not give the month of publication.

25. Editorial

```
"Price Support Goes South." Editorial. Burlington Free Press 5
     June 1990: A10.
```

If signed, list the author's name first.

26. Letter to the editor and reply

```
Kempthorne, Charles. Letter. Kansas City Star 26 July 1992: A16.

Massing, Michael. Reply to letter of Peter Dale Scott. New York
     Review of Books 4 Mar. 1993: 57.
```

27. Review

```
Kramer, Mimi. "Victims." Rev. of 'Tis Pity She's a Whore. New
     York Shakespeare Festival. New Yorker 20 Apr. 1992: 78-79.

Rev. of Bone by Faye Myenne Ng. New Yorker 8 Feb. 1992: 113.
```

Documenting electronic sources

Electronic sources include both *databases,* available in portable forms such as CD-ROM, diskette, or magnetic tape, and *online* sources accessed with a computer connected to the Internet.

The Works Cited entries for electronic **databases** (newsletters, journals, and conferences) are similar to entries for articles in printed periodicals: cite the author's name; the article or document title in quotation marks; the newsletter, journal, or conference title; the number of the volume or issue; and the year or date of publication (in parentheses); the number of pages, if available.

Portable databases are much like books and periodicals. Their entries in Works Cited lists are similar to those for printed material except that you must also include the following items.

◆ The medium of publication (CD-ROM, diskette, magnetic tape)

◆ The name of the vendor, if known (this may be different from the name of the organization that compiled the information, which must also be included)

◆ The date of electronic publication, in addition to the date the material originally may have been published (as for a reprinted book or article)

28. Periodically updated CD-ROM database

```
James, Caryn. "An Army as Strong as Its Weakest Link." New York
    Times 16 Sep. 1994: C8 New York Times Ondisc. CD-ROM.
    UMI-Proquest. Oct. 1994.
```

If a database comes from a printed source such as a book, periodical, or collection of bibliographies or abstracts, cite this information first, followed by the title of the database (underlined), the medium of publication, the vendor name (if applicable), and the date of electronic publication. If no printed source is available, include the title of the material accessed (in quotation marks), the date of the material if given, the underlined title of the database, the medium of publication, the vendor name, and the date of electronic publication. If you have difficulty determining some of the information requested in these guidelines, simply follow the guidelines as closely and consistently as possible.

29. Nonperiodical CD-ROM publication

```
"Rhetoric." The Oxford English Dictionary. 2nd ed. CD-ROM.
    Oxford: Oxford UP, 1992.
```

List a nonperiodical CD-ROM as you would a book, adding the medium of publication and information about the source, if applicable. If citing only part of a work, underline the title of the selected portion or place it within quotation marks, as appropriate (as you would the title of a printed short story, poem, article, essay, or similar source).

30.   Diskette or magnetic tape publication

```
Lanham, Richard D. The Electronic Word: Democracy, Technology,

    and the Arts. Diskette. Chicago: U of Chicago P, 1993.

Doyle, Roddy. The Woman Who Walked Into Doors. Magnetic tape. New

    York: Penguin Audiobooks, 1996.
```

List these in the Works Cited section as you would a book, adding the medium of publication (e.g., "Diskette or Magnetic tape").

Documenting **online** or Internet information follows the same basic guidelines as documenting other texts—*who* said *what, where,* and *when.* However, some differences need to be noted. In citing online sources from the World Wide Web or electronic mail (*email* per MLA, or *e-mail* per APA) two dates are important—the date the text was created (published) and the date you found the information (accessed the site). When both publication and access dates are available, provide them both. However, many WWW sources and most *synchronous communications* (IRCs, MUDs, and MOOs) are often updated or changed, leaving no trace of the original version, so always provide the access *date* which documents that this information was available on that particular date. Thus, most electronic source entries will end with an access date immediately followed by the electronic address: 23 Dec. 1997 <http://www.cas.usf.edu/english/walker/mla.html>. The angle brackets < > identify the source as Internet.

The following guidelines are derived from the MLA Web site <http://www.mla.org>. To identify a **World Wide Web** source, include all the relevant items in the following order, each followed by a period, except date of access.

- ◆ *Author* (or *editor, compiler,* or *translator*). If known, full name, last name first (if unknown, include alias).

- ◆ *Title.* Include title of poems, short stories, articles in quotation marks. Include title of posting to discussion list or forum in quotation marks followed by *Online posting.* Underline book titles.

- ◆ *Editor, compiler,* or *translator.* Include name, if not cited earlier, followed by appropriate abbreviation, *Ed., Com., Tran.*

- ◆ *Print source information.* Same as printed citation.

◆ *Title of scholarly project, database, personal,* or *professional site* (under-lined); if no title, include description such as *Home page.* Include name of editor if available.

◆ *Identifying number.* For a journal, include volume and issue number.

◆ *Date of electronic publication.*

◆ *Discussion list information.* Include full name or title of list or forum.

◆ *Page, paragraph,* or *section numbers.*

◆ *Sponsorship* or *affiliation.* Include the name of any organization or insti-tution sponsoring this site.

◆ *Date of access.* Include date you visited this site.

◆ *Electronic address.* Include within angle brackets < >.

31. Scholarly project

The Education of Henry Adams. University of Virginia American
   Studies Program. Feb. 1996. U. Virginia. 8 Mar. 1998
   <http://www.xroads.virginia.edu/~HYPER/HADAMS/ha_home.html>.

32. Personal or professional site

Fulwiler, Anna. Home page. 1 Feb. 1998 <http://www.uvm.edu/
   ~afulwile>.

Yellow Wall-Paper Site. U. of Texas. 1995. 4 Mar. 1998
   <http://www.cwrl.utexas.edu/~daniel/amlit/wallpaper/
   wallpaper.html>.

33. Book

Twain, Mark. The Adventures of Tom Sawyer. Internet Wiretap
   Online Library. Carnegie-Mellon U. 4 Mar. 1998
   <http://www.cs.cmu.edu/Web/People/rgs/sawyr-table.html>.

34. Poem

Poe, Edgar Allan. "The Raven." American Review, 1845. Poetry
   Archives, 8 Mar. 1998. <http://tqd.advanced.org/3247/
   cgi-bin/dispoem.cgi?poet=poe.edgar&poem=88.html&frame=none>.

MLA

35. Article in a journal

Erkkila, Betsy. "The Emily Dickinson Wars." <u>Emily Dickinson
    Journal</u> 5.2 (1996): 14 pars. 8 Mar. 1988
    <http://www.colorado.edu/EDIS/journal/index.html>.

36. Article in a reference database

"Victorian." <u>Britannica Online</u>. Vers. 97.1.1 Mar. 1997.
    <u>Encyclopedia Britannica</u>. 2 Mar. 1998
    <http://www.eb.com:180>.

37. Posting to a discussion list

Beja, Morris. "New Virginia Woolf Discussion List." Online
    posting. 22 Feb. 1996. <u>The Virginia Woolf Society</u>, Ohio
    State U. 4 Mar. 1998 <gopher://dept.English.upenn.edu:70/
    0r0-1858-?Lists/20th/vwoolf>.

38. File transfer protocol (FTP), telnet, or gopher site

King, Jr., Martin Luther. "I Have a Dream Speech." 28 Aug. 1963.
    30 Jan. 1996 <telnet://ukanaix.cc.ukans.edu>.

Clinton, William Jefferson. "Remarks by the President at the
    Tribute Dinner for Senator Byrd." Washington: Office of
    the White House Press Secretary, 17 July 1994. 17 Jul.
    <gopher://info.tamu.edu.70/00/.data/politics/1994/byrd.0717>.

Use the abbreviations *ftp, telnet, gopher* or *http* as appropriate in the site address.

39. Email, listserv, or newsgroup (USENET) message

Fulwiler, Toby. "A question about electronic sources." 23 Jan.
    1998. Email to the author. U. of Vermont.

Robert Harley. "Writing Committee meeting." 24 Jan. 1998.
    Distribution list. U. of Vermont. 25 Jan. 1998.

Answerman (Mathes, Robert). "Revising the Atom." 2 Mar. 1997.
    4 Mar. 1997 <alt.books.digest>.

If you quote a personal message sent by somebody else, be sure to get permission before including his or her address on the Works Cited page.

40. Synchronous communications (MUD, MOO, IRC)

StoneHenger. <u>The Glass Dragon MOO</u>. 6 Feb. 1995. 6 Feb. 1995
    <telnet://surf.tstc.edu>.

Harnack, Andrew. "Words." Group discussion. 4 Apr. 1996.
    12 June 1996 <telnet://moo.du.org/port=8888>.

After posting date, include type of discussion (e.g., personal interview, group discussion), followed by a period.

Documenting other sources

41. Cartoon

Davis, Jim. "Garfield." Cartoon. <u>Courier</u> [Findlay, OH] 17 Feb.
    1996: E4.

Roberts, Victoria. Cartoon. <u>New Yorker</u> 13 July 1992: 34.

42. Film or videocassette

<u>Casablanca</u>. Dir. Michael Curtiz. Perf. Humphrey Bogart and
    Ingrid Bergman. Warner Bros., 1942.

<u>Fast Food: What's in It for You</u>. Prod. Center for Science.
    Videocassette. Los Angeles: Churchill, 1988.

Begin with the title, followed by the director, the studio, and the year released. You may also include the names of lead actors, producer, and the like between the title and the distribution information. If your essay is concerned with a particular person's work on a film, lead with that person's name, arranging all other information accordingly.

Lewis, Joseph H., dir. <u>Gun Crazy</u>. Screenplay by Dalton Trumbo.
    King Bros., 1950.

43. Personal interview

Holden, James. Personal interview. 12 Jan. 1996.

Morser, John. Professor of Political Science, U of Wisconsin.
    Telephone interview. 15 Dec. 1997.

Begin with the interviewee's name and specify the kind of interview and the date. You may identify the interviewee's position if relevant to the purpose of the interview.

44. Published or broadcast interview

Sowell, Thomas. "Affirmative Action Programs." Interview. <u>All things</u>
    <u>Considered</u>. Natl. Public Radio. WGTE, Toledo. 5 June 1990.

```
Steingass, David. Interview. Counterpoint 7 May 1970: 3-4.
```

For published or broadcast interviews, begin with the interviewee's name. Include appropriate publication information for a periodical or book and appropriate broadcast information for a radio or television program.

45. Print advertisement

```
Cadillac DeVille. Advertisement. New York Times 21 Feb. 1996,
     natl. ed.: A20.
```

Begin with the name of the product, followed by the description *Advertisement* and publication information for the source.

46. Unpublished lecture, public address, or speech

```
Graves, Donald. "When Bad Things Happen to Good Ideas." National
     Council of Teachers of English Convention. St. Louis,
     21 Nov. 1989.
```

Begin with the speaker, followed by the title (if any), the meeting (and sponsoring organization, if needed), the location, and the date. If there is no title, use a descriptive label (such as *Speech*) with no quotation marks.

47. Personal or unpublished letter

```
Friedman, Paul. Letter to the author. 18 Mar. 1992.
```

Personal letters and email messages are handled nearly identically in Works Cited entries. Begin with the name of the writer, identify the type of communication (e.g., *Letter*), and specify the audience. Include the date written, if known, or the date received. To cite an unpublished letter from an archive or private collection, include information that locates the holding (for example, *Quinn-Adams Papers. Lexington Historical Society. Lexington, KY.*).

48. Published letter

```
King, Jr., Martin Luther. "Letter from Birmingham Jail." 28 Aug.
     1963 Civil Disobedience in Focus. Ed. Hugo Adam Bedau.
     New York: Routledge, 1991. 68-84.
```

Cite published letters as you would a selection from an anthology. Specify the audience in the letter title (if known). Include the date of the letter immediately after its title. Place the page number(s) after the publisher information. If you cite more than one letter from a collection, cite the entire collection in the Works Cited list, and indicate individual dates and page numbers in your text.

49. Map

```
Ohio River: Foster, KY, to New Martinsville, WV. Map. Huntington:
     U.S. Corps of Engineers, 1985.
```

Cite a map as you would a book by an unknown author. Underline the title and identify the source as a map or chart.

50. Performance

Bissex, Rachel. Folk Songs. Flynn Theater. Burlington, VT.

    14 May 1990.

Rumors. By Neil Simon. Dir. Gene Saks. Broadhurst Theater, New

    York. 17 Nov. 1988.

Identify the pertinent details such as title, place, and date of performance. If you focus on a particular person in your essay, such as the director or conductor, lead with that person's name. For a recital or individual concert, lead with the performer's name.

51. Audio recording

Young, Neil, comp., perf. Mirror Ball. CD. In part accompanied

    by members of Pearl Jam. Burbank: Reprise, 1995.

Marley, Bob, and the Wailers. "Buffalo Soldier." Legend.

    Audiocassette. Island Records, 1984.

Depending on the focus of your essay, begin with the artist, composer, or conductor. Enclose song titles in quotation marks, followed by the recording title, underlined. Do not underline musical compositions identified only by form, number, and key. If you are not citing a compact disc, specify the recording format. End with the company label, the catalog number (if known), and the date of issue.

52. Television or radio broadcast

"Emissary." Star Trek: Deep Space Nine. Teleplay by Michael

    Pillar. Story by Rick Berman and Michael Pillar. Dir.

    David Carson. Fox. WFLX, West Palm Beach. 9 Jan. 1993.

If the broadcast is not an episode of a series or the episode is untitled, begin with the program title. Include the network, the station and city, and the date of broadcast. The inclusion of other information—such as narrator, writer, director, or performers—depends on the purpose of your citation.

53. Work of art

Holbein, Hans. Portrait of Erasmus. The Louvre, Paris.

    The Louvre Museum. By Germain Bazin. New York: Abrams,

    n.d., 148.

McIntyre, Linda. Colors. Art Institute of Chicago.

Begin with the artist's name. Follow with the title, and conclude with the location. If your source is a book, also give pertinent publication information.

47d · Student paper: MLA style

Full-sentence outline of "The Two Freedoms of Henry David Thoreau"

Thesis statement: The writings of Henry David Thoreau inspire modern readers by arguing for freedom from government intervention and freedom from social conformity.

    I.   "Civil Disobedience" advocates political freedom while <u>Walden</u> argues for social freedom.

   II.   "Civil Disobedience" ("CD") advocated freedom from government interference in daily life.

      A. The premise of "CD": "That government is best which governs least."

      B. Thoreau is arrested for not paying poll tax and is put in jail.

         1. Thoreau protests war with Mexico and institution of slavery.

         2. Doctrine of passive resistance is articulated in "CD."

      C. Thoreau argues against all forms of slavery in "Slavery in Massachusetts" and "A Plea for John Brown."

      D. Influence of "CD" is felt throughout world.

         1. "CD" inspires Gandhi and the movement for Indian independence.

         2. "CD" is basis for British Labour Party platform.

         3. "CD" supports underground resistance to Nazi Germany.

         4. "CD" influences American civil rights movement.

  III. <u>Walden</u> (<u>W</u>) is written to argue against social conformity and for the value of simple living.

      A. Thoreau confronts the "essential facts of life."

         1. <u>W</u> provides example of economical living.

         2. <u>W</u> provides example of living alone.

      B. Thoreau lives deliberately at Walden Pond.

         1. Thoreau tends a bean patch.

         2. Thoreau chases loons.

      C. Living at Walden Pond is not an option today.

  IV. The ideals articulated in <u>Walden</u> and "Civil Disobedience" inspire modern readers.

MLA

NAME	Andrew Turner
INSTRUCTOR	Professor Stephany
COURSE	English 2
DATE PAPER DUE	3 October, 199X

1/2″

1″

Turner 1

WRITER'S LAST NAME AND PAGE NUMBER APPEAR ON EACH PAGE.

DOUBLE SPACED

WRITER OPENS WITH THESIS.

The Two Freedoms of Henry David Thoreau

Henry David Thoreau led millions of
people throughout the world to think about
individual freedom in a new way. During
his lifetime, he attempted to live free
of unjust governmental constraints as well
as conventional social expectations. In
his 1849 essay "On the Duty of Civil
Disobedience," he makes his strongest case
against governmental interference in the
lives of citizens. In his 1854 book
Walden: or, Life in the Woods, he makes
the case for living free from social
conventions and expectations.

DO NOT JUSTIFY RIGHT-HAND MARGIN.

WRITER IDENTIFIES TWO WORKS TO BE EXAMINED.

ABBREVIATED TITLE IS USED AFTER WORK HAS BEEN IDENTIFIED BY FULL TITLE.

Thoreau opens "Civil Disobedience"
with his statement that "that government
is best which governs not at all" (222).
He argues that a government should allow
its people to be as free as possible,
providing for the needs of the people
without infringing on their daily lives.
Thoreau explains, "The government does not
concern me much, and I shall bestow the
fewest possible thoughts on it. It is not
for many moments that I live under a

ONLY THE PAGE NUMBER IS NEEDED WHEN SOURCE IS INTRODUCED IN THE SENTENCE.

1″

MLA

Turner 2

SHORT TITLE IS ADDED TO PAGE NUMBER BECAUSE TWO WORKS BY THE AUTHOR APPEAR ON WORKS CITED PAGE.

government." ("Civil" 238). In other words, in his daily life he attends to his business of eating, sleeping, and earning a living and not dealing in any noticeable way with an entity called "a government."

Because Thoreau did not want his freedom overshadowed by governmental regulations, he tried to ignore them. However, the American government in 1845 would not let him. He was arrested and put in the Concord jail for failing to pay his poll tax--a tax he believed unjust because it supported the government's war with Mexico as well as the immoral institution of slavery. Instead of protesting his arrest, he celebrated it and explained its meaning by writing "Civil Disobedience," one of the most famous English-language essays ever written. In it, he argues persuasively that "under a government which imprisons any unjustly, the true place for a just man is also a prison" (230). Thus the doctrine of passive resistance was formed, a doctrine that advocated protest against the government by nonviolent means:

PAGE NUMBER ONLY IS USED BECAUSE THE CONTEXT IDENTIFIES THE WORK.

INDENTED 10 SPACES → How does it become a man to behave toward this American government today? I answer that

Turner 3

QUOTATION OF MORE THAN 4 LINES PRESENTED IN BLOCK FORMAT.

he cannot without disgrace be associated with it. I cannot for an instant recognize that political organization as my government which is the slave's government also. (224)

SIGNAL PHRASE INTRODUCES THE NAME OF THE SECONDARY-SOURCE AUTHOR.

According to Charles R. Anderson,

PARTIAL QUOTATION IS WORKED INTO SENTENCE IN A GRAMMATICALLY CORRECT WAY.

Thoreau's other writings, such as "Slavery in Massachusetts" and "A Plea for Captain John Brown," show his disdain of the "northerners for their cowardice on conniving with such an institution" (28). He wanted all free American citizens, north and south, to revolt and liberate the slaves.

In addition to inspiring his countrymen, Thoreau's view of the sanctity of individual freedom affected the lives of later generations who shared his beliefs. "Civil Disobedience" had the greatest impact because of its "worldwide influence on Mahatma Gandhi, the British Labour Party in its early years, the underground in Nazi-occupied Europe, and Negro leaders in the modern south" (Anderson 30). For nearly one hundred fifty years, Thoreau's formulation of passive resistance has been a part of the human struggle for freedom.

Turner 4

Thoreau also wanted to be free from the everyday pressure to conform to society's expectations. He believed in doing and possessing only the essential things in life. To demonstrate his case, in 1845 he moved to the outskirts of Concord, Massachusetts, and lived by himself for two years on the shore of Walden Pond (Spiller et al. 396-97). Thoreau wrote Walden to explain the value of living simply, apart from the unnecessary complexity of society: "Simplicity, simplicity, simplicity! I say, let your affairs be as two or three, and not a hundred or a thousand" (66). At Walden, he lived as much as possible by this statement, building his own house and furniture, growing his own food, bartering for simple necessities, attending to his own business rather than seeking employment from others (Walden 16-17).

Living at Walden Pond gave Thoreau the chance to formulate many of his ideas about living the simple, economical life. At Walden, he lived simply in order to "front only the essential facts of life" (66) and to center his thoughts on living instead of on unnecessary details of mere livelihood. He developed survival skills

ABBREVIATED POPULAR TITLE IS LISTED AFTER WORK'S FIRST REFERENCE.

IDENTIFICATION FOR WORK WITH MORE THAN THREE AUTHORS.

PAGE NUMBERS FOR PARAPHRASE ARE INCLUDED.

SHORT TITLE IS ADDED TO PAGE NUMBER BECAUSE TWO WORKS BY THE AUTHOR APPEAR IN THE LIST OF WORKS CITED.

MLA

that freed him from the constraints of
city dwellers whose lives depended on a
web of material things and services

**PAGE
NUMBERS
ALONE ARE
SUFFICIENT
WHEN
CONTEXT
MAKES THE
SOURCE
CLEAR.**

provided by others. He preferred to "take
rank hold on life and spend my day more as
animals do" (117).

While living at Walden Pond, Thoreau
was free to occupy his time in any way
that pleased him, which for him meant
writing, tending his bean patch, and
chasing loons. He wasn't troubled by a
boss hounding him with deadlines or a wife
and children who needed support. In other
words, he wasn't expected to be anywhere
at any time for anybody except himself.
His neighbors accused him of being selfish
and did not understand that he sought most
of all "to live deliberately" (<u>Walden</u> 66),
as he felt all people should learn to do.

Then as now, most people had more
responsibilities than Thoreau had, and
they could not just pack up their
belongings and go live in the woods--if
they could find free woods to live in.
Today, people are intrigued to read about
Thoreau's experiences and are inspired by
his thoughts, but few people can actually
live or do as he suggests in <u>Walden</u>. In
fact, most people, if faced with the

Turner 6

prospect of spending two years removed
from society, would probably think of it
as a punishment or banishment, rather than
as Thoreau thought of it, as the good
life.

Practical or not, Thoreau's writings
about freedom from government and society
have inspired countless people to reassess
how they live their lives. Though unable
to live as he advocated, readers everywhere remain inspired by his ideal, that
one must live as freely as possible.

**WRITER'S
CONCLUSION
REPEATS
THESIS
ASSERTION.**

Turner 7

Works Cited

Anderson, Charles Roberts, ed. <u>Thoreau's
  Vision: The Major Essays</u>. Englewood
  Cliffs: Prentice, 1973.

Spiller, Robert E., et al. <u>Literary
  History of the United States:
  History</u>. 3rd ed. New York: Macmillan,
  1963.

Thoreau, Henry David. "On the Duty of
  Civil Disobedience." Walden <u>and</u>
  <u>"Civil Disobedience</u>." New York:
  Signet-NAL, 1960. 222-240.

---. <u>Walden: or, Life in the Woods</u>. Walden
  and <u>"Civil Disobedience</u>." New York:
  Signet-NAL, 1960. 7-221.

**HEADING
CENTERED**

**WORK WITH
MORE THAN
THREE
AUTHORS
CITED WITH
FIRST
AUTHOR'S
NAME AND
"ET AL."**

**ALL DOUBLE
SPACED**

◄—1″—► **INDENTED
5 SPACES
FROM MARGIN**

**FORMAT
FOR WORKS
WITHIN AN
ANTHOLOGY
INCLUDES THE
INDIVIDUAL
WORK'S
INCLUSIVE
PAGINATION.**
◄—1″—►

**AUTHOR'S
NAME IN
ADDITIONAL
ENTRIES IS
REPLACED
WITH
HYPHENS,
FOLLOWED BY
A PERIOD.
ENTRIES ARE
ALPHABETIZED
BY TITLE.**

APA

48 ◆ APA DOCUMENTATION

Most disciplines in the social sciences and related fields use the name-and-date system of documentation put forth by the American Psychological Association (APA). The disciplines of education and business also use this system. This citation style highlights dates of publication because the currency of published material is of primary importance in these disciplines. Because collaborative authoring is common in the social sciences, listing all authors is customary. For more about the foundations and purposes of the APA system, see the *Publication Manual of the American Psychological Association,* 4th ed. (Washington: APA, 1994). The numbered entries that follow introduce and explain some of the conventions of this system.

48a   In-text citations

1.   Single work by one or more authors

◆ Whenever you quote, paraphrase, or summarize material in your text, give both the author's last name and the date of the source. For direct quotations, provide specific page numbers. Page references in the APA system are always preceded, in text or in the reference list, by the abbreviation *p.* or *pp.* to designate single or multiple pages.

◆ Supply authors' names, publication dates, and page numbers (when listed) in parentheses following the cited material. Do not repeat any of these elements if you identify them in the text preceding the parenthetical citation.

```
Exotoxins make some bacteria dangerous to humans
(Thomas, 1974).

According to Thomas (1974), "Some bacteria are only harmful
to us if they make exotoxins" (p. 76).

We need fear some bacteria only "if they make exotoxins"
(Thomas, 1974, p. 76).
```

◆ For a work by two authors, cite both names.

```
Smith and Rogers (1990) agree that all bacteria producing
exotoxins are harmful to humans.

All known exotoxin-producing bacteria are harmful to humans
(Smith & Rogers, 1990).
```

The authors' names are joined by *and* within your text, but APA convention requires an ampersand (&) to join authors' names in parentheses.

APA

DIRECTORY FOR APA DOCUMENTATION GUIDELINES

IN-TEXT CITATIONS (48A)

1 Single work by one or more authors
2 Two or more works by the same author published in the same year
3 Unknown author
4 Corporate or organizational author
5 Authors with the same last name
6 Quotation from an indirect source
7 More than one work in a citation
8 Long quotation set off from text

FOOTNOTES (48B)

THE REFERENCE LIST (48C)

DOCUMENTING BOOKS

1   Book by one author
2   Book by two or more authors
3   More than one book by the same author
4   Book by a corporation, association, organization, or foundation
5   Revised edition of a book
6   Edited book
7   Book in more than one volume
8   Translated or reprinted book
9   Chapter or article in an edited book
10 Anonymous book
11 Government document

DOCUMENTING PERIODICALS

12 Article in a journal paginated by volume
13 Article in a journal paginated by issue
14 Magazine article
15 Newspaper article

DOCUMENTING ELECTRONIC SOURCES

16 CD-ROM
17 Computer software
18 Online journal articles
19 File transfer protocol (Ftp), telnet, or gopher site
20 Synchronous communications (MOO, MUD, IRC)
21 World Wide Web (www) site
22 Email and listserv messages

DOCUMENTING OTHER SOURCES

23 Film, recording, and other nonprint media
24 Interviews and other field sources

◆ For a work by three to five authors, identify all the authors by last name the first time you cite a source. In subsequent references, identify only the first author followed by *et al.* ("and others").

> The most recent study supports the belief that alcohol abuse is on the rise (Dinkins, Dominic, Smith, Rogers, & White, 1989). . . . When homeless people were excluded from the study, the results were the same (Dinkins et al., 1989).

◆ If you are citing a source by six or more authors, identify only the first author in all the references, followed by *et al.*

2. Two or more works by the same author published in the same year

To distinguish between two or more works published in the same year by the same author or team of authors, place a lowercase letter (*a, b, c,* etc.) immediately after the date. This letter should correspond to that in the reference list, where the entries will be alphabetized by title. If two appear in one citation, repeat the year.

> (Smith, 1992a, 1992b)

3. Unknown author

To cite the work of an unknown author, identify the first two or three words of the entry as listed on the Reference page. If the words are from the title, enclose them in quotation marks or underline them, as appropriate.

> <u>Statistical Abstracts</u> (1991) reports the literacy rate for Mexico at 75% for 1990, up 4% from census figures 10 years ago.

> Many researchers now believe that treatment should not begin until other factors have been dealt with ("New Evidence Suggests," 1987).

4. Corporate or organizational author

Spell out the name of the authoring agency for a work by a corporation, association, organization, or foundation. If the name can be abbreviated and remain identifiable, you may spell out the name only the first time and put the abbreviation immediately after it, in brackets. For subsequent references use only the abbreviation.

> (American Psychological Association [APA], 1993)
> (APA, 1994)

APA

5. Authors with the same last name

To avoid confusion in citing two or more authors with the same last name, include each author's initials in every citation.

```
(J. M. Clark, 1994)
(C. L. Clark, 1995)
```

6. Quotation from an indirect source

Use the words *as cited in* to indicate quotations or information in your source originally from another source.

```
Lester Brown of Worldwatch believes international
agriculture production has reached its limit and that
"we're going to be in trouble on the food front before
this decade is out" (as cited in Mann, 1993, p. 51).
```

7. More than one work in a citation

◆ List two or more sources within a single parenthetical reference in the same order in which they appear in your reference list. If you refer to two or more works by the same author, list them in chronological order with the author's name mentioned once and the dates separated by commas.

```
(Thomas, 1974, 1979)
```

◆ List works by different authors in alphabetical order by the author's last name, separated by semicolons.

```
(Miller, 1990; Webster & Rose, 1988)
```

8. Long quotation set off from text

Start quotations of forty or more words on a new line, and indent the block five spaces from the left-hand margin. Indent the first line of the second or any subsequent paragraphs (but not the first paragraph) five additional spaces. Double-space all such quotations, omit quotation marks, and place the parenthetical citation after any end punctuation, with no period following the citation.

Footnotes   48b

Footnotes are used to provide additional information that will be of interest to some readers but also likely to slow down the pace of your text or obscure your point for other readers.

◆ Footnotes should be as brief as possible; when the information you wish to add is extensive, present it in an appendix.

APA

- Number footnotes consecutively on a page following the Reference list on a page headed "Footnotes."

- Type footnotes double spaced, and indent the first line of each as you would a paragraph.

48c The reference list

All works mentioned in a paper should be identified on a reference list according to the following general rules of the APA documentation system.

Format After the final page of the paper, title a separate page "References" with no underlining or quotation marks. Center the title one inch from the top of the page. Number the page in sequence with the last page of the paper.

Double-space between the title and the first entry. Set the first line flush with the left-hand margin; indent the second and all subsequent lines of an entry 5 to 7 spaces (or one default tab) from the left margin in a "hanging indent." (Papers submitted for publication use the paragraph indent format, with the first line indented five spaces and subsequent lines flush with the left margin, but most instructors prefer the hanging indent format. Always check with your instructor.)

Also double-space both between and within entries. If your reference list exceeds one page, continue listing your references in sequence on an additional page or pages, but do not repeat the title "References."

Order of entries Alphabetize the list of references according to authors' last names, using the first author's last name for works with multiple authors. For entries by an unknown author, alphabetize by the first word of the title, excepting nonsignificant words (*A, An, The*).

Format for entries The three most common of several variations on general formats are the following.

BOOKS

          ONE SPACE   ONE SPACE   ONE SPACE

    Author(s). (Year of publication). Book title. City of

INDENT 5
SPACES ——publication: Publisher.

JOURNAL ARTICLES

          ONE SPACE   ONE SPACE   ONE SPACE

    Author(s). (Year of publication). Article title. Journal

INDENT 5
SPACES ——Title, volume number, inclusive page numbers.

MAGAZINE AND NEWSPAPER ARTICLES

```
            ONE SPACE              ONE SPACE
              |                      |
Author(s). (Year, month of publication). Article title.
INDENT 5
 SPACES ———Publication Title, inclusive page numbers.
```

Authors   List the author's last name first, followed by a comma and the author's initials (not first name). When a work has more than one author, list all authors in this way, separating the names with a comma. When listing multiple authors for a single work, place an ampersand (&) before the last author's name. A period follows the author name(s).

Titles   List the complete titles and subtitles of books and articles, but capitalize only the first word of the title and any subtitle, as well as all proper nouns. Underline the titles of books, magazines, and newspapers, but do not underline article titles or place quotation marks around them. Place a period after the title. Make sure punctuation is underscored, also.

Publishers   List publishers' names in shortened form, omitting words such as *Company*. Spell out the names of university presses and organizations in full. For books, use a colon to separate the city of publication from the publisher.

Dates and page numbers   For magazines and newspapers, use commas to separate the year from the month and day, and enclose the publication dates in parentheses: (*1954, May 25*). Inclusive page numbers should be separated by a hyphen with no spaces: *361-375*. Full sequences should be given for pages and dates (not *361-75*). If pages do not follow consecutively (as in newspapers), include subsequent page numbers after a comma: *pp. 1, 16*. Note that *pp.* precedes the page numbers for newspaper articles but not for journal articles.

Abbreviations   State and country names are abbreviated, but months are not. Use U.S. postal abbreviations for state abbreviations (but omit them for cities well known for publishing: Baltimore, Boston, Chicago, Los Angeles, New York, Philadelphia, and San Francisco).

Following are examples of the reference list format for a variety of source types.

Documenting books

1.   Book by one author

Benjamin, J. (1988). The bonds of love: Psychoanalysis, feminism, and the problem of domination. New York: Prometheus.

2.   Book by two or more authors

Zweigenhaft, R. L., & Domhoff, G. W. (1991). Blacks in the White Establishment? A Study of Race and Class in America. New Haven, CT: Yale University Press.

Include all authors' names in the reference list, regardless of the number of authors associated with a particular work.

3. More than one book by the same author

List two or more works by the same author (or the same author team listed in the same order) chronologically by year, earliest work first. Arrange any such works published in the same year alphabetically by title, placing lowercase letters after the dates. In either case, give full identification of author(s) for each reference listing.

Bandura, A. (1969). <u>Principles of behavior modification.</u> New York: Holt, Rinehart, and Winston.

Bandura, A. (1977a). Self-efficacy: Toward a unifying theory of behavioral change. <u>Psychological Review,</u> 84, 191-215.

Bandura, A. (1977b). <u>Social learning theory.</u> Upper Saddle River: Prentice-Hall.

If the same author is named first but listed with different co-authors, alphabetize by the last name of the second author. Works by the first author alone are listed before works with co-authors.

4. Book by a corporation, association, organization, or foundation

American Psychological Association. (1994). <u>Publication manual of the American Psychological Association</u> (4th ed.). Washington: Author.

Alphabetize corporate authors by the corporate name, excluding the articles *A, An,* and *The.* When the corporate author is also the publisher, designate the publisher as *Author.*

5. Revised edition of a book

Peek, S. (1993). <u>The game inventor's handbook</u> (Rev. ed.). Cincinnati: Betterway.

6. Edited book

Schaefer, Charles E., & Reid, S. E. (Eds.). (1986). <u>Game play: Therapeutic use of childhood games.</u> New York: Wiley.

Place *Ed.* or *Eds.,* capitalized, after the singular or plural name of the editor(s) of an edited book.

7. Book in more than one volume

Waldrep, T. (Ed.). (1985-1988). <u>Writers on writing</u> (Vols. 1-2). New York: Random House.

For a work with volumes published in different years, indicate the range of dates of publication. In citing only one volume of a multivolume work, indicate only the volume cited.

```
Waldrep, T. (Ed.). (1988). Writers on writing (Vol. 2). New
    York: Random House.
```

8. Translated or reprinted book

```
Freud, S. (1950). The interpretation of dreams (A. A. Brill,
    Trans.). New York: Modern Library-Random House. (Original
    work published 1900)
```

The date of the translation or reprint is in parentheses after the author's name. Place the original publication date in parentheses at the end of the citation, with no period. In the parenthetical citation in your text, include both dates: (*Freud 1900/1950*).

9. Chapter or article in an edited book

```
Telander, R. (1996). Senseless crimes. In C. I. Schuster &
    W. V. Van Pelt (Eds.), Speculations: Readings in culture,
    identity, and values (2nd ed., pp. 264-272). Upper Saddle
    River: Prentice-Hall.
```

The chapter or article title is not underlined or in quotation marks. Editors' names are listed in normal reading order (surname last). Inclusive page numbers, in parentheses, follow the book title.

10. Anonymous book

```
Stereotypes, distortions and omissions in U.S. history
    textbooks. (1977). New York: Council on Interracial Books
    for Children.
```

11. Government document

```
U.S. House of Representatives, Committee on Energy and Commerce.
    (1986). Ensuring access to programming for the backyard
    satellite dish owner (Serial No. 99-127). Washington: U.S.
    Government Printing Office.
```

For government documents, provide the higher department or governing agency only when the office or agency that created the document is not readily recognizable. If a document number is available, list it in parentheses after the document title. Write out the name of the printing agency in full rather than using the abbreviation *GPO*.

Documenting periodicals

In citing periodical articles, use the same format for listing author names as for books.

12. Article in a journal paginated by volume

Hartley, J. (1991). Psychology, writing, and computers: A review of research. Visible Language, 25, 339-375.

If page numbers are continuous throughout volumes in a year, use only the volume number, underlined, following the title of the periodical.

13. Article in a journal paginated by issue

Lowther, M. A. (1977). Career change in mid-life: Its impact on education. Innovator, 8(7), 1, 9-11.

Include the issue number in parentheses if each issue of a journal is paginated separately; do not use the abbreviation *p.* or *pp.*

14. Magazine article

Garreau, J. (1995, December). Edgier cities. Wired, 158-163, 232-234.

For nonprofessional periodicals, include the year and month (not abbreviated) after the author's name; do not use the abbreviation *p.* or *pp.*

15. Newspaper article

Finn, P. (1995, September 27). Death of a U-Va. student raises scrutiny of off-campus drinking. The Washington Post, pp. D1, D4.

If an author is listed for the article, begin with the author's name, then list the date (spell out the month); follow with the title of the newspaper. If there is a section, combine it with the page or pages, including continued page numbers as well, using the abbreviation *p.* or *pp.*

Documenting electronic sources

APA conventions for documenting fixed electronic sources such as CD-ROMs, diskettes, and magnetic tapes list author, date, and title followed by the type of electronic source [CD-ROM] and the complete information for the corresponding print source if available.

16. CD-ROM

A specific example of this format is as follows:

Krauthammer, C. (1991). Why is America in a blue funk? [CD-ROM]. Time, 138, 83. Abstract from: UMIACH file: Periodical Abstracts Item: 1126.00

17. Computer software

```
HyperCard (Version 2.2) [Computer software]. (1993). Cupertino,
    CA: Apple Computer.
```

Provide the version number, if available, in parentheses following the program or software name. Add the descriptive term computer software in brackets and follow it with a period. Do not underline names of computer programs.

Documenting On-line Sources

APA provides three general formats for listing on-line (World Wide Web or e-mail) sources which closely follow the conventions for their printed equivalents. (Keep in mind that all APA citations follow the general structure of *who* said *when, what,* and *where.*)

ON-LINE PERIODICAL

```
Author(s) (date of publication). Article title. Periodical title
    [description of Internet source], Volume (issue). Access
    date: Electronic address
```

ON-LINE PUBLICATION

```
Author(s) (date of publication). Chapter title. Title of full
    work. Access date: Electronic address
```

ON-LINE BOOK

```
Author(s) (date of publication). Title of full work. Access date:
    Electronic address
```

For more details than the following examples can provide, consult the APA web page at http://www.apa.org/journals/webref.html.

18. On-line journal articles

```
Kapadia, S. (1995, November). A tribute to Mahatma Gandhi: His
    views on women and social exchange [19 paragraphs].
    Journal of South Asia Women's Studies [On-line serial],
    1 (1). Retrieved December 2, 1995 from the World Wide Web:
    http://www.shore.net/~india/jsaws
```

Indicate the number of paragraphs in brackets after the title and add the term *On-line serial* in brackets between the journal name and the volume number.

19. File transfer protocol (Ftp), telnet, or gopher site

```
Altar, T. W. (1993). Vitamin B12 and vegans. Retrieved May 28,
    1996: ftp://wiretap.spies.com/Library/Article/Food/b12.txt

Clinton, W. (1994, July 17). Remarks by the President at the
    tribute dinner for Senator Byrd. Washington: Office of the
    White House Press Secretary. Retrieved February 12, 1996:
    gopher://info.tamu.edu.70/00/.data/politics/1994/byrd.0717
```

After the access date, supply the ftp, telnet, or gopher search path.

20. Synchronous communications (MOO, MUD, IRC)

```
Harnack, A. (1996, April 4). Words. Group discussion. Retrieved
     April 5, 1996: telnet://moo.du.org/port=8888
```

21. World Wide Web (www) site

```
Williams, Scott. (1996, June 14). Back to school with the quilt.
     AIDS Memorial Quilt Website. Retrieved June 14, 1996:
     http://www.aidsquilt.org/newsletter/stories/backto.html

Chicago prep star Fields seriously injured in crash. (1996,
     February 27). ESPN Sportszone. Retrieved March 12, 1996:
     http://www.sportszone.com/gen/top/0707241001.html
```

22. E-mail and listserv messages

Under current APA guidelines, electronic conversations are not listed on the references page. Cite e-mail and listserv messages in the text as you would personal letters or interviews.

```
R.W. Williams, personal communication, January 4, 1998.
```

Documenting Other Sources

23. Film, recording, and other nonprint media

```
Curtiz, M. (Director). (1942). Casablanca [Film]. Hollywood, CA:
     Warner Bros.
```

Alphabetize a film listing by the name of the person or persons with primary responsibility for the product. Identify the medium in brackets following the title, and indicate both location and name of the distributor (as publisher). Other identifying information, such as the director, should appear in parentheses.

24. Interviews and other field sources

These are identified in the text in parentheses (name, place, date) but are not listed on the References page. See model 17.

48d Informational research paper: APA style

The research essay "Green Is Only Skin Deep: False Environmental Advertising," by Elizabeth Bone, was written in response to an assignment to identify and explain one problem in contemporary American culture. Bone's essay is documented according to the conventions of the American Psychological Association (APA). This sample includes title page, abstract, and outline page; check with your instructor to find out if these are required for course papers.

ABBREVIATED TITLE (OPTIONAL)

Green   1

**PAGE NUMBERING
BEGINS ON TITLE
PAGE.**

**TITLE PAGE IS
CENTERED AND
DOUBLE-SPACED.**

Green Is Only Skin Deep: **TITLE**

False Environmental Marketing

Elizabeth Bone   **AUTHOR**

Professor John Clark   **INSTRUCTOR**

English 1   **COURSE**

December 6, 199X   **DATE**

APA

ABSTRACT SHOULD BE PRINTED ON A SEPARATE PAGE FOLLOWING THE TITLE PAGE

Green   2

HEADING CENTERED

DOUBLE-SPACED

Abstract

NO PARAGRAPH INDENT

THE ABSTRACT SUMMARIZES THE MAIN POINT OF THE PAPER.

Most Americans consider themselves environ-mentalists and favor supporting environmentally friendly or "green" companies. However, companies use a number of false advertising practices to mislead the public about their green practices and products by (1) exaggerating claims, (2) masking false practices behind technical terminology, (3) mis-sponsoring green events, (4) not admitting responsibility for real problems, (5) advertising green by association, and (6) solving one problem while creating others. Consumers must be skeptical of all commercial ads and take the time to find out the truth behind advertising.

APA

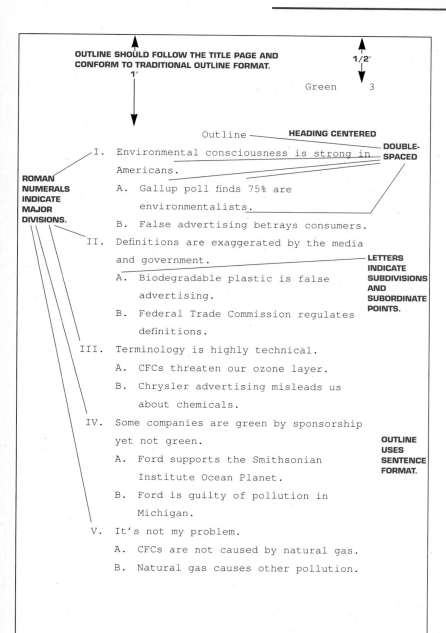

OUTLINE SHOULD FOLLOW THE TITLE PAGE AND
CONFORM TO TRADITIONAL OUTLINE FORMAT.
1″

1/2″

Green   3

Outline ——— HEADING CENTERED

I. Environmental consciousness is strong in Americans. —— DOUBLE-SPACED

ROMAN NUMERALS INDICATE MAJOR DIVISIONS.

   A. Gallup poll finds 75% are environmentalists.

   B. False advertising betrays consumers.

II. Definitions are exaggerated by the media and government. —— LETTERS INDICATE SUBDIVISIONS AND SUBORDINATE POINTS.

   A. Biodegradable plastic is false advertising.

   B. Federal Trade Commission regulates definitions.

III. Terminology is highly technical.

   A. CFCs threaten our ozone layer.

   B. Chrysler advertising misleads us about chemicals.

IV. Some companies are green by sponsorship yet not green.

   A. Ford supports the Smithsonian Institute Ocean Planet. —— OUTLINE USES SENTENCE FORMAT.

   B. Ford is guilty of pollution in Michigan.

V. It's not my problem.

   A. CFCs are not caused by natural gas.

   B. Natural gas causes other pollution.

APA

APA

Green   4

   VI. Many companies are green only by
       association.
      A. Advertising has nothing to do with
         product.
      B. Chevrolet logo implies relationship.
  VII. Some companies are singled-minded in
       their environmentalism.
      A. Chevron employees do good in
         Mississippi.
      B. Chevron pollutes Santa Monica Bay.
 VIII. Environmental image does not match
       reality.
      A. Earth First! educates consumers.
      B. Federal Trade Commission regulates.
      C. Consumers beware!

↕ 1/2″

Green   5

TITLE IS REPEATED FROM TITLE PAGE

Green Is Only Skin Deep:

False Environmental Marketing

A recent Gallup poll reported that 75%
of Americans consider themselves to be environmentalists (Smith & Quelch, 1993). In the
same study, nearly half of the respondents
said they would be more likely to purchase a
product if they perceived it to be environmentally friendly or "green." According to
Smith and Quelch (1993), since green sells,
many companies have begun to promote themselves as marketing products that are
either environmentally friendly or manufac-
tured from recycled material. Unfortunately, many of these companies care more
about appearance than reality.

The most common way for a company to
market itself as pro-environment is to
stretch the definitions of terms such as
"biodegradable" so that consumers believe
one thing but the product delivers something
else. For example, so-called biodegradable
plastic, made with cornstarch, was introduced to ease consumers' fears that plastic
lasts forever in the environment. However,
the cornstarch plastic broke down only in
specific controlled laboratory conditions,
not outdoors and not in compost bins. The
Federal Trade Commission has updated its

AUTHOR'S NAME, DATE, AND PAGE NUMBERS ARE IN PARENTHESES

DOUBLE SPACED

INFORMATIONAL THESIS IS AT END OF FIRST PARAGRAPH.

FIRST EXAMPLE OF FALSE ADVERTISING IS INTRODUCED.

APA

regulations to prevent such misrepresenta-
tions, so that now Glad and Hefty trash bags
are no longer advertised as biodegradable
(Carlson, Grove, & Kangun, 1993).

The use of technical terms can also
mislead average consumers. For example,
carbon fluoride compounds, called CFCs, are
known to be hazardous to the protective
layer of ozone that surrounds the earth, so
their widespread use in air conditioners is
considered an environmental hazard (Decker &
Stammer, 1989). Chrysler Corporation adver-
tises that it uses CFC-free refrigerant in
its automobile air conditioners to appeal to
environmentally concerned consumers ("Ozone
layer," 1994). However, Weisskopf (1992)
points out that the chemical compounds that
replace CFCs in their air conditioners pose
other environmental hazards that are not
mentioned.

Another deceptive greening tactic is
the sponsoring of highly publicized environmental events such as animal shows, concerts, cleanup programs, and educational exhibits. For example, Ocean Planet was a
well-publicized exhibit put together by the
Smithsonian Institution to educate people
about ocean conservation. Ford Motor Company
helped sponsor the event, which it then used

SECOND EXAMPLE IS GIVEN.

AUTHOR QUOTED BY NAME IN THE TEXT IS FOLLOWED BY PUBLICATION YEAR IN PARENTHESES.

TRANSITIONS KEEP THE READER ON TRACK.

APA

Green   7

in its car advertisements: "At Ford, we feel
strongly that understanding, preserving, and
properly managing natural resources like our
oceans should be an essential commitment of
individuals and corporate citizens alike."
("Smithsonian Institution's Ocean Planet,"
1995, p. 14).

   While sponsoring the exhibit may be a
worthwhile public service, such sponsorship
has nothing to do with how the manufacture
and operation of Ford automobiles affect the
environment. In fact, Ford was ranked as
among the worst polluters in the state of
Michigan in 1995 (Parker, 1995).

   Some companies court the public by mentioning environmental problems and pointing
out that they do not contribute to those
problems. For example, the natural gas industry describes natural gas as an alternative to the use of ozone-depleting CFCs
("Don't you wish," 1994). However, according
to Fogel (1985), the manufacture of natural
gas creates a host of other environmental
problems from land reclamation to carbon-
dioxide pollution, a major cause of global
warming. By mentioning problems they don't
cause while ignoring ones they do, companies
present a favorable environmental

SHORTENED TITLE IS USED WHEN NO AUTHOR IS CREDITED ON REFERENCE PAGE.

APA

image that is at best a half truth, at worst
an outright lie.

Other companies use a more subtle approach to misleading green advertising.
Rather than make statements about environmental compatibility, these companies depict
the product in unspoiled natural settings or
use green quotations that have nothing to do
with the product itself. For example, one
Chevrolet advertisement shows a lake
shrouded in mist and quotes an environmen-

QUOTATION OF FEWER THAN 40 WORDS IS INTEGRATED INTO THE TEXT.

talist: "From this day onward, I will restore the earth where I am and listen to
what it is telling me" ("From this day,"
1994). Below the quotation is the Chevy logo
with the words "Genuine Chevrolet." Despite
this touching appeal to its love of nature,
Chevrolet has a history of dumping toxic
waste into the Great Lakes (Allen, 1991).
Has this company seriously been listening to
what the earth has been telling it?

The most common manner in which companies attempt to prove they have a strong environmental commitment is to give a single
example of a policy or action that is considered environmentally sound. Chevron has
had an environmental advertising campaign
since the mid-1970s. Most recently their ads

Green   9

feature Chevron employees doing environmental good deeds (Smith & Quelch, 1993). For
example, a recent ad features "a saltwater
wetland in Mississippi at the edge of a pine
forest . . . the kind of place nature might
have made," and it goes on to explain that
this wetland was built by Chevron employees
("The shorebirds who found," 1990). However,
during the time this advertisement was running in magazines such as Audubon, Laganga
(1993) points out that Chevron was dumping
millions of gallons of nasty chemicals (car-
cinogens and heavy metals) into California's
Santa Monica Bay, posing a health risk to
swimmers. The building of the wetland in one
part of the country does not absolve the
company for polluting water somewhere else.

It should be clear that the environmental image a company projects does not
necessarily match the realities of the
company's practice. The products produced by
companies such as Chrysler, Ford, General
Motors, and Chevron are among the major
causes of air and water pollution: automobiles and gasoline. No amount of advertising can conceal the ultimately negative
effect these products have on the environment (Kennedy & Grumbly, 1988). According to

ELLIPSIS POINTS INDICATE MISSING WORDS IN QUOTATION.

PAGE NUMBER IS NOT LISTED WHEN IT IS LISTED ON REFERENCE PAGE.

APA

APA

Shirley Lefevre, president of the New York

Truth in Advertising League: ——————— **COLON IS USED TO INTRODUCE A LONG QUOTATION.**

DOUBLE SPACED   It probably doesn't help to single out

one automobile manufacturer or oil

company as significantly worse than the

INDENTED 5 SPACES   others. Despite small efforts here and

there, all of these giant corporations,

as well as other large manufacturers of

metal and plastic material goods, put

profit before environment and cause more

harm than good to the environment.

(personal communication, May 1995)   **INTERVIEW CONDUCTED BY AUTHOR IS NOT LISTED ON THE REFERENCE PAGE.**

Consumers who are genuinely interested

in buying environmentally safe products and

supporting environmentally responsible com-

panies need to look beyond the images pro-

jected by commercial advertising in maga-

zines, on billboards, and on television.

Organizations such as Earth First! attempt

to educate consumers to the realities by

writing about false advertising and exposing

the hypocrisy of such ads ("Do people al-

low," 1994), while the Ecology Channel is

committed to sharing "impartial, unbiased,

multiperspective environmental information"

with consumers on the Internet (Ecology,

1996). Meanwhile the Federal Trade Commis-

Green   11

SECOND CITATION OF MORE THAN THREE AUTHORS IS SHORTENED TO FIRST AUTHOR'S NAME AND "ET AL."

sion is in the process of continually up-
grading truth-in-advertising regulations
(Carlson, et al., 1993). Americans who are
truly environmentally conscious must remain
skeptical of simplistic and misleading commercial advertisements while continuing to
educate themselves about the genuine needs
of the environment.

THESIS IS REPEATED IN MORE DETAIL AT END.

APA

Green   12

HEADING CENTERED

References

AUTHORS ARE LISTED ALPHABETICALLY.

DOUBLE SPACED

Allen, F. E. (1991, March 10). Great Lakes

cleanup enlists big volunteers. The Wall

Street Journal, p. B1.

INITIALS ARE USED FOR FIRST AND MIDDLE NAMES.

Carlson, L., Grove, S. J., & Kangun, N. (1993).

A content analysis of environmental

advertising claims: A matrix methods

approach. Journal of Advertising, 22 (9),

27-39.

ONLY FIRST WORD AND PROPER NAMES ARE CAPITALIZED IN ARTICLE TITLE.

"P." OR "PP," IS NOT USED TO INDICATE PAGES IN A PROFESSIONAL JOURNAL

Decker, C., and Stammer, L. (1989, March 4).

Bush asks ban on CFC to save ozone. Los

Angeles Times, p. A1.

Do people allow themselves to be that gullible?

DATE FOLLOWS AUTHOR (OR TITLE IF NO AUTHOR IS IDENTIFIED).

(1994, September). Earth First! 9, 6.

Don't you wish we could just do this to CFC's

natural gas advertisement? (1994,

December 7). Audubon, 12, 7.

The ecology channel. (1996). [Information posted

on-line]. Retrieved November 20, 1997 from

the World Wide Web: http//www.ecology.com/

Fogel, B. (1985). Energy: choices for the

future. New York: Franklin Watts.

BOOK AND PERIODICAL TITLES ARE UNDERLINED.

From this day onward I will restore the earth

where I am. (1994, November-December).

INDENTED 5 SPACES

[Chevrolet advertisement]. Audubon, 11-12,

18-19.

Kennedy, D., & Grumbly, T. P. (1988). Automo-

tive emissions research. In Watson, A.,

APA

Green   13

"P." OR "PP." IS USED FOR PAGE NUMBERS IN BOOKS OR POPULAR PERIODICALS.

Bates, R. R., & Kennedy, D. (Eds.). <u>Air pollution, the automobile, and public health</u> (pp. 3-9). Cambridge, MA: National Academy Press.

LaGanga, M. (1993, February 4). Chevron to stop dumping waste near shoreline.

TITLES OF PERIODICAL ARE NORMALLY CAPITALIZED.

<u>Los Angeles Times,</u> pp. A1, A10.

The ozone layer has protected us for 1.5 billion years: It's time we returned the favor. (1994, November-December). [Chrysler advertisement]. <u>Audubon, 11-12,</u> 40-41.

Parker, L. (1995 March 28). GM, Ford among top

TITLE IS USED WHEN NO AUTHOR IS IDENTIFIED IN THE SOURCE.

polluters in state. <u>Detroit News,</u> p. A2.

The shorebirds who found a new wetland. (1990, July). <u>Audubon, 7,</u> 38.

Smith, N. C., & Quelch, J. A. (1993). <u>Ethics in marketing.</u> Boston, MA: Richard D. Irwin.

Smithsonian Institution's Ocean Planet: A special report, (1995, March). <u>Outdoor Life, 3,</u> 13-22.

Weisskopf, M. (1992, February 23). Study finds CFC alternatives more damaging than be-lieved. <u>The Washington Post,</u> p. A3.

49 ◆ OTHER DOCUMENTATION STYLES

49a Chicago style (CMS)

In addition to literature and languages, the disciplines in the humanities include history, philosophy, religion, and the fine arts. The most widely used documentation system in these fields is the traditional system found in *The Chicago Manual of Style,* 14th ed., published by the University of Chicago Press (Chicago: 1993). Although it is more elaborate than the stripped-down newer systems, the Chicago style (CMS) is the least obtrusive from a reader's point of view. Still, the Chicago style probably should not be used in English and literature classes. The numbered entries on pages 406−407 explain this style's conventions.

DIRECTORY FOR CHICAGO (CMS) DOCUMENTATION GUIDELINES: ENDNOTES AND FOOTNOTES

DOCUMENTING BOOKS: FIRST REFERENCE

1. Book by one author
2. Book by two or more authors
3. Revised edition of a book
4. Edited book and one volume of a multivolume book
5. Translated book
6. Reprinted book
7. Work in an anthology or chapter in an edited collection
8. Article in a reference book
9. Anonymous book

DOCUMENTING PERIODICALS: FIRST REFERENCE

10. Article, story, or poem in a monthly or bimonthly magazine
11. Article, story, or poem in a weekly magazine
12. Article in a daily newspaper
13. Article in a journal paginated by volume
14. Article in a journal paginated by issue
15. Review

DOCUMENTING OTHER SOURCES: FIRST REFERENCE

16. Personal interview
17. Personal or unpublished letter
18. Work of art

DOCUMENTING SUBSEQUENT REFERENCES TO THE SAME WORK

19. Subsequent references to a work

CMS

CMS

In-text citations

◆ Mark each quotation, paraphrase, and summary of source material by inserting a raised (superscript) Arabic number immediately after the sentence or clause. The superscript number follows all punctuation except dashes. Numbers run consecutively throughout the text.

> Frank Lloyd Wright's "prairie style" was character-
> ized initially by the houses he built around Chicago "with
> low horizontal lines echoing the landscape."[1] Vincent
> Scully sees the suburban building lots for which Wright
> was designing as one of the architect's most important in-
> fluences.[2]

◆ For each superscript number, there is a corresponding note, either at the end of the paper or at the foot of the page on which the number appears.

> 1. "Wright, Frank Lloyd," <u>The Concise Columbia Encyclopedia,</u>
> 1st ed.

> 2. Vincent Scully, <u>Architecture: The Natural and the Manmade</u>
> (New York: St. Martin's, 1991) 340.

Positioning notes and the bibliography

Endnotes are typed as one double-spaced list at the end of the text. The endnote format is easy to deal with, and it allows you to add or delete notes and change numbering with less fuss than footnotes entail.

The **endnote page** follows the last page of text. It and subsequent pages are numbered in sequence. The title *Notes* appears centered without quotation marks, one inch from the top of the page. Double-space before the first entry, within entries, and between entries. Entries go in the order of the note numbers in your paper. Indent the first line five spaces; subsequent lines within entry are flush with the left-hand margin.

Footnotes enable readers to find information at a glance. Footnotes appear in a single-spaced list at the bottom of the page on which the footnotes occur, four lines of space below the last line to text.

Numbers appear aligned with the entry, followed by a period and one space before the first word. Indent the first line five spaces.

Some instructors also require a separate, alphabetically arranged **bibliography.** If you include all the sources you consulted, head the list *Works Consulted.* Use the same format given for a Works Cited list in the MLA documentation chapter (see 47c).

CMS

Documenting books: First reference

1. Book by one author

1. Lewis Thomas, <u>Lives of a Cell: Notes of a Biology Watcher</u> (New York: Viking, 1974), 76.

2. Book by two or more authors

2. Toby Fulwiler and Alan R. Hayakawa, <u>The Blair Handbook</u> (Boston: Blair-Prentice, 1994), 234.

3. Revised edition of a book

3. S. I. Hayakawa, <u>Language in Thought and Action</u>, 4th ed. (New York: Harcourt, 1978), 77.

4. Edited book and one volume of a multivolume book

4. Tom Waldrep, ed., <u>Writers on Writing</u>, vol. 2 (New York: Random House, 1988), 123.

5. Translated book

5. Albert, Camus, <u>The Stranger</u>, trans. Stuart Gilbert (New York: Random House, 1946), 12.

6. Reprinted book

6. Zora Neale Hurston, <u>Their Eyes Were Watching God</u> (1937; reprint New York: Perennial-Harper, 1990), 231-32.

7. Work in an anthology or chapter in an edited collection

7. John Donne, "The Good-Morrow," in <u>The Metaphysical Poets</u>, ed. Helen Gardner (Baltimore: Penguin, 1957), 58.

8. Article in a reference book

8. "Behn, Aphra," <u>The Concise Columbia Encyclopedia</u>, 1983 ed.

An alphabetically arranged book requires no page numbers. Begin with the author of the entry, if known.

9. Anonymous book

9. <u>The World Almanac and Book of Facts</u> (New York: World Almanac-Funk & Wagnalls, 1995).

Documenting periodicals: First reference

10. Article, story, or poem in a monthly or bimonthly magazine

10. Robert A. Linn and Stephen B. Dunbar, "The Nation's Report Card Goes Home," <u>Phi Delta Kappan</u>, October 1990, 127-43.

11.   Article, story, or poem in a weekly magazine

11.   John Updike, "His Mother Inside Him," <u>New Yorker</u>, 20 April 1992, 34-36.

12.   Article in a daily newspaper

12.   Jane E. Brody, "Doctors Get Poor Marks for Nutrition Knowledge." <u>New York Times</u>, 10 February 1992, national edition, p. B7.

13.   "Redistricting Reconsidered," <u>Washington Post</u>, 12 May 1992, national edition, p. B2.

13.   Article in a journal paginated by volume

14.   Joseph Harris, "The Other Reader," <u>Journal of Advanced Composition</u>, 12 (1992): 34-36.

14.   Article in a journal paginated by issue

15.   Helen Tiffin, "Post-Colonialism, Post-Modernism, and the Rehabilitation of Post-Colonial History," <u>Journal of Commonwealth Literature</u>, 23, no. 1 (1988): 169-81.

15.   Review

16.   Mimi Kramer, "Victims," review of <u>'Tis Pity She's a Whore</u>, as performed at the New York Shakespeare Festival, <u>New Yorker</u>, 20 April 1992, 78-79.

Documenting other sources: First reference

16.   Personal interview

17.   John Morser, personal interview, 15 December 1993.

17.   Personal or unpublished letter

18.   Paul Friedman, letter to author, 18 March 1992.

18.   Work of art

19.   Hans Holbein, <u>Portrait of Erasmus</u>, The Louvre, Paris, page 148 in <u>The Louvre Museum</u>, by Germain Bazin (New York: Abrams, n.d.).

Documenting subsequent references to the same work

19.   Subsequent references to a work

The second and any subsequent times you refer to a source, include the author's last name followed by a comma, a shortened version of the title, a comma, and the page number(s).

20.   Thomas, <u>Lives</u>, 99.

21.   Harris, <u>The Other Reader</u>, 35.

SAMPLE PAGE WITH ENDNOTES

Owsley 2

recorded "in exultant tones the universal neglect that had overtaken pagan learning."[2] It would be some time, however, before Christian education would replace classical training, and by the fourth century, a lack of interest in learning and culture among the elite of Roman society was apparent. Attempting to check the demise of education, the later emperors established municipal schools, and universities of rhetoric and law were also established in major cities throughout the Empire.[3]

Owsley 12

Notes

1. Rosamond McKitterick, The Carolingians and the Written Word (Cambridge: Cambridge University Press, 1983), 61.

2. J. Bass Mullinger, The Schools of Charles the Great (New York: Stechert, 1911), 10.

3. James W. Thompson, The Literacy of the Laity in the Middle Ages (New York: Franklin, 1963), 17.

4. O. M. Dalton, introduction, The Letters of Sidonius (Oxford: Clarendon, 1915), cxiv.

5. Pierre Riche, Education and Culture in the Barbarian West (Columbia: University of South Carolina Press, 1976), 4.

6. Riche, Education, 6.

Kelly 5

The Teatro Olimpico was completed in 1584, the statues, inscriptions, and bas-reliefs for the frons-scena being the last details completed. Meanwhile, careful plans were made for an inaugural, which was to be a production of Oedipus in a new translation.[10] Final decisions were made by the Academy in February 1585 for the seating of city officials, their wives, and others, with the ruling that "no masked men or women would be allowed in the theatre for the performance."[11]

The organization of the audience space was "unique among Renaissance theaters, suggesting . . . its function as the theater of a 'club of equals' rather than of a princely court."[12] The Academy is celebrated and related to Roman grandeur by the decoration over the monumental central opening, where its motto, "Hoc Opus," appears.[13] It is difficult to make out the entrances.

10. J. Thomas Oosting, Andrea Palladio's Teatro Olimpico (Ann Arbor: UMI Research Press, 1981), 118–19.
11. Oosting, Palladio's Teatro, 120.
12. Marvin Carlson. Places of Performance: The Semiotics of Theater Architecture (Ithaca: Cornell University Press, 1989), 135.
13. Simon Tidworth, Theaters: An Architectural and Cultural History (London: Praeger, 1973), 52.

CMS

49b Documentation styles in the sciences

The applied sciences (chemistry, computer science, mathematics, physics), the life sciences (biology, botany, zoology), and the medical sciences (medicine, nursing, general health) all use a number system of documentation.

Number citation

In the number system of citation, writers indicate their sources by using a number, either in parentheses or as a superscript, that corresponds to a numbered list of sources at the end of the paper. Math and the life sciences generally prefer parenthetical numbers; chemistry, physics, the medical fields, and computer science generally prefer superscript numbers.

When an author's name is used in the sentence, the number goes in parentheses or in superscript immediately after the name.

```
Linhoffer (3) reported similar results.

Linhoffer[3] reported similar results.
```

If no author's name appears, the number goes right after the use of the source material. In using parenthetical numbers, science writers may include the author's last name before the number in parentheses.

```
(Smith, 3)
```

Numbers cited in the text may appear in one of two arrangements. In **sequential arrangement,** the first source mentioned in text is "1," the second source is "2," and so on. Any subsequent reference to that source uses the same number. (Sequential arrangement is preferred in chemistry, computer science, physics, the life sciences, and medicine.)

In **alphabetical arrangement,** numbers are assigned according to the alphabetical order of the authors' last names on the reference page. Thus, a reference to an author named Smith might be "12," even though it is the first source cited in text, because eleven other names precede it in the list of references. (Mathematicians prefer alphabetical arrangement.)

Reference lists

The Literature Cited or References section provides publication information for all sources cited in the text. Select the format appropriate to your discipline, or consult your instructor.

CBE style

The life sciences (biology, botany, zoology, anatomy, and physiology) follow the documentation system recommended in *The CBE Manual,* 6th ed.

SCI

(New York: Cambridge UP, 1994), published by the Council of Biology Editors.

◆ In-text citations are numbered sequentially and placed in parentheses.

◆ The list of references is called "Literature Cited," "References Cited," or "References." Entries use the following general styles.

BOOKS

1. Winfree, A. T. The timing of biological clocks. 2nd ed. New York: Scientific American Library; 1987:102-110.

Titles are not underlined (or italicized), and only the first word is capitalized. The publisher's name is followed by a semicolon. The date is followed by a colon with no space before or after it if page numbers are included.

PERIODICALS

2. Brown, S. G.; Wagsten, M. V. Socialization processes in a female lowland gorilla. Zoo Biol. 5:269-280; 1986.

Article and journal titles are in roman type, with no underlining (or italics) and no quotation marks. No space precedes or follows the colon between volume and page numbers. If an issue number is required, it goes right after the volume number in parentheses.

ACS style

Documentation style in chemistry is based on that given in *The ACS Style Guide: A Manual for Authors and Editors* (Washington, DC: American Chemical Society, 1986).

◆ In-text citations use superscript numbers and are arranged either sequentially or by author name and date.

◆ The reference list uses the title "Literature Cited," and entries use the following general styles.

BOOKS

1. Siggia, S.; Hanna, J. G. Quantitative Organic Analysis via Functional Groups, 4th ed.; R. E. Krieger: Malabar, FL, 1988; pp. 55-60.

PERIODICALS

2. Scott, J. M. W. J. Chem. Ed. 1992, 69, 600-602.

Article titles are left out. If an issue number is required, it goes right after the volume number in parentheses. No spaces are used between date, volume, and page numbers for periodicals. Use all digits for page sequences.

AIP style

Physics follows the style of the *AIP Style Manual,* 4th ed. (New York: American Institute of Physics, 1990).

- ◆ In-text citations are numbered sequentially using superscript numbers.

- ◆ The reference page is titled "References." Entries use the following general styles.

BOOKS

[1] Pagels, H. R. <u>Perfect Symmetry: The Search for the Beginning of Time</u> (Bantam, New York, 1986), pp. 78-86.

PERIODICALS

[2] Crawford, F. S. Am. J. Phys. 60, 751-752 (1992).

Article titles are omitted. If issue numbers are required, they go right after the volume number in parentheses followed by a comma. The date comes last.

ESL INDEX

Terms in italics are listed in the Glossary of Usage, pages 135–150.

INDEX

A

a, an, 135
Abbreviations, 309–12
  acronyms, 248, 312
  of geographic names, 311–12
  initials, 312
  Latin, common, 312
  following names, commas to set off,
    258
  numbers with, 308, 310
  punctuation of, 247, 248
  in reference lists, 385
  of titles and degrees, 309–10
  in Works Cited list, 359
Ability, designations of, 132
Abridged dictionary, 120
Absolute phrases, 238–39, 252
Abstract nouns, 107–8, 221
Academic journals. *See* Journal
  writing
accept, except, 135
Acronyms, 248, 312
ACS style, 411–12
Actions, 28
Action verbs, 111
Active voice, 164
  defined, 112, 228
  sentence vitality and, 107, 113
  unnecessary shifts between passive
    voice and, 217
adapt, adopt, 135
Adding new material, 65
Addresses:
  abbreviations in, 311–12
  in business letters, 317, 319
  commas with, 258
  numbers in, 308
Adjective clauses, 95, 240, 253
Adjectives:
  commonly confused with adverbs,
    204–5
  comparative form, 207–9, 230
  compound, hyphens in, 303
  coordinate, 255
  defined, 203, 229
  descriptive, 230
  double negatives and, 206
  forming, 204

  infinitive phrases as, 238
  irregular, 209
  kinds of, 230–31
  limiting, 230–31
  after linking verbs, 205–6
  nouns as, 231
  participial phrases as. *See* Participial
    phrases
  positive form, 207, 230
  predicate, 236
  prepositional phrases as, 237
  proper, 231
  separating from independent
    clauses with commas, 252
  superlative form, 207–9, 230
  verbals as, 229
Adverb clauses, 240, 251
Adverbs:
  commonly confused with
    adjectives, 204–5
  comparative form, 207–9, 230
  conjunctive, 92, 93, 160–61, 231,
    233
  defined, 203, 229–30
  double negatives and, 206
  forming, 204
  infinitive phrases as, 238
  irregular, 209
  kinds of, 231
  after linking verbs that function as
    action verbs, 206
  negators, 231
  positioning, 210–11
  positive form, 207, 230
  prepositional phrases as, 237
  prepositions as, 232
  relative, 231
  separating from independent
    clauses with commas, 252
  superlative form, 207–9, 230
  verbals as, 229
adverse, averse, 135
advice, advise, 135
affect, effect, 136
Afterword, 76
Age, designations of, 132
Agents, 228
aggravate, 136

PLANNING NOTES

RESEARCH NOTES

WRITING NOTES

REVISING NOTES

◆ EDITING SYMBOLS

ABB	abbreviation **42**		**PASS**	passive voice **16c**
AD	adjective/adverb **26**		**REF**	pronoun reference **25a**
AWK	awkward		**REP**	repetitious **17c**
BIAS	biased language **19**		**S-V AGR**	subject-verb agreement **24**
CAP	capital letter **38**		**SHIFT**	distracting shift **28a-e**
CASE	pronoun case **25c**		**SLANG**	slang **18d**
CLICHE	cliché **18g**		**SP**	spelling **37**
COH	coherence **13c**		**SUB**	subordination **14c-d**
CON	conciseness **17**		**T**	verb tense **28b**
CONCL	conclusion **12b**		**TONE**	tone **1d**
COORD	coordination **14a-b**		**TRANS**	transition **13c**
CS	comma splice **22**		**??**	unclear
D	diction **16a-b; 18**		**U**	unity **13a**
DEV	development **6-9**		**US**	usage glossary **20**
DIR	indirect **17e-f**		**VAR**	variety **15b-d**
DM	dangling modifier **27c**		**VERB**	verb **23**
DOC	documentation **47-49**		**VITAL**	vitality **16**
EMPH	emphasis **15a**		**W**	wordy **17a-d**
FRAG	sentence fragment **21**		**WC**	word choice **18**
FS	fused sentence **22**		**WW**	wrong word **18b**
GR	grammar **21-29**		**'**	apostrophe **34**
HYPH	hyphen **39**		**[]**	brackets **36d**
INC	incomplete construction **28h**		**:**	colon **33**
			,	comma **31**
ITAL	italics (underlining) **40**		**—**	dash **36b**
JARG	jargon **18e**		**...**	ellipsis points **36c**
LC	lowercase letter **38**		**!**	exclamation point **30c**
LOG	logic **8c**		**()**	parentheses **36a**
MIXED	mixed construction **28f-g**		**.**	period **30a**
MM	misplaced modifier **27a**		**?**	question mark **30b**
MOOD	verb mood **23f**		**" "**	quotation marks **35**
MS	manuscript format **43b**		**;**	semicolon **32**
NUM	number **41**		**/**	slash **36e**
OPEN	opening **12a**		⌒	close up space
¶	paragraph **13**		**#**	add space
//	parallelism **14f-g**		**∧**	insert
P	punctuation **30-36**		⸜	delete
P-A AGR	pronoun antecedent agreement **25b**		∼	transpose
			X	obvious error

EDITING NOTES